Perspicuous Presentations

Perspicuous Presentations

Essays on Wittgenstein's Philosophy of Psychology

Edited by

Danièle Moyal-Sharrock
Birkbeck College, University of London

First published 2007 by
PALGRAVE MACMILLAN
Houndmills, Basingstoke, Hampshire RG21 6XS and
175 Fifth Avenue, New York, N.Y. 10010
Companies and representatives throughout the world

PALGRAVE MACMILLAN is the global academic imprint of the Palgrave
Macmillan division of St. Martin's Press, LLC and of Palgrave Macmillan Ltd.
Macmillan® is a registered trademark in the United States, United Kingdom and other
countries. Palgrave is a registered trademark in the European Union and other countries.

ISBN-13: 978-0-230-52748-5   hardback
ISBN-10: 0-230-52748-5   hardback

This book is printed on paper suitable for recycling and made from fully managed and
sustained forest sources. Logging, pulping and manufacturing processes are expected to
conform to the environmental regulations of the country of origin.

A catalogue record for this book is available from the British Library.

Library of Congress Cataloging-in-Publication Data

Perspicuous presentations : essays on Wittgenstein's philosophy of psychology / edited by
    Danièle Moyal-Sharrock.
        p. cm.
     Includes bibliographical references (p.) and index.
     Contents: Wittgenstein on fear / John V. Canfield – Wittgensteinian grammar &
philosophy of mind / Stépohane Chauvier – The importance of being thoughtful / Lars
Hertzberg – Wittgenstein on "experiencing meaning" / Jacques Bouveress – Revisiting "the
unconscious" / Wes Sharrock – Wittgenstein and the foundations of cognitive
psychology / Rom Harré – Dispositions or capacities?: Wittgenstein's social philosophy of
mind / Christiane Chauviré – The myth of the "outer": Wittgenstein's redefinition of
subjectivity / Sandra Laugier – Wittgenstein on "the sort of explanation one longs
for?" / Frank Cioffi – Patterns in the weave of life: Wittgenstein's "Lebensmuster" / Jean-
Jacques Rosat – Wittgenstein on psychological certainty / Danièle Moyal-Sharrock – Criteria
and defeasibility: when good evidence is not good enough / Eric J. Loomis – "Tennis
without a ball": Wittgenstein on "secondary sense" / Michel ter Hark – The cradle of
language: making sense of bodily connexions / Stephen J. Cowley – Getting clear about
perspicuous representations: Wittgenstein, Baker & Fodor / Daniel D. Hutto.

     ISBN-13: 978-0-230-52748-5 (cloth)
     ISBN-10: 0-230-52748-5 (cloth)

     1. Psychology-Philosophy. 2. Wittgenstein, Ludwig, 1889-1951. I. Moyal-Sharrock Danièle,
1954-

B138.P422 2007
192-dc22   2006052961

10   9   8   7   6   5   4   3   2   1
16   15 14 13 12 11 10 09 08 07

Printed and bound in Great Britain by
Antony Rowe Ltd, Chippenham and Eastbourne

This volume is dedicated to my dear friend, Jack Canfield, who – in the interstices of his Buddhist retreats – showed me how we come to language.

Contents

Tables and Figures

Table

Figures

Preface

Perspicuous Presentations focuses on the penetrating contributions Wittgenstein made to several areas in the philosophy of psychology – contributions that have had repercussions in psychology, psychiatry, sociology and anthropology. It also introduces to the English-speaking world eminent French Wittgensteinians whose work I have admired over the years, all the while deploring the insulating effect of the language-barrier. To bring them to richly deserved attention, I have translated some of their characteristically illuminating papers for this volume. They appear alongside the latest work of more familiar scholars here either engaged in tackling difficult topics of Wittgenstein's philosophical psychology, or inspired by his work to challenge confusions prevailing in the philosophy of mind and in cognitive psychology. While revealing differences in approach and interests, this coming together of some of the best minds on the subject discloses a surprising degree of consensus, and gives us the clearest picture yet of Wittgenstein as a philosopher of psychology.

John V. Canfield has not only splendidly elucidated Wittgenstein's philosophy of psychology; he has given it impetus and helped it spread its wings so that it now reaches such disciplines as developmental psychology, the sciences of education, and anthropology. Canfield's insights have enriched Wittgenstein's. *Perspicuous Presentations* is also in celebration of this.

Notes on Contributors

Jacques Bouveresse is Professor of Philosophy of Language and Epistemology at the Collège de France (Paris). He is the author of numerous books on Wittgenstein, including *Le Mythe de l'intériorité* (The Myth of the Inner) (1976), *Wittgenstein Reads Freud* (1991/1995), *Wittgenstein, la philosophie et le langage* (2002), and *Wittgenstein et les sortilèges du langage* (Wittgenstein and the Bewitchments of Language) (2003). His most recent work is in philosophy of religion, *Croire et ne pas croire. Sur la croyance, la foi et la vérité* (Believing and Not Believing: On Belief, Faith and Truth).

John V. Canfield is Emeritus Professor at the University of Toronto. He has written numerous outstanding articles on Wittgenstein, and is the author of *Wittgenstein: Language and World* (1981) and *The Looking-Glass Self* (1990). He edited the 15-volume collection, *The Philosophy of Wittgenstein*, and is co-editor (with Stuart Shanker) of *Wittgenstein's Intentions* (1993). Professor Canfield is also editor of the *Philosophy of Meaning, Knowledge and Value in the Twentieth Century* (Routledge History of Philosophy). He has just completed *Becoming Human: The Development of Language, Self and Self-Consciousness* (2007).

Stéphane Chauvier is Professor of Philosophy at the University of Caen Basse-Normandie. His main areas of research and publication are metaphysics, first-person epistemology and philosophy of politics. He is the author of *Dire 'je': essai sur la subjectivité* (Saying 'I': An Essay on Subjectivity) (2001), *Qu'est ce qu'une personne?* (What is a Person?) (2003) and *Justice et droits à l'échelle globale* (Justice and Rights on the Global Scale) (2006). He is also the editor of *Gareth Evans* (2004).

Christiane Chauviré is Professor of Philosophy at the Sorbonne (Paris), where she teaches epistemology and philosophy of language. Besides numerous articles, she is the author of *Ludwig Wittgenstein* (1989), *Peirce et la signification* (Peirce and Meaning) (1995), *La Philosophie dans la boîte noire. Cinq pièces facile sur Wittgenstein* (Black-Box Philosophy: Five Easy Pieces on Wittgenstein) (2000), *Voir le visible: la seconde philosophie de Wittgenstein* (Seeing the Visible: The Philosophy of the Second Wittgenstein) (2003), *Le Moment anthropologique de Wittgenstein* (2004) and *L'œil mathématique. Essai sur la philosophie mathématique de Peirce* (The Mathematical Eye: Essay on Peirce's Mathematical Philosophy) (forthcoming).

Frank Cioffi is Honorary Professor of Philosophy at the University of Kent at Canterbury. He is the author of *Freud and the Question of Pseudoscience* (1998) and *Wittgenstein on Freud and Frazer* (1998). His most recently published papers are 'Wittgenstein and the Riddle of Life' (2004), 'The Evasiveness of Freudian Apologetic' (2004) and 'Overviews: What Are They Of and What Are They For?' (2007).

Jeffrey Coulter is Professor of Sociology at Boston University. His interest has been in the philosophy of mind, especially the criticism of contemporary cognitivism, on which he has published several books, and recently co-edited a special issue of the journal *Theory, Culture and Society* (2007). He is currently working on an extensive study of the 'ecological psychology' of J. J. Gibson. His most recent book is *Mind in Action* (1989).

Stephen J. Cowley is Senior Lecturer in Developmental Psychology at the University of Hertfordshire. He does most of his empirical work in South Africa where he holds an Honorary position at the University of KwaZulu-Natal. Among recent publications that span Linguistics, Developmental Science and Social Robotics are: 'Grounding Signs of Culture: Primary Intersubjectivity in Social Semiosis' (2004), 'Language and Biosemiosis: A Necessary Unity?' (2006), and 'What Baboons, Babies and Tetris Players Tell Us about Interaction: A Biosocial View of Norm-Based Social Learning' (2006). His research focus falls on how language transforms humans by bringing them into contact with each other while using a heterogeneous range of cultural practices and artefacts.

Michel ter Hark is Professor of History of Philosophy and the Behavioural and Cognitive Sciences at the University of Groningen, the Netherlands. His publications include *Beyond the Inner and the Outer: Wittgenstein's Philosophy of Psychology* (1990) and *Popper, Otto Selz and the Rise of Evolutionary Epistemology* (2004). He is currently working on two books, one on the history of cognitive science, the other on Wittgenstein's notion of secondary sense.

Rom Harré taught Philosophy of Science for many years at Oxford, where he is Emeritus Fellow of Linacre College. He currently teaches at Georgetown and American Universities in Washington DC. He has published widely on topics in the philosophy of physics and chemistry. Recently he has turned to studies in discursive psychology, a new development closely related to philosophy of mind. His most recent book, with Michael Tissaw, is *Wittgenstein and Psychology* (2005).

Lars Hertzberg is Professor of Philosophy at Åbo Akademi University, Finland, where he has taught since 1980. He has published numerous articles, primarily on Wittgenstein, philosophy of mind, and language and ethics, some of which were collected in *The Limits of Experience* (1994). He is currently preparing *The Ethical Will*.

Daniel D. Hutto is Professor of Philosophical Psychology at the University of Hertfordshire. He has published on a wide range of topics relating to the philosophy of psychology and philosophical methodology. He is the author of *The Presence of Mind* (1990), *Beyond Physicalism* (2000), *Wittgenstein and the End of Philosophy* (2003, 2nd edn 2006) and *Folk Psychological Narratives* (2007).

Sandra Laugier is Professor of Philosophy at the University of Amiens (France), where she teaches philosophy of language, philosophy of science and moral philosophy. Her publications include *L'anthropologie logique de Quine* (1992), *Du réel à l'ordinaire* (From the Real to the Ordinary) (1999) and *Recommencer la philosophie: la philosophie américaine aujourd'hui* (Restarting Philosophy: American Philosophy Today) (1999), as well as the edited volumes: *Wittgenstein, métaphysique et jeux de langage* (2001), *Husserl et Wittgenstein: de la description de l'expérience à la phénoménologie linguistique* (2004). Her most recent publication is: *Ethique, littérature, vie humaine* (2006). She is the translator of Stanley Cavell into French, and has also translated works by Quine and Emerson.

Eric Loomis is Assistant Professor of Philosophy at the University of South Alabama. His articles include 'Logical Form and Propositional Function in the *Tractatus*' (2006), 'Empirical Equivalence in the Quine-Carnap Debate' (2007) and 'Necessity, the A Priori, and the Standard Meter' (1999). He is currently working on a book with Cory F. Juhl entitled *Analyticity*.

Danièle Moyal-Sharrock is Lecturer at Birkbeck College, University of London. She is the author of *Understanding Wittgenstein's 'On Certainty'* (2004), and the editor of *The Third Wittgenstein: The Post-Investigations Works* (2004) and *Readings on Wittgenstein's 'On Certainty'* (2005). She is also the translator, into French, of Wittgenstein's *On Certainty* (2006). She is currently preparing a collection of her essays on Wittgenstein in French: *Wittgenstein: Lectures fortes* (Wittgenstein: Uncompromising Readings).

Jean-Jacques Rosat is Lecturer at the Collège de France (Paris). He has co-edited *Wittgenstein: les mots de l'esprit. Philosophie de la psychologie*

(Wittgenstein: The Words of the Mind) (2001), *Wittgenstein, dernières pensées* (Wittgenstein: Last Thoughts) (2002), and *L'empirisme logique à la limite. Schlick, le langage et l'expérience* (The Limits of Logical Empiricism: Schlick: Language and Experience) (2006). He is currently working on *La Description de l'expérience: psychologie, phénoménologie et langage ordinaire dans la philosophie de Wittgenstein* (The Description of Experience: Psychology, Phenomenology and Ordinary Language in Wittgenstein's Philosophy).

Wes Sharrock is Professor of Sociology at the University of Manchester. His main interest is in the philosophical confusions of the social sciences, understood in terms of Wittgenstein's philosophy. He also has an interest in the field of 'computer supported cooperative work' and has made studies of software engineering, printing and child therapy. His publications include *Thomas Kuhn*, with R. Read (2002) and *Perspectives in Sociology* (5th edn, 2006).

Abbreviations of Works by Wittgenstein

AWL   *Wittgenstein's Lectures: Cambridge, 1932–1935,* from the notes of A. Ambrose and M. MacDonald, ed. A. Ambrose. Oxford: Blackwell, 1979.

BB   *The Blue and Brown Books,* 2nd edn. Oxford: Blackwell, 1969.

CE   'Cause and Effect: Intuitive Awareness', in PO, 371–426.

CV   *Culture and Value,* ed. G. H. von Wright in collaboration with H. Nyman, trans. P. Winch, amended 2nd edn. Oxford, Blackwell, 1980.

GB   'Remarks on Frazer's *Golden Bough*', in PO, 119–55.

LC   *Lectures & Conversations on Aesthetics, Psychology and Religious Belief,* from the notes of Y. Smithies, R. Rhees and J. Taylor, ed. C. Barrett. Oxford: Blackwell, 1966.

LE   'A Lecture on Ethics', in PO, 37–44.

LFW   'Lectures on Freedom of the Will', from the notes of Yorick Smythies, in PO, 426–44.

LPP   *Wittgenstein's Lectures on Philosophical Psycholy, 1946–47,* notes by P. T. Geach, K. J. Shah and A. C. Jackson, ed. P. T. Geach. Hassocks: Harvester Press, 1988.

LWI   *Last Writings on the Philosophy of Psychology. Volume I,* ed. G. H. von Wright and Heikki Nyman, trans. C. G. Luckhardt and Maximilian A. E. Aue. Oxford: Blackwell, 1982.

LWII   *Last Writings on the Philosophy of Psychology. Volume II,* ed. G. H. von Wright and Heikki Nyman, trans. C. G. Luckhardt and Maximilian A. E. Aue. Oxford: Blackwell, 1982.

NB   *Notebook, 1941–1916,* ed. G. H. von Wright and G. E. M. Anscombe, trans. G. E. M. Anscombe. Oxford: Blackwell, 1961.

OC   *On Certainty,* ed. G. E. M. Anscombe and G. H. von Wright, trans. D. Paul and G. E. M. Anscombe, amended 1st edn. Oxford: Blackwell, 1997.

PG   *Philosophical Grammar,* ed. R. Rhees, trans. A. Kenny. Oxford: Blackwell, 1974.

PI   *Philosophical Investigations,* trans. G. E. M. Anscombe. 2nd edn. Oxford: Blackwell, 1997.

PLP   *The Principles of Linguistic Philosophy*, by F. Waismann, ed. R. Harré, 2nd edn. London: Macmillan, 1997. Preface by Gordon Baker.

PO   *Philosophical Occasions: 1912–1951*, ed. J. C. Klagge and A. Nordman. Indianapolis: Hackett Publishing, 1993.

PR   *Philosophical Remarks*, ed. R. Rhees, trans. R. Hargreaves and R. White. Oxford: Blackwell, 1975.

RC   *Remarks on Colour*, ed. G. E. M. Anscombe, trans. L. L. McAlister and Margaret Schättle. Oxford: Blackwell, 1980; 1st edn 1977.

RFM   *Remarks on the Foundations of Mathematics*, ed. G. H. von Wright, R. Rhees and G. E. M. Anscombe, trans. G. E. M. Anscombe, 3rd revised edn. Oxford: Blackwell, 1978.

RPPI   *Remarks on the Philosophy of Psychology*, vol. I, ed. G. E. M. Anscombe and G. H. von Wright, trans. G. E. M. Anscombe. Oxford: Blackwell, 1980.

RPPII   *Remarks on the Philosophy of Psychology*, vol. II, ed. G. H. von Wright and H. Nyman, trans. C. G. Luckhardt and M. A. E. Aue. Oxford: Blackwell, 1980.

TLP   *Tractatus Logico-Philosophicus*, trans. D. F. Pears and B. F. McGuinness. London: Routledge & Kegan Paul, 1961.

VOW   L. Wittgenstein and F. Waismann, *The Voices of Wittgenstein: The Vienna Circle*, ed. G. Baker, Foreword by B. McGuinness, trans. G. Baker, M. Mackert, J. Connolly and V. Politis. London and New York: Routledge, 2003.

WVC   *Ludwig Wittgenstein and the Vienna Circle*, shorthand notes recorded by F. Waismann, ed. B. F. McGuinness. Oxford: Blackwell, 1979.

Z   *Zettel*, ed. G. E. M. Anscombe and G. H. von Wright, trans. G. E. M. Anscombe. Berkeley: University of California Press, 1970.

A main source of our failure to understand is that we do not command a clear view *of the use of our words.* – *Our grammar is lacking in this sort of per-spicuity. A perspicuous presentation produces just that understanding which con-sists in 'seeing connexions'. Hence the importance of finding and inventing* intermediate cases.

The concept of a perspicuous presentation is of fundamental significance for us. It earmarks the form of account we give, the way we look at things.

Philosophical Investigations §122

Introduction: 'I'll teach you differences!'

> Hegel seems to me to be wanting to say that things which look different are really the same. Whereas my interest is in showing that things which look the same are really different. I was thinking of using as a motto for my book a quotation from *King Lear*: 'I'll teach you differences.'
>
> Wittgenstein to Drury[1]

Wittgenstein's philosophical genius owes much to his having assimilated this lesson of *King Lear's*: Beware of *faux amis!* That is, he perceived that most of our philosophical misconceptions result from our conflating sentences that *are identical* – or at least have *the same form* – but in fact *mean* different things. Wittgenstein's genius lies in his extraordinary ability to see crucial differences in what, to us, *looks the same*. The motto would has been apt: Wittgenstein does teach us differences.

It could be said that, from the first (*Tractatus*) to the last (*On Certainty*), Wittgenstein crusaded against the *face-value* of language. Why is this a philosopher's crusade? Because the attempt to demarcate the merely contingent from the necessary is a philosopher's task, and Wittgenstein realized that this task was obstructed, not by any metaphysical obstacles, but by the very nature of language, which allows us to use the same sentence in different capacities. This economy comes with a disadvantage: sentences do not wear their status on their sleeve: the status of words or sentences is not visible from their form. Hence the Tractarian denunciation of ordinary language as misleading: the same words can be used in different ways and therefore have different statuses (TLP: 3.323), but this is not visible in language, and so the most fundamental confusions occur, of which philosophy is full (TLP: 3.324).[2] Wittgenstein's continuing crusade was to remind us of this, and to denounce the ravages on philosophy of *misleading appearance*:

> When something seems queer about the grammar of our words, it is because we are alternately tempted to use a word in several different ways. And it is particularly difficult to discover that an assertion which the metaphysician makes expresses discontentment with our grammar when the words of this assertion can also be used to state a fact of experience.
>
> (BB: 56–7)

We are thus alerted to differences that can often *only* be revealed by a perspicuous examination of *use*. Correct analysis, writes Wittgenstein, would require that 'we destroy the outward similarity' between the metaphysical proposition and the experiential one (BB: 55),[3] or between other such *Doppelgänger*. To 'destroy the outward similarity' is not, however, to modify our vocabulary, but simply to make a perspicuous presentation of how this outward similarity is a superficial and misleading one: to show that, *whatever its appearance*, it is the *use* of a sentence or word that determines its meaning[4] and, more pertinently for philosophers, its (grammatical or logical) *status*:

> A language-game: Report whether a certain body is lighter or darker than another. – But now there's a related one: State the relationship between the lightness of certain shades of colour .... The form of the propositions in both language-games is the same: 'X is lighter than Y.' But in the first it is an external relation and the proposition is temporal, in the second it is an internal relation and the proposition is timeless.
>
> (RC I: 1)

Two uses, two statuses. It is *form* that the philosopher must learn to overlook, and *use* that she must learn to look for: the use will then give her the status. And having that, she will avoid the kind of category mistake that takes a grammatical statement (e.g. 'Other minds exist') for an empirical one (e.g., 'Ghosts exist'), thereby giving rein to scepticism about other minds; or the kind of category mistake that takes an expressive utterance for a descriptive one, thereby generating a 'mythology of the inner'. And she will avoid facile generalizations that seek to encapsulate essence.

Indeed we are, in our philosophical zeal, too quick to generalize, and in so doing neglect the particular, especially when it has *the same form* as the general. Countering this, writes John Canfield, Wittgenstein 'moves always in the direction of the particular'. In his contribution to this volume, 'Wittgenstein on Fear', Canfield shows Wittgenstein doing what any philosopher of language might do: he gives us an account of the concept of fear through an analysis of utterances like 'I am afraid'. And yet, notes Canfield, Wittgenstein's approach inverts the traditional approach:

> it is a type of analysis that differs deeply from other types. Instead of trying to bring the many cases of fear-talk under the same general account, it seeks to fracture any general account into a multitude of different uses. Instead of understanding the many in terms of one, understand the one in terms of the many.

In retracing Wittgenstein's analysis of the concept of fear, Canfield delineates the ways in which the utterance 'I am afraid' can be functionally equivalent to, for example, a cry of fear, a report on how one feels, a reflection on one's present state; and shows that a 'fine-tuned look at what it is to speak of fear' can only be arrived at through a consideration of use:

> Each use of 'I am afraid' occurs within a language-game that is different from the others. These contrasts are obscured by the blanket expression 'I am afraid'. Conceptual clarification will result from a realization that those words hide differences of use.

And it is by becoming aware of the different language-games with 'fear', of what the language-games involved in fear-talk are like, says Canfield, that we are made aware of 'the misleading nature of the question about what fear really is'.

There is nothing that fear *really* is. Fear is not *essentially* anything. But this does not mean that we cannot give an account of fear, make perspicuous presentations of it; speak about a *concept* of fear and distinguish it from other concepts. In his philosophical psychology, as elsewhere, Wittgenstein provides us with such *perspicuous presentations.*[5] These presentations – be they descriptions of our use of words or (re)classifications of our concepts – are *perspicuous* precisely because to get to meaning or to status, Wittgenstein, wary of *faux amis*, looked beyond appearance to use. Moreover, he did not stop at a single use, but *surveyed* our uses: this is also what is conveyed by the expression *übersichtliche Darstellung*; or, in Canfield's words: *understanding the one in terms of the many*. So that, philosopher that he is, Wittgenstein does not *remain* in the particular;

but gestures in the direction of the general. Yet it is *only* by having scrutinized, attended to, the particular, that the philosopher can, profitably for philosophy, gesture towards the general.

That Wittgenstein did survey, and indeed sought an *overview* of, psychological concepts is the subject of Stéphane Chauvier's chapter, 'Wittgensteinian Grammar and Philosophy of Mind'. In opposition to *austerely* Therapeutic readers who take Wittgenstein to show only what the mind is *not*, whilst seeking to cure us of the desire to question ourselves on the nature of the mind and of mental phenomena, Chauvier provides us with a mapping of Wittgenstein's writings on philosophical psychology drawn directly from his grammar of psychological concepts, which lets surface the outline of a *positive* conception of mind. This Chauvier dubs a *semantic non-reductionism*. And here, pre-empting a possible charge of linguistic idealism against Wittgenstein, Chauvier takes care to clarify the distinction between physical and grammatical impossibility.

In his chapter, 'The Importance of Being Thoughtful', Lars Hertzberg rejects the traditional assumptions that the essence of thinking is concentrated in processes of thought underlying, and separable from, its manifestations in speech and conduct, and that humans are the paradigm of what it means to be a thinking being. Assumptions which make looking at the wide variety of ways in which the word 'thinking' is used superfluous. Following Wittgenstein, Hertzberg argues that the word 'thinking' does not refer to any specific mental process, and that there is no specific capacity for engaging in thought that may or may not set us apart from animals or machines. Instead, Hertzberg suggests we envisage thought in terms of 'achievement' and 'attribution' aspects. The achievement aspect has to do with the ability to succeed in intellectually demanding tasks; the attribution aspect with the kinds of thoughts, attitudes, motives, that may be attributed to different individuals and animals. In philosophical discussions about thinking, the achievement and attribution issues are often confused. Philosophers argue as if the achievement issue were more basic: if an animal is able to solve some problem, this shows that we can attribute intellectual powers to it. But in fact the question of attribution must be addressed before the question of achievement can even be raised, so that what looks to us like a 'failure' on the part of an animal to solve some problem is really a failure on our part for having attributed it to the animal as a 'problem' in the first place.

In Chapter 4, Jacques Bouveresse elucidates Wittgenstein's abstruse notion of 'experiencing meaning'. He clarifies how Wittgenstein's remarks on 'experiencing meaning' contribute to our understanding the difference between meaning something and saying something, and how the difference is improperly rendered by the overly simplified picture of two parallel processes taking place in two distinct milieus. We must rid ourselves of this picture, warns Bouveresse, if we want to understand the radically different and much more complicated relationship between saying and meaning something. According to the pneumatic conception, in order to have a meaning, a word must first have a soul, but as Bouveresse makes clear, this does *not* hold for the meaning blind: for them words do have a meaning and are used, as they are by us, meaningfully; but they do not also have a soul. They 'only', so to speak, have a meaning. Bouveresse suggests that in his remarks on the problem of meaning blindness, Wittgenstein is seeking a more correct evaluation of what it is that these words are lacking, and by the same token, what it is that is lacking in the person uttering them.

In 'Revisiting "the Unconscious"', Wes Sharrock and Jeff Coulter examine some of the controversies that have attended the concept of 'the unconscious' in the human sciences, particularly the cognitive sciences. The concept of 'the unconscious' has become a central *presupposition*, it is assumed that we 'unconsciously' supplement the conscious steps we take, so that *some* appeal to 'the unconscious' and to what happens there has become not only right but positively unavoidable in any explanation of behavioural phenomena. The idea that the 'unconscious mind' (increasingly identified with the *brain*) must be postulated to engage in the formation of hypotheses, on the basis of inferential processes, using stored data, was further boosted by Chomsky's linguistic theorizing and Fodor's philosophical psychology. With these, appeals to 'the unconscious' involve a personification of the brain and its operations that result in the absurd projection of person-level predicates to parts of persons' bodies: hence, it is *brains* that formulate, test and confirm hypotheses, that analyse, interpret, follow rules and so on. Sharrock and Coulter endorse Ryle's rejection of the Chomskian picture of child language learning in which the child's life, in its interactions with others, is entirely absent. Indeed, the last thing that cognitivists turn to, deplore Sharrock and Coulter, is the stream of life, and they suggest that this is due to a preoccupation with a particular *form* of explanation, an overwhelming fixation on the *a priori* form which a satisfactory explanation must take. They recommend a Wittgensteinian 'return to the surface' of things, to where all that is needed for the elucidation of those facets of human conduct, which cognitivism consigns to the 'invisible inner', is in plain view.

In his chapter on 'Wittgenstein and the Foundations of Cognitive Psychology', Rom Harré suspects a connection between the 'presuppositions' of cognitive psychologists and Wittgenstein's 'hinges' in *On Certainty*. Among proposals, in cognitive psychology, for the non-causal principles of order – enduring mental structures of which we are not aware, but which shape (somehow) the contents of experience and patterns of social action – are various cognitive entities, such as schemata, rules and scripts. Inasmuch as these words serve to refer both to the mental entities themselves, and to their representations, Harré sees a link between them and 'hinges'. Though Wittgenstein's purpose was different from the purposes of cognitive and social psychologists, Harré sees his treatment of the sources of orderliness in human affairs as illuminating for psychology. Harré takes the concept of 'hinge' to refer to whatever is the source of stable linguistic and social practices, with respect not only to fixing the meanings of words but also to the correctness and propriety of actions, and raises the question of how hinge *propositions* are related to hinges, and what might be the point of enunciating them. He notes the ambiguities in the way hinge propositions are presented as if they were the hinges themselves, and relates this to an error which he claims is endemic among psychologists: 'they often mistake the expression of a cognitive or social hinge for the hinge itself, and go on to misread the grammar of the hinge proposition reporting a non-propositional norm as if it were a causal hypothesis. Experiments are then devised to look for evidence for it.' What Harré calls the 'rule problem' presents itself in two versions: (a) What are norms when they are not verbally formulated rules in the imperative mood?; and (b) What sort of beings could rules express? In a refusal to countenance such monsters as 'unformulated rules', Harré attempts to clarify the problematic status of these 'rules'.

Although Wittgenstein uses the term 'disposition' in his classifications of psychological concepts, he is not satisfied with it. In 'Dispositions or Capacities? Wittgenstein's Social Philosophy of Mind', Christiane Chauviré explains this reticence as something of a shortcoming on Wittgenstein's part: he misses out on a useful concept because he only envisages a mechanistic conception of the disposition, and never conceives of it on a more acceptable organic and teleological model, *à la* Peirce. Chauviré wonders why commentators have never found peculiar this reductionist assimilation of a disposition to a mechanism, as if it went without saying. She traces back Wittgenstein's disqualification of the disposition to his early conception of language as a calculus, and links it to his denunciation of possibility as a 'shadowy reality'. She then shows how Wittgenstein replaces the notion of disposition with that of capacity: the mastery of a technique or know-how, inculcated by training or instruction and deployed entirely in practice. So that if, in matters relating to the philosophy of mind,

Wittgenstein seems estranged from pragmatists and dispositionalists like Peirce and Bourdieu, he is much closer to them in matters of social philosophy, upholding as he does an anti-intellectualistic conception of the practical sphere, and indeed a kind of social philosophy of mind.

In 'The Myth of the *Outer*: Wittgenstein's Redefinition of Subjectivity', Sandra Laugier suggests that Wittgenstein's writings on philosophical psychology be understood as a reworking of his quest for a non-psychological self, which results in his redefining the subject – of both language and experience – as no longer the point without extension of the *Tractatus*, or the metaphysical subject, or the subject of psychology. Wittgenstein's exposure of 'the myth of the inner' should not be read as a wholesale rejection of the inner and the mental, but as a rethinking of inner-outer dualism, and as an attempt to challenge the kind of exaltation we have about the inner life being *private*. However, Laugier joins Stanley Cavell in finding something misleading in the familiar interpretation of Wittgenstein's exploding of the myth of privileged access to our sensations (e.g.,knowing our own pain better than we know someone else's), for at stake here is not so much one's access to the other, as the difficulty, indeed anxiety, in accessing one's own inner life. In affirming the other's *accessibility*, Wittgenstein is led to produce a theory of *inaccessibility*, or at least self-ignorance. The sceptical problem is transformed: no longer a scepticism about *other minds*, or about knowledge of others, it becomes a problem about *access* to others, for which the obstacle is not otherness or privacy, but the impossibility for oneself to access one's self.

In his powerful chapter on 'the sort of explanation one longs for!', Frank Cioffi suggests that the reason for Wittgenstein's juxtaposition of issues in aesthetics and psychoanalysis, which so intrigued G. E. Moore, is that in both these areas, our inquiries with respect to the feelings, thoughts and impulses aroused cannot be answered by empirical explanation or hypothesis, but only by 'further descriptions' – that is, by similes or some other mode of felicitous reformulation of our experience. Wittgenstein devalues empirical enquiry where its outcome can have no bearing on what is really of interest to us: our impressions and how to evince and evoke them more adequately. Indeed, he charges Freud for offering causal hypotheses as solutions when what is called for is rather clarifying what was at the back of the patient's mind. But Cioffi does not leave it there: he asks if there are not cases when a discourse made up of hypotheses *would be* preferable to one made up of further descriptions. The question here is at what point the content of a mental state becomes interesting enough in its own right to warrant its clarification or elaboration rather than scrutiny of its causal-diagnostic implications. Cioffi's reply is that it is the character of our interest and not the conceptual character of the explanation that differentiates these cases. He concludes that where explanation will not meet our needs, 'another genre of epistemic achievement – a succinct graspable expression of our predicament, a "synoptic view" of it – might'. There is a distinctive non-empirical, but nonetheless epistemic, preoccupation with the self: the self as an object of scrutiny presenting a multiplicity of aspects requiring articulation. A Wittgensteinian overview of these aspects, he suggests, would facilitate self-understanding. However, self-understanding may no more bring our disquietude to a term than explanation did. What we may have longed for in such cases is neither the discourse that explains the self nor one which leaves us with a graspable view of its nature, but 'peace'.

One of Wittgenstein's crucial contributions to philosophical psychology, affirms Jean-Jacques Rosat, is to have revealed the conceptual traps laid by *spatial* pictures of the mind (box of secrets, *inner* space), and *optical*, indeed *cinematographic* ones (a roll of film unwinding before the light of a projector, or a stream of consciousness). In 'Patterns in the Weave of Life: Wittgenstein's *Lebensmuster*', Rosat examines Wittgenstein's use of Henry James's metaphor of 'patterns in a carpet', in which Wittgenstein compares life to a carpet or a weave on which emerge, in intertwined patterns, human feelings and behaviours: for example, pain, joy, grief, hope. These 'patterns of life', as Wittgenstein calls them, have distinct motifs, physiognomies, duration and so on. The point of this new comparison is that on a carpet all is, in principle, visible, open to view; if a pattern is not visible to us, this is not because it is hidden, but because we cannot discern it. The course of human life is made up of the interweaving of these 'patterns of life' in an infinite but *constantly varied* repetition. This, then, leaves room for a good deal of irreducible indeterminacy, and guarantees that no single occurrence of, say, hope or joy presents all the characteristics of hope or joy. Each *token* is necessarily incomplete. However, our tendency is to want to complete what mere description seems to leave incomplete, and Wittgenstein warns us against this *illusion of theory*: 'Here *is* the whole. (If you complete it, you falsify it.)' (RPP I: 257). The tendency to complete the pattern with a picture of the inner is what makes us slide from the rough ground of description to pseudo-theoretical constructions with scientific pretensions, what Wittgenstein calls *metaphysics*; and he sees the James-Lange theory as typical of a theory that completes the pattern. Rosat shows how Wittgenstein's picture of patterns in a weave both stems from and corrects James's picture of a stream of consciousness.

As is well known, Wittgenstein pointed out an asymmetry between first- and third-person psychological statements: the first, unlike the latter, involve observation or a claim to knowledge and are constitutionally open to uncertainty. In my own contribution, 'Wittgenstein on Psychological Certainty', I challenge this asymmetry and Wittgenstein's own affirmation of the constitutional uncertainty of third-person psychological statements, and argue that Wittgenstein ultimately did too. I first show that, on his view, most of our *third-person* psychological statements are non-cognitive; they stem from a *subjective* certainty: a certainty which, though not the result of an epistemic process, is not invulnerable to error in that it is a kind of *assumption*. I then trace Wittgenstein's realization that some third-person psychological certainties are not merely subjective but 'objective' (which means, as he uses the word, that they are logically indubitable): in some cases, we can be as logically certain that someone else is in pain as we are about ourselves being in pain. This positively reinforces Wittgenstein's rebuttal of other-mind scepticism. I conclude with a response to objections about the legitimacy of calling an assurance that is *logical* (i.e., that does not have uncertainty or doubt on its flipside) a 'certainty', by suggesting that the flipside is to be found in pathological cases, and most pertinently here, in cases of *dyssemia*: a rare disorder affecting the ability to *properly* express or recognize basic physical expressions of feeling.

In his chapter, 'Criteria and Defeasibility', Eric Loomis tackles the problem of psychological certainty and imponderable evidence from a different angle. He begins by reminding us that with his notion of criterion, Wittgenstein proposed a form of non-inductive evidence which would partially constitute the meaning of those statements for which it serves as evidence. Providing a cogent explication of the notion of a criterion has proven a long-standing challenge, yet providing such an explication is important to our appraisal of Wittgenstein's work in the philosophy of psychology. For if the notion of non-inductive evidence as he used it is indefensible, many of his remarks on the philosophy of mind and language are undercut, since they require acknowledging a distinction between inductive correlations and meaning-constituting, non-inductive evidence. Loomis argues that our best hope for making sense of the notion of criterial evidence remains the simple one of treating it as logically entailing the truth of certain statements in the absence of a defeater. He shows how contemporary developments in fallibilist epistemology can help us to clarify this idea.

In 'Tennis without a Ball', Michel ter Hark deals with Wittgenstein's little-understood notion of 'secondary sense'. We are first shown in what respects secondary sense differs from metaphor. Unlike metaphor, secondary sense cannot be paraphrased into (quasi-)literal terms; and, unlike metaphor, it presupposes the command and understanding of the primary sense of the words in a strong sense. Confusing secondary sense with primary sense lies at the root of philosophical and foundational debates in psychology. Indeed, to ignore the logical dependency of the secondary sense of a word on its primary sense and to see the former, much as the latter, as language referring to objects and facts, may just as easily lead one to behaviourism as to mentalism or dualism. Ter Hark then puts the notion of 'secondary sense' to work in three different areas: synaesthesia, mental calculation and pretend play. He observes that in these areas there is a temptation to treat these concepts not in a secondary, but in a primary way – that is, it is tempting to suppose that these concepts refer to different sorts of processes in the mind or brain – and he shows why this is mistaken. A detailed and critical discussion of experimental psychological investigations into the nature of children's pretend play is interwoven in the text.

In his chapter, 'The Cradle of Language: Making Sense of Bodily Connexions', psychologist Stephen Cowley attempts to bridge the gulf separating investigations of mind from those of language by using the method of 'micro-investigations' – a method which, he claims, shows that Wittgenstein's conceptual clarifications can be used for the real-time investigation of human biomechanics. Micro-investigations are observational acts that draw on shared customs, and can be used in tracing how minded activity arises from behaviour. Hypothetically, given a record of every movement that influences a child, observations might help clarify what makes us human. In taking this view, however, it must be stressed that events use – not just experiential time – but relationships, interactions and, above all, vocal and visible gesture. Accordingly, to give a sense of these complex dynamics, Cowley develops a thick description of events. Specifically, he uses micro-investigation to scrutinize an event involving a 9-month-old baby, tracing why the baby comes to *feel like* fetching a block. Cowley delineates and makes critical use of John Canfield's illuminating sketches of development which scrupulously avoid cognitivism and present a purely descriptive anthropological study of how infants find their way into language-games.

Dan Hutto's chapter, 'Getting Clear About Perspicuous Representations: Wittgenstein, Baker and Fodor', offers new insights into the important role perspicuous representations play in Wittgenstein's philosophy. Ultimately, Hutto's aim is to show that the approaches of therapeutic and theoretically minded philosophers, respectively exemplified by Baker and Fodor, are in fact extremely limited and beset with internal difficulties. Though endorsing some of Baker's central insights about the nature and use of perspicuous representations in Wittgenstein's philosophy, Hutto firmly rejects many of his conclusions about the end of philosophy. He agrees with Baker that Wittgenstein was set against the very idea of philosophical 'theorizing', but denies that this led him (or ought to lead anyone) to promote a purely therapeutic philosophy. Hutto supplies reasons for preferring an account of Wittgenstein's approach to philosophy that emphasizes its clarificatory ambitions, and shows how perspicuous and other forms of representations have been misused in attempts at so-called philosophical theorizing. He concludes by proposing that it is only by steering clear of *both* theoretical and extreme therapeutic approaches that it is possible to prosecute a positive philosophy – one that employs perspicuous representations to bring 'relevant connections' to light for the purposes of enabling us to understand and reflect on aspects of various domains of human being.

Notes

1. In a letter (Drury, 1967), 69.
2. Cf. also: 'It was Russell who performed the service of showing that the apparent logical form of a proposition need not be its real one' (TLP: 4.0031).
3. 'What we did in these discussions was what we always do when we meet the word "can" in a metaphysical proposition. We show that this proposition hides a grammatical rule. That is to say, we destroy the outward similarity between a metaphysical proposition and an experiential one, and we try to find the form of expression which fulfils a certain craving of the metaphysician which our ordinary language does not fulfil and which, as long as it isn't fulfilled, produces the metaphysical puzzlement' (BB: 55).
4. 'For it is not the "thought" (an accompanying mental phenomenon) but its *use* (something that surrounds it), that distinguishes the logical proposition from the empirical one' (RC III: 19; my emphasis).
5. 'A main source of our failure to understand is that we do not *command a clear view* of the use of our words. – Our grammar is lacking in this sort of perspicuity. A perspicuous representation produces just that understanding which consists in "seeing connexions". Hence the importance of finding and inventing *intermediate cases*. The concept of a perspicuous representation is of fundamental significance for us. It earmarks the form of account we give, the way we look at things. (Is this a *"Weltanschauung"*?)' (PI: 122). The German is 'übersichtliche Darstellung'; I prefer translating *Darstellung* as *presentation* rather than *representation* to avoid connotations of a rendering from one language or form of symbolism to another, which I do not believe Wittgenstein intended.

1
Wittgenstein on Fear

John V. Canfield

Wittgenstein's later philosophy treats language as custom. That we have taken up such and such speech practices can be seen as part of our natural history, and thus his comment:

> What we are supplying are really remarks on the natural history of human beings ... .
>
> (PI: 415)

The result of that approach is a philosophical anthropology – a matter of delineating the language customs that constitute speech. What makes this philosophical is twofold. It focuses on concepts of significance in philosophy and the social sciences, with the aim of removing confusions underlying our intellectual endeavours. And, as opposed to a purely empirical inquiry, it proceeds in part by making up language customs related to the actual ones under study.[1] These possible practices serve as templates. Held up against strands of actual usage they help us see the contours of the concepts we are interested in. Wittgenstein's work is further distinguished by its direction. Instead of moving toward the abstract, seeking accounts that rely on general ideas such as, in the case of the emotions, 'quale', or 'cause', he moves always in the direction of the particular.

When we turn to the details of Wittgenstein's depiction of our natural history we will often find ourselves baffled – unsure of what he is saying and why he says it. I believe the effort to understand him will be well repaid: his writings provide a window through which we can see something of what it is like to be human.

In this chapter I am interested in Wittgenstein's treatment of the emotions, and in particular *fear*. The remarks I shall attempt to elucidate are drawn from Part II of the *Philosophical Investigations*, and from the note-books that are its source.[2]

I A problem

In reading through Wittgenstein's observations on fear I was struck by an apparently minor exegetical problem, the subsequent discussion of which leads to a number of more significant interpretive questions. Wittgenstein writes in the *Investigations*:

> But here is the problem: A cry [of fear, for example] which cannot be called a description, which is more primitive than any description, for all that serves as a description of the inner life.
>
> (PI: p. 189b)

My initial response to this obscure claim was perplexity over the phrase, 'But here is the problem'. Why should the point made about that primitive cry constitute a problem for Wittgenstein? For the sentence after the colon apparently invokes his familiar appeal to the natural or instinctive behaviour that serves as a source of certain utterances – those he calls *Äusserungen*. That an untutored, primitive cry of fear might serve as, or do the same communicative job as, an apparent description like 'I am afraid' would not seem problematic to him. Conversely, it seems that 'I am afraid' might in some cases be a transformation into language of the primitive cry of fear. In short, we are dealing here with a familiar circle of Wittgensteinian ideas, so why should what he says after the colon in PI: p. 189b constitute a problem for him?

The answer is that it doesn't; it is not a problem for him but for his interlocutor – the persona he is always arguing with. To see why it is a problem for that person we should turn to the manuscript where the quotation in question has its original home. In Wittgenstein's manuscripts from 1948 and 1949 (as given in LW I), PI: p. 189b appears as LW I: 45 and is preceded by the following section that does not appear in the *Investigations* and that may indeed seem quite irrelevant to 189b:

> Does the sentence 'Napoleon was crowned in the year 1804' really have a different meaning depending on whether I say it to somebody as a piece of information, or in a history test to show what I know, or etc., etc.? In order to understand it, the meanings of its words must be explained to me in the same way for each of these purposes. And if

the meaning of the words and the way they're put together constitute the meaning of the sentence, then ...

(LW I: 44)

These remarks seem to appear out of nowhere, and so the question arises of the relationship, if any, between them and LW I: 45 (or PI: p. 189b). What is the content of §44? It assumes a common, if unpolished, view of the nature of language. The meaning of the words that make up a sentence, and the way they are put together, yield its meaning. A sophisticated version of such an account is found, for example, in the semantic theory of Jerry Fodor and the late Jerrold Katz. Once the sense of the words is fixed, and the syntax of the sentence within which they occur is given, we can go on to use the sentence in various ways. We can use the assertion about Napoleon in a history of the period or, say, as a true/false question on an exam; in either case it will have the same meaning.

Obviously that account of §44 does not immediately yield an answer to our question about the relationship between it and §45. To get an answer we must continue to work our way back through the manuscript remarks. §43 – a long passage I will not quote in full – makes a point that will be familiar to students of Wittgenstein's remarks on psychology, although it has its own mysteries. The idea is that a sentence like 'I am afraid' can have a large variety of uses. This idea is evident in §43 and in many other places. For example in the *Investigations* he writes:

> I say 'I am afraid'; someone else asks me: 'What was that? A cry of fear; or do you want to tell me how you feel; or is it a reflection on your present state?'

(PI: p. 187g.)

In that passage he goes on immediately to list a number of further ways in which 'I am afraid' might be used.

§43 contains reflections on that multiplicity of ways of taking 'I am afraid'. If 'I am afraid' may be used in many different ways, how can we find out how it is used in a given case? He remarks that the question will 'almost never be asked' because, he suggests, the tone in which it is pronounced and its context give an answer. For, he says:

> ... from these we will deduce whether he is making fun of his own fear, perhaps, or whether he is discovering it in himself, so to speak,

or whether he is confessing it to us reluctantly, but for the sake of candour, or whether he is uttering it like a scream, etc.

(LW I: 43)

It is at this point that his interlocutor steps in to make the point that will lead to a resolution of our perplexity about the relationship between §44 and §45:

– And don't the words, no matter how they are uttered, give me information about the same state of affairs, namely, his state of mind?

(LW I: 43)

That's not Wittgenstein speaking, but his *alter ego*. §44, the strange and seemingly out of place rumination on 'Napoleon was crowned ...', serves just to back up the interlocutor's point, by indicating how plausible it is to separate meaning from use. Apparently, 'Napoleon was crowned ...' signifies the same state of affairs in the world, no matter whether it appears in a history book or on a final exam. Similarly, the interlocutor would have it, 'I am afraid', in virtue of the meaning of its constituent words and their order, always serves to describe a 'state of mind'.

Here, then, is the thesis Wittgenstein sets himself against: No matter how it is used (as confession, cry, whatever), 'I am afraid' is a description of a state of mind. We are now in a position to understand what is going on in §45. We are not dealing there with an utterance of 'I am afraid'. Rather, Wittgenstein's example is a 'cry of fear' – something 'more primitive than any description'. He is thinking, of course, of examples like someone's – or some animal's – natural expression of pain. This does not belong to language, and yet language can build upon it, as when a person learns to substitute something like the conventional signal 'ouch' for a cry of pain untouched by custom. Similarly for natural expressions of fear; they may issue forth in a way not shaped by custom. Such a cry of fear, Wittgenstein observes, can 'serve as a description of [an] inner state'. The cry and what he would call the *Aüsserung* 'I am afraid' are functionally equivalent.[3] Each can serve to draw an observer's attention to someone's fear-state. We now have before us the context for the remarks we have been examining. We are inclined to think that all uses of 'I am afraid' report the speaker's state of mind. That they do is the objection raised in §43, and explained further in §44. Use is one thing, meaning another: all utterances of 'I am afraid' constitute descriptions of the speaker's mental state. But §45 presents a putative counter-example to that thesis. The argument behind the apparent counter-example runs as follows:

1. A cry of fear does not equal a description of a state of mind.
2. A cry of fear does equal 'I am afraid' (in the case where the latter is an *Aüsserung*).
3. Therefore 'I am afraid' does not (in this case) equal a description of a state of mind.

The counter-example suggested in §43 is a cry of fear that is in some significant way equivalent to the *Aüsserung* 'I am afraid'. This reading of §45 relies on making explicit Premise (2), the unstated presupposition of §45. That Wittgenstein would affirm (2) is suggested by remarks like the following:

> Meaning, function, purpose, usefulness – interconnected concepts.
>
> (LW I: 291)

A cry of fear can serve the same purpose as the corresponding *Aüsserung*, have the same usefulness or function. We might say that in the sense of meaning tied to purpose, usefulness and function, the cry and the *Aüsserung* can be said to be equal in meaning. Thus the cry of fear, while not a description of the inner life, nevertheless serves as one, in that it performs the same job a description might. Namely it draws the other person's attention to the fact that the agent is afraid. An utterance of 'I am afraid' might do the same. Nonetheless, not all such utterances are descriptions of the inner life, because some of them have the same status as a cry of fear, something that is no description. So, in sum, the problem-setting example I spoke of is a cry of fear that is in some strong sense equal to 'I am afraid', *qua Aüsserung*. Neither is a description of the inner life, although both could function as such by serving to communicate the idea that a person is afraid.

Note that there is an innocent and a metaphysical way of reading the phrase 'description of the inner life'. On the latter, one thinks that an emotion like fear can be observed inwardly: fear is a mental object we can introspect and report on. On the former, to say 'He is afraid' might in some cases rightly be called a description of the person's inner life, but only in that it reports the occurrence of a certain emotion – it speaks, for example, of Jones's fear. As we shall see for the case of fear-talk there are a large number of different ways of thus innocently describing someone's inner life.

II 'I will teach you differences'

The examination of §45 brings us up against a hallmark aspect of Wittgenstein's discussion of fear: the idea – in effect denied by the interlocutor at §43, with the denial reinforced at §44 – that there are a significant number of different ways 'I am afraid' may be understood, different language-games in which the sentence or its equivalents appear. This emphasis on differences shows itself plainly in the distinction between uses of 'I am afraid' that are *Aüsserungen* and those that are not. That contrast is a central one, but there are numerous other variations in the use of fear-language. Wittgenstein emphasizes such alternatives in several lists he gives, some of them already quoted. That multi-concept view of fear raises a number of hard questions. First, is it indeed true that there are significantly different uses of fear assertions? It is far from obvious that the items in the various listed ways of speaking of fear do all differ significantly. Second, if they do differ, how exactly do they do so? And why would it be important to recognize those differences?

To begin, I will set out some more of the alleged variations Wittgenstein refers to. In the quote given earlier from PI: p. 187g, he distinguishes three things: a cry of fear, a report on how one feels, and a reflection on one's present state. Note that it is not obvious that the latter two are different.

The list of differences given in §43 has already been quoted. There the speaker may be making fun of his fear, or reporting on his discovery of it, or confessing it, or, our old favourite, uttering it like a scream. And again, in PI: p. 188a (immediately following PI: 187g) there is this list:

> We can imagine all sorts of things here, for example:
> 'No, no! I am afraid!'
> 'I am afraid. I am sorry to have to confess it.'
> 'I am still a bit afraid, but no longer as much as before.'
> 'At bottom I am still afraid, though I won't confess it to myself.'
> 'I torment myself with all sorts of fears.'
> 'Now, just when I should be fearless, I am afraid!'
>
> (PI: p. 188a)

Wittgenstein goes on to make the crucial remark that for each of these utterances 'a special tone of voice is appropriate and a different context'.[4] He then makes this observation:

> It would be possible to imagine people who as it were thought much more definitely than we, and used different words where we use only one.
>
> (PI: p. 188a)

If we say that to have mastery of a concept is to be able to use a corresponding word in the appropriate language-game, then each item in Wittgenstein's list exemplifies a different concept. Each use of 'I am afraid' occurs within a language-game that is different from the others. These contrasts are obscured by the blanket expression 'I am afraid'. Conceptual clarification will result from a realization that those words hide differences of use.

To repeat, one may well doubt whether the examples listed or alluded to really belong to distinct language-games. Concerning the items in the above quoted long list from PI: p. 188a, for example, one is hard put to see significant differences. The task now is to bring those various contrasts to light. I begin by taking up briefly Wittgenstein's idea of a conceptual genealogy:

> I should like to speak of a genealogical tree of psychological concepts
> (RPP I: 722)

In establishing parts of such a genealogy for *fear* we are not limited to observations on actual language-games and their surroundings; rather, one can construct relevant imaginary cases (see LW I: 19, for example). While it would take some arbitrary decisions to place all of the items listed at PI: p. 188a in an 'A begat B, B begat C ...' hierarchy, some points along such a line are plain. We are to start at the logically most primitive level and work our way up, so let us begin with our pre-linguistic hominid forebears. What form of life might stand as a foundation for their subsequent various uses of fear-talk? What is the context out of which such talk might emerge? Two elements stand out. First, a world containing fearful objects, such as predators, poisonous snakes, angry fellow creatures. Second, inborn ways of expressing fear. So at the bottom level of our genealogical sketch stand human-like creatures who lack speech but who often encounter fearful things, and in doing so react in ways we would recognize, given the context, as expressions of fear, or fear behaviour. For example, a certain hesitation or drawing back, a scream, or panicked flight. Here we are at the genealogical stage suggested by Wittgenstein's remark:

> That someone can scream doesn't mean that he can tell somebody something in a conversation.
> (LW I: 46)

Now we must add speech. It is easy to imagine a people who use a certain sound to indicate that the person spoken of is afraid – indeed, let the sound be 'Afraid!' In an appropriate context we see someone acting fearfully and draw this fact to another's attention by a look, and the word 'Afraid'. Given the proper linguistic surroundings we can imagine this use supplemented as required by other words, yielding 'He is afraid!', 'Jones is afraid!' and so on. There are various ways such signals might be useful to a people. They might be employed to pass on the fact of the possible presence of something fearful, or to explain a person's hesitant behaviour. Given a more sophisticated surrounding, they might justify our scorn for someone, or serve to ameliorate his failure to do something.

So far, then, the use of '... afraid' is tied to behaviour. That fact gives point to Wittgenstein's statement:

> What does 'being afraid' mean? If I wanted to define it at a *single* showing – I should *play-act* fear.
>
> (PI: p. 188d)

We have been speaking of other-directed uses of fear-talk – 'He is afraid', 'Jones is afraid'. Where should we put 'I am afraid' in our genealogical hierarchy? Which comes first, 'He/Jones is afraid' or 'I am afraid'? I assume, in the latter case, that we are dealing with an *Aüsserung* – the 'I am afraid' that is an embodiment in language of a natural fear-reaction. A child raised in a culture where people use the word 'afraid' to attribute fear to others one day spontaneously says 'Afraid!' in a situation where earlier it would have just jumped back in fear. On one scenario this utterance would not have happened unless the word was already in use in the culture to refer to the fear of others.

The child's first-person uses differ from its third-person ones in that the former are not made on the basis of observation. I do not see my reflection, notice that I am acting in a fearful manner, and on that basis say 'I am afraid'. I will speak here of a non-observational use of fear-talk. In the story as presented the first-person use develops on the back of the other-directed one. 'He is afraid' is logically prior to the non-observational 'I am afraid'.

So far our genealogy seems clear: an assumed pre-linguistic world containing fearful things and agents who react fearfully to them, followed by, first, the development of 'He is afraid' as governed by criteria involving behaviour in a context, and second by the introduction of a non-observational, first-person use of 'I am afraid'. Note, however, that the development of other- and first-person uses might have gone the other way. Conceivably, a people might have first evolved a custom-governed use of a word *qua* fear-*Aüsserung*, and then subsequently employed the same word in other-person descriptions. Thus there are two possible genealogical lines. To ask which one in fact obtained goes beyond conceptual clarification; the task rather is to see what our concepts are by studying various ways they might have grown.

Before we can attempt to delineate other points on some possible genealogical tree, it is necessary to get clearer about differences holding among some of the other examples Wittgenstein has alluded to. To begin, consider the threefold way of taking 'I am afraid' given at PI: p. 187g, which I cite again for convenience:

> What was that? A cry of fear, or do you want to tell me how you feel; or is it a reflection on your present state?

An instance from Kleist's play *Prince Friedrich of Homburg* seems to fit the second of those stated alternatives:

> *Elector*: But Natalia is so quiet. What's bothering my sweet child?
> *Natalia*: I'm afraid, dear uncle.
> *Elector*: And yet [you are] no less safe now than [you were in your] mother's arms.[5]

If, as Wittgenstein emphasizes, 'describing my state of mind is something I do in a particular context' (PI: p. 188f), what is the background for Natalia's utterance? The Elector and his subordinates are preparing plans for a decisive battle the next day, and as part of that, he is going over arrangements for the evacuation of his wife and his niece Natalia to a safe haven, across the Havel River, where 'no Swedes will dare to let themselves be seen'. He notices that his niece, who is present at these preparations, is bothered and asks why. She reports, naturally enough given the context, that she is afraid, and he replies by reassuring her. Now, how does Natalia's utterance differ from uses of 'I am afraid' like the third alternative cited in PI: p. 187g concerning reflection on one's present state? One differentiating feature comes to light when we consider the question: 'on what basis does Natalia put forward her fear-assertion?' Sometimes a person might reflect on what he has been doing and how he has been reacting all day, and come thus to utter the words 'I am afraid'. We might call this a memory-based use. But nothing like that happens in the Natalia case, we may assume. There is no shifting through the past day's events; no rehearsing or evaluating them in memory in order to comprehend her present state. Rather there is just the context as set out, the question and the natural, spontaneous answer 'I am afraid'. It would be misleading to call that answer a reflection on the person's mind state.

Rather, Natalia's utterance is closer to an *Aüsserung qua* cry of fear. To get an example of the latter sort we can imagine that in her flight to safety she is faced with the necessity of running through a field under bombardment; drawing back, unable to precede, she cries out (as in PI: p. 188a), 'No, no! I am afraid!' Her original 'I am afraid' is like such an *Aüsserung* in that it is not made on the basis of a criterion; it is spontaneously uttered. It is unlike an *Aüsserung* in that the latter will issue forth when the person is suddenly faced with some danger, whereas before speaking Natalia was aware for some time of her plight. Furthermore, Natalia's 'I am afraid' was said in response to a question; *Aüsserungen* are not so given forth. In contrast to Natalia's original utterance, there is no calm comment on her emotion, nor is there reported a memory-based reflection on her state of mind.

Kleist's play can provide a further contrasting use of 'afraid'. The Prince, a proud and glory seeking man, has been condemned to death for disobeying the Elector's orders. He bears up well under this but then, temporarily out of prison, comes face to face with the freshly dug grave that awaits him on the morrow. Faced with this stark sign of immanent death he goes to pieces, losing his honour and courage, and vowing to do anything to escape death. In that context we can imagine his saying 'I am afraid' as a reaction to the thought of the firing squad. Here the utterance 'I'm afraid!' is, we might say, thought-based. The Prince is not reacting to the sight of some danger, as in the case of the field under bombardment. An empty grave in itself poses no threat, but the thoughts it inspires may be terrible ones.

After the list of different uses cited at PI: p. 188a Wittgenstein writes:

> It would be possible to imagine people who as it were thought much more definitely than we, and used different words where we use only one.

Let us follow up on that suggestion. In the Natalia example, instead of 'I am afraid', those more conceptually astute people might substitute 'I am facing danger'. Here one should not object that 'I am facing danger' is hardly equivalent to 'I am afraid', since a heroic person might acknowledge the danger and yet be without fear. For in the example, the words 'I am facing danger' are just what the precise people say when we would say, with Natalia, in the same sort of context and with the same tone of voice, 'I am afraid'. It would be wrong to read our understanding of 'I am facing danger' into the usage of the precise people. The same point holds for the other examples looked at below. The Prince's 'I am afraid' might become, 'I can't bear these thoughts!' For the memory-based case, 'I am uneasy'. For my speaking of someone else's fear: 'He is fear-behaving' and for an *Aüsserung*, simply 'Fear!' To add in one more type of case, recall Wittgenstein's raising the possibility of a use of fear-talk that applies only to non-human animals (cf. LW I: 10).

I turn now to some further differences from the list in PI: p. 188a. 'I am afraid', might be used to say in effect 'I torment myself with all sorts of fears'. Tone of voice: a slightly embarrassed honesty. Context: I am expecting her to arrive after travelling through rebel-held territory. I say to myself things like: She may be captured, she's weak and may fall ill, she may step on a mine ... And I find myself unable to cease entertaining those thoughts or expressing those worries. We might say 'I am afraid' is, for those precise-thinking people, 'I self-torment'. One difference between this case and that of the Prince and his grave is this: the Prince's fearful thoughts come at once in a great rush, and he is undone. The self-tormentor's bad thoughts started early (from no particular source) and last through the day or days.

Consider the case 'I am afraid. I am sorry to have to confess it.' For people to be able to speak that way requires they possess the concept *confess*. That requires in turn standards of behaviour; roughly speaking, one can only confess if what one did was somehow unworthy. So: 'How do you feel about being ordered to the front?'; 'I am afraid. I am sorry to have to confess it.' This comes close to the Natalia example. We create an alternative to that instance by imagining that Natalia's culture has a low opinion of those who say they are afraid; to say it is to lose face. This new use then requires only a certain tone of voice, and a context of the sort just suggested. Natalia-2 who inhabits that context, simply says 'I am afraid' with a confessing tone of voice. The precise-speakers might say instead 'I confess-fear'.

'I am still a bit afraid, but no longer as much as before.' Knowing I must undergo an operation, someone asks me if I am afraid; I answer as above. When I first learned of the necessity for the operation, I was overcome by dread. But now I have studied the matter and have been reassured by trustworthy people that the operation is low risk. Hence my remark. But how do I recognize that I am still a bit afraid? Well, I still worry a bit about it, despite those reassurances. It's on my mind. I think about it; I know it is coming and I am uneasy. On what basis do I say that earlier I was much more afraid? I remember being stunned at the news, and being unable to think of anything else.

Having a wrong model in mind may confuse us here. We may think of diminished fear on the model of diminished pain. Yesterday my headache was devastating; today it is much less intense. I remember its past intensity and am aware of its present diminished force. The example of fear doesn't work that way. It was the thought of a highly dangerous operation that overwhelmed me, not some intense mind-state; I was afraid of the operation, not of my feelings about it.

'At bottom I am still afraid, though I won't confess it to myself.' There are different cases. In one imaginable instance the cause or occasion of fear is no longer present. Perhaps in the operation example later tests have shown that there is no need for surgery; the problem can be treated with drugs. But though the person knows this, he is still afraid. On what basis might he say that he is? Perhaps he is aware that his former care-free attitude to life has changed. Now, unlike earlier, little things can disturb him. This case, so far, is like the memory-based example, except that the agent must dig deeper, be more subtle and sophisticated, must rely more on nuance. What is the force of the 'I won't confess it to myself?' part of the example? It may seem nonsensical. If he says he won't confess it to himself, he must already know it, so how could he self-confess it. Here self-confession seems like self-deception; both seem at first impossible, but only because one is working with the wrong pictures. We think the self-confessor must both know what is confessed and, on the basis of the confession, come to know it. So how might 'I won't confess it to myself' be actually used. Perhaps in such a context as this: The speaker won't ask himself the question 'Am I afraid?' He turns his mind away from it, thinking 'Don't go there!'

It might be useful to indicate some of the differences I have elicited by placing them in one possible genealogical order, as follows:

(1) Way of life: danger, and fear-reaction
(2) Cry of fear
(3) 'Fear!' (other directed; simple behavioural criterion)
(4) 'Fear! (self-directed; no criterion; *Aüsserung*)
(5) 'He is afraid' (as in (3))
(6) 'I am afraid!' (as in (4))
(7) 'I am afraid' (Natalia case: no criterion)
(8) Prince/grave; thought-based
(9) Reflective fear; 'I am uneasy'
(10) 'I self-torment'
(11) 'I confess fear'
(12) 'Fear, but I won't confess it'

The use in line (3) can arise, given the context cited in lines (1) and (2). 'Fear!' in line (4) is an *Aüsserung*. Line (5) is just an enlargement of the

'Fear' of line (3), and similarly for lines (6) and (4). Differences between (7), (8) and (9) have been cited. Lines (11) and (12) are noteworthy for their reliance on quite sophisticated cultural features. The two major conceptual gaps that emerge are between *Aüsserungen* and descriptions, (between (4) and (9)) and between thought-based fear (8) and the no-thought variety as in (6).

III   Paths through life

In light of the examples we have canvassed, no one could deny that there are different uses of words like 'fear' or 'afraid'. But are those differences significant, and is the existence of significantly different language-games (if there are such) itself significant? There may be differences, but so what?

To address the first question, consider some of the differences and similarities among the various language-games. They all require a fearful context, or the assumption of one – though these can vary as concerns their weight. Certain tones of voice – expressing joy for example – are admissible in no straightforward or, as it were, first-level first-person cases. On the other hand there is a whole class of cases I have not considered that are marked especially by tone of voice, as when someone says 'I'm afraid' playfully, jokingly, ironically, indeed even joyfully, in response to a pretend, playful threat. As for differences, some are *Aüsserungen*, some are not; some involve self-observation, some do not; some arise spontaneously, some only with prompting; some are thought-driven, some not; some require sophisticated presuppositions, such as the existence in the culture of the practice of confession, or of witty self-deprecation, or self-deception, whereas some are simple and basic, related to our gut-reactions to suddenly sensed danger. We could highlight these differences by imagining various peoples, some of whom have this language-game with fear, some that, some this subset, some that and so on. Now, are these differences significant? Well yes, if you want a fine-tuned look at what it is to speak of fear.

Is the existence of those differences itself significant? There are two reasons for thinking it is. One concerns the question that lies behind Wittgenstein's examination of 'fear':

> We ask: 'What does "I am frightened" really mean? What am I thinking when I say it?'
>
> (PI: p. 188c)

This asks after the correct general or theoretical account of fear. That the query is central to any examination of fear, whether conceptual or empirical, doesn't need arguing. Even those who would abandon our normal understanding of 'fear' for a scientific version would want to know at least this much about what 'I am frightened' really means, namely that science in the fullness of time will tell us the answer.

Immediately after stating the question Wittgenstein goes on to say: '... of course we find no answer, or one that is inadequate'. Why does this question have no adequate answer? The reason is that we assume that the fear reported upon in 'I am afraid' is the referent of 'fear' and that there is only one thing fear is. The task of the psychologist or other researcher is then to say what that one thing is. That referential understanding is natural, intuitive. But as the examples I have discussed show, this notion of a common referent is mistaken. There are many distinct uses of 'fear' or 'afraid'. We must change the question. Instead of 'What is the one thing we speak of when we speak of fear?', we should ask 'What is it like to speak of fear?' That is, what are the language-games involved in fear-talk like?

Thus becoming aware of different language-games with 'fear' is significant in that it reveals the misleading nature of the question about what fear really is. The case of the blind men and the elephant comes to mind. The creature is snake-like, rope-like, wall-like, depending on what comes to hand. To the seeing person the animal is all of those, and more.

We might think of Wittgenstein's account of fear, in so far as I have presented it, as an analysis of utterances like 'I am afraid'. However, it is a type of analysis that differs deeply from other types. Instead of trying to bring the many cases of fear-talk under the same general account, it seeks to fracture any general account into a multitude of different uses. Instead of understanding the many in terms of one, understand the one in terms of the many.

I add that this talk of analysis, as well as the fable of the blind men, can be misleading. In response to a citation of differences, theorists of fear might simply connect the allegedly distinct uses by the word 'or' and thus, apparently, arrive at a correct account of fear that admits the differences. So a theorist like Robert Solomon might say (not that he would want to) that his thought-based account of an emotion like fear is correct, but just not all inclusive; there are other forms fear can take. Such a response would elide the radical difference between such an account of fear and Wittgenstein's. The difference consists in the two parties' profoundly various take on the nature of language.

Someone might object, 'What does an examination of use of Wittgenstein's sort have at all to do with the question "What is fear?" The issue, after all, is not how we use certain words but how things really are.' The reply is that observing language-games does show us how things really are. *This* is how humans move through life. We are not dealing with mere words, but with patterns of action and interaction in the world.

Another objection would hold that I have left feelings out of account. A treatment of fear that omits consideration of what the speaker is feeling may seem wrong-headed in the extreme. While there certainly are various feelings characteristic of fear, they are, however, neither necessary nor sufficient for being afraid. Not sufficient, in that the mere existence of the feeling itself, devoid of any of the usual contexts and manifestations of fear, would not count as fear. Not necessary, in that someone, say, screaming and fleeing in terror from a bombing attack, would count as having fear even in the absence of any of those alleged feelings. An understanding of fear-talk must focus on context, behaviour, expression, tone of voice and truth-criteria. Rather than placing feeling at the foundation of our concept of fear, we are to understand the feeling in terms of those characteristics.

Canvassing different language-games concerning fear helps free us from the conviction that fear is some one thing, some state of mind, for example. It shows us the many faces of fear. But that noticing of differences also has a positive aspect, other than that of telling us what fear is. Marking differences in language-games for 'fear' or 'afraid', and like terms, helps us understand ourselves by making clear the different fear-word employing paths through life people take. In general as a child grows it must take on various culturally constrained ways of proceeding through life. Some of these action patterns are linguistic. It learns to say 'hello' and 'goodbye', to ask for things and tell its intentions. Eventually it learns to take part in a huge number of language customs. Its language learning takes place in some or other broad biological and cultural way of life.

The form of life provides the various possibilities for individual, tribal or national existence. If you enter *this* path in *this* culture, you become a warrior or hunter, if this other path in this other culture, a midwife or shaman or brain surgeon, and so on. The pathways must be there in the life-way. Custom and culture constrain our possibilities of interacting with others – something Sartre failed to realize when he spoke of our absolute freedom.[6] You can't undertake to practice, say, the Apache custom of mother-in-law avoidance all by yourself; for a non-Apache people your repeated refusal to be in the same social space as her would only be weird. Language-games, as I have assumed from the beginning, are further cultural givens, fine-tuned ways of proceeding through life. To recognize their features is, as indicated at the beginning of this paper, to see something of what it is like to be human.

Notes

1. See, for example, PI: p. 230a.
2. The latter have been published as RPP I and II, and LW I and II.
3. On this, c.f. D. Moyal-Sharrock, '"Words as Deeds": Wittgenstein's "spontaneous utterances" and the Dissolution of the Explanator Gap', *Philosophical Psychology* 13:3 (September 2000), 355–75.
4. Cf. also, PI: 188f: 'Describing my state of mind (of fear, say) is something I do in a particular context. (Just as it takes a particular context to make a certain action into an experiment.)/ Is it, then, so surprising that I use the same expression in different games? And sometimes as it were between the games?'
5. Heinrich von Kleist, *Prince Friedrich of Homburg*, trans. Diana Stone Peters and Frederick G. Peters (New York: New Directions, 1978), 16.
6. Cf. Jean-Paul Sartre, *Being and Nothingness*, trans. Hazel E. Barnes (New York: Philosophical Library, 1956), 439ff.

2
Wittgensteinian Grammar and Philosophy of Mind

Stéphane Chauvier

The thousands of remarks on philosophical psychology made by Wittgenstein during the last six years of his life[1] have an objective that may be called therapeutic. In bringing psychological concepts back from their philosophical to their ordinary use,[2] Wittgenstein explicitly sought to dissolve the prestige of some of the pictures on which traditional philosophy of mind was reared, particularly the picture of the inner; that is, of inner phenomena to which a subject would have privileged access.

Some contemporary interpreters of Wittgenstein believe this therapeutic objective to be Wittgenstein's *only* objective in these remarks. For these 'New Wittgensteinians', Wittgenstein in his philosophy of psychology is not a mere therapeute, but an *austere* therapeute.[3] He seeks to show what the mind is *not*, whilst attempting to cure us of the desire to question ourselves on the nature of the mind and of mental phenomena. Much like an eel slipping through our fingers, Wittgenstein's thought is seen as offering no grip on any positive reading of his philosophical psychology – on any reading involving *theses*. In opposition to this view, I will propose a mapping of Wittgenstein's writings on philosophical psychology drawn directly from his 'grammar' of psychological concepts, and which lets surface the outline of a positive conception of the mind.

Clearly, Wittgenstein did not delineate a 'philosophy of mind' in the sense this expression is understood by contemporary philosophy. But this is not, I suggest, because his 'austerity' prevented him from engaging in this type of investigation, but because the conception of mind Wittgenstein did come to could only have been reached via an analysis of the *grammar* of psychological concepts.[4] So that the meaning of his 'grammatical' remarks cannot be reduced to their *pars destruens*.

1   Use versus theses on use

Let us begin by stating the obvious: Wittgenstein's remarks on philosophical psychology are remarks on the ordinary use of psychological concepts, but they are not themselves an ordinary use of these concepts. It is one thing to use language; it is another to study, examine, analyse the use of language; for example, it is one thing to use the concept of belief; another, to study, examine, analyse our uses of the concept of belief. Even where Wittgenstein's remarks contain fragments of language use, it is clear from the context that these fragments are not first-order uses of language. Moreover, Wittgenstein rarely refers to fragments of language use without then *characterizing* that use. A case in point is the fundamental distinction between expression (*Äusserung, Ausdruck*), information (*Meldung*) and description (*Beschreibung*). Focusing on the contrast between, say, 'I believe it is raining' and 'I believed it was raining' draws out a difference that the words 'expression' and 'information' can then be used to name. And to then say that some psychological concepts are sometimes used in sentences that are expressions and sometimes in sentences that are descriptions or reports is a statement that does not *make use* of the psychological concept of belief, but that *bears on its use*.

Psychological language games are then the *theme* of Wittgenstein's philosophical investigations. They constitute its object of study; it is *about* them that Wittgenstein formulates his 'remarks'. This means that it is at least possible to credit Wittgenstein, if not with substantial philosophical theses, then with theses relative to the grammar of psychological concepts, theses stating a grammarian's knowledge. Wittgenstein did not restrict himself to quoting fragments of the ordinary use of psychological concepts; he mentioned them, observed them and characterized them; he laboured to order them and drew lessons from this examination.

I suggest that the quasi-totality of the subject-matter of Wittgenstein's remarks on philosophical psychology can be summarized in two master 'grammatical' theses. I will call the first of these *the thesis of the equivocality of the concept of mind*.[5] This thesis states that psychological concepts constitute, at best, a family; that there is no common genus which would allow us to define the whole range of psychological concepts using a genealogical tree. The second master thesis is related to the first; I will call it the *thesis of asymmetry*. This thesis complements the previous one by stating what all psychological concepts have in common in spite of their equivocality and which therefore justifies their belonging to the same family: an asymmetry between their present tense first-person and third-person uses, as well as between their first-person present and past tense uses.

Whatever for now their precise meaning, it should be clear that these two theses are genuine theses; that is, they are statements that may be true or false. They are not themselves grammatical truths; rather, they are truths *about* the grammar of our concepts. What makes them true or false; what functions as truth-makers of these theses, are the uses – our uses – of psychological concepts.

Moreover, these two theses play a genuinely architectonic role, not in the sense that they are the foundations of anything, but simply in that they *explain* what Wittgenstein does in most of his remarks. So that if we were to pick at random any of the thousands of remarks that make up his philosophical psychology, we would find that in most cases Wittgenstein was deliberately engaged in showing differences: (a) between *pairs* of psychological concepts (e.g., the concept of pain from that of depression; seeing *vs.* seeing as); or (b) between different uses of a single concept (e.g., distinguishing expressive from descriptive uses of the concept of pain or belief). What I shall attempt to show here is that, in the intersection of these two theses, a philosophy of mind, or at least the germ of such a philosophy, can be seen emerging from the very lap of grammar.

2   The thesis of the equivocality of the concept of mind

This passage from the Geach transcription of a Wittgenstein lecture serves to illustrate the thesis of the equivocality of the concept of mind:

> *Wittgenstein*: Yes. Pain – knowledge – intention – they all belong to psychology. But what is it like to say that?
> *Geach*: As doctors deal with hearts and malaria.
> *Wittgenstein*: … My distinctions are not like the distinctions of botanical variety: they are distinctions of category. We are not dealing in nuances; it is like the difference between King and Queen in chess.
>
> (LPP: 59–60)

Here, Wittgenstein is suggesting that when we qualify as 'psychological' phenomena like pain, knowledge, intention – in contrast to physical phenomena – the inevitable suggestion is that we are dealing with species of a common genus; perhaps even with modes or modifications of a common substance. Whereas, in fact, as regards the psychological, no candidate for the status of common genus or of common substance proves satisfying. This is especially true, insists Wittgenstein, of the concept of experience, *Erlebnis*.[6] Clearly, then, his view is that differences between psychological concepts are too great for these to be viewed as species of a common genus. Differences between psychological concepts are categorial, not specific: the concept of *mind* is no more a 'common genus' than the concept of *being*, in Aristotle.

The idea that the realm of the psychological constitutes a family rather than a genus is a particularization of a more general, well-known Wittgensteinian theme; but if we are to take this idea further, we must insist on what is implied in recognizing that a concept works like a family resemblance concept. Let us consider the classical example of the concept of game (PI: 66). Wittgenstein rejects the idea that the meaning of a word can be expressed by means of a unitary definition stating the necessary and sufficient conditions of any game. We are then tempted to say that he rejects the traditional notion of *essence*, which, since Aristotle, is thought to be what such a definition defines. But this does not mean that Wittgenstein rejects the idea that there is a difference between a game and a non-game, or between a game and a serious activity. What he does reject is the manner in which it is claimed this difference is *known*. We know what a game is, not when we know a unitary definition of the word 'game', but when we are able to survey the extension of the concept of game; that is, when we know the circumstances of the use of the concept of game. It is possible, however, to distinguish a practical from a theoretical knowledge of such circumstances. A *practical* knowledge might simply consist in the aptitude to use the concept of game correctly in any of the circumstances that motivate such a use. But what would be a *theoretical* knowledge of such circumstances? It would consist in something like a catalogue of the similarities and differences of these circumstances which, while having something of the impossible unitary definition of essence, would nevertheless replace it by what Wittgenstein calls *Übersicht*, 'a synoptic view'.

This means that a single operation – call it *conceptual differentiation* – fulfils two functions simultaneously. For one, it makes clear that a given concept is a family resemblance concept by showing that the differences between pairs of elements preclude the localization of a common generic trait. Here, conceptual differentiation has a negative or therapeutic function: it reveals the inadequacy of certain unitary pictures. At the same time, however, conceptual differentiation itself *constitutes* the adequate mode of knowing the family in question in that it effects an ordering between members of the family. Therefore, it has also a positive or constructive function.

We can now return to the particular case of psychological concepts. A significant number of Wittgenstein's remarks on philosophical psychology is dedicated, if not to the *demonstration* of the thesis of equivocality, then to its exhibition or 'monstration'. For Wittgenstein, the point is to reveal that between psychological concepts, there are differences that preclude our ordering them in accordance with the canon of the Porphyrian tree. But while this endeavour has a negative aim – which is to reveal the inadequacy of certain unitary pictures – it has also a positive aim or effect: to procure an adequate knowledge of things psychological, an *Übersicht* of psychological concepts.[7]

That Wittgenstein did indeed seek such an overview of psychological concepts is attested by his allusion in several remarks to what he himself calls a 'plan for the treatment of psychological concepts'.[8] In such remarks, we are offered a mode of ordering the observations dispersed in the remarks as a whole. Of course, it would be entirely inappropriate to say that, in his search for 'synopticity', Wittgenstein managed to reduce all psychological concepts to a determined number of *classes*. There are no such classes precisely because intermediary concepts can always be found. And yet in our exploration of Wittgenstein's diverse attempts at ordering, we shall see emerging, if not a tripartition of psychological concepts, certainly three clusters of concepts, between which isolated cases occur but which nevertheless form three clear shapes in the landscape of the philosophy of mind.

The first cluster brings together concepts of 'sensations' (*Sinnesempfindungen*) (RPP II: 63) and 'impressions' (*Eindrücke*) (RPP I: 836): 'smell', 'hearing', 'sight', 'being in pain' are included in this cluster. Although these concepts exhibit important differences, particularly those having to do with perception ('hearing' or 'sight') and sensation ('being in pain', 'stretching out one's arm'), they all have a common trait, which is that it makes sense to ask the person expressing them in the first person questions related to their duration, intensity and clarity – which gives credence to the picture of something inwardly experienced; what contemporary philosophers call *qualia*.

A second cluster subsumes what Wittgenstein sometimes calls 'mental states' (*Seelenzustände*) (RPP II: 177) and more often, 'emotions' (*Gemütsbewegungen*) (RPP II: 148): for example, joy, sadness, depression, anger, fear. Here, it makes sense to question the individual expressing them in the first person about their duration and their course; not, however, about their localization. Nor does it make sense to speak about them in terms of the spatial detection of an object, or in terms of bodily pain:

> I am inclined to say: emotions can *colour* thoughts; bodily pain cannot. Therefore let us speak of sad thoughts, but not, analogously, of toothachey thoughts.
>
> (RPP II: 153)

The third cluster is one on which the whole weight of interpretation rests, and about which it might be said that one of its characteristics is Wittgenstein's apparent difficulty in assigning it a categorial term. In some remarks, Wittgenstein speaks of 'directed emotions' (*gerichteten Gemüts-bewegungen*) and of 'attitudes' (*Stellungnahmen*) (RPP I: 836). Elsewhere, he suggests the term 'dispositions' (RPP II: 45, 57), but only to indicate a little later about the concept of intention, which, however, belongs to that cluster, that the expression 'mental disposition' is 'misleading as much as one does not perceive such a disposition within himself as a matter of experience' (RPP II: 178). One notes here an obvious difficulty on Wittgenstein's part in characterizing the concepts in this cluster, which include knowing, understanding and belief, as well as intending, hoping and willing. The shared characteristics are negative: it never makes sense to question someone who expresses knowledge, belief, intention or hope, and so on, about the internal duration of what she is expressing (which indicates that the use of these concepts is not linked to characteristic experiences, as is the case with sensory impression concepts); and there are no characteristic facial or bodily expressions associated with the use of these concepts, as is the case with emotion concepts. This third cluster is therefore both firmly distinct from the first two, as well as categorially indeterminate.

It must be reiterated that these three clusters are mere clusters, not genuine species or classes; for not only are there important internal differences in each cluster, there are also concepts that are not exclusive to any one of them. The concept of representation, for instance, belongs both to the third and first clusters; that of hope to the third and second. It is clear, however, that Wittgenstein makes use of specific criteria in his differentiation of psychological concepts, as for example: the (im)possibility of linking their use to something experiential or to characteristic forms of expression, shouts, gestures or facial expressions; or of spatially situating them; or of deliberately prompting them. So that even if there are substantial enough differences to preclude subsuming psychological concepts under the same genus (whilst assigning them specific or modal differences), an order can nonetheless be discerned within the realm of the psychological – an order that would be more aptly formalized by a graph than by a tree, but an order nevertheless, which suffices to provide us with a synoptic view of the psychological realm. As to our second thesis – the thesis of asymmetry – it allows us to articulate all these differences, whilst giving shape to the notion of *Übersichtlichkeit*.

3   The thesis of asymmetry

The thesis of asymmetry is the counterpart of the thesis of equivocality and it functions as a kind of centripetal force. Although there is no common genus, no common concept of mind, there is a common characteristic of all psychological concepts when they are used in verbal form: a first/third-person present tense asymmetry, and a first-person present tense/first-person past tense asymmetry.[9]

What does the thesis of asymmetry amount to? Wittgenstein presents it as an *epistemic* asymmetry: to judge that someone else is angry, I must observe his behaviour, but to judge that I am angry, I need not observe myself; it is enough that I *be* angry.[10] In more traditional terminology, we would say that this marks a difference in the modes of knowing the object of judgment. And yet, although Wittgenstein characterizes the asymmetry of psychological verbs by means of an epistemic variable (observation), I suggest that the asymmetry with which he is concerned is not an epistemic one.

The asymmetry evoked by Wittgenstein is meant to discriminate between psychological and non-psychological verbs – for instance, between suffering and writing.[11] The question is: why is 'I am suffering' psychological and 'I am writing a letter' physical? If the asymmetry Wittgenstein is concerned with were epistemic, the answer would be: because I *know* that I am writing in the same way I know that someone else is writing, whereas I do not *know* that I am suffering in the same way I know that someone else is suffering. This response might appeal to a distinction made by Wittgenstein in the *Blue Book* between two uses of the word 'I', which he calls 'the use as object' and 'the use as subject' (BB: 66). In 'I am suffering', the use of 'I' is subjective, and this accounts for the asymmetry with 'He is suffering'; whereas in 'I am writing', the use of 'I' is objective, therefore producing no epistemic asymmetry with 'he is writing'; and so, 'to write' is not a psychological verb.

Yet this account cannot be right; for if it were, the distinction between psychological and physical verbs would have to be grounded on a distinction between uses of 'I' (a verb would be psychological when the 'I' that accompanies it in the present tense is 'subjective', and physical when the 'I' that accompanies it in the present tense is 'objective'), which is not the one in the *Blue Book* (where the criterion is that of a supposed immunity against an error of identification: the use of 'I' is objective whenever it makes sense to doubt whether it is really me doing something or other). But does Wittgenstein anywhere else, in any of his remarks, suggest, about psychological verbs, that their use in the first-person present tense is characterized by the impossibility of being mistaken about the 'subject' of the verb? Rather, on Wittgenstein's view, what characterizes *all* first-person present tense uses of psychological verbs is that the question of truth and falsity, and the correlative question of certainty and doubt, *are not pertinent*. The use of a psychological verb in the first-person present tense can constitute a lie or a pretence, but it cannot be false or, therefore, true.[12] When, in pain, I cry out 'I am in pain', this judgment is neither true nor false. The alternative is rather: either I express my pain, or I simulate pain. For we do not say of someone who is imitating that he is making a mistake or saying something false. He *is* simply not the person he is imitating.

It therefore follows that the asymmetry definitive of psychological verbs cannot be an epistemic asymmetry, and so talk of 'observation' is, from this standpoint, misleading. Wittgenstein's central idea, with respect to the thesis of asymmetry, is that first-person uses of psychological verbs are precisely not acts or judgments having to do with knowledge. The asymmetry characteristic of psychological verbs is logical or, rather, *pragmatic;* it resides in what we might call the kind of *language act* per-formed by first- and third-person utterances of a psychological verb. For Wittgenstein, the reason there is no asymmetry between 'I am writing' and 'He is writing' is that in the first case, I am *describing* what I am doing just as in the second case, I am *describing* what someone else is doing. In both cases, I am describing or, as it can also be said, I know. On the other hand, the asymmetry between 'I am suffering' and 'he is suffering' is that, in the first case, I am *expressing* my pain, whereas in the second, I am *describing* someone's state, how she is feeling. The asymmetry is there-fore logical, or rather pragmatic; not epistemic. There is an asymmetry between the kind of language act accomplished in the first and third person when a psychological verb is used, whereas no such asymmetry obtains with non-psychological verbs.

This interpretation is reinforced by the fact that Wittgenstein did not consider the use of present tense psychological verbs in the first person to be necessarily different in nature from their use in the third person. Indeed, depending on context, the utterance 'I am afraid' can just as well constitute a *description* of my fear, as an *expression* of it.[13]

The characteristic thing about psychological verbs, then, and that which opposes them to 'physical' verbs, is that they can be used to perform the specific language acts that Wittgenstein calls 'expressions': a verb is psy-chological if it can be of expressive use. Suppose there were no expressive use: what would be the difference between 'I am sad' and 'He is sad'? In the first case, I would be describing my emotional state to someone; in the other, I would be describing someone else's emotional state. The difference would be a purely epistemic one and it would take us back to the traditional Cartesian thesis that what characterizes the first person is its epistemic authority. Could we speak of asymmetry here? No more than we could say there is an asymmetry in knowing there is a fire somewhere because we are seeing smoke or because we are seated in the front row. An epistemic difference is not an asymmetry in that it is possible – mentally or physically – to reconcile both points of view (e.g., by taking the person who was too far to see the fire, closer to it). By contrast, asymmetry occurs with regard to, say, expressing one's sadness: for only I can express my sadness;[14] someone else can only describe it, or know about it.

We can therefore conclude that what the thesis of asymmetry implies is the existence of a kind of language act ('expression') which occurs only when a psychological verb in the first person is used. *Only those verbs whose first-person present tense use can be expressive are psychological verbs.* Only psychological verbs can be thus used. And from the fact that they can be thus used, their grammar is asymmetrical, for we are doing different things when expressing our fear and when describing someone else's; whereas we are doing the same thing when describing what we are doing and describing what someone else is doing. It is in this sense that the asymmetry in question is logico-pragmatic, and not epistemic.

4 Attributive versus expressive use of psychological concepts

Reflecting on Wittgenstein's conceptual differentiation, what we first see emerging is an outline of that 'therapy' which is clearly central to his philosophy of psychology. First, conceptual differentiation results in divesting some psychological concepts of the generic function invested in them by philosophers. This is the case of the concept of thought, about which Wittgenstein shows that its specialized grammar cannot have the transversal character implied by the celebrated Cartesian dictum: to think, that is: to doubt, to understand, to affirm, to deny, to want, to not want, to imagine, to feel.[15] The same goes for the concept of experience, present only in some, and certainly not all, psychological concepts. Second, the distinction between expressive and descriptive or informative uses of psychological concepts helps dilute the prestige of the inner/outer picture, which relies on a misapprehension of the asymmetry: that is, the belief that 'I am in pain' and 'He is in pain' both describe inner states, only in one case directly and in the other indirectly. If 'I am in pain' is seen for what it is: an expressive – not a descriptive – language act, the contrast disappears which initially led us to believe that the description of others' mental states is but a diminished knowledge of what we know ourselves directly from within. The contrast between 'I am in pain' and 'He is in pain' is not epistemic but logico-pragmatic, so that the difference is not between two modes of knowledge, but between something that is knowledge and something that is not. It is a categorial, not a specific, difference.

Although it is undeniable that an exploration of the grammar of psychological concepts affords us a negative lesson and that it might even be said that the organizational mode of Wittgenstein's grammatical exploration converges towards this anti-climactic goal, a therapeutic effect is *not* the only effect these remarks have on the reader. To see this more clearly, we shall now intersect the two lines of analysis discussed, that which conceptually differentiates pairs of concepts and that which conceptually differentiates uses of a single concept. This intersection produces a kind of double-entry table; on one side of which we get a column of psychological concepts which might be ordered, going from concepts whose use affords an experiential dimension (e.g., the concept of pain) to concepts whose use affords no experiential dimension (e.g., concepts of belief or intention), with various intermediary cases. On the other side, two lines, at least, can be drawn from each of these concepts corresponding to their (expressive and attributive) uses: *grosso modo* first- and third-person uses. At first glance, the information provided by this 'table' seems grammatical, or, we might say, metalinguistic. Our knowledge is a grammarian's knowledge and a grammarian is more concerned with analysis than with synthesis, with differences more than with similarities. However, this grammarian's knowledge holds a lesson of rather more significance once we pay attention to the kind of information gleaned from the observation of the expressive use of psychological concepts.

First, we should note that the psychological concepts whose grammar Wittgenstein is exhibiting are not only encountered in psychology books, but first and foremost in ordinary use.[16] As Wittgenstein himself insists, it is not for psychology to teach us that, for example, human beings see,[17] hope or are afraid. Psychology studies the 'phenomena' that are associated with concepts;[18] for instance, how something we perceive changes, how human beings go from hope to despair or how they conquer their fears, but the psychologist could not focus his attention on these phenomena if the concepts of seeing, hoping and being afraid were not available to her in a pre-scientific way. These concepts constitute the ground or background of psychology which, for that very reason, depends on a correct understanding of these concepts.

Psychological concepts, then, are to be found in the speech and behaviour of human beings. Moreover, they are not encountered in isolated fashion, like dictionary terms, but in the various uses we make of them. This especially means that psychological concepts are not only used by us with a descriptive or attributive goal, but also in an expressive mode; and this is true, it should be noted, of *all* psychological concepts, whatever cluster they belong to.

But what does it mean to say that a psychological concept is used expressively? Essentially, it means that the utterance in question is not an attribution of a psychological state to a subject, whether that subject is ourselves or another. It also means, then, that in this kind of use,[19] the psychological word does not serve to *designate* or *nominate* a private content.[20] This is another way of saying that, *in this kind of use, there is no logical room for a distinction between a word and what it designates* or, more generally, for a distinction between the psychological concept and the phenomenon, or 'mental thing'.

To help us shed light on this, let us contrast two different cases. First, the exploration of the grammar of colour concepts. What does this consist in? Schematically speaking, in noting the circumstances in which we use these concepts, in recording what it makes sense to say of colours and, particularly, what we judge to be impossible about them – for example, that the same patch can be both red and blue at the same time. Impossibilities are crucial in grammatical exploration because they can reflect the rules that underlie the use of concepts. But not all impossibilities are grammatical. To help us decide which kind of impossibility we are dealing with – grammatical or physical – we must imagine colour concept systems different from ours and see what becomes of these impossibilities. We can imagine people for whom two shades of blue are two radically and incompatibly different colours, or people who have concepts that connect colour and shape,[21] so that for them a red square and a red circle are two different qualities. These kinds of variations provide us with exclusively *grammatical* information, information bearing on our colour concepts. We become aware of the system of measurement we use, the standard we apply, but our knowledge remains restricted to the sphere of concepts, the grammatical sphere.[22]

Let us now imagine possibilities pertinent to our exploration of the grammar of psychological concepts in their *attributive* uses. First, imagine people whose attributive use of psychological concepts would not be similar to ours; for example, people who would say only of someone who is bleeding that he is in pain (cf. RPP II: 599); or people who would make no difference between being really in pain and simulating pain. In such cases, we would be inclined to say that these people have an idea of pain that is different from ours and that it is correlated with forms of life other than ours. Alternatively, imagine people who would make no attributive use whatsoever of their psychological concepts, but only an expressive use. These beings might, for example, have a concept of belief, but use it only in the first person, and perhaps only in the first-person present tense (cf. RPP II: 279). What we come to learn, then, in engaging in this kind of conceptual variation, is again something concerning the grammar of *our* concepts. We let the 'grammatical' in our psychological concepts come through:

> Can there be a justification 'in reality' for the grammatical peculiarities of psychological verbs? The concepts we have show what *selection* of phenomena we make – what *interests* us.
>
> (LPP: 52)[23]

It would appear, then, that the same applies to our examination of psychological concepts as to that of our colour concepts; that the knowledge these examinations afford us is purely a grammarian's knowledge: what we discover is how we describe the world, and we do this by looking for contrasts with deviant conceptual systems. But here, we are being too hasty; for, as we shall now see, an exploration of the *expressive* use of psychological concepts does *not only* yield grammatical knowledge.

We distinguish between hoping and fearing, between 'I hope he comes' and 'I fear he will not come', but imagine people who had only one concept at their disposal: that of hopefear. These people would say things like 'I hopefear he comes'. In such a case, there would be no logical room for saying something like: 'These people's idea of fear and hope is different from ours.' What we should say is that these people know neither hope nor fear, but something else that we would characterize as a quietist or neutral attitude to the future.

Now, can we imagine beings that have no concept of hope? And compare that to imagining beings that have no concept of dog? In the latter case, we would say that such beings do not know dogs; that, for them, dogs do not exist; that their life is such that it does not demand that they pay attention to dogs. But we would obviously not conclude that in a world peopled by such beings, dogs do not exist. Yet what would we say of beings that have no concept of hope? We could not say that these beings do not know hope, although hope exists in their world unnoticed by them. What we would have to say is that, in the world inhabited by these beings, hope does not exist, full stop:

> Can only those hope who can talk? Only those who have mastered the application of a language? The signs of hope are modes of this

complicated pattern of life. (If a concept applies to the character of handwriting, it has no application to beings that do not write.)

(LW I: 365)

This suggests an obvious difference between the kind of information gleaned in a grammatical exploration of colour concepts, or of psychological concepts in their attributive use, and that gleaned when we explore expressive uses of psychological concepts. In the first two cases, our knowledge remains purely grammatical in that it bears on the way we describe a certain realm of experience, on our conceptual system, our mode of representation. In the case of the expressive use of psychological concepts, however, our knowledge bears *both on concepts and on what these concepts are expressions of.* In its expressive use, the concept of belief does not amount to a manner of apprehending a certain content, plus a way of behaving towards that content. In its expressive use, the concept of belief articulates an act of belief, so that *the concept is expressive of that of which it is the concept.* It follows that, in observing the expressive uses of the concept of belief, what we are observing, if not the belief itself, is at least an internal component of the belief itself.

5   The *conceptual dependence* of psychological phenomena

Let us now attempt to develop this idea further. To say that psychological concepts are expressive of that of which they are the concept is not to say that they *designate* a certain type of act, operation or behaviour which would accompany their use, but that their use *is* that about which they are a concept. A dog *is* not the use of the concept of dog. The use of the concept of dog is a description of what we see, information about what there is, or a fragment of zoological science. On the other hand, an expressive use of the concept of hope or belief constitutes an *instance* of hope or belief, or, at least, essential *moments*[24] of these, in that the use of the concept is not reducible to the proffering of a sentence, but also adapts itself to a range of behaviours, and even experiences. A difference between remembering and hoping is that we remember the past, but have hope in the future. This is, in a way, a grammatical difference. To say: 'I remember that Pierre will come', and then start waiting impatiently for Pierre is a-grammatical; but if we put these words in a real mouth, if we watch them issue from a human body, then what we are observing is not only an a-grammatical use; what we are observing is a real mental act which has been mislabelled: an act of hope which has been labelled 'remembering'.

To say, therefore, that psychological concepts in their first-person present tense use are expressive of what they are the concept of is to say that psychological concepts are internally implicated in their corresponding mental states. Would there be dogs in the world if we had no concept of dog? Of course there would. Having a concept of dog implies only that our life is one that takes an interest in dogs. But would hope exist if we did not have a concept of hope? This is explicitly denied by Wittgenstein. We do not need the concept of hope merely to formulate our hope, but also to make it known to others; and to express it – where expressing it means deploying it, articulating it, giving it human shape. In a way, it would be right to say that a life without the concept of hope would be a life that had no interest in hope, but it would also be a life without hope. We could say, then, that psychological phenomena are *conceptually dependant*.

But what exactly is the nature of this dependence? If hope or pain are essentially in need of their concept, why do they thus need it? Is it that pain needs the concept of pain in order to exist or only in order to manifest itself? Is the concept *ratio essendi* or *ratio cognoscendi* of what it is a concept of? Wittgenstein's remarks prompt two different, but interrelated, responses.

First, we saw that a distinction must be made – though it is a distinction that is difficult to acknowledge or accept – between concepts whose expressive use has an experiential aspect and those that do not. There is an experience of pain, but no experience of understanding, intention, belief; with all kinds of intermediary situations. Consequently, as Wittgenstein notes, the concept of pain is not necessary to suffering,[25] whereas the concepts of hope and intention are respectively necessary to hoping and intending:

> Anyone with a soul must be capable of pain, joy, grief, etc. etc. And if he is also to be capable of memory, of making decisions, of making a plan for something, with this he needs linguistic expression.
>
> (LW II: 67)

This remark, written by Wittgenstein in 1950, is fundamental to our interpretation. It clearly states that in the case of memory, resolution and promise, 'linguistic expression' is necessary for a person to remember, decide, promise or promise to herself. But it also indicates that 'expression' cannot here be understood in the usual sense of: outwardly manifesting what is inner and logically distinct from its externalization. Expression through language is not an exteriorization by language, but a constitution by language. What is thus constituted is something which, in an essential way, manifests itself. We might say that psychological phenomena are conceptually dependent *strictly speaking*, when their existence is consti-tuted by expressive and egological uses of their concept.

There would then be, by contrast, other psychological 'states' that would not be conceptually dependant. More precisely, states of mind or mental states that could exist in a being even though it did not have corresponding con-cepts and, moreover, would not have 'linguistic expression' at its dis-posal. An animal can feel pain or wait for its master although it has no 'linguistic expression' at its disposal. But this conclusion lets one of Wittgenstein's other points escape us. For although, strictly speaking, it is true that only 'dispositions' belonging to the third cluster are concep-tually dependant, it is also right to say that, for Wittgenstein, all psy-chological 'states' are conceptually dependant.

To show this, we must return to the contrast between expressive and attributive uses of psychological concepts. A point made constantly by Wittgenstein is that, in their third-person uses, psychological concepts are employed on the basis of behavioural criteria. To master the concept of pain in its attributive uses is to be able to identify certain behav-iours as pain-behaviours. But here, there is a problem. On the one hand, Wittgenstein asserts that children learn psychological concepts in their expressive mode: learning to master the concept of pain is learning to broaden one's pain-behaviour by including in it the expressive use of the concept of pain.[26] On the other hand, however, psychological concepts are truly mastered only when the child is also able to use them attribu-tively; that is to apply them on the basis of behavioural criteria. The prob-lem here is that in one case the concept is assimilated with no application criteria, whereas in the other, it is linked to criteria. Of course, we might be tempted to say that we have here to do with two distinct concepts that merely share the same linguistic label, say pain; but in the case of us humans, it is actually a single concept that is at work here. Wittgenstein provides two convergent explanations for this.

First: when we learn to use the word 'pain', we do not learn that some-thing we are perceiving is called 'pain'; we do not learn this word in the manner of an Augustinian baptism. We simply learn to experience our pain in a certain way, to express it in a certain way. To learn the concept of pain consists as much in learning to *say* something as in learning to *behave* in a certain way when we are having a particular experience. And, as Wittgenstein says, there is a difference between learning to name some-thing and learning to do something, be it with language: 'For doing is something that one can give someone an *exhibition* of' (RPP I: 655). We might say, then, that the child learns what to do with his pain; that is, in this case, he learns to react to it in a certain way, to express it, but also to talk about it ('Where does it hurt?'; 'Does it hurt a lot?' etc.). The point, then, is simply that when we have acquired the mastery of a certain arti-ficial behaviour, we acquire, at the same time, the ability to recognize that behaviour in others. When a child has learned to draw, she acquires the ability to recognize when someone else is drawing, or that someone else is doing something close to drawing. This ability to go from behaviour in action to the observation of behaviour is steered by the child's learning of the verb in all its persons (cf. LW I: 874).

This explanation of the transition from the expressive to the attribu-tive use of a psychological concept is not the only one suggested by Wittgenstein. Another explanation appeals to the notion of primitive behaviour; to a kind of natural precondition for the transition from the expressive to the attributive use:

> Believing that someone is in pain, doubting whether he is, are so many natural kinds of behaviour towards other human beings; and our lan-guage is but an auxiliary to and extension of this behaviour. I mean: our language is an extension of the more primitive behaviour. (For our *language-game* is a piece of behaviour.)
>
> (RPP I: 151)

> What, however, is the word 'primitive' meant to say here? Presumably, that the mode of behaviour is *pre-linguistic*: that a language-game is based *on* it: that it is the prototype of a mode of thought and not the result of thought.
>
> (RPP I: 916)

What can this mean, if not that the attributive use of psychological con-cepts must itself be conceived as a mode of *behaviour vis-à-vis* others, as the cement of a meaningful community for which dispositions such as compassion would be the instinctive preconditions?[27] When the child learns to make an attributive use of psychological concepts, she has not thereby become a theoretician: to understand, or to feel compassion for, are human ways of *being*.

Reverting to our initial problem, it seems then that the distinction between conceptually dependant and conceptually independent psycho-logical phenomena is pertinent only in that it marks the difference between phenomena that have an experiential aspect and those that do not. Otherwise, it must be said that *all* psychological phenomena, inasmuch as they are characteristic of a *human* mind, are conceptually dependant; indeed, even those states of mind that possess what we might call an experiential *germ* are not ex-pressed, in the ordinary sense, by their encounter with language, but internally modified by that encounter.

It can indeed be said that learning the *expressive* use of the concept of pain or of fear broadens, articulates and, as it were, humanizes primitive behaviour (cf. LW I: 45–6; RPP I: 479). Of course, one can suffer or be afraid without a concept, but to have the concept is not merely to be equipped with a way of communicating our experience to others. To have the concept changes our relationship to the experience itself, qualitatively modifies what it is, for us, to be in pain or to be afraid. One can be afraid without words, but one can also be afraid *with words*. One does diverse things with language, and being afraid with words is one of them. The fear of someone who utters 'I am afraid' is not distinct from his utterance. Nor is it, however, entirely in his utterance. But the fact is that his utterance – the meaning of his utterance as much as its tone –is an integral part of his fear, so that the fear of a being who has no concept of fear is narrower than that of a being who does. The utterance is part and parcel of the fear and, for that reason, the fear that includes such an utterance – as a 'moment' or a part of it – is qualitatively different from the speechless fear of a dog.

It is also true that learning the *attributive* use of a concept as an extension of its expressive use modifies, broadens and articulates our primitive empathic behaviour. The attributive use of the concept is not, or at least not initially, a theoretical behaviour *vis-à-vis* others. It first constitutes an extension of the more primitive, prelinguistic, behaviour that is the root of our capacity to understand others and decipher their behaviour. So that the individual who is able to judge that others are afraid does not simply make use of a contingent appendix of her own capacity to be afraid. Rather, it is what she experiences or can experience as fear that finds itself qualitatively broadened by her capacity to recognize fear in the behaviour of others and to worry about it.

It is not, therefore, *only in certain cases* that the capacity to have certain types of mental behaviour depends on 'linguistic expression'. The fact that we are speaking beings makes it such that 'linguistic expression' affects the whole of our mental life. When a state of mind is endowed with what can be called an *experiential moment*, that moment is not the content of the state or its intentional object, but a mere *circumstance* to which the adoption of a corresponding linguistic behaviour is linked; and it is the articulated whole – consisting of the experience, the expressive use of the concept, as well as the corresponding behaviour – that constitutes the complete state of mind. Not only in cases like intending, hoping or wishing is a psychological state or operation conceptually dependant; all our psychological states, inasmuch as they are human, are thus dependant.

6 Wittgenstein's 'semantic non-reductionism'

We can now thus summarize our thesis: Wittgenstein's 'grammatical' claim, according to which there are expressive uses of psychological concepts, is the flip side of a more substantial claim; that of the conceptual dependency of psychological phenomena. An expression is not an externalization, *a fortiori* a designation; it is an essential moment of human behaviour which can, for that very reason, be called 'mental' (*seelisch*). It is in this sense that a positive picture issues from the core of grammar, which can then no longer be read as mere philosophical therapy.

Wittgenstein's final remarks contain an explicit outline of this picture of the mind. He writes that meeting a human being who did not have a soul would simply mean being face to face with a human body whose behaviour is that of an automaton – that is, its behaviour would be predictable and rigid, for 'unforeseeability must be *an* essential property of the mental. Just like the endless multiplicity of expression' (LW II: 65). Consequently, having a soul or a mind and being capable of expressive behaviour are one and the same thing.[28] A little further, Wittgenstein adds that '[p]erhaps language, along with tone of voice and the play of features, is the most subtly gradated behaviour of men' (LW II: 66). The expressive behaviour alluded to here cannot be understood as a mere externalization of inner processes. Indeed, a few remarks earlier, Wittgenstein notes that '[t]he inner is tied up with the outer not only empirically, but also logically' (LW II: 63). What is more, the behaviour in question comprises, essentially and centrally, linguistic behaviour, the use of language. The only conclusion, a syllogistic one, is the following: to have a soul or a mind, for a *human* being, is not only to use language, but to use language expressively.

No doubt, this is but a tiny picture, a vignette, of the mind. Yet it suffices, if not to credit Wittgenstein with a philosophy of mind, at least to interpret his views, in the terminology of the philosophy of mind, as a form of *semantic non-reductionism*.[29]

To start with, Wittgenstein's position clearly implies a rejection of any form of reductionism in that inasmuch as, say, my hope that Peter will come tomorrow *essentially contains* the concepts that allow me to express it, no cerebral event or mental experience is susceptible of being identical to it. For, the use of a concept, or the meaning of a word is intersubjective. To hope is to use the concept of hope meaningfully; and to make a meaningful use of the concept of hope will no doubt involve cerebral or mental events, but it cannot be identical to them, for no absolute feature can be identical to a relational one. Of course, this is not to say that the study of the brain is not pertinent, even in psychology, to the study of 'psychological phenomena'; but it is so only in the sense that it is important for the kicker in rugby to know the direction of the wind. That a lesion in a part of her brain prevents an individual from recognizing certain familiar faces informs us about the neural conditions required for someone to recognize a face, but the recognition of a face is not itself a neuronal process, and the defective neuronal process would itself have no importance for beings that had no *interest* in recognizing faces.

More generally, a human mind is not an entity in a human body, whether that entity be the brain itself or mental contents. The concept of mind is applicable to a human being as a whole; even, says Wittgenstein, to a human body: a mind is not something in a body; a mind is a body that is capable of expressive behaviour. A human body has various organs, of which, notably, a brain. Obviously, the brain is involved in our diverse sensorial experiences, as also in our capacity to use language; but neither cerebral processes nor experiences constitute the mental behaviour of a human body. If the precondition for recollection were a cerebral trace or mental picture, to recall would be, above all, to *refer* to a past event. A dog which would have stored a mental image of its master would recall its master only if it could *refer* to him via the concept of memory and the temporal inflection of the verb. No doubt, mental images can have a causal role in the dog's behaviour; they can, for instance, explain why it bites some people and sniffs others, but the mental images that inhabit us are not the *cause* of our memories, wishes or feelings of familiarity. The occurrence of these images is the *circumstance* that leads us to make use of the concept of memory or of wishing, or to formulate a memory or a wish. We might almost speak here of occasionalism. We have learned to become mental beings on the basis of certain experiences, pictures or external circumstances. But just as the blue sky does not constitute my belief that the sky is blue or even the cause of that belief, an experience, a picture, *a fortiori* a cerebral event, does not constitute a recollection or a wish, or the cause of the fact that I remember or that I wish.

If Wittgenstein's position thus implies a rejection of any form of reductionism, it is, then, itself necessarily a form of non-reductionism. And he has sufficiently reminded us of the fallacious root of our belief in a Cartesian ego to prevent us thinking that his non-reductionism might be of a metaphysical ilk. So that, on our view, the only adequate description that remains of Wittgenstein's insistence that we *learn* the use of psychological concepts is what we have termed a semantic non-reductionism. In the same way we learn to dance, we also learn to wish, to believe and so on; that is, to make meaningful use of these concepts and tie them to actions, emotions, experiences. We cannot dance without legs; and no doubt, we could not wish or believe without a brain. But the legs are not the cause of the dance – the dance is not deducible from the legs, but comes from without, to the point of becoming second nature – and the same goes for 'mental behaviour'. It is because the mind constitutes a range of conceptually articulated behaviour that it is irreducible to neurological or mental processes, without being a separate metaphysical entity:

> Operating with concepts permeates our life. I see some sort of analogy with a very general use of keys. If for instance one always had to open a lock in order to move something.
>
> (LW II: 51)

The mistake made by philosophers is not that they have wanted to talk about the mind. It is to have talked about it as if it were some entity external to language and *designated* by language. The mind is not hidden; nothing is hidden. The mind is *constituted* by pragmatic uses of psychological concepts, so that in observing the *words* of the mind, it is the *life* of the mind that we apprehend.

Notes

1. RPP I and II; LW I and II; cf. also LPP.
2. 'When philosophers use a word – 'knowledge', 'being', 'object', 'I', 'proposition', 'name' – and try to grasp the essence of the thing, one must always ask oneself: is the word ever actually used in this way in the language-game which is its original home? – / What we do is to bring words back from their metaphysical to their everyday use' (PI: 116).
3. On these interpretations, cf. Crary and Read (2000), and Bouveresse, Laugier and Rosat (2002).
4. 'Essence is expressed by grammar' (PI: 371).
5. With reference to the debate, in the history of metaphysics, between partisans of the equivocality of the notion of being and partisans of the univocality of the notion of being.
6. 'The concept of experience: Like that of happening, of process, of state, of something, of fact, of description and of report. Here we think we are standing on the hard bedrock, deeper than any special methods and language-games. But these extremely general terms have an extremely blurred meaning. They relate in practice to innumerable special cases, but that does not make them any

solider; no, rather it makes them more fluid' (RPP I: 648). Cf. also: 'Ought I to call the whole field of the psychological that of "experience"? And so all psychological verbs "verbs of experience"?' (RPP I: 836).

7. 'The genealogical tree of psychological phenomena: I strive, not for exactness, but for a view of the whole [*Übersichtlichkeit*]' (RPP I: 895); cf. also 'What is it, however, that a conceptual investigation does? Does it belong in the natural history of human concepts? – Well, natural history, we say, describes plants and beasts. But might it not be that plants had been described in full detail, and then for the first time someone realized the analogies in their structure, analogies which had never been seen before? And so, that he establishes a new order among these descriptions. He says, for example, "compare this part, not with this one, but rather with that" ... and in so doing he is not necessarily speaking of derivation; nonetheless the new arrangement might also give a new direction to scientific investigation' (RPP I: 950).

8. RPP I: 836; cf. also RPP II: 62–3, 148, 152–3.

9. Cf. '[The] characteristic [of psychological verbs] is this, that their third person but not their first person is stated on grounds of observation' (RPP I: 836); 'Psychological verbs characterized by the fact that the third person of the present is to be identified by observation, the first person not' (RPP II: 63); 'The salient thing [about the psychological verb] is the asymmetry; "I think", unlike "he thinks", has no verification' (LPP: 49).

10. 'After all I know that when I am angry, I simply don't need to learn this from my behaviour. – But do I draw a conclusion from my anger to my probable action? One might also put it like this: my relation to my *actions* is not one of observation.' (RPP I: 712.). Cf. also LW II: 10: 'My words and actions interest me in a completely different way than they do someone else. (My intonation also, for instance.) I do not relate to them as an observer.'

11. 'I want to say first of all that with the assertion "It's going to rain" one expresses belief in that just as one expresses the wish to have wine with the words "Wine over here!" One might also put it like this: "I believe p" means roughly the same as "p" and it ought not to mislead us that the verb "believe" and the pronoun "I" come in the first proposition. We merely see clearly from this that the grammar of "I believe", is very different from that of "I write"' (RPP I: 472).

12. In response to Danièle Moyal-Sharrock's objection that in admitting lying, we must necessarily be admitting truth and falsity, I would reply that, here, a distinction must be made between the falsity of a mistake and that of a lie. In any case, lying is best thought of as kind of simulation or make-believe; to lie is not to think about something false, but to make-believe (simulate) something false.

13. 'We surely do not always say someone is *complaining* because he says he is in pain. So the words "I'm in pain" may be a cry of complaint, and may be something else. (Something similar holds for expression of fear and other emotions.) / But if 'I'm afraid' is not always like a cry of complaint, and yet sometimes is, then why should it *always* be a description of my state of mind?' (LW I: 35–6.)

14. Strictly speaking, however, this utterance is senseless, but it facilitates understanding!

15. Cf. Descartes, *Meditations on First Philosophy, Second Meditation*, lines 20–2.

16. 'Psychological concepts are just everyday concepts. They are not concepts newly fashioned by science for its own purpose, as are the concepts of physics and chemistry. Psychological concepts are related to those of the exact sciences as the concepts of the science of medicine are to those of old women who spend their time nursing the sick' (RPP II: 62).

17. Cf. LW II: 71 and 100.

18. 'I would like to say. Psychology deals with certain *aspects* of human life. / Or: with certain phenomena. – But the words "thinking", "fearing", etc. etc. do *not* refer [*bezeichnen*] to these phenomena' (RPP II: 35). Cf. also RPP II: 133.

19. Though we shall see that the expressive use determines all other uses.

20. 'One could say that "seeing", "imaging", and "hoping" are simply not words for phenomena. But of course that doesn't mean that the psychologist doesn't observe phenomena' (RPP II: 77).

21. Cf. RPP I: 545 and 547.

22. 'We have a colour system as we have a number system./ Do the systems reside in *our* nature or in the nature of things? How are we to put it? – *Not* in the nature of numbers or colours'; 'Then is there something arbitrary about this system? Yes and no. It is akin both to what is arbitrary and to what is non-arbitrary' (RPP II: 426–7).

23. Or, more clearly still: 'If I am to describe the dimensions of objects in this room, I may use all sorts of units. One says: the unit is arbitrary. In a way, the concept is like a unit; if provides a way of describing' (LPP: 48.)

24. I am here using 'moment' in the Hegelian or Husserlian sense, that is, as designating the constitutive parts of a certain type of whole.

25. 'That is to say: when someone manifests a state of mind, he might also have had that state of mind without manifesting it. That is a rule' (RPP I: 157). 'That is a rule', it seems to me, means: it is a criterion of use of the concept of state of mind. But this is not to say that a real, nontrivial, difference is also thereby captured.

26. For example, PI: §244; RPP I: 131, 146, 313.

27. 'I wouldn't say either of myself (or of others) that we understood manifestations of life that are foreign to us. And here, of course, there are degrees' (RPP II: 30).

28. 'If one sees the behaviour of a living thing, one sees its soul' (PI: 357).

29. For the opposition between reductionism and non-reductionism which we shall use here, cf. Parfit (1987), 210.

3
The Importance of Being Thoughtful

Lars Hertzberg

Part I   Thinking as the magic wand

I.1

Even before I knew what philosophical bewilderment is, I remember being bewildered by the following question: supposing that what happens in our minds is governed by nothing but mechanical laws of association, how is it that we are capable of thinking *to a purpose*; that is, to find relevant and correct solutions to the various problems we face? It must, I thought, be a matter of chance if a chain of blind associations is to lead me to a good answer. I should, apparently, have to know in what direction I need to be going even before I get started. But if I could know that, on the other hand, what would I need the thinking for?

Here I was, I think, in the grip of a philosophical picture, one that has in effect dominated philosophical thought about human reason in the modern age, if not longer. According to this picture, reason or thought involves the exercise of a specific cognitive capacity, one that underlies, and is separable from, its manifestations in speech and conduct. This picture has been widely influential in Western philosophy and psychology, and is deeply entrenched in common ways of thinking and speaking. On this view, the human capacity for thought is required in order to explain certain pervasive features of human life, features that, it is believed, would be utterly mysterious in its absence. In this vein, the psychologist Donald Hebb refers to 'man's mental capacities and the behaviour they make possible, the behaviour that most clearly distinguishes him from other animals'.[1]

But here is the conundrum: how is the faculty itself to be explained? It has, it seems, to fulfil two requirements that seem hard to reconcile with one another. On the one hand, it is assumed that engaging in thought is always advantageous: someone who tries to think things through is guaranteed to be better placed for solving any given problem than if she had not tried: this activity, as it were, has the direction of success built into it. On the other hand, since thinking is taken to constitute a mechanical, impersonal process, the ability to think well about things is given to anyone willing to spend the time and effort; it does not require any special talent or training. The ability to think, then, is a huge asset, yet at the same time it is universally available. Descartes notoriously tried to escape this conundrum by arguing that the human capacity to function rationally is to be explained by postulating that human beings are endowed with a supernatural capacity of reasoning. Is there any way of resolving the dilemma without invoking the supernatural?

The role of thinking as a process underlying the human capacity for insightful action is one of two themes that have characterized philosophical thought about thinking in the modern era. We might speak about this as the idea of the power of thought. But there is also another theme: that of the *powerlessness* of thought. This is the notion, famously formulated by Hume, according to which thought or reasoning cannot by itself supply the motive force for human action. This notion is closely connected with the idea of a sharp distinction between reason and the passions; or, as it has sometimes been phrased, between cognition and will, or between intellect and character. The passions are dynamic; thought by itself is inert. We share passions with the animals – instrumental thought is what makes us unique.

The power of thought, on this view, is purely instrumental; *considered as an instrument*, on the other hand, thought is immensely powerful. In fact, the idea of thinking as an impersonal process governs our idea of what thinking can achieve, and our idea of what thinking can achieve supports the notion that it has to be an impersonal process. This complex of ideas is for the most part taken for granted in our reflecting on the nature of thought. It tends to become a filter through which philosophers regard the phenomena of thought, making us focus on phenomena that seem to fit the paradigm and to ignore those that do not. In this way, the complex becomes self-verifying. We have, we believe, a solution to the question how people are able to function rationally and effectively: they do so *by thinking*. But then it remains to be explained how thinking does it. What we need to do in order to get out of the conundrum, I want to suggest, is to give up the belief that thinking provides the solution; indeed, we should give up the belief that we *need* a solution, that there is such a problem as that of rational action which can and needs to be solved. Wittgenstein, I will argue, gives us some of the materials we need in order to rid ourselves of this picture. In what follows, I shall be trying to think about the problem along some of the lines suggested by him.

In the next section, I shall review Wittgenstein's critique of the idea of thinking as a separate process. In Part II, I discuss the notion that thinking is what distinguishes human beings from animals. I argue that the issue gets confused by the failure to distinguish between two ways of approaching the question of the capacity for thought. In Part III, I discuss the importance of thought, showing how it can be understood once we rid ourselves of the idea of thinking as involving the exercise of a specific capacity.

I.2

In *Philosophical Investigations*, Wittgenstein questions one of the core presuppositions of the picture we have just described: the idea that thinking, in essence, is a specific activity or process. On this view, when, for instance, we speak or act thoughtfully, the thinking is to be regarded as a process accompanying our words or actions, the way the piano might accompany a singer:

> When I think in language, there aren't 'meanings' going through my mind in addition to the verbal expressions: the language is itself the vehicle of thought.
>
> (PI: 329)

> Is thinking a kind of speaking? One would like to say it is what distinguishes speech with thought from talking without thinking. – And so it seems to be an accompaniment of speech. A process which may accompany something else, or can go on by itself.
>
> Say: 'Yes, this pen is blunt. Oh well, it'll do.' First, thinking it; then without thought; then just think the thought without the words. ... what constitutes thought here is not some process which has to accompany the words if they are not to be spoken without thought.
>
> (PI: 330)

> Thinking is not an incorporeal process which lends life and sense to speaking, and which it would be possible to detach from speaking, rather as the Devil took the shadow of Schlemiehl from the ground.
>
> (PI: 339)

The playing could be carried out without the singing; on the other hand, if we were asked to carry out the thinking accompaniment without the words or actions (and note: without even imagining words or actions to ourselves) we would be nonplussed. Furthermore, the fact that in speaking, I am thinking about what I am saying must of course show itself in what I say, it is not an uncertain inference to a separate, hidden process:

> Speech with and without thought is to be compared with the playing of a piece of music with and without thought.
>
> (PI: 341)

Accordingly, concentrating on what goes on in the thinker's mind while speaking, or at some other definite time, is not a fruitful way of getting clear about the use of the word 'think'. However, we are not readily prepared to relinquish the picture of thinking as a peculiar process. We defend it by various stratagems. Thus, even where someone sees the solution to a complex problem in a flash, or immediately decides on a complex course of action, we tend to assume that what makes the response possible has to be some underlying instantaneous cognitive occurrence. Thus, the following account by Hebb seems to correspond to what many of us would take to be a natural view of the role of thought:

> This sudden thinking-of-the-answer or 'seeing the light' is of course well known in human problem-solving ... [T]he sudden solution has a special interest because the sharp break in behaviour identifies for us the moment at which a reorganization of thought-processes has occurred. ... [I]nsight can be defined, essentially, as the *functioning of mediating processes in the solution of problems*, and from this point of view it is clear that some mode or degree of insight is present in all problem-solving by the higher animal.
>
> (1958: 204)

Wittgenstein remarks:

> Suppose we think while we talk or write – I mean, as we normally do – we shall not in general say that we think quicker than we talk; the thought seems *not to be separate* from the expression. On the other hand, however, one does speak of the speed of thought; of how a thought goes through one's head like lightning; how problems become clear to us in a flash, and so on. So it is natural to ask if the same thing happens in lightning-like thought – only extremely accelerated – as when we talk and 'think while we talk'. So that in the first case the clockwork runs down all at once, but in the second bit by bit, braked by the words.
>
> (PI: 318)

One reason why we find it hard to give up the idea that thinking must consist in a process (whether protracted or instantaneous) is that it seems to us that the problems that thinking is called upon to solve are too complex for anyone simply to 'see' the solution right away. Hence thinking, it seems, must have a structure like a calculus, it must consist of steps. The subliminal speed becomes symbolic of the non-clockable phenomenon. But then one might ask: if occasionally we can go through the process in a flash, why do we not do it all the time?

Sometimes we may hit on the answer after some time, perhaps after we have stopped thinking about the matter – as, for instance, in trying to put a name to a familiar face. Here we are inclined to say that a thought process must have taken place, only it was hidden. What we are assuming is that we *could* have done it consciously, only we did not need to. We may even marvel at the feats of our subconscious mind. But what do we actually take to have happened here? Suppose we tried to put the name to the face, as it were, consciously rather than subconsciously: how would we go about it? What steps would we take? It would appear that there is nothing happening in this case that could explain *how* the mind goes about it in the other case. Hence it is not at all clear what is supposed to be hidden in 'the hidden process'. (If we find it astounding that the subconscious mind can look for the name all by itself, should we not find it even more astounding that most of the time it comes up with the name *right away*?) The idea of a hidden process that might as well have been overt is simply based on a preconceived notion of what thinking *must* be like. (Actually, the picture should perhaps be reversed: in the conscious case we try to do intentionally what normally happens of itself – as when we breathe.)

I.3

Wittgenstein's discussion about thinking in *Philosophical Investigations* opens with the following remark:

> In order to get clear about the meaning of the word 'think' we watch ourselves while we think; what we observe will be what the word means! – But this concept is not used like that.
>
> (PI: 316)

Here we are obviously to imagine quotation marks around the first sentence: this is Wittgenstein's imaginary interlocutor speaking, giving expression to the natural view. Wittgenstein's response is to tell us to focus on how the word 'think' is actually used (and, he might have added, its cognates, such as acting thoughtfully or thoughtlessly, etc.) In PI: §340, Wittgenstein writes:

> One cannot guess how a word functions. One has to *look at* its use and learn from that.
> But the difficulty is to remove the prejudice which stands in the way of doing this. It is not a *stupid* prejudice.
>
> (PI: 340)

In fact, as Wittgenstein remarks elsewhere,[2] thinking is a 'widely rami-fied' concept: it has a large variety of uses. In reflecting on the 'nature of thought', rather than attending to the variety of those uses, we operate with an indistinct notion of a faculty or process which, it appears, is called upon to carry out a large variety of tasks, and hence must possess some formidable powers. As Wittgenstein remarks:

> We talk of processes and states and leave their nature undecided. Sometime perhaps we shall know more about them – we think. But that is just what commits us to a particular way of looking at the matter. For we have a definite concept of what it means to learn to know a process better.
>
> (PI: 308)

(Of course, *among* the different uses of the word 'think', there are some in which it does refer to an activity occurring in time. We shall come back to that point later.)

Here, again, there is a self-sustaining complex of thought: we assume that the essence of thinking is concentrated in what we call processes of thought (which, we believe, can be studied by observing what happens in our minds while we are thinking); this, in turn, means that we do not need to look at the wide variety of ways in which the word 'thinking' is used; hence nothing will disconfirm our conviction that this is what thinking really is.

Part II Achievement versus attribution

II.1

It is widely assumed that the relation between human beings, animals and inanimate objects can best be understood in terms of the capacity for thought. *Thought*, we think, is the key to human existence. Some philoso-phers, like Descartes, have claimed that human beings are unique among created beings in having it. Others will maintain that animals share in it to a smaller or larger extent, while many have thought that machines do too, or that they may come to do so as a result of future developments in artificial intelligence. Despite these disagreements, there seems to be a wide consensus among philosophers and others concerned with the field that there is a determinate issue here concerning who (or what) is capable of thought and who (or what) is not, and what this capacity consists in. In fact, a whole new branch of study, cognitive science, is based on this assumption.[3]

In any case, humans are seen as the paradigm of what it means to be a thinking being. But suppose Wittgenstein is right in suggesting that there is no such thing as specific thought processes, hence no specific faculty generating them? Where does this leave the whole issue? Is that the end of human uniqueness? Or does it simply mean that thinking is not a useful key to what is distinctively human? What specifically is there about the human mind that makes it paradigmatic of the ability to think? Unquestionably people do live differently from animals; that is, there are features common to all human cultures that distinguish them from any non-human forms of life; but then, would not the same be true if we singled out any other animal species and compared it with all the rest? Or, if we feel that there is something unique about human uniqueness, is not that simply due to the fact that this happens to be our own species?

What precisely is it that thinking is supposed to achieve? The primary expression of the human capacity for thought, it is usually taken for granted, is the ability to function rationally and effectively, and in particular the ability to solve the various practical or intellectual problems that cross our path. The capacity is also taken to manifest itself in the use of language; that is, in the ability to choose words and construct sentences to express what one wants to say, or the ability to use words to refer to absent objects, to past or future events or to abstract entities, or the ability to use and understand sentences one has never heard before; again, it may involve the ability to take account of absent objects or imagined possibilities in one's actions, or the ability to act imaginatively rather than mechanically or by rote.

II.2

In fact, there are two separate aspects to the difference that thought is assumed to make; we might distinguish between the 'achievement' aspect and the 'attribution' aspect. The achievement aspect is a matter of smartness: it has to do with the ability to succeed in intellectually demanding tasks. Thus, human beings may be more skilled than dogs in finding their way through a particular kind of maze, just as one kid may do better than another (and a dog may do it better than a sheep). Of course, there are other tasks at which most dogs will outperform most humans, such as picking up a scent or jumping a fence, but these are not taken to require a capacity for thought.[4]

The attribution aspect, on the other hand, has to do with the difference between the kinds of thoughts, attitudes, motives, and so on that will be attributed to different individuals and animals. For instance, we will not wonder what our dog might be thinking about recent developments on the stock market, or whether in his opinion the colour of the wallpaper clashes with that of the curtains. We would not even entertain the idea of his having such thoughts except as a joke. In this spirit, Wittgenstein writes

> One can imagine an animal angry, frightened, unhappy, happy, startled. But hopeful? And why not?
>
> A dog believes his master is at the door. But can he also believe his master will come the day after to-morrow? – And *what* can he not do here? – How do I do it? – How am I supposed to answer this?
>
> Can only those hope who can talk? Only those who have mastered the use of a language. That is to say, the phenomena of hope are modes of this complicated form of life.
>
> (PI: p. 174)[5]

Wittgenstein suggests that the claim that the dog cannot feel hope may seem bewildering. It makes us wonder how *we* bring it off. What may confuse us here is the notion that we are talking about an achievement: we can do it but the dog fails no matter how hard he tries. Part of what contributes to the confusion is the use of the modal 'can'. Conceivably the point could have been better made by simply saying that a dog '*does* not believe his master ...', '*does* not hope', or better yet: '*we do not say* that the dog believes ... or hopes'.[6] The negation here is not an ordinary one, as though we were simply denying that dogs ever do feel hope. The remark is meant to remind us that we never have *occasion* to say that a dog hopes for this or that; *nor, accordingly, to deny it.*[7]

In saying this, however, Wittgenstein is not pointing to the existence of certain rules of sense prohibiting the attribution of hope to dogs and other non-speaking creatures. The idea of a prohibition makes it seem as if there is something we might want to say but are not allowed to. We should rather get to a point where we no longer feel the wish to say certain things.[8] As long as we feel the wish to say it, however, we are still in the grips of the problem (' ... it is much easier to bury a problem than to solve it' PI: 351). Of course, what is crucial here does not have to do specifically with the concept of hope. If someone insists that his dog hopes for things, let him. What we come to see, rather, is that a word such as 'hope' has its life in certain surroundings, rather than being dependent on assumptions about hidden states or processes. Saying that dogs do not hope and saying that their form of life differs from ours in certain respects are, as it were, two ways of saying the same thing, rather than the latter being the ground for the former.[9] Analogous points can of course be made in many other instances; say, concerning the kinds of thing we may say of an infant, of someone living in a past era or an alien culture and so on. And in all these cases, it should be noted, our attention is being drawn to a *continuum* of cases, not to a dichotomy.

II.3

There is another way of expressing what is, I believe, basically the same point. This way of putting it is suggested by a very illuminating essay by David Cockburn (1994), in which he discusses the following remark by Wittgenstein:

> 'But doesn't what you say come to this: that there is no pain, for example, without *pain-behaviour*?' – It comes to this: only of a living human being and what resembles (behaves like) a living human being can one say: it has sensations; it sees; is blind; hears; is deaf; is conscious or unconscious.
>
> (PI: 281)

According to Cockburn, this remark is misleading if it is taken to say that one might point to certain conditions in which one would be justified or unjustified in attributing sensations to a being. It has often been assumed that Wittgenstein's response to the 'other minds' problem is to be read along these lines: the question whether another person really feels pain is solved by pointing to the fact that he displays the kind of behaviour that is the criterion of being in pain. This response, of course, would be a good example of what it means to 'bury' a problem: one would have the feeling of being left with a worry, but having been deprived of the means of expressing it. Cockburn's point is that this relation should be turned around: seeing the behaviour of the animal as (relevantly) similar to ours *means* seeing it as expressive of pain, perception, fear, consciousness, and so on:

> That we can see these similarities between the behaviour of flies and squids and that of human beings is a *reflection* of, not a condition of,

our ability to ascribe the pain or fear. We might then, with some justice, reverse Wittgenstein's remark, writing instead: 'Only of what has
sensations; sees; is blind; hears; is deaf; is conscious or unconscious
can one say that it is a living human being or resembles (behaves like)
a living human being.'

(1994: 148)

The need for this reversal becomes obvious if we consider, on the one
hand, the ease with which we may detect, say, attentiveness, anger or
worry, in the behaviour of a dog, and, on the other hand, the great difference, in purely physical terms, between the face and body of a human
being and those of a dog. Cockburn goes on to point out that we cannot
specify the forms of behaviour in which pain, grief or fear can be seen
(except, of course, with the help of the words 'pain', 'grief' or 'fear') and
he links this to the fact that we cannot specify in advance how we will
be moved by another's behaviour. What furthermore contributes to the
impossibility of doing so, of course, is the role of the surroundings for our
response (say, the way the presence of an *object* of anger or fear is part of
what enables us to see someone's reaction as an expression of anger or fear).

I would agree that this is the direction in which Wittgenstein's remark
needs to be taken. It may seem as if the argument is circular: 'we attribute
pain or anger to dogs because we do'; but this would be a misapprehension: there is no argument being given here, just a reminder of how one
speaks about and lives with dogs.

II.4

In philosophical discussions about thinking, the achievement and attribution issues are often confused.[10] This, I would suggest, contributes to the
intractability of the nature of thought. Philosophers often argue as if the
achievement issue were more basic: if an animal is able to solve some problem, that shows that we can attribute intellectual powers to it. A case in
point is Köhler's famous experiments with chimpanzees, whose ability
to get at a banana hanging beyond reach by fitting two sticks together has
been taken to show the presence in them of higher intellectual capacities. However, if we are to compare different living beings with respect to
their capacity to solve various problems, we must evidently assume that
the situation they are placed in faces them all with one and the same
problem. This seems to presuppose that it is possible to decide what problem an animal is facing in any given situation by simply observing the
situation itself. What is or is not a problem, in other words, is somehow
determined *a priori*. But this is clearly wrong. It hardly makes sense to try

to decide whether an animal is faced with a problem or what the problem is without taking into account how it lives and does things. In other words, the question of attribution must be addressed before the question of achievement can even be raised. On the whole, it could be said, something will not constitute a problem for an animal unless it is the sort of thing the animal is, on the whole, equipped to resolve; unless attempts at dealing with problems of this kind are part of the animal's life.

What looks to us like a 'failure' on the part of an animal to solve some problem, maybe a problem that most of us would solve in passing, then, is misdescribed if we take it to show that there is a comparable task at which humans do better than animals; what it may show, rather, is that humans are better at thinking about *human* things.

A writer who lays great store by the achievement aspect is Peter Singer, who appeals to other cases of smart behaviour on the part of apes in his effort to show that some animals are, as he phrases it, 'rational and self-conscious beings', and that they should therefore enjoy some of the same rights as human beings (1979: 95).[11] In his novel *Elizabeth Costello*, J. M. Coetzee portrays someone who draws what appears to be an alternative conclusion from the line of argument adopted by Singer:

> In my reading of the scientific literature ... efforts to show that animals can think strategically, hold general concepts or communicate symbolically, have had very limited success. The best performance the higher apes can put up is no better than that of a speech-impaired human being with severe mental retardation. If so, are not animals, even the higher animals, properly thought of as belonging to another legal and ethical realm entirely ...?

To which Elizabeth Costello responds:

> ... let me just make one observation: that the programme of scientific experimentation that leads you to conclude that animals are imbeciles is profoundly anthropocentric. It values being able to find your way out of a sterile maze, ignoring the fact that if the researcher who designed the maze were to be parachuted into the jungles of Borneo, he or she would be dead of starvation in a week. In fact I would go further. If I as a human being were told that the standards by which animals are being measured in these experiments are human standards, I would be insulted. It is the experiments themselves that are imbecile.[12]

Whether Elizabeth Costello should be understood as representing the author's views is a question we need not address here. In any case, she is arguing eloquently that, if the tests were to be purged of their inherent anthropocentrism, the question who is the best achiever would be thrown entirely open.

In fact, once we recognize the distinction between the attribution issue and the achievement issue, there no longer seems to be any reason for focusing on problem-solving in reflecting on the relation between animals and human beings (or between machines and human beings, come to that). The question to what extent a companionship between human beings and animals (of various kinds) is intelligible, or what claims various animals have on our concern, must be conceived in much broader terms. Thus, one might suppose that Jane Goodall's account of three young chimpanzees devastated by the death of their mother would have a much greater bearing on how we relate to them than any number of smart tricks they can perform.[13] Switching the perspective around to the issue of attribution changes the character of the whole question. Basing the issue of fellowship on tests of smartness makes it appear as if it all turns on some hidden but measurable property that can be scientifically tested, whereas the matter should really hinge on one's openness to the lives of animals. In fact, as Costello suggests, calling the tests anthropocentric is too generous; they are really quite narrowly modelled on the concerns of late modern Western academics.

As for the idea of thinking machines, it seems clear that the whole discipline of artificial intelligence is based on trying to derive attribution from achievement. The idea that machines might be thinkers gets its purchase from successes in programming machines for the performance of specific tasks. But where it comes to having a life in which various matters take on significance, how *could* it be produced through computer programming?

II.5

Even if we concede that a distinction needs to be made between attribution and achievement, however, we may still be strongly inclined to believe that there must be some common ground to the various mental powers of which human beings seem in such sovereign possession, and which animals (depending on our predilections) may or may not be taken to possess. This common ground is often characterized as the capacity for abstract, conceptual or symbolic thought, or as an ability to form representations of things (objects, states of affairs) for oneself.

According to Singer, 'the most natural way' of explaining the chimpanzees' skill in a certain complex task is to say that they have 'grasped the concept' relevant to the task. And he writes:

> If an animal can devise a careful plan for obtaining a banana, not now but at some future time ... that animal *must* be aware of itself as a distinct entity, existing over time.
>
> (1979: 96; my emphasis)

Consider, for instance, Köhler's chimps who managed to get at the bananas by fitting sticks into one another or piling boxes on top of each other and climbing up. If a chimp finds the banana lying right there in front of him, on the other hand, rather than hung up beyond reach, and if he simply reaches out for the banana and puts it in his mouth, we would probably not be inclined to conclude that the performance had to be preceded by an act of thought. In this case, we feel, there is no gap, as it were, between the task and what is required for its solution, one that would need to be bridged by an act of thinking. The question, however, is how one decides which tasks involve 'gaps' and which do not. Any attempt to establish this would evidently be circular, since the evidence used for showing that thought processes have occurred is precisely the ability to carry out tasks that are assumed to require a capacity for thought.

In fact, some problems that might appear to us to be prime examples of what requires thinking do not, apparently, involve any 'gaps' for certain individuals. I am thinking, for instance, of so-called *savants* (often people suffering from Asperger's syndrome), who can immediately and without apparent effort give the solution to complex problems, such as determining whether some large number is a prime or on what weekday a certain distant date will fall. The fact that these abilities seem to us inexplicable is due to an *a priori* conception of what thinking must be like.[14]

In *Remarks on the Philosophy of Psychology*, Wittgenstein makes a reference to Köhler's experiments:

> Now imagine ... one of Köhler's monkeys, who wants to get a banana from the ceiling, but can't reach it, and thinking about ways and means finally puts two sticks together, etc. Suppose one were to ask, 'What must go on inside him for this to take place?' – This question seems to make some sort of sense. And perhaps someone might answer that unless he acted through chance or instinct, the monkey must have seen the process before his mental eye.
>
> (RPP II: 224)

Wittgenstein is drawing attention to the way we use the inferential 'must' in speaking about what must have preceded the animal's performance. The word 'must' here is a give-away, betraying the *a priori* character of this whole line of thinking.

In *The Brown Book* (the German version), Wittgenstein imagines someone claiming that two people who responded differently to a command 'must have carried different pictures of the concepts in their soul', and says that his reply to that person would be: 'What you say can either be a hypothesis for explaining the facts I have described, or a *simile* under which you represent these facts; but it is not something that *follows* from the facts.' (BrB: 210; my translation). It is clear, however, that Singer does not simply wish to propose a simile under which we can regard the chimp's behaviour, but rather he means us to infer the existence of some independent state explaining that behaviour. However, the status of such a hypothesis is unclear: obviously, there can be no independent method for checking on its correctness (nor does Singer recognize the need for such a check). The inference has nothing to recommend it but our inclination to accept it: the animal's supposed higher processes are doomed to remain forever in this inferential limbo.

The idea of inner representations as independent states that explain the individual's ability to carry out certain tasks or to be related to past or future events or to abstract entities (whether those states are assumed to be in some sense mental – conscious or unconscious – or physiological) is grounded in nothing apart from the philosophical picture which convinces us that such states *must* exist. There can be no independent method of establishing the presence or investigating the nature of such states. Indeed, all we can say about them is that they must have precisely those characteristics that they need for the task they are required to fulfil. The concept of representation is the receptacle for this unknown, unknowable 'something'.

Part III Proving thoughtful

III.1

I have been arguing, following Wittgenstein's suggestions, that the word 'thinking' does not refer to any specific mental process, that there is no specific capacity for engaging in thought that may or may not set us apart from animals and/or machines. It might be thought that Wittgenstein is ignoring the importance we actually attach to thinking. After all, there are certain demanding tasks we would not undertake without giving the matter some careful thought; we admonish people to think of what they are doing; we praise people for being thoughtful and criticize them for their thoughtlessness; and so on. In fact, Wittgenstein does discuss the importance we attach to thought in (*Philosophical Investigations*) PI: 466–70. He asks, with a tinge of irony:

> Does man think, then, because he has found that thinking pays? –
> Because he thinks it advantageous to think?
> (Does he bring his children up because he has found it pays?)

> (PI: 467)

Wittgenstein is ironic about the idea that our habit of thinking things through might, as a whole, be based on our having decided that it pays. That would be circular: it would entail that we had figured out that it is a good idea to figure things out. He does acknowledge that some of our thinking is done because we have found that it pays. Thus, he admits that boilers do not explode as often as they used to after we started calculating their dimensions; nevertheless, they still do explode from time to time. On the other hand, all our thinking is not like calculating the dimensions of boilers. Thinking before acting often means getting mentally prepared for a task, 'gathering one's thoughts'. What this comes down to varies from case to case: the thinking we engage in, say, before making a ski jump is quite different from that we engage in before taking a language proficiency test, or giving a class on induction, or jilting our boyfriend, or painting a floor, or reversing with a trailer, or asking the boss for a raise. Yet it is a feature of human nature, we might say, that we often feel a need to gather our thoughts before doing one of these things.[15] Sometimes, too, experience will have told us that in many cases, if we simply rush into the situation unprepared, the whole thing may end up in disaster. Still, many of us also perform a lot of things just as well or even better without preparation.

It is clear, then, that in many cases we do engage in a 'clockable' activity called 'thinking about X', and that we find it important to do so. There are actually many other kinds of thought activities (or experiences) as well, such as reminiscing, daydreaming, or being haunted by images or memories, say, after witnessing an accident – the kinds of thought for which one will occasionally be offered a penny. However, even where thinking about X is something that goes on during a specific period of time, there is nothing *about* what is going on during the time which establishes the link to X. The idea that there would be something 'from which' one knows what the thought is about is problematic: whose knowledge is here in question? If you are able to guess what I am thinking about this may be due to my demeanour or the circumstances, but if you *ask* me, on the other hand, *I* do not have to infer or guess what I am thinking about from anything, not even from what was going through my mind. If I want to be open about it, I just tell you.[16] (Nor, if by thinking about a problem I come up with a solution to it, is there any determinate characteristic my thinking would have to have had for it really to have been what led to the solution.) This seems to be the point of Wittgenstein's remark:

> If God had looked into our minds he would not have been able to see there whom we were speaking of.
>
> (PI: p. 217)[17]

This point seems to be suggested in the following passage:

> Well, what does one include in 'thinking'? What has one learnt to use this word for? – If I say I have thought – need I always be right? – What *kind* of mistake is there room for here? Are there circumstances in which one would ask: 'Was what I was doing then really thinking; am I not making a mistake?'
>
> (PI: 328)

Even where the thinking consists in something that occurs at a certain time, then, there is nothing about that which it consists in that determines it as the thinking it is; any more than in bringing up a child there is some specific feature of what I am doing which *makes it* bringing up a child. Deciding that thinking about matters is or is not, on the whole, a useful practice makes no more sense than deciding that bringing up one's children is or is not useful, not least because it is unclear what abstaining from either of these would amount to.

III.2

The words 'thought' and 'thinking', however, also have uses that are unambiguously laudatory. When someone is writing a paper in philosophy, for instance, her aim is to put forward a thoughtful account of the matters under discussion. In other words, she hopes that her presentation or argument will be found convincing and original, and that it will not contain any gross oversights that would expose her to criticism for thoughtlessness. Whether she will succeed at this or not will, in a sense, be out of her hands. It will depend in part on her ability to think of illuminating comparisons or contrasts, of foreseeing possible objections or misunderstandings, and so on. There is nothing she could undertake that would *insure* her against such criticism. And, even if her contemporaries find her paper helpful and convincing, later readers may find her reasoning hopelessly flawed because of some crucial oversight. Thus, what once seemed thoughtful may do so no longer.

What would not be debatable, on the other hand, is that the writer will have expended such and such an amount of time thinking about the issues. In that sense, a lot of thought may have gone into the writing of the paper. Pointing this out, however, would be no defence against a possible accusation of thoughtlessness. If anything, a writer, if forced to admit that her reasoning was thoughtless, might be all the more ashamed to let on just how much thinking had gone into the writing of her piece, with all the false starts, all the fumbling in the dark, and so on. The ability to avoid an accusation of thoughtlessness, then, is in no direct proportion to the amount of thought given to a matter.

A person's thoughtfulness will show itself, among other things, in what she *takes* to be a problem, as well as in her *way* of thinking the problem through. A really thoughtful person might not even need to spend much time on the problem,[18] someone less thoughtful might not realize there was a problem there to think about, or she might rack her head over it to no avail. (The character of one's thoughtlessness, we might say, is inseparable from the particular person one is.) Actually, thinking things through, like most other performances, will depend for its success on being done *with* thought: to think well we need to think thoughtfully.

The laudatory use of 'thoughtfulness' has nothing to do with the contrast between human beings and 'thoughtless brutes'. When someone is criticized for her thoughtlessness, her achievement is contrasted with that of other, more thoughtful individuals, or with her own performance on some other occasion. Only of a speaker would we ever say that she is speaking without thinking: we would not say this of a parrot or a babbling infant.

When Wittgenstein concludes the discussion of the idea of thinking as a process accompanying speech or action by suggesting that '[t]houghtless speech and speech that is not thoughtless' should rather 'be compared with the playing of a piece of music thoughtlessly or in a way that is not thoughtless' PI: 341), what he has in mind is evidently this laudatory use. Playing thoughtfully is close to playing expressively, with feeling. In a way, Wittgenstein's formulation is misleading. He gives the impression that playing with thought and thoughtlessly are exhaustive alternatives. 'Thoughtful' and 'thoughtless', rather, are contrary opposites.[19] Not any old poor performance would be called thoughtless. A beginner, for instance, is not yet in a position to play thoughtlessly: one needs to have attained at least some degree of proficiency to come up for this particular brand of criticism. But neither of course will the beginner's playing be called *thoughtful*, however much he may wrinkle his brows over the score. Wittgenstein himself gives a hint of this elsewhere:

> Only under quite special circumstances does the question arise [*variant*: make sense] whether one spoke *thinkingly* or not.
>
> (RPP II: 233)

It might be thought that Wittgenstein's point here has some analogies with Gilbert Ryle's suggestion that the verb 'to think', in many cases, should be thought of as having an adverbial use, that is, as referring to the manner in which someone goes about things, rather than to a separate process. According to Ryle, for someone to do something while thinking of what he is doing is to do what he is doing, as Ryle puts it, 'with his wits about him':

> To X, thinking what one is doing, is not to be doing both some X-ing and some separately doable Y-ing; it is to be X-ing ... on purpose, with some tentativeness, some vigilance against some known hazards, some perseverance and with at least a modicum of intended or unintended self-training.
>
> (1979: 24)[20]

However, I do not believe that this is what Wittgenstein is trying to say. *Philosophical Investigations* (PI: 316), the first part of which was quoted above, ends by suggesting that observing oneself thinking in order to get clear about the meaning of the word 'think'

> would be as if without knowing how to play chess, I were to try and make out what the word 'mate' meant by close observation of the last move of some game of chess.

There are of course many different ways of mating: any move, given the right context, could be a mate. But neither is mating a certain *way of performing a move*: rather, it is a move which holds a certain position in the game. It is internally connected with the notion of winning a game. All the other moves get their sense from the attempt to mate and from trying to prevent one's opponent mating. Similarly, what counts as my thinking of the solution to a problem is dependent on the context, the nature of the problem, what counts as a solution, and so on.

In fact, there is an ambiguity in Ryle's account. In saying that someone is acting 'with his wits about him', 'with some tentativeness, some vigilance against some known hazards', one may either be describing his manner of proceeding, drawing attention to certain characteristic features of a kind, say, that an actor might portray, or one may be praising his performance: 'He really had his wits about him, spotting that moose on the road', or 'She is a truly vigilant proof reader: she's hardly ever missed an error.' In the latter cases, no reference is made to the *manner* of acting. There is no manner of proceeding that could make me immune to the accusation that I had been acting thoughtlessly. In fact, *contra* Ryle, in some cases a person's thoughtfulness, 'presence of mind', will show itself precisely in his acting decisively and without hesitation.[21]

III.3

What leads us astray here, as I have been arguing, is the influence exerted by the active verb 'to think' in conjunction with the picture of human action with which it is connected. The grammar of the verb 'to think' leads us to suppose that our ability to perform in a thoughtful manner must be based on some activity that we carry out, some effort we undertake or some process that takes place within us. As touched on in the introduction, we assume that this is a neutral, inert, mechanical, impersonal procedure by which conclusions are deductively or inductively derived from premises independently supplied. It is taken to be 'impersonal' in the sense that it is routinely accessible and yields the same results to anyone willing to make the effort; it is 'inert' in the sense that thought by itself cannot supply the motive force for human action. However, as we have seen, the actual use of expressions like 'thoughtful', or 'with thought', is radically different from this. This shows the usefulness of Wittgenstein's advice to look at the way the word 'think' *functions* rather than simply guess at it (PI: 340).[22] On some uses of the word, thinking does not necessarily put us in a better position to succeed in what we are doing. On some other uses, thinking is linked to success, but that is only because success is a condition for calling a performance thoughtful. It is the confusion of these uses that makes us think that there is a specific mental activity that enables us to act wisely and well.

The picture of thought as a method with the direction of success built into it seems to involve the following steps, each one of which, I would contend, is false:

1. to figure something out is to construct a chain of argument leading to the relevant conclusion;
2. all valid arguments, when fully spelled out, have the form of deductive or inductive reasoning;

3. reasoning deductively or inductively is an algorithmic process; that is, it can be carried out purely mechanically;
4. if we do something mechanically it follows that a machine could do it (and, if a machine can do something, it follows that we could do it mechanically).

The picture is a mixture of the kinds of mental stretching, bending and sorting we sometimes go through in order to get straight about some matter, and the kind of thing we would tell someone in order to defend our judgment or bring them over to our position. Constructing an argument is something we typically do in a dialogue; say, when our judgment is being challenged, or when we try to bring someone over to our position. The argument we present depends on what we think will carry conviction; this is dependent on whom we are talking to and the context of the conversation. We *may* argue our case by retracing the steps by which we arrived at the position; but then again we may choose some other tactic. In many cases, there may be no steps to retrace. In any case, an argument's being convincing has nothing to do with its being overtly or implicitly deductive: what it means for something to be a good argument depends on what needs to be said in the situation at hand, not on certain formal criteria.[23]

Once the idea of thinking as a mechanical process is abandoned, this enables us to surrender the Humean postulate that reason can only be concerned with the choice of means. The Humean dichotomy is artificial and tends to cripple our efforts to get a clear view of the uses of the word 'thought'. In fact, some of the most emphatic uses of that word are ones that involve a reflection on a person's character, as when we blame someone for thinking only of himself, or when we praise a person's thoughtfulness, say, in choosing the perfect gift for someone else's birthday. Similarly, when a musical performance or a philosophical essay is praised as being thoughtful, this does not mean that we have a standard in mind against which the performance or the essay is being assessed. When regarded under the dichotomy of means and ends, however, uses like these will be shunted aside as metaphorical or, at best, peripheral.

'Thinking' is not the only word with regard to which our understanding is hampered by the dichotomy between intellect and character. Similar observations hold of a wide range of so-called cognitive concepts, for example, knowledge, understanding,[24] reason, sense, attention, awareness, imagination and remembering. Thus, try to imagine the occasions on which some of the following things might be said:

'Can't you be more reasonable?'
'I don't understand you at all!'

'You don't know what I'm going through!'
'I can't believe you forgot your promise!'
'You should try to be more attentive to her!'

Someone making one of these utterances will not normally be concerned with the addressee's success or failure in applying a cognitive skill to a problem confronting him. The criticism is not, typically, of a kind that is to be avoided by acquiring some crucial piece of information or by considering some argument more carefully. But neither, of course, would it clarify matters to suggest that in using these locutions we are really *not* speaking about matters of thought or understanding at all; that these words are only being used metaphorically, and that what we are talking about are really just matters of choice, preference or feeling. Rather, in these locutions, intellect and character seem to be inseparably intertwined: the cases invoked in them are ones in which character is *expressed* in a person's way of perceiving, attending to or thinking about the situation at hand.

III.4

Let me conclude with a few remarks about the concept of reason. Reason and rationality hold a place of honour in much of Western thought about human existence. Wittgenstein, on the other hand, never accorded these concepts so much as a passing interest.[25] This, I would claim, is no accident. The received idea of the central role of reason (or rather the received ideas, since there is hardly any generally accepted account of precisely *why* reason is important) is closely bound up with the notion of thought as involving a specific process. Philosophers' uses of the word 'reason' tend to be very distant from the way reason is spoken about in most human affairs. In ordinary parlance, a reasonable fellow is someone it is easy to come to terms with. In trying to persuade someone to change his mind we plead with him: 'Please be reasonable!'; if we are successful, we may say 'He finally saw reason'. Being reasonable, on the whole, seems to be a matter of attitude; the reasonable individual is not given to excesses, whether in taking risks, in forming judgments, or in dealing with other people. It is very much a golden-mean type of virtue. Above all it should be clear that being reasonable is not a purely intellectual or cognitive matter (if such a thing exists).

Sometimes observations like these are countered by an attempt to distinguish between reason and rationality. It is then conceded that while *reason* does involve the kind of attitude I have suggested here, *rationality* is a matter of pure intellect. A rational person, it will be suggested, is 'thought-governed': she is skilled and persistent in employing thought in choosing means to given ends (and, it is perhaps added, is not easily deflected from whatever courses of action thinking recommends). However, if I have been right in suggesting that the notion of a specific ability for thought is unintelligible, it is unclear what kind of quality is actually being described here. It might be suggested that the rational person is someone who approaches issues in a characteristic way: she limits her concerns in an attempt to get a systematic grip on things (thus if she is a business executive she might be someone who keeps her eyes on the bottom line to the exclusion of everything else). In this way, rationality may come to be associated with a quality of single-mindedness or ruthlessness. On this account, too, rationality boils down to a matter of attitude; though, in distinction from reason, it is not obvious why rationality, thus understood, should in itself be considered a virtue.

In the absence of a notion of thought as a specific goal-seeking activity, it seems hard to formulate an intelligible account of reason that would explain why it should be considered to be of central importance in human life. It is not, I hope, too unfair to suggest that academic philosophers may have had an ulterior motive for bringing reason to the fore. After all, reason is usually taken to be the arena on which their most important contribution to our shared life is made. Thus, in defending the importance of reason they were, they thought, defending their place in our culture. From Wittgenstein's point of view, these ideas were based on a misunderstanding; besides, any such motive would have been totally alien to him.[26]

Notes

1. Hebb (1958), 200. Hebb is not consistent in claiming that the mental capacities of human beings distinguish them from other animals; elsewhere, he assumes that human beings share the capacity for thought with the 'higher' animals (ibid.: 48).
2. RPP II: 216, 220. The translation of the first sentence of 216 is very loose, to put it mildly. 'Wenn man auch das denkende Arbeiten, ohne alles reden, in unsere Betrachtung einbezieht, so sieht man, dass unser Begriff "denken" ein weitverzweigter ist' would be better rendered as follows: 'If one also includes working thoughtfully, without any talking, in our consideration, one sees that our concept "thinking" is a widely ramified one.'
3. For an example of the way these issues tend to be argued, see Gilbert Harman (1973), 176 ff. Harman makes two characteristic moves here. First, he surreptitiously moves from saying that computers behave *as if* they made inferences to saying that they do. Second, he uses this 'datum' to argue that human beings can, by analogy, be said to make unconscious inferences.

4. In fact, it is not all that easy to find tasks at which humans will outperform dogs, if one does not include tasks involving the use of language or hands. A connected problem is that a number of unspoken assumptions may already be packed into the notion of an 'intellectually demanding task'. We shall get back to the issue presently.

5. Also, cf. PI: 250: 'Why can't a dog simulate pain? Is he too honest? Could one teach a dog to simulate pain? Perhaps it is possible to teach him to howl on particular occasions as if he were in pain, even when he is not. But the surroundings which are necessary for this behaviour to be real simulation are missing.'

6. In a philosophical discussion someone may insist that for all we know, dogs may entertain hopes, or maybe even thoughts about the stock market. So in a sense it is true that 'people *do* say such things'. The point of interest, however, is that people do not find occasion to make such remarks in the course of their lives with dogs.

7. Recent new reports hail the 'discovery' that some animals laugh (cf. http://news.nationalgeographic.com/news/2005/03/0331_050331_animallaughter.html). This gives the misleading impression that what will count as laughter is given once and for all. What is of real interest in this connection, rather, are the circumstances of an animal's life in which there would be a place for speaking of it as laughing.

8. On these issues, cf. PI: 342–62. On the nature of appeals to what makes sense, see also Cora Diamond, 'What Nonsense Might Be' in Diamond (1991) and 'Rules: Looking in the Right Place' in Diamond (1989); Edward Witherspoon, 'Conceptions of Nonsense in Carnap and Wittgenstein' in Crary and Read (2000). I have discussed the issue in Hertzberg (2001).

9. Norman Malcolm, in 'Thoughtless Brutes', claims, against Descartes, that we often attribute thoughts to a dog (Malcolm 1972–73). His examples, however, are ones in which the word 'believes' might have been substituted for 'thinks', rather than cases of thinking something through, coming to think of something, etc. This does not undermine his argument against Descartes, however.

10. Whether this is due to the legacy of Descartes I do not know. What characterized his thinking about these issues is that he subsumed all the aspects of the mind under the concept of thought, thus suggesting that the capacity for thought was the key to the distinctively human. Cf. Alanen (2003), 78.

11. For other examples, see Singer's review article, 'Bandit and Friends', *New York Review of Books*, 9 April 1992.

12. J. M. Coetzee, *Elizabeth Costello* (London: Secker & Warburg, 2003), 107f. This discussion is in response to a lecture by Costello in which she imagines the chimpanzee's reaction to Köhler's experiment; a masterful illustration of the way in which the problem presented by one and the same situation might be understood in radically different ways by certain people and certain apes.

13. Quoted in Cockburn (1994), 149.

14. For an account of such a case, see 'The Twins' in Sacks (1985), 185–203.

15. In this connection, we might also reflect on the following remark: 'How can one learn the truth by thinking? As one learns to see a face better if one draws it' (Z: 255).

16. D. W. Hamlyn, somewhat uncharacteristically, seems to overlook this point in his essay 'Thinking'. He argues that 'the application to the object of thought of

the concepts involved in the thought ... requires a ground – something that can act as the focus for that conceptual understanding, in that it has something of that significance for us. That significance may well be idiosyncratic, but it must exist, and it is what philosophers have been getting at when they have spoken of images, etc. functioning as symbols' (Hamlyn, 1976: 111f.). What he is apparently arguing is that I must have a basis for what I claim to be thinking about. Though he admits that it need not be a display of the object itself, still it must be some feature that is linked, for me, to that object. Here one might ask, first, whether on Hamlyn's account I might *mis*identify the object of my thought, and, second, what is the basis of his claim that such a ground *must* exist.

17. In this connection, we might consider a newspaper report (*The Guardian*, 12 February 2005) about one of the autistic savants we spoke about previously. Under the headline 'A Genius Explains, the story says: 'Daniel Tammet ... can perform mind-boggling mathematical calculations at breakneck speeds ... Tammet is calculating 377 multiplied by 795. Actually, he isn't "calculating": there is nothing conscious about what he is doing. He arrives at the answer instantly.' Still, 'unlike other savants ... Tammet can describe how he does it.' This is how: '[since the age of three] he has been able to see numbers as shapes, colours and textures. The number two, for instance, is a motion, and five is a clap of thunder. "When I multiply numbers together, I see two shapes. The image starts to change and evolve, and a third shape emerges. That's the answer. It's mental imagery. It's like maths without having to think."' *Some explanation!* one feels like saying.

18. In some cases giving thought to matters is even a *substitute* for thoughtfulness. This point is well illuminated by Oliver Sacks, who discusses the way in which autistic individuals will sometimes have to bring thought to bear on problems that to most normal people will just resolve themselves as a matter of course. In the title essay in his book, *An Anthropologist on Mars*, he says about Temple Grandin, a highly intelligent autistic woman: 'This implicit knowledge [of social conventions and codes, of cultural presuppositions of every sort], which every normal person accumulates and generates throughout life on the basis of experience and encounters with others, Temple seems to be largely devoid of. Lacking it, she has instead to "compute" others' intentions and states of mind, to try to make algorithmic, explicit, what for the rest of us is second nature' (Sacks, 1995: 258). Apparently, one mark distinguishing some autists from most non-autists is that what is a matter of thought for one group is not so for the other, and vice versa. Sacks's point should be clear, although one might question his way of expressing it, since the terms 'explicit' and 'implicit' suggest that these are matters that we could all put into words, if called upon to do so. In fact, of course, the thought that everything we need to be able to command if we are to act successfully could in principle be put into words, let alone be made 'algorithmic', is an illusion.

19. This point is noted by Oswald Hanfling in 'Thinking' (2002), 136.

20. See also Ryle's essay 'Thinking and Reflecting' in (Ryle 1990): esp. p. 468. This volume contains a number of useful discussions of the concept of thinking.

21. It is important to note the difference between the sense of thoughtfulness I have been describing, and the sense of the word in which it is a synonym of 'pensive'; i.e., in which it carries the meaning 'being wrapped in thought'. These are at opposite ends of a scale: my being pensive may explain my acting

thoughtlessly. Of course, just as I was being thoughtless in one regard, I may at the same time have been thoughtful in some other.

22. Cf. also RPP II: 234.

23. The idea that formal logic provides a model for good reasoning is effectively criticized by Don S. Levi in his book *In Defense of Informal Logic* (Dordrecht: Kluwer Academic Publishers, 2000).

24. I discuss some 'non-intellectual' uses of the word 'understand' in Hertzberg (2005).

25. It is true that in *On Certainty* the concept of 'the reasonable individual' has a certain role; but even there, it is characteristically different from the role it is ordinarily given in philosophy: it does not occur there as a philosopher's notion.

26. Earlier versions of this chapter were presented at a Wittgenstein conference at the University of Minnesota in October, 1996, and at the research seminar at Åbo Academy in the spring of 2004. I wish to thank the participants in those seminars for their comments. Work on this essay was financed in part by the Academy of Finland, project number 210162.

4
Wittgenstein on 'Experiencing Meaning'

Jacques Bouveresse

1 The meaning of words and the meaning we give them

In *The Origins of Analytic Philosophy*, Michael Dummett suspects Husserl of holding the view that the meaning of a word in discourse is each time determined by an act of meaning on the part of the speaker, which has all the trappings of a Humpty Dumpty decision: what a word means is what we want it to mean at the moment we use it; and we can, in principle, make it mean what we like. All depends on what the speaker has *put* behind her words, much as what a face communicates depends on what the person we are looking at has put behind it, with the difference that a face can also involuntarily and unconsciously express many things – which language could not do if what is expressed would each time have to be a meaning intention that the speaker first had and then sought to transmit.

The drawback of such a conception is that it renders unintelligible the way in which an intention of meaning can be made public and communicated by the words in which it is expressed. The '*sense-animated* expression', as Husserl calls it, owes its sense to meaning-conferring acts; and to make *these* 'known to the hearer is the prime aim of our communicative intention, for only in so far as the hearer attributes them to the speaker will he understand the latter' (1913/2001: 192, 193). Husserl expresses himself in a curious way here, as if the principal aim of discourse were to inform the hearer of the meaning-conferring acts produced by the speaker while she spoke rather than of the object of her discourse; that is, what she meant to say and did say when she used words as she did. If taken literally, this would be grossly circular: we would have to concede both that we can only succeed in knowing what someone else means by the words she uses if we first know what those words mean, and that we can only know that sort of thing if we know what meaning-conferring act was effected by the speaker at the moment of utterance.

It could be shown without too much difficulty that Dummett's suspicion, undoubtedly encouraged by Husserl's manner of expression, is not really justified. Yet it is worth highlighting the problem that such accounts as Husserl's would pose if taken literally: meaning something cannot both completely determine the meaning of what was said and be itself, as seems to have to be the case, part and parcel of what was said (which includes aspects such as intonation), as well as of the linguistic and extralinguistic context of the utterance, and other diverse factors. The German word *Weiche* can be used as a verb, noun or adjective, and Wittgenstein's oft-reiterated pun: '*Weiche, Wotan, weiche!*'[1] relies on the possibility of understanding it both as a verb in the imperative and as an adjective. The sentence can therefore be interpreted either as a command to Wotan to withdraw, or as an answer to his question about whether we preferred our eggs hard or soft-boiled. It is of course possible to use an ambiguous word in such a way that the sentence and context compel the hearer to understand the word one way, while at the same time understanding it ourselves in another. But how are we to describe what goes on in such a case, and what is likely to be communicated?

It seems, at first glance, also possible to use a sentence that unquestionably has meaning in a meaningful way, whilst actually giving it no meaning. This is the case considered by Wittgenstein of someone who would utter the sentence 'Die Rose ist rot' whilst giving, or at least trying to give' 'ist' the meaning of 'ist gleich', the meaning not of the copula, but of the equal sign (PI: p. 175). The upshot seems to be that the meaning disintegrates for the speaker, but not for the hearer. And the question which then arises is: in order to grasp the meaning of what was said, must the hearer understand that the speaker deliberately meant nothing? Wittgenstein considers fundamentally suspect the notion that the meaning of a sentence can both consist in the meaning of its constitutive words and simply decompose or undo itself, as in the example just cited. What is true here, says Wittgenstein, is simply that 'one might tell someone: if you want to pronounce the salutation "Hail!" expressively, you had better not think of hailstones as you say it!' (ibid.). Indeed, it is true that we should avoid doing this if we want to pronounce those words expressively, but to say as much is not to say that if we do it, we will not be understood, or that there is something else – the real meaning of the word in the given context – about which we must necessarily be thinking.

What is the margin of freedom between what I say and what I might mean? And to what extent does what I might have meant constitute the interesting and important thing here? Consider one of Wittgenstein's favourite English examples: the sentence 'Time flies', in which 'time' can function as a noun, or as a verb in the imperative, and 'flies' as a verb and as a noun:

> ... in conversation, I sigh: 'Time flies!'[2] and then whisper 'if you've got nothing more interesting to do'. One gets the impression each time that it is impossible to effect the two irreconcilable moves of thought. If the first words ['Time flies!'] are understood as a sigh, then the others ['if you've got nothing better to do'] lose their context. And if we were to imagine a situation in which we meant the words as an order ['Time flies!'], whilst uttering them as a sigh, it could not be the sigh 'Time flies!'

(Ms 133; DMS translation)

> It is perfectly possible to pronounce words suitably to a particular situation, and hence with such-and-such a meaning, but at the same time to *think* another interpretation. So that for me, unbeknownst to the other, the words have a peculiar meaning.

(RPP I: 671)

> If asked, I shall perhaps explain this meaning, without this explanation's having come before my mind earlier. So what had my state of mind, as I spoke the words with the double meaning, to do with the words of the explanation? Here there is obviously no such thing as the explanation's fitting the phenomenon.

(RPP I: 672)

> 'If you had asked me, *this* is the answer I'd have given you.' That signifies a state; but not an 'accompaniment' of my words.

(RPP I: 675)

> Ask yourself again: what interests us in knowing how someone meant this word, this sentence? Is it really a, so to speak, organic phenomenon concomitant with speech that we are interested in? And why? – Because we can draw empirical conclusions from this concomitant phenomenon? ...
>
>   No, I did not get the explanation of what I meant from any illustration, nor did I read it off another phenomenon. But naturally this does not suggest that I did not 'really' mean that which I am explaining

I meant. For that would mean yet something else. (It is precisely a particular kind of explanation and temporal indication.)

(Ms 133: 48–50; DMS translation)

The problem here is that when, say, to remove all ambiguity and prevent possible misunderstanding, I give an explanation of the kind: 'I meant ...', I can no more suggest that that explanation had presented itself to me at the time I uttered the words than I can find a correlation between that explanation and what might have occurred at the same time in my mind. In his *Lectures on Philosophical Psychology, 1946–1947*, Wittgenstein says, about that sort of example:

> 'Time flies!' You may see a clock and flies and sigh 'time flies!' – what is it that you couldn't do – that really contradicts meaning the sigh? – If I ask a man what he meant, you wouldn't expect him to say: Only the context can show. This suggests an experience. But his saying what he visualized is quite independent.
>
> (PLP: 56)

Indeed, were we to ask a person what he meant, he would not say that only the context could have shown it, but that he had decided the meaning and that he knows perfectly what he had decided at that moment. And this suggests an experience or action of a certain kind. But what makes us so certain that one of these must have occurred?

As noted, Wittgenstein said about the explanation 'I meant ...' that it is a particular type of explanation because it is not inferred from anything that really happened but from something that could have happened: if I had been asked, I would have given such-and-such an answer. And this is a special kind of temporal indication because it refers to the past – indeed, points to a precise moment in the past – but fails to point to some particular thing that in fact did happen at the said moment. Suppose you used the word 'Napoleon' in a sentence:

> If you were asked 'Did you just now precisely mean the man who won the Battle of Austerlitz?', you will say 'yes'. 'So you meant this man as you uttered the sentence in which his name occurs!' – Yes, but perhaps only in the sense in which I also knew that in mathematics $2 + 2 = 4$. That is, not as if at that moment a particular process that might be called 'meaning something' had taken place, even if perhaps certain pictures associated to that meaning and which might have been different for another meaning of the word 'Napoleon' did accompany

the utterance. Perhaps the reply: 'Yes, I meant the victor of Austerlitz' is a further step in the account. What is misleading in this step is the past tense, which seems to give a description of what happened 'in me' as I uttered the sentence. Whereas the past tense really only applies to the sentence, which was uttered earlier.

(Ms. 111: 25–6; DMS translation)

In many, perhaps the majority, of cases, when I say that at the moment I uttered the word 'Napoleon', what I meant was the victor of Austerlitz, this is not very different from simply saying that I knew that in our language the word designates him, and that we understand it to mean him when the word is so used. But this thing I *knew* is not a thing about which it might be said that I know it at any given moment, and that the fact of my knowing it must have translated itself, at the moment in question, into the occurrence of a particular event or process in my mind. It is in this sense that the use of the past tense: 'I meant ...' is misleading.

The question that Wittgenstein returns to again and again is precisely that of knowing how and why what someone meant, interpreted in the sense of 'the meaning he had in mind at the moment he spoke', is supposed to interest us. And what he contests is precisely that what seems to us crucial in the process of linguistic communication – that is, the mental act of meaning something by which a speaker confers a determined meaning to the words he uses, and the correlative act of understanding by which the hearer succeeds, if all goes well, in attributing the same meaning to them – is indeed crucial:

'The person who says this can mean the word in one way or another.' etc. We imagine, therefore, that the word or in any case the sentence, is accompanied by something mental, and that this accompaniment is the important thing, which places the words in one relation or another to reality. And now this manner of speaking can indeed be misleading, but that does not mean that something false is stated. (Infinitesimal calculation.) For it remains true that I can utter the words 'That is red' as a definition and as an indication of colour.

So where lies the error or the erroneous picture? – We use a primitive picture and see in it the explanation of something that puzzles us.

(Ms 131: 67–8; DMS translation)

There is of course an important difference, fully acknowledged by Wittgenstein, between uttering words in a meaningful way and merely uttering them. We are tempted to say that something must be taking place in the first case that does not take place in the second. In *Philosophical Investigations*, Wittgenstein envisages three possible and natural ways to describe the situation, and concludes that they are in fact equivalent:

> Whether I say that in the first case they have depth; or that something goes on inside me, inside my mind, as I utter them; or that they have an atmosphere – it always comes to the same thing.
>
> (PI: 594)

We are inclined to say, particularly when doing philosophy, that when we characterize the difference between the three cases by saying that in the first case something goes on in me or in my mind, we are giving the real explanation of what the other two forms of expression merely metaphorically describe. However, Wittgenstein suggests that what we are in fact doing in the first case is merely using another picture, one which is on a par with the other two; moreover, it is a primitive picture and has therefore every chance of turning out to be misleading.

In fact, the anti-mentalism generally imputed to Wittgenstein does not consist, as is often thought, in his refuting the reality attributed to the mental (although, as he notes, this reality is most of the time merely postulated *post factum* in the mode of something that *must* have happened at the moment the words were uttered in order for them to have meaning, indeed the very meaning they have). Rather, Wittgenstein's anti-mentalism consists in the shift of perspective that makes of *the language-game itself* the first and fundamental thing: that which does not have to be explained – indeed, cannot be – by the real or supposed mental experiences which are, in each case, supposed to make it possible, and are in fact nothing but mere accompaniments of the language-game. In order to play the crucial role attributed to it, the mental would have to enter the linguistic process in a very determined form – that of a series of episodes of meaning something linked to the words used, and capable of combining so that *the sentence as a whole* can end up meaning something. But this conception of things relies on a serious misapprehension of the real grammar of the expression 'meaning something', as well as of the real nature of the relationship between what is said and what is meant. Moreover when, after the fact, one looks for the thing that, in principle, should have occurred in the mind for words to acquire and communicate meaning, one generally finds no real trace of what one is looking for. Although the utterance of a word with a determinate meaning intention can be accompanied by diverse mental experiences, and a change of intention have a correlate corresponding to those experiences,

Wittgenstein insists that none of the experiences we can think of *is* the intention or can explain what the intention is.

Experiences of meaning are experiences linked to meaning, but any meaning something and meaning intention with which the word is used in particular circumstances are not themselves experiences of any kind. And, even if they were – that is, if at the moment of speaking, we had a specific mental experience of something like the word's possibilities of use, complemented, in the case of an ambiguous word, by a decision in favour of one of them – we would still have to ask ourselves what the role and importance of such experiences in linguistic communication consist in:

> For if it is like this, if the possible uses of a word do float before us in half-shades as we say or hear it – this simply goes for *us*. But we communicate with other people without knowing if they have this experience too.
>
> (PI: p. 181)

And so the meaning someone gives their words can only be accessible if it resides in the words themselves and the use made of them, not in the mental experiences accompanying that use in the speaker's mind.

To take another of Wittgenstein's favourite examples, is it reasonable and necessary to suppose that, when the German word *Bank* is used to mean 'financial institution' rather than 'bench', the difference is marked by a particular meaning-conferring mental act thanks to which it carries the first and not the second sense? The distinction made by Wittgensein between meaning intention proper and the experienced content that accompanies and illustrates it (in the case at hand, e.g., the picture in the speaker's mind of a particular bank) is reminiscent of one of Husserl's 'essential distinctions': that which must be made between meaning intention and its optional 'fulfilment'. But Wittgenstein's remarks also compel us to ask whether the presence of a meaning intention can be seen as necessarily linked to the performance of a certain act which, it seems, we ought to be able to retrace *post factum*. In other words, the question is whether it is true, as Husserl believes, that 'the articulate sound-complex' only first becomes 'a spoken word or communicative bit of speech, when a speaker produces it with the intention of "expressing himself about something" through its means'; that is, when he first 'endow[s] it with a sense in *certain acts of mind*, a sense he desires to share with his auditors' (1913/2001: 189; emphasis added). Wittgenstein would certainly not question that speaking a language can be described as an intentional activity, but this does not mean: an activity consisting in the performance of acts of intention that must always accompany words and which give them meaning. Therefore, he not only rejects the idea that understanding could be constituted of experiences linked, more or less passively, to the use of words (as suggested by the causal theory of meaning, which he rejected in the early 1930s), he also denies that understanding is – in the speaker who uses words that he understands in a particular way as well as in the hearer who must be able to understand them in the same way – a specific mental activity that complements use and makes it so that, in use, signs really become signs and, as phenomenologists say, acquire the capacity of 'directedness'. As Wittgenstein himself suggests: to suppose that each time we mean something with a word, a particular act of meaning-something must have been effected is as curious as supposing that each time I recognize a familiar object in my environment, a particular act of recognition must occur (cf. PI: 602–3). When I remember the meaning intention with which I used a word, I do remember something, indeed something of which I can be completely certain; but this something is not an episode of my mental life. The two questions 'Tell me, what was going on in you when you uttered the words ...?' and 'Tell me what you meant by the words ....' require and receive two completely different answers: ' "Tell me, what was going on in you when you uttered the words ...?" – The answer to this is not: "I was meaning ...."!' (PI: 675). And of course, nor is the answer to the question 'What did you mean?': 'Such and such things were going on in me while I was speaking.'

2   Against the dualist conception of the action of language

In saying that it is use itself which, in a way, constitutes the life of the sign, Wittgenstein is attempting to rid us of the temptation 'to think that the action of language consists of two parts; an inorganic part, the handling of signs, and an organic part, which we may call understanding these signs, meaning them, interpreting them, thinking' (BB: 3). It is because we think we need something capable of giving life to the sign that we resort to the idea that the essential thing, at the moment of use, must occur in the mind. Wittgenstein affirms the contrary: in order to breathe life into the sign, use does not need a mental complement without which it would be nothing but sign manipulation uninhabited by thought. It wrongly seems to us that the connection between the words we use and what they are about requires something which is of a different nature from their use; as if the connection could only be established by certain things that our mind *does*, over and above what we say. And in suggesting that what our minds do here is something incommensurable with anything of the order of mere sign manipulation, what we mean is that it is something which we must, more or less, give up trying to understand; indeed, that the mind can do, with means proper to it, things that, although perfectly real, familiar and even banal, seem to us impossible: 'This is partly', remarks Wittgenstein, 'what makes us think of meaning or thinking as a peculiar *mental activity*; the word "mental" indicating that we mustn't expect to understand how these things work' (BB: 39). We look for a way of explaining how the words we utter can be meaningful, but we do it in a way that does not eliminate – on the contrary, it ratifies and glorifies – unintelligibility.

From the conceptual, as well as the empirical, point of view, meaning something is not a specific experience we have of the meaning of words as we are speaking them. It does not consist of a kind of procession of meanings in the mind or in the mind's eye. But this is not to say that the use of words in speech cannot be accompanied by experiences that we might call 'meaning experiences' (*Bedeutungserlebnisse*). When Wittgenstein evokes these, it is mostly to emphasize how small in importance and pertinence they are in contrast to the interesting and meaningful uses of expressions like 'meaning something' or 'understanding' (say, 'understanding a word in such and such a way' (cf. RPP I: 358 and 687)). This is precisely the point illustrated by the thought experiment in which Wittgenstein imagines human beings suffering from 'meaning blindness' (*Bedeutungsblindheit*): people who use words exactly as we do, but without having any of the characteristic sensations, impressions and experiences that, for us, are indissolubly linked to word use. What such people would lack is what authors like William James consider to be constitutive of our capacity to grasp a sentence as meaningful, as something radically different from a series of vocal sounds that 'mean nothing'. For Wittgenstein, on the other hand, the specific *Erlebnis* that can be associated with the pronunciation of a word is, in many respects, the thing that counts least:

> When I supposed the case of a 'meaning-blind' man, this was because the experience of meaning seems to have no importance in the *use* of language. And so because it looks as if the meaning-blind could not lose much. But it conflicts with this, that we sometimes say that some word in a communication meant one thing to us until we saw that it

meant something else. First, however, we don't feel in this case that the experience of the meaning took place while we *were hearing the word*. Secondly, here, one might speak of an experience rather of the sense of the sentence, than of the meaning of a word.

The picture that one perhaps connects with the utterance of the sentence 'The bank is far away', is an illustration of *it* and not of one of its words.

If someone insists that when he hears and understands an order, a piece of information etc., he mostly does not experience anything at all, at least not anything that determines the sense for him – might this man not say nevertheless in some form or other that he had taken the first words of the sentence like *this* and later altered the way he took them? – But what would he say that *for*? It might explain a particular reaction on his part. He heard, e.g. that N was dead and believed that this meant his friend N; then he realizes that it is not so. At first he looks upset; then relieved – And it is easy to see what kind of interest such an explanation may have.

(RPP I: 202–4; cf. RPP II: 242)

Because for a meaning-blind person the hearing of words is not accompanied by any particular experience, he will not say that he first experienced the word in one way, then in another. He will probably, however, be able to speak of another kind of change which did occur and which explains the reaction he had. In fact, Wittgenstein is not sure about what ought to be said in such a case:

What am I to say now – that the meaning-blind man is not in a position to react like that? Or that he merely does not assert that he *then* experienced the meaning – and so, that he merely does not use a particular picture?

(RPP I: 205)

This suggests that when *we* say that we had a particular experience of meaning, we may be doing nothing more than using a certain picture. Wittgenstein does not at all deny that words like 'meaning' (or *'meinen'*) can also, in certain cases, refer to an experience that occurred at a given moment. This is what happens, for instance, when I say that all of a sudden I understood that such-and-such a meaning was to be given to the word or the rule, and knew from that moment on how I was to continue. The problem arises precisely from the fact that the word 'meaning' can be used to refer both to a particular, dated event or episode of our mental life and to something very different, and we do not know how to make these two things compatible. In *Lectures on Philosophical Psychology*, Wittgenstein makes the following remark:

> I say: the meaning of a word is the technique of its use. How, then, can a word mean something momentarily, when I hear or say it? The meaning seems to be something that accompanies the word often but not always. There seem to be degrees of meaningfulness. If I say 'Open the window', 'window' has meaning; if you repeat 'window, window ...' the meaning vanishes.
>
> (LPP: 55)

There can be no doubt then that meaning can also be something that is present at the moment the word is pronounced, or that can be more or less present, or that can be present for a time and then no more. A problem resulting from the fact that we speak of meaning in this temporal way is that when we look closer at what we are doing, we realize that to say: 'When I uttered the word, it had for me this or that meaning' generally means 'If you had asked me the question, I would have said that ...'. Here, then, we are making a use of the conditional that is both essential and disconcerting. Wittgenstein notes that describing changes in our *experience* is very different from describing changes in our *knowledge*. To say that I knew this and now do not, makes little sense (except perhaps to relate the fact that we can forget something we had known), but we can certainly use a word giving it one meaning at one time, and another at another time. And yet, says Wittgenstein:

> Change of meaning seems to be more like a change of knowledge than a change of experience. If you ask, 'What happened in you when you changed your meaning?', the answer is 'What changed is the answer I would have given if you had asked me what I meant!' So when I said 'Now I know', what changed was that now I could have given a new answer.
> But this description of change in subjunctives seems queer.
>
> (LPP: 59)

It seems queer because it describes a change that is *supposed to have occurred* in terms of a change that *could have occurred* if certain conditions had been met. Wittgenstein adds:

> The use of the subjunctive for change of meaning – 'if you had asked me five minutes ago I should have said ...' – shows that it isn't a change in the same sense as change of picture.
>
> (LPP: 60)

The fact that what I need here are two different descriptions of the use of the same word, which I could have given and which essentially contribute to the explanation, means that we have here to do with two entirely different kinds of change. As concerns the change of experience, it can – as, for example, a change of the picture we had in mind – be described with the help of categorial propositions, and it does not essentially imply the possibility of giving one or more explanations of meaning. Of course, unlike us, the meaning-blind person will not be tempted to account for, still less identify, the change of meaning with a change of experience. She will simply say something like: 'When I first used the word "Bank" I was talking about a financial institution, and when I used it the second time I was talking about a bench.'

The difficulty here is that when I say that I used the word to mean first one thing and then another, that mode of expression evokes the idea of two experiences occurring at different moments in my mind, although, generally speaking, we find nothing really corresponding to this. What is characteristic of assertions like 'When I used those words, I meant ...' is, as noted earlier, that they refer to a particular moment, without thereby pointing out a particular mental experience that occurred *at that moment* and which we could recall (PI: pp. 216–17). Wittgenstein does not at all question our right to say, for example, that at the moment we heard the words, we understood them in such and such a way: 'Is it (in the end) an illusion, if I believed that the other's words had this sense for me at *that* time? Of course not! Any more than it is an illusion to believe that one has dreamed something before waking up' (RPP I: 201). There is an analogy between the case of someone who says: 'When I used a word, I knew that I was doing it in such and such a way', and someone who recounts a dream and says: 'At that moment, I saw such and such a person come in and knew it was my father.' In both cases, we might be tempted to consider that what presents itself as an account of something that really happened is in fact the result of a memory loss upon awakening; so that the explanations I am likely to give with respect to what I meant resemble the account of a dream:

> What if someone were to say: The plot of a dream is a strange disturbance of memory; it gathers together a great number of memories from the preceding day, from days before that, even from childhood, and turns them into the memory of an event which took place while a person was sleeping.
>   Indeed, all of us are familiar with instances in which we blend several days' memories into *one*.
>
> (LW I: 656)

But Wittgenstein is not here suggesting that this is how we should treat accounts of dreams or of meaning something. What he says is that in order for me to legitimately affirm that, when I uttered, say, the name N, I meant such and such a person, it is not necessary that I be able to remember a particular experience which linked the word to that person and to her alone. I do not need to remember an experience of this kind in order to be able to say that I remember having used the word to mean such and such a person. As to the comparison with dreaming, whether it be justified or not, we should note that it appears regularly in Wittgenstein's considerations of this type of problem. In the *Investigations*, he says about the conception that our *meaning something* (which occurs in the mental sphere and privately) is what gives the sentence its sense: 'How could this seem ludicrous? It is, as it were, a dream of our language' (PI: 358).

Indeed, the comparison with dreaming also naturally comes to mind when considering cases in which we feel we are failing to express with clarity something that is clear in our minds:

> There really are cases in which the sense of what we mean is much clearer in our mind than can be expressed in words. (This happens to me very often.) It is then as if we remembered a dream very distinctly but could not recount it; as if we saw very clearly before us the picture of a dream, but could not describe it well enough for the other to also see it. In fact, for the person writing (me) the picture often remains behind the words, so that the words seem to me to describe it.
>
> (Ms 138: p. 2a; DMS translation)

To use the word 'Bank' to refer to a financial institution and not a bench is indeed to use it with a certain intention, an intention we can legitimately affirm we had at the moment we used the word. But the intention is precisely not an experience:

> But what makes it different from an experience? – Well it has no experiential content. For the contents (e.g. images) which often go hand in hand with it, are not the intention itself – And yet neither is it a disposition, like knowing. For the intention was present when I said 'Bank'; now it is no longer present; but I have not forgotten it.
>
> (RPP II: 243)

The intention was there at a given moment, as were also the events of the dream. Which is to say that in cases of this kind, reference to the past is not illegitimate; it is the attempt to see it as referring to a specific experience supposed to have occurred in the past that is:

'When you started speaking, I thought you meant ...'. With this utterance, one refers to the past – Do we do this by mistake? – Of course not. As little as when we recount: 'Just before waking up, I had a dream: ...'.
Naturally, we also say: 'You understood me right from the start. I could see it in your face.'

(Ms 131: pp. 3–4; DMS translation)

Here, Wittgenstein notes that if the speaker's meaning something can be assimilated to a dream that he is able to recount after the fact, so can the hearer's understanding: he should be able to recount that he had understood what was being said to him in such and such a way, perhaps erroneously at first, and then correctly.

What justifies a *rapprochement* with dreaming is that in both cases there is a kind of paradox. *Post factum*, one says 'I meant ...'; although, in a way, at the time we meant nothing or, in any case, we find nothing that really corresponds to what we would in principle expect to find. Similarly, one says *post factum*:

'Why in a dream do we call *this* "knowing"?' – We don't call anything 'knowing' in a dream; rather we say 'In my dream I knew ...'.

(LW I: 63)

The analogous question we might be tempted to ask in the case of meaning something is: 'Why do we call this a meaning something accompanying the utterance of words in discourse?', whereas in fact, all we say is: 'When I uttered the words, I meant ...'. Yet Wittgenstein does not want to question the legitimacy of the use of the concept of 'knowledge' regarding things that occur in dreams. He notes, without questioning it, that not only is the concept of knowledge also used that way, but that this is a very special use, almost categorially different from ordinary use: one can say 'In my dream I saw a shining gold ball and *knew* it was hollow', but it would be senseless to say this sort of thing in normal circumstances (cf. RPP I: 249).

I will not here consider the question of whether Malcolm was right or wrong to attack, from what he believed was a Wittgensteinian perspective, the 'orthodox' conception according to which dreaming is a mental activity of a certain type, indeed the very activity of mind in sleep. Malcolm thought that 'the idea that someone might reason, judge, imagine, or have impressions, while asleep, is a meaningless idea in the sense that we have no conception of what could establish that these things did or did not occur' (1959: 49–50); and Malcolm adds that

> ... sometimes a man may wake up with the impression that certain incidents occurred and may be in doubt as to whether those incidents belonged to a dream or to reality. To find out that it was a dream is to find out that those incidents did *not* occur. To learn, in this sense, that a certain event occurred in a dream is not to learn that the event took place while one slept, but just the reverse, namely, that the event did not take place at all – which shows how misleading is the form of words 'It occurred in a dream!
>
> (1959: 50–1)

I am not at all sure that Wittgenstein would have endorsed this verificationist approach, accepted the idea that the manner of self-expression criticized by Malcolm comprises anything deceitful, or contested that dreaming can be a real experience, if a very particular one, in which one can speak of things that are lived, perceived, judged or known.

3 The paradoxical temporality of meaning something

Wittgenstein sums up the difficulty we have with meaning something in the following remark:

> In saying 'When I heard this word, it meant ... to me' one refers to a *point of time* and to a *way of using the word*. (Of course, it is this combination that we fail to grasp.)
>   And the expression 'I was then going to say ... .' refers to a *point of time* and to an *action*.
>
> (PI: p. 175)

Perhaps even more than '*meinen*', the verb 'to mean' is an action verb and, in the sentence considered, it seems to have to refer to something that was done at a given moment. Wittgenstein notes that the remarkable thing here is the reference to a point in time, and that that is what the 'meaning blind' would lose. We are especially inclined to postulate the occurrence of a particular meaning-conferring act when using – either in a sense determined by contrast to another, or in two senses determined successively – a word that has several senses ('Mr Scott is not a Scot').

But when an identical sentence is used in different circumstances – so that the word 'Bank' clearly means one thing at one time, and another at another time – 'must something special go on in hearing the sentence if you are to understand it? Don't all *experiences* of understanding get covered up by the use, by the *practice* of the language-game?' (RPP I: 184). And, we might add, doesn't the person who utters the sentence also have all the experiences of meaning-profferal? And can we say that cases of this kind justify the supposition that a word is used in each case in the sense we give it at the moment we use it? Wittgenstein takes the example of the sentence '"I have no doubt that that often happens." – If you say this in a conversation, can you really believe that in speaking you distinguish between the meanings of the two words "that"?' (RPP I: 191). If we compared the coming of the meaning into one's mind to a dream, we could say, notes Wittgenstein, that our ordinary talk is dreamless; and the meaning-blind person would then be 'one who would always talk dreamlessly' (RPP I: 232).

The meaning-blind person, as described by Wittgenstein, is someone who, unlike us, is incapable of getting a particular characteristic feeling or impression from an isolated word. Considering, for example, the German word *sondern* at one time as a verb and at another as a conjunction, he will not say that these two different ways of considering it are accompanied by two specific experiences that are equally different. Yet, for reasons just indicated, once the words are considered in use, the difference between us may well be a negligible one.

4   The meaning blind

Here are some of the differences which, on Wittgenstein's view, might exist between human beings suffering from meaning blindness and ourselves. They would entertain with their language a relation different from the one we have with ours. They would, for example, be deprived of the feeling that a word has, over and above its meaning, a physiognomy or a character – something that is particularly visible in the case of certain proper names that end up absorbing, as it were, their meaning in themselves, in such a way as to become indissociable from what they represent. The meaning blind would be insensitive to anything that might make a word absolutely irreplaceable (in a poetical context, for instance). Someone who would not understand that we can be attached to a word to the point of thinking that no other word will do is someone who we would undoubtedly call 'prosaic'; and, asks Wittgenstein, 'is that what the "meaning-blind" would be?' (RPP I: 342). He says of the meaning blind – one of whose characteristics would be, for example, the inability to feel that the ending 'a' changes character when the name 'Maria' is used as the name of a woman or as that of a man – that 'we could think he would be insensitive to certain effects of music or poetry' (MS 131: pp. 36–7). A meaning-blind person would also be incapable of feeling the very strong impression that is sometimes prompted by a modification of the spelling of a word. Generally, 'If for you spelling is just a practical question, the feeling you are lacking in is not unlike the one that a "meaning-blind" man would lack' (RPP II: 572).

It is undoubtedly the case that the meaning of a word is something that may not only be known, but also lived with more or less intensity, and the meaning blind would be deprived of this second possibility. But this only means that they could not be initiated to certain of our language-games, not that they could not speak our language:

"If you didn't *experience* the meaning of the words, then how could you laugh at puns?" [<In English> Hairdresser and sculptor.][3] – We do laugh at such puns: and to that extent we could say (for instance) that we experience their meaning.

(LW I: 711)

For the meaning blind, language would be deprived of the essential relation to feeling that it seems to have in verbal jokes. Wittgenstein even suggests that we could not speak of meaning that is lived if we could not play with meaning in a way that prompts laughter. The relationship that the meaning blind would have with language would then not only seem more prosaic and instrumental, but also more detached and, perhaps, more intellectual than ours. The meaning-blind person could, like us, use an ambiguous word in its different senses and say that she has used it in one sense or the other; but she would lack what we might call the 'feeling', characteristic of ambiguity, that we have when two senses meet and fuse, as it were, in the same term, as is the case with some puns.

In *Lectures on Philosophical Psychology, 1946–1947*, Geach notes: 'One is very much tempted to say there is an act of meaning when there is a pun'; to which Wittgenstein answers: 'The temptation is this. A word is like a railway station where a lot of lines cross. It is as though the experience were a vibration showing which way we might travel' (LPP: 57). And in puns, it seems we have the specific experience of someone who would be simultaneously pulled in two divergent directions leading to two very different places; and it is also this kind of experience that the meaning blind would lack. On the same topic, Wittgenstein speaks also of the comical effect that a bizarre tool would have on us, which was constituted of two utterly disparate parts and had two completely different uses. Kraus says of one of the 'Austrian "kings of steel": "He was a man of iron and he stole"' (*Er war ein Mann von Eisen und stahl*). We are almost tempted to say that, in order to grasp the pun, we must hear the same word '*Stahl*' simultaneously with its first letter as a capital ('He was a man of iron and steel'), and in lower case ('He was a man of iron and he stole'), and with two disparate and discordant meanings: one noble, the other deprecating.

In spite of attempts made here by Bergson, Freud and others, I am not suggesting that this kind of observation is an explanation of why the sentence makes us laugh. About the tool which would be a bizarre combination of two disparate functions, for example a poker that would have the exact shape of a certain weapon, so that the handle of the poker would be the head of the weapon and the handle of the weapon the front end of the poker, Wittgenstein has this to say:

> This shape could make on many people the impression of a pun. But we might well recognize the double use without the sensation of a pun.
> That the words 'Time flies' have a double use does not necessarily have a comical effect on us. But we are inclined to say: the expression jumps from one meaning to the other. (Like the drawing of a cube from one meaning to the next.) As if both expressions had in common only the letters, whilst something else, the real body of the expression, was other.

(Ms 131: pp. 39–40; DMS translation)

We can say then that the meaning blind would not experience, as we do, the characteristic sensation procured by the fact that meaning, in cases of this kind, commutes, as it were, from one sense to another without ever stopping on one or the other. But that a word has a double use, and that we know this, does not explain why, when a word is used in both senses simultaneously, this can produce a comic effect.

5   Conclusion

Wittgenstein is often accused of having no interest in the mental, especially in particular mental experiences that might be linked to the use of words. But a cursory glance at *Remarks on the Philosophy of Psychology* shows that, in fact, it is replete with remarks on the subject. Wittgenstein obviously does not suggest that when we speak, nothing happens in the mind that merits consideration. What he says is very different. It can, I believe, be summarized in two principal points:

1. No doubt, meaning something is very different from saying something, and is surely not reducible to it, but the difference is not properly rendered by the overly simplified and even primitive picture of two parallel processes taking place in two distinct milieus. Indeed, from a philosophical point of view, that is the worst possible rendering of the difference. We must therefore seek to rid ourselves of this picture or model if we want to understand the radically different and much more complicated relationship between saying and meaning something.
2. From this, must we conclude that philosophy is only interested in the outer expression and not in what is called the inner, which would be verbally externalized by the outer expression? Wittgenstein writes: '"You say that he only says it, nothing goes on in him at that time." I answer: "The word 'only' is misleading, as also the fact of speaking of an inner concomitant process"' (Ms: 130: p. 3, DMS translation). So that what goes on and what matters cannot be reduced to the simple utterance of words. But it is wrong to think that the only way of imagining the other thing or the necessary complement is through the picture of an inner process accompanying the utterance of words. Once this model is adopted, it becomes virtually impossible to be attentive to what really goes on and to describe it correctly.

A little earlier, Wittgenstein had written: 'I am opposed to the pneumatic conception. That is, in so far as it is a conception of the gaseous character of the soul. The converse of the pneumatic conception is the behaviourist conception; and both are bad' (Ms: 130: p. 3, DMS translation). It may be difficult to believe that Wittgenstein could have considered the behaviourist conception to be just as bad as its rival conception, and yet, from all he says it is clear that he could not have done otherwise. This is not without some relation to the problem of meaning blindness.

Partisans of the pneumatic conception maintain that a word cannot only have a meaning; it must also have a soul or, more precisely, in order to have a meaning, it must first have a soul. Wittgenstein writes: 'Remember what is said: each word has not only a meaning but also a soul' (Ms 131: 30, DMS translation). It might be said that, for the meaning blind, words do have a meaning and are used, as they are by us, meaningfully; but they do not also have a soul. They have 'only' (as we are tempted to say as if something essential were missing here) a meaning. In his remarks on the problem of meaning blindness, it seems to me that Wittgenstein is looking to replace this idea by a much less philosophical, more realistic and if possible more correct evaluation of what it is that these words are lacking, and by the same token, what it is that is lacking in the person uttering them.

Notes

1. The reference is to the opera singer who had to sing 'Weiche, Wotan, weiche' ('Depart Wotan, depart') and to whom the other singer on the stage had just whispered 'Do you like your eggs soft (*weiche*) or hard?' [Editors' Note RPP I: 77]
2. Here, read 'time' as a verb, and 'flies' as a noun.
3. The English joke: 'What is the difference between a hairdresser and a sculptor? – A hairdresser curls up and dyes, and a sculptor makes faces and busts.'

5
Revisiting 'The Unconscious'

Wes Sharrock and Jeff Coulter

For some years, we have been engaged in reflecting upon and writing about a range of issues in the social and behavioural sciences from a Wittgensteinian perspective.[1] In what follows, we seek to revisit some of the controversies which have attended the theoretical invocation of the concept of 'the unconscious' in the human sciences, especially the cognitive sciences.

What is 'the unconscious'?

Henri Ellenberger entitled his well-known major study of Freud *The Discovery of the Unconscious*,[2] and Ernest Jones wrote: 'It is generally held that Freud's greatest contribution to science ... was his conception of an *unconscious mind*.'[3] We do not accept that by inventing a nominalized usage of the ordinary concept of someone's being 'unconscious', or of someone's having done something 'unconsciously' (an adjectival and an adverbial use respectively), Freud discovered anything at all. Inventing a nominal use where before there had been none ('unconscious', yes, but not '*the* unconscious') is not akin to any empirical discovery, but marks a change in our forms of representation. To what effect, with what sorts of justification, and with what consequences, are matters which will concern us here.

Of course, the intellectual history of this conception has been notoriously fraught with dissent. William James wrote: 'The "unconscious" is the sovereign means of believing whatever one likes in psychology and of turning what might become a science into a tumbling ground for whimsies' (1890: 163). His views were reflected (in diverse ways) throughout the entire span of the behaviouristic hegemony in psychology, even though James was not himself a behaviourist.

95

Freud's own use of his conceptual innovation varied, but there are two consistently distinctive ways in which he deployed it: the 'descriptive' way, in which what is 'unconscious' pertains to what is effectively 'latent', and the 'dynamic' way, in which 'the unconscious' is a component of an explanatory theory of various dimensions and characteristics of human conduct, both rational and pathological. In the former deployment, Freud addresses such phenomena as memories and dispositions which are not always 'present to consciousness' or 'latent', whereas in the theoretical, explanatory (and hence the more innovative) contexts of its use, Freud is attempting to explain dream phenomena, slips of the tongue, post-hypnotically 'suggested' activities for which their agents cannot adduce the reason which formed part of the 'suggestion', neurotic symptoms and other cases.[4] For Freud, 'the unconscious' becomes a sort of psychological zone, space, repository, place, site or location for a wide range of theoretically projected mechanisms, states, operations and processes. This marks out his chief theoretical claim to having founded a new science of mind, one which, while maintaining certain fundamental themes from the Cartesian tradition (nicely documented by Ilham Dilman[5]), is radically deterministic and eventually, as MacIntyre (1958: 16–24) stresses, *materialistic* in its 'ultimate' theoretical appeal to the neurophysiological 'substratum' to which, Freud maintained, his major theoretical constructs, including the operations, states and processes of/in the 'unconscious mind', will one day be reduced. Nonetheless, as MacIntyre also observes:

> Freud retains from the Cartesian picture the idea of the mind as something distinct and apart, a place or a realm which can be inhabited by such entities (*sic*) as ideas. Only he makes dominant not 'the conscious' mind but 'the unconscious'.
>
> (1958: 45)

Elsewhere, MacIntyre remarks that, in many significant respects, in Freud, 'The unconscious is the ghost of the Cartesian consciousness' (ibid.: 73).

The 'cognitive' unconscious

With the rise of the 'cognitive sciences' (cognitive psychology, psycholinguistics and related fields), the concept of 'the unconscious' became a central presupposition, although in these contemporary intellectual contexts the rationales for its use differ somewhat from its psychoanalytic predecessors. We think it useful to be reminded by Elder that:

> Freud adopts the concept of the unconscious not because what appears to consciousness is *false* but because consciousness is 'incomplete', 'discontinuous', or, taken by itself, 'unintelligible', because the data of consciousness are *insufficient* to account for the known phenomena of psychical life.
>
> (1994: 35)

For example, since a good deal of our commonplace inferential reasoning is enthymematic, it has been argued that we must have recourse to 'unconscious' supplementations to the conscious steps we take in order to explain the role of the 'unstated premise(s)'. Another reason for invoking 'unconscious mental processes' has been the effort to explain rule-governed grammatical speech where the 'rules' are not a feature of a speaker's awareness as a condition for being able to speak grammatically. This is, of course, Chomsky's position. As nicely summarized by Dennett:

> ... what you consciously represent to yourself is at best indirect evidence of what might be explicitly represented in you unconsciously. So far as cognitive science is concerned, the important phenomena are the explicit unconscious mental representations. Thus when Chomsky[6] talks about the explicit representation of one's grammar in one's head, he certainly doesn't mean the conscious representation of that grammar. It is presumed to be unconscious and utterly inaccessible to the subject. But he also means that it is not merely tacit in the operation or competence of the system .... He means to take the hard line: the grammar is itself unconsciously but explicitly represented in the head.
>
> (1987b: 218)

Before we explore this particular issue more extensively, we think it worthwhile to consider some quite basic lines of argument designed to encourage us to think along these lines, that is, designed to give us the impression that *some* appeal to 'the unconscious' and to what happens there is not only right but positively unavoidable if we seek to explain a variety of behavioural phenomena. Dennett gives us the example of 'getting a joke' where the information required to grasp its humorous point is not explicit in its formulation. Consider this one (from Pylyshyn via Dennett (1987c: 76)): 'A man went to visit his friend ... and found him with both ears bandaged. "What happened?" asked the man, and his friend replied, "I was ironing my shirt when the telephone rang." – "That explains one ear, but what about the other?" – "Well, I had to call a doctor!" ' Dennett proceeds to argue that for anyone who 'got' the joke, various unmentioned details need to be known but such knowledge, if made explicit during the hearing of the joke, would hinder its appreciation. However, since such knowledge must be 'drawn upon' in order to 'get' the joke, the information involved must be 'in the head' but unconsciously so, and whatever use is made of it must also be unconscious. For Dennett, 'there must be an information-sensitive process in each individual that takes them from the seen [or heard] words to the chuckle' (1987c: 77). Since as everyone knows, 'explaining' a joke is both a tedious and usually humourless endeavour, and doing so contemporaneously with hearing a joke is most likely to deprive the joke of its humour altogether, Dennett believes that such informational items as, for example, people usually answer a telephone when it rings, they do so by putting the receiver to the ear, etcetera, etcetera, being prerequisite for 'getting the joke', *must* (note his emphasis) be unconsciously stored and unconsciously accessed.

A major difficulty with this account is that 'explaining a joke' is far from being any sort of prerequisite for 'getting a joke' and, as noted, is itself a pretty humourless (or humour-detracting) procedure. It also reifies what is presupposed in understanding something into something accompanying the hearing of what is understood. However, the issue we wish to address here is the *form* of the appeal to 'the unconscious'. Echoing MacIntyre's comment above, it is clear that whatever is (going on) *in* 'the unconscious' is modelled on the notion that some tasks ordinarily can require consciously and explicitly *representing* things to ourselves.

Take the calculation 5 times 19 (= 95), and contrast it with 5 times 5 (= 25). For most of us who learned the multiplication table by rote in our early years, the latter calculation is presumably a matter of the by-rote production of the solution unmediated by any sequence of explicit representations and their manipulation, whilst the former probably requires one of two sorts of explicit sequences. One sequence is imagining manipulating the numerals accordingly: 5 times 9 is 45 (by-rote for those who mastered the elementary multiplication table), 5 times 1 is 5 (again by-rote), then explicitly imagine shifting the 4 (from the 45) to be added to the 5, yielding 9. (As kids, we learned to call this procedure that of 'carrying'). Now we have the left-over 5 to the right of the newly arrived-at 9 to its left, yielding 95. Another (more economical) sequence of steps would be to realize that 5 times 20 is 100, that 19 = (20–1), thus 5 times 19 is 5 times 20 (which is 100) minus 5 times 1 (which is 5), yielding 95.

(For more elaborate calculations (e.g., those involving longer strings of numerals) there are some esoteric algorithms available which some of us may not be aware of as a matter of our ordinary computational practice.) Such manipulations of imagined numerals, their relative locations and so on, comprise what is often referred to as 'mental arithmetic' or 'calculating in the head'. However, when one studies many contemporary appeals to 'the unconscious', one finds descriptions of symbol manipulations wholly analogous to those we can give for ones of which we are routinely aware (as in the case just discussed). Hence MacIntyre's remark: 'The unconscious is the ghost of the Cartesian consciousness' (1958: 73). Moreover, many such appeals to the manipulation of symbols or of 'explicit representations' are posited as *necessary* for the performance of a range of tasks and practices in our lives (recall Dennett's use of 'must' in his discussion of the joke and its comprehension), such that issues of 'mere' *empirical* evidence can seem otiose. Unlike many psychoanalytical claims about, and appeals to, 'the unconscious', which generate disputes as to their evidentiary support and the (determinate) possibility of evaluating such evidence and arriving at a truth-claim (on which see Frank Cioffi's illuminating discussion of the Popper-Grunbaum dispute[7]), most cognitivist claims and appeals are essentially *aprioristic* in character. Dennett summarizes thus:

> Ryle said, aprioristically, that we *couldn't* be mental-representation-manipulators; Fodor and others have said, aprioristically, that we *must* be.
> (1987c: 225)

Now, this is not quite right regarding Ryle, who certainly would not have denied (indeed, even acknowledged) the sort of scenario we depicted above regarding calculating in other-than-by-rote ways and in other-than-on-paper ways, but it is certainly true that Ryle rejected what he termed the 'intellectualist legend' according to which *all* of our rational, intelligent conduct requires the postulation of internal, 'mentally represented' theories.

Stuart Shanker offers the following comments about the *non-psychoanalytic* conception of 'the unconscious' and its quite distinctive origins in his discussion of the 'cognitive' unconscious, the domain of 'unconscious inference':

> This notion of 'unconscious inferences' owed much to Helmholtz's inferential theory of perception. According to the standard empiricist theory of perception which shaped Helmholtz's thinking, there is a 'gap' between the retinal patterns of stimulation that we experience

and the objects that we see. This 'gap', Helmholtz argued, must be filled by 'cerebral inferences': i.e., the brain must frame *hypotheses* on the basis of the data it has stored from past experiences and the information it is currently processing .... But then, why not extend the argument to the problem of creativity? Insight, no less than perception, could be treated as the end-result of 'unconscious inferences'. One could thus explain the 'Aha phenomenon' as the result of the fact that, although one is not consciously thinking about a problem, the brain continues to work away on it. Should it hit upon a solution, this will be instantly recognized by the faculty of consciousness.

(1998: 126)

The speculations of the mathematician Henri Poincaré as to the 'derivation' of what appeared to him to have been sudden spontaneous insights into deep mathematical problems[8] fuelled the idea that, in Hadamard's terms, 'there can be no doubt of the necessary intervention of some mental process unknown to the inventor, in other terms, of an unconscious one.'[9] The idea that the 'unconscious mind' (increasingly being identified with the *brain*) must be postulated to engage in the formation of hypotheses on the basis of inferential processes using stored data is given a further boost in the latter half of the twentieth century by Chomsky's linguistic theorizing and Fodor's (Chomskian) philosophical psychology. Citing the work of Gregory (a neo-Helmholtzian psychologist of perception)[10] approvingly, Fodor observes:

> ... perceptual integrations are most plausibly viewed as species of inferences-to-the-best-explanation, the computational problem in perceptual integration being that of choosing the best hypothesis about the distal source of proximal stimulations.

(1975: 50)

Focusing upon linguistic phenomena, Fodor elaborates as follows:

> If, for example, *e* [an expression] is a token of a sentence type, and if understanding/perceptually analyzing *e* requires determining which sentence type it is a token of ..., then on the current [cognitivist] view of understanding/perceptually analyzing, a series of representations of *e* will have to be computed. And this series will have to include, and distinguish between, representations which specify the acoustic, phonological, morphological, and syntactic properties of the token.

(1975: 51)

Note the extreme intellectualizations here being posited as *requirements* of mundane activities and accomplishments, along with their correlative discursive idealizations. More on these topics later. The ensuing critical discussion will be addressed, *seriatim*, to the various issues raised in this section.

From the 'unconscious mind' to neural metaphysics

Since virtually no one explicitly proclaims himself to be a 'classical Cartesian dualist', insisting on the radical distinction between mind and body (with brains being components of bodies); and since, in our puta- tively post-Cartesian intellectual scene, materialism now rules, appeals to 'the unconscious' have become place-holders for the ultimate site or locus for its postulated operations – the brain. However, this move has engendered some quite striking conceptual confusions. The first is the proclivity to adopt a body/brain dualism, such that the body retains the status that it had in behaviourism, and the brain becomes the residency of 'mental' operations. This involves a personification of the brain and its operations. No one would dream of claiming, even as a 'theoretical' move, that a brain could ride a bicycle, but the neo-Cartesians suppose that *the body* does the pedalling and the turning of the handlebars as it is instructed by the intellectual operations of the brain, so then it seems that it is the brain that *is* riding the bicycle, but this is only because what would normally be ascribed to persons is transferred to the brain. It is transparently absurd: people ride bicycles. Nonetheless, it appears that the notion that it is *brains* which can formulate, test and confirm/disconfirm hypotheses, that it is *brains* which can analyse, interpret, decide, follow rules and so forth, has been far less readily denounced as an absurd pro- jection of person-level predicates to parts of persons' bodies. Dreyfus has been a notable exception here; he will have none of it:

> The brain is clearly an energy-transforming organ. It detects incoming signals; for example, it detects changes in light intensity correlated with changes in texture gradient. Unfortunately for psychologists, however, this physical description, excluding as it does all psychological terms, is in no way a *psychological* explanation. On this level one would not be justified in speaking of human agents, the mind, intentions, percep- tions, memories, or even of colours or sounds, as psychologists want to do. Energy is being received and transformed and that is the whole story.
>
> (1992/1999: 177)

Some time ago, one of us compiled several objections to the sort of theorizing, characteristic of Helmholtz, Gregory, Chomsky and Fodor, depicted above.[11] In particular, the point was made that such theorizing confuses physical with 'symbolic' or 'conceptualized' phenomena in so far as all start out depicting *everything* seen and heard in purely physical terms – thus, sounds, words, utterances and expressions (for example, Fodor's '*e*'s) are initially construed solely as acoustic wave forms, and witnessed scenes, objects and events in the environment are initially construed as quanta of light energy (photons), with the former interacting with receptors in the cochleae and the latter interacting with the photoreceptors in the retinae. These interactions involve the transduction of energies and the generation of ions into the cortex via networks of nerve cells. Perception and comprehension are then argued to be the end-products of internal, unconscious processings, computings, and so on, operating on – well, on what? Electrochemical impulses? Ionic discharges between neurons? The entire line of argument collapses into incoherence. However, Good replied as follows:

> He [Coulter] believes that acoustics are the business of the cochlea and that the hearer does not need to compute the representations that Fodor proposes because the hearer has no reason to be interested in them … . This … is only sensible if we accept Coulter's proposal that hearers have nothing to do with ears, since it is plain that it is not meanings that arrive at ears but acoustic wave-forms. However, Coulter must allow for some kind of commerce between the ears and the hearer if the hearer is to hear and his argument necessarily cannot rule out the possibility that that commerce might be predicated on a series of operations that can be most usefully characterized in terms of the framework of contemporary phonology and the like.
>
> (1985: 99)

It is palpably false to conclude from the argument against Fodor that it commits one to the absurd idea that 'hearers have nothing to do with ears'. It had been duly noted that the transduction of acoustic energy by the receptors of the cochleae facilitate the hearer's ability to hear anything whatsoever. Put Good's argument the other way around: presumably it implies that no one ever really hears what anyone else says, one only hears the sounds people make. Good arrives at his caricature because of his *own* inclination to preserve a behaviourist conception of what is empirically detectable, separating the sound waves that are produced in and by saying something from what one says in and by producing those sound waves. Sensory neurophysiology has a perfectly plain and clear, if complex, picture of the processes facilitating our auditory capacities, *the mechanics of reacting to sound waves*, and it is to this science, *and only to this science*, that we must look for an explanation of 'how hearers are able to hear'. The question of 'what is heard' is a person-level, not a neurophysiological, question, and it will involve conceptualizations of what G. H. Mead nicely termed 'the symbolic environment'. Good thinks that we need more, along Fodor's lines, because he thinks that 'meanings' do not reach the ears when acoustic wave-forms do.

This is doubly confused. First, it is usually when someone gives an explanation of what something means/meant that we can be said to have 'heard what it meant'. It is by no means the case that *every* instance of hearing something *intelligible* is a matter of, or involves, 'hearing what it meant', although to have 'heard what was said', if what was said made sense, can in an anodyne manner be said to have been a case of having 'heard what was meant'. But there aren't *two* things going on here! In a sense, then, although not in the one which Good intended, it may be true that only rarely do 'meanings' reach our ears. But Good thinks that this entails that we as hearers must *supplement* the work done (indeed, unconsciously) by our central nervous system in order to hear something intelligible, something that 'makes sense'. Such supplementation will involve complex computations over explicit representations. (He does not say how we *as hearers*, as persons, can do this in the face of the fact that we are not aware of so doing, so presumably this too must be cast into the pit of the unconscious ....) The necessity for such concoctions is an artefact of the initial attachment to the empiricist myth of the given in its behaviourist form, leaving the impression that a description of the physical properties of the input is an *exhaustive* description of that input, rather than a bare, aspectual one. Thus, the interior supplementary workings are deemed necessary in order to reconnect the theoretically stripped input with other aspects of it, those of which cognitive theorists are well aware by virtue of their enculturation – such as the linguistic and intelligible features – and upon which they depend in order to envisage credible forms for those putatively supplementary processes. This reveals the fact that cognitive theory has no clear understanding of the relationship between the person and the brain and hence cannot provide a role for us *as hearers*, as persons. The postulated processes must be dispatched to the unconscious, since it is plain that *we hearers* do not carry out such processes, but this is not because there is *evidence* that such processes are taking place – who knows what the brain processes that are going on are doing? – but rather there is only the theoretically induced necessity to bridge the gap between what are, in reality, two different descriptions of one and the same input, namely, to borrow Ryle's terms, a thin one and a thick one. Good ends up in the grip of the parallel-track misconception of comprehension according to which to understand an utterance is (1) to hear it as a string of sounds (or to read it as a sequence of graphemic marks), and (2) to assign a structural linguistic interpretation to a string that already has acquired a determinate acoustic composition, as though identifying sounds and the words they constitute could proceed independently and serially.

Fodor gives this game away in his unfortunate pairing of 'understanding' with 'perceptually analysing' in the earlier quotation from his discussion of linguistic comprehension. Understanding, as Wittgenstein and Ryle taught us, is *not* a process word, being akin to an achievement or a capacity, whereas 'analysing' (like 'interpreting') is a time-bound process. Good follows Fodor into the same conceptual mistake. One facet of this mistake is the mereological fallacy, that of ascribing a predicate to a part which can logically only be ascribed to a whole (in this case, the 'whole' is the living creature). This is not a matter of the use of tropes such as synecdoche or metonymy: it encompasses a related raft of confusions, as Bennett and Hacker illustrate in considerable detail in their recent major study of the philosophical foundations of cognitive neuroscientific theory.[12] One of Wittgenstein's more obscure passages in his *Philosophical Investigations* is actually a move to alert us to the temptation of making a mereological error:

> It comes to this: only of a living human being and what resembles (behaves like) a living human being can one say: it has sensations; it sees; is blind; hears; is deaf; is conscious or unconscious.
>
> (PI: 281)

The ascription of 'unconscious mental processes' (modelled after 'conscious' ones, as we have noted[13]) to the human *brain* is an example of the mereological fallacy in cognitive science. As Bennett and Hacker observe:

> The tissues of the brain, like the brain itself, are neither conscious nor unconscious, neither awake nor asleep. The 'work' done by the brain is not done consciously and deliberately, but nor is it done unconsciously and without deliberation. For the brain cannot do anything consciously *or* unconsciously, since it is not a conscious creature with the capacity to be conscious or to be conscious *of anything* .... The fact that we are not conscious of the activities of our brains does not imply that *we* are engaged in them unconsciously; but nor does it imply that

the brain is engaged in these activities unconsciously. For only a creature that can do something *consciously* can also be said to do something *unconsciously*.

(2003: 270)

Just as a bus, which is certainly incapable of vision, cannot be said therefore to be *blind*, since only a being which *could* have (had) the capacity of vision can be so described, so also is it the case that brains, which satisfy no criteria for *their* being able to see or to fail to see something, can themselves be neither conscious *nor* unconscious, be engaged in neither conscious *nor* unconscious activities or operations. Naturally, this is not to deny that our brains enter into states and undergo processes (e.g., catalyzing enzymes, generating ionic discharges, etc.) of which we as persons are unaware in the sensory meaning of that term. However, none of the actual electrochemical events that take place in our brains are at issue in the cognitivist accounts. After all, these are *events*, not actions.

The cognitivist commitment to a *form* of explanation

Ryle mocked the Chomskian picture of child language learning (as expressed in Zeno Vendler's work) because human life, as children live it, in relations with others, is entirely absent from that picture,[14] and in dealing with cognitivism one persistently encounters this same problem. The last thing that cognitivists have on their minds is the exploration of the actual character of individuals' doings in the midst of their daily affairs. We think that the reason for this is to be found in a preoccupation with a particular *form* of explanation. This preoccupation functions in theoretical mode as a form of self-handicapping, meaning that those subservient to it must pretend that they do not understand things which they patently do understand. It is undoubtedly intended to serve the requirements of rigour and this in turn signifies that pre-theoretical understandings can have no more than probative status prior to confirmation (or disconfirmation) by the best explanation of the preferred kind. Harold Garfinkel, in turn, mocked the frame of mind which follows from this – the idea that there is a need to remove the walls the better to see what keeps the roof up (1967: 22). This explains the absence of the 'hurly burly' of human life from any *explicit* part of the story which the cognitivists contrive. Stephen Stich[15] attempts to formulate a principled expression of this attitude, striving to explain how the things that human beings do with their time gets in the way of the kind of understanding that a genuine cognitive science must seek. However, we claim that this attitude results only in a *pretence* that our ordinary understandings are in a state of theoretical quarantine, for they are actually in pervasive (if unacknowledged) use throughout the enterprise, and unavoidably so in the portrayal of the 'phenomena' that are grist for the explanatory mill.

The main interest in their phenomena for the cognitivists is that they should provide the materials for a demonstration that there is a need for their preferred form of explanation. That is, 'we', the naïve pre-theoretical participants in human affairs must realize that we do not *really* understand what we might imagine to be the most plain and intelligible things that endlessly confront us in our daily lives. The measure of our lack of understanding is not, however, to be found in any sort of *puzzlement* which the empirical occurrence of these 'phenomena' recurrently causes us, but in the fact that *whatever* kinds of understandings we might have, these do not – as almost assuredly they will not – conform to the *a priori* conception being fostered as to what it is to understand something that the theorist is applying. In other words, it is the preconceived form of explanation that is used both to manufacture the demand for explanation and to fill the need so created. Because of the overwhelming fixation on the *a priori* form which a satisfactory explanation must take, we see why the attention is entirely focused upon the explanatory part of the enterprise and why the *explananda* are given only perfunctory attention. In this vein, John F. Kihlstrom proposes that:

> ... a good deal of mental activity is unconscious in the strict sense of being inaccessible to phenomenal awareness under any circumstances. In conversational speech, for example, the listener is aware of the meaning of the words uttered by the speaker but not of the phonological or linguistic principles by which the meaning of the speaker's utterance is decoded. Similarly, during perception the viewer may be aware of two objects in the external environment but not of the mental calculations performed to determine that one is closer or larger than the other.
>
> (1987: 1447)

Further,

> In the case of skill learning, the process is initially accessible to consciousness – as indicated, for example, by the novice sailor's overt or covert rehearsal of the steps involved in tying a knot – and later becomes unconscious by virtue of practice – as indicated by the inability of many musicians, athletes and typists to describe their skill to others, and by the fact that conscious attention to them actually interferes

with their performance. Employing a metaphor from computer science, this process is described as knowledge compilation, suggesting that the format in which knowledge is represented has been changed.

(Kihlstrom, 1987: 1447)

First, notice how such argumentation seeks to recruit to its own partisan position facts that are utterly commonplace to all and available entirely independently of the cognitivist framework. Endless repetition of Chomsky's claims about innate phonological and linguistic principles adds nothing *empirical* to the familiar fact that children take to language naturally. Equally, that practice produces fluency in a performance is, in its variegated forms, familiar to all parents, music teachers, sports coaches and innumerable others. In other words, *everything* hinges upon a *rhetorical* construal of platitudes. For example, the Chomskian notion that the information that English is a 'subject–predicate' language is 'buried deep within the brain' just fails to notice the fact that explaining the nature of 'subject' and 'predicate' does not involve laying out a set of *discoveries* made by grammarians, but involves explaining what it means to identify a given expression in a sentence as 'the subject' and another one as 'the predicate', and to understand what it is about these expressions that licenses such attributions. In other words, what is involved is coordinating what speakers of the language perfectly well understand and can express in vernacular terms about the sentences they construct with the jargon of grammarians, and 'subject' and 'predicate' there feature more as stipulations as to how sentence parts are to be named than they do as the product of any kind of empirical discovery. The subject–predicate relation identifies a *rule* of sentence formation in English (and some other natural languages) and *not* a causal generality about the behaviour of English speakers. The jargon of grammarians is not buried in the depths of anyone's brain, but is simply confined within the boundaries of the practice of formal grammar instruction. Hence, while it may be true to say that 'most speakers of English will not say "English" in response to a request to name a subject–predicate language, nor will they hit the buzzer in a game show in response to name a subject–predicate language',[16] this is because they would not understand the question, not because they cannot gain access to the 'depths' of their brains. It is not as though someone who does not understand that English is a subject–predicate language has attempted some sort of introspective examination of their 'consciousness' and has come back empty-handed. After all, any inspection pertinent to understanding what makes English a subject–predicate language would be some – relatively few – samples of English sentences (which is all that

Chomsky has, in any case). The Chomskian pattern of inference has extended into cognitive neuroscience to buttress claims about the role of the brain in the production and comprehension of sentences. Kosslyn and Koenig remark:

> The [neural] subsystems used to understand single words are also used to understand sentences, but this ability also requires the use of subsystems that compute relations among words. The relations among words are restricted in part by syntactic factors. That is, each word is assigned to a form class (such as noun, verb, adjective, adverb, and article), and the rules of grammar specify the ways in which form classes can be combined to produce sentences.
>
> (1995: 238)

Here we have a fanciful projection of an acquired (and even somewhat *specialized*) *human* capacity to parse sentences to the workings of the human brain, even though, presumably, people (with brains) could speak and understand each other *before* there was such an enterprise as grammatical parsing, and people with *no* grammatical knowledge whatsoever are not precluded from speaking and understanding one another. Even Chomsky has not embraced the peculiar notion that English speakers are born with an 'innate knowledge' of the syntactic parts of speech of their natural language!

What Chomsky and those who follow him really seek to argue is that what we as persons are unaware of are the 'mental processes' of manipulating the sentence-forming procedures of the language. This idea has its roots in the prior conception that when we produce sentences we are really 'translating' a thought into a linguistic structure, one which clothes the thought in words. However, as Wil Coleman has pointed out (in personal communication), the suggestion of psychological processes at work in rule manipulation of the sort Chomsky envisages is an illusion. It is an artefact of the manner in which Chomsky presents his (early) formalization of linguistic rules, a formalization that involves what he calls 'rewrite rules' and which, laid out in a linear sequence, can create the (false) impression that there is a dynamic sequence through which 'S' (the 'thought') is successively transformed into a grammatical structure and then into a phonologically and semantically realized expression. Chomsky's formalizations could better be construed as akin to equations from the point of view of expositing their actual character, for that is all they are. Their programme is to specify the only permissible forms in which English words can be combined into sentences. The idea of unconscious manipulations bridging the gap between 'thought' and 'utterance' only reproduces Chomsky's neo-Cartesian mentalism and is a merely gratuitous postulation in relation to his formal linguistic *descriptions*.

Knowledge, rules and skills

In so far as the speaking of a language is a rule-governed activity, then it can hardly be the case that I understand what someone says to me independently of the relevant rules – in so far as the sense of what he or she says is determined (fixed, not caused) by those rules, then clearly my understanding of what is said to me requires my recognition of how the words which facilitate saying such things fit together, are articulated in terms of those same rules. In watching a game of cricket, I see that the batsman is out or not. The umpire has raised his finger. This observation presupposes that I am aware of (sensitive to) the rule of cricket that the umpire is the final arbiter of whether a batsman is out or not. 'Aware' here does not imply some occurrently conscious state, some consultation of a 'mental representation' of the cricket rule book, some secondary operation of checking what the umpire's raised finger signifies in cricket according to the rules of cricket, *in addition to* my observing the umpire raise his finger. Being 'aware' rather than being affiliated to 'understand' is all too often affiliated to the usage of 'conscious' in the sense of 'paying attention'. I am perfectly well aware of the cricket rule since, after all, my applying it in making my observation about the batsman involves my understanding of it, but I am not 'conscious of' the rule, in the sense that I am not paying any attention to it.

Part of cognitivism's need for 'the unconscious' results from the fact that it is inclined to multiply the number of activities involved in doing many things, making 'the unconscious' nothing other than a warehouse for all of those theoretically postulated, but empirically undemonstrated, processes generated in the course of their misrepresentations of the use of language and of the character of everyday activities. The example of the umpire's finger might seem inapposite in so far as the 'cognitive unconscious' is about *procedural* matters, but the example is meant to make a point about the way in which 'awareness' of the rule is integral to the understanding of what the situation is, and the same point applies to my grasping the meaning of the words that I and those I listen to use in saying what we say. I may not be aware of the (linguistic) fact that the words which make up this sentence are to be identified as 'noun', 'verb', and the like, in the vocabulary of grammarians, nor need I be aware that this sentence would differ from that one in a way that would be described by a grammarian as anaphoric, but this does not mean that I can be other than sensitive to the ways in which these words act as the 'parts of speech' that they are, for I am sensitive to the grammar of English. I understand what is said such that, for example, I can understand perfectly well that 'he' in a sentence refers to the 'John' mentioned earlier, whereas in some other sentence it would not. I can point to the features of the sentence (the absence of any other possible referent, etc.) which assure me that this is so, but I could not, of course, state these facts in the technical terms – or jargon – in which the linguist could state them. The grammarian's task is to capture what I know (inserting 'tacitly', 'unconsciously', etc., only muddies the waters here), to identify just those things that I am sensitive to in forming my own remarks and understanding those of others.

It is perfectly reasonable to say that tying a knot 'becomes unconscious by virtue of practice', but not in the context of such a presumptively biased portrayal as: 'in the case of skill learning, the process is initially accessible to consciousness ... and later becomes unconscious'. The difference is not between something which is 'accessible to consciousness', something that one can be aware of, and something that is unconscious and therefore *no longer* accessible to consciousness. The difference, in the case of tying a knot, is that when learning to do this one must *pay a great deal of attention* to how the activity is done, whereas, after one has learned how to do it, one can do the activity without paying any particular attention to it. However, this distinction, between practising and mastering, in the way that I tie my shoelaces does not involve my handing over the tying of the shoelaces to some other agency (the unconscious). Tying my shoelaces is not done unconsciously, though it is done without my being conscious of what I am doing in doing it.

There are, then, many contexts in which the conscious/unconscious dichotomy does not properly apply. In the normal case, *I* – not my unconscious – tie my shoelaces, and I *just* tie my shoelaces, doing so *neither* consciously *nor* unconsciously. Initially I pay a great deal of attention to how shoelaces are tied, but eventually learn how to tie them without needing to pay attention to how they are tied. But I can if I wish pay attention to how I tie my shoelaces, so how I tie my shoelaces is 'accessible to consciousness', although not through 'accessing the unconscious' but just by paying attention where I do not ordinarily do so.

John Hyman (1999: 436) has protested that many philosophers tend to think of knowledge as the capacity to give answers to questions (although, in their defence, it might be that they simply consider that a good example of someone's knowing something might be their capacity correctly to answer a question). According to Kihlstrom, a person's skills

... later become unconscious by virtue of practice – as indicated by the inability of many musicians, athletes, and typists to describe their skills to others, and by the fact that conscious attention to them actually interferes with their performance.

(1987: 1452)

It certainly seems as if being unable to answer questions about how one does something is the hallmark of 'the cognitive unconscious'. However, it is actually an open question as to whether musicians, athletes and typists are unable to 'describe their skills', since so much depends upon the kind of descriptive task that they are being given.

The descriptive skills of the grammarian and the phonologist are highly specialized, and there is no question but that speakers of a language, just in virtue of their capacity to speak, would be unable to describe their linguistic skills in a way which would satisfy the requirements of such experts. Second, we must not suppose that being able to 'describe' a certain skill is a requirement for being aware – in the sense employed above in the cricketing example – of what is involved in those skills. One perhaps cannot give an impromptu 'description' of a skill in the form that the cognitivist demands, but one can certainly *show* someone else in what one's skill(s) consist. One can readily show someone else how one fastens one's shoelaces. One can interlace commentary with such a showing: for example, 'you need to ensure that the ends are equal like this', 'this goes under there', 'tug firmly on both ends',and so on. To accept Kihlstrom's point would be to make a mystery of the existence of music, athletic coaches, typing teachers and the rest. It is not, then, as if the skilled performer's skills operate beyond the reach of the performer, in some inaccessible domain of 'the unconscious', or as if a performer's inability to 'describe' those skills reflects a return, empty-handed, from some frustrated introspective foray. The skills of 'description' may also, in important part, involve those of 'reflection' and, again, *these* skills may not be available to some otherwise skilled performers.

There can arise a difficulty in paying attention to the skills involved in something that one is doing and simultaneously producing a performance involving those skills, where 'pay attention' means something like 'reflect upon and self-consciously examine, making attempts at observation'. That efforts to do this will, in some cases, at least disrupt the performance has more to do with the fact that the point of acquiring considerable proficiency in the exercise of a capacity is to ensure that one can devote all one's attention to the task which the employment of that skill enables one to execute. The effort to devote attention elsewhere – whether to a concurrent investigation of *how* one is doing whatever one is doing or to some other activity – will be disruptive of the task in hand, since it will dilute the attention necessary for that task. When typing, one's attention is wholly engaged with what one is writing, is focused upon the screen, not upon the backs of one's hands. This says more about the way in which *attention is integrated with particular skills* than it does about any general division between 'the conscious' and 'the unconscious'. It is, contrastively, less difficult to pay attention to how one is placing one's hands and feet at the controls of a car whilst driving without detracting from the amount of care required for safe driving.

To avoid further Good-like misconstruals, we wish to note that these remarks are made entirely without prejudice to whatever neuroscience may find out about the part that brains play in people's performances, for fault has been found here with the ways in which such performances have been characterized to begin with. In conclusion, then, we would observe, in a spirit similar to that of William James as quoted earlier, that 'The Unconscious' has become a repository for otiose 'secondary' shadow activities or operations. We recommend a 'return to the surface' of things, for it is there, as Wittgenstein has taught us, in plain view, that we can, in principle, find all that we need for the elucidation of those facets of human conduct which cognitivism consigns to the 'invisible inner'.

Notes

1. Several of our writings have appeared in the journal *Theory and Psychology* over the past decade.
2. Henri Ellenberger, *The Discovery of the Unconscious* (London: Allen Lane, 1970).
3. As cited by Alasdair C. MacIntyre in MacIntyre (1958), 6; emphasis in original.
4. For a thorough discussion of these points, see Elder (1994), 34–7 *et seq.*
5. See Ilham Dilman ' "Unconscious Mind": A Contradiction in Terms?', in his *Freud and the Mind* (Oxford: Basil Blackwell, 1984), ch. 4.
6. In his, *Rules and Representations* (New York: Columbia University Press: 1980).
7. Frank Cioffi 'Psychoanalysis, Pseudoscience, and Testability', in his *Freud and the Question of Pseudoscience* (Chicago, IL: Open Court/Carus, 1998), ch. 9.
8. See especially his 'Mathematical Creation', in *The Foundations of Science* (New York: The Science Press, 1929).
9. Jacques Hadamard, *The Psychology of Invention in the Mathematical Field* (New York: Dover Publications, 1945), 20. As cited in Shanker (1998), 124.
10. Richard L. Gregory, *Eye and Brain: The Psychology of Seeing* (New York: McGraw-Hill). Cf. his 'The Confounded Eye', in R. L. Gregory and E. H. Gombrich (eds), *Illusion in Nature and Art* (London: Duckworth, 1973).
11. Cf. Coulter (1985).

12. Cf. especially 'The Mereological Fallacy in Neuroscience', in their *Philosophical Foundations of Neuroscience* (Oxford: Blackwell, 2003), 68–107.
13. 'Processes' such as: analysing, disambiguating, contextualizing, parsing, computing and representing, etc.
14. Gilbert Ryle, 'Mowgli in Babel', in Konstantin Kolenda (ed.), *On Thinking* (New Jersey: Rowman & Littlefield, 1979).
15. From *Folk Psychology to Cognitive Science: The Case Against Belief* (Cambridge, MA: Bradford Books, 1983).
16. Ian Ravenscroft, *Philosophy of Mind: A Beginner's Guide* (Oxford: Oxford University Press, 2005), 162.

6
Wittgenstein and the Foundations of Cognitive Psychology

Rom Harré

The recent reassessment of the 'shape' of Wittgenstein's philosophy has opened up a new way in which his philosophical insights can be relevant to current developments in Cognitive Psychology. I shall follow Moyal-Sharrock (2004b, 2004a) in calling the last phase of his writings, the 'third Wittgenstein'.

The advent of cognitive psychology has brought two important concepts under pressure. How is the notion of 'rule' to be understood in contexts in which the word is used to refer to influential cognitive 'somethings' which may never be formulated? With this query goes another. 'What is the appropriate range of convenience for the concept of "proposition"? Can it range beyond the limits of statements which can only be true or false?' These queries intersect in a third and puzzling question: 'In what sense, if any, are rules propositions?'

I follow the convention suggested by Moyal-Sharrock: LW1 is the Wittgenstein of the *Tractatus Logico-Philosophicus*; LW2 the Wittgenstein of the *Blue and Brown Books* and the first part of the *Philosophical Investigations*; LW3 is the Wittgenstein of the second part of the *Investigations* together with *On Certainty*.[1] For LW1 logic is the exclusive grammar of rational, empirically grounded discourses. For LW2 the scope of meanings and rules is widened to include much that was excluded by LW1. For LW3 the use of 'rule' to verbally express normative constraints on thought, speech and action, is supplemented by other concepts for expressing the character of normative constraints that shape forms of life, notably that of a 'hinge'. Moyal-Sharrock (2004a: 87) and Stroll (1994: 146) take it that LW3 develops his account of the grounds of regulatively constrained speech, thought and action, in such a way as to move further away from verbally expressed sources of order towards human ethology and non-linguistic practices. Stroll (1994: 146) lists acting, being trained in communal practices and instinct as non-intellectual foundations for forms of life. I believe these constraints are stronger, indeed in many cases amounting to normative framings of speech and action.

Cognitive psychology is the study of human perception, thought and action as it accords with certain non-causal principles of order. At the beginning of the 'cognitive revolution' of the twentieth century these were presumed to be enduring mental structures of which people were not aware, but which shaped (somehow) the contents of experience and patterns of social action. Among the proposals for this role were various cognitive entities, for instance schemata, rules and scripts. From the beginning, these words did duty both for referring to the mental entities themselves, and for the representations of such entities in the writings of psychologists. This suggests that there should be some interplay between Wittgenstein's insights with respect to 'hinges' and the presuppositions of cognitive psychologists, and any ambiguities that the double use of the 'rule' terminology brings with it. Philosophers and psychologists enunciate hinge propositions, each for their own purposes. Both are trying to bring to light some of the presuppositions of practices. Though Wittgenstein's purpose may have been different from the purposes of cognitive and social psychologists, his treatment of the sources of orderliness in human affairs can be illuminating for psychology. The reason for turning to this work of Wittgenstein's for guidance is well put by Moyal-Sharrock: '... the message of *On Certainty* is precisely that knowledge does not have to be at the basis of knowledge ... underpinning knowledge ... [are] pragmatic certainties that can be verbally rendered for heuristic purposes' (2004a: 10). To apply this insight to psychology we need only add practices to the second occurrence of knowledge in the above quotation.

I shall be taking the concept of 'hinge' to refer to whatever is the source of stable linguistic and social practices, with respect not only to the fixing of the meanings of words but also the correctness and propriety of actions. Though he uses the actual word 'hinge' rarely, it seems to me that LW3 writes of propositions in the role of hinges in preference to using the explicitly normative and performative expression 'rules' to express his transforming insight that the linguistic implications of the use of the metaphor of 'grammar' as the collective term for normative constraints is still too restrictive. The progression from the logicism of LW1 through the rule-based account of normativity offered by LW2 needed to be taken one step further. Towards the end of Section V of the second part of the *Investigations*, Wittgenstein considers talk of presuppositions.

In discussing making sense of some practical activity as 'presupposing this or that', he says:

> Should we ever really express ourselves like this: 'Naturally I am presupposing that ...'? – Or do we not do so only because the other person already knows that? Doesn't presupposition imply doubt? And doubt may be entirely lacking. Doubting has an end.
>
> (PI: p. 180)

By the time he was writing the later paragraphs of *On Certainty*, Wittgenstein stresses that it is 'our acting' that lies at the bottom of the language game – and 'not certain propositions' (cf. Moyal-Sharrock, 2004a: 98). Presuppositions are too proposition-like.

This raises the question of how hinge *propositions* are related to hinges, and what might be the point of enunciating them. We can start with the least controversial reading of this pair of terms. Hinge propositions are not themselves hinges but are a convenient way of making hinges explicit, whatever sorts of beings they may be. It seems to me that there are ambiguities evident in *On Certainty* and the writings of some of the most perceptive commentators in that sometimes hinge propositions are presented as if they were the hinges themselves. LW2's use of 'rule' is already problematic. On his view, taken strictly, a rule as an instruction cannot be a proposition. Throughout his work Wittgenstein was clear that such rules were not subject to assessments of truth and falsity. Of course, a form of words may be serving as a description of a presumptive rule, and then it would be a proposition, since it might be used to describe the rule truly or falsely. This recourse is not open for those cases in which rules are instructions, since they are imperatives. It seems to me that these troubles are parallel to the ambiguities that are evident in cognitive psychology over the grammars of such words as 'schemata', 'paradigm', 'norm', 'rule' and so on.

In short, discursively formulated normative constraints, for example rules in the imperative mood, are to be contrasted with non-discursively formulated normative constraints, such as customary habits. Both could be described verbally. As verbal expressions of the norms such sentences would fall into the domain of propositions since they could be assessed as to whether they were true or false representations of either kind of norm.

Hinges and propositional hinges

Recent studies of LW3 by Stroll (1994) and Moyal-Sharrock (2004a) suggest that for the Wittgenstein of *On Certainty* non-propositional hinges are the deepest and most entrenched influences in shaping forms of life. Hinges are not instructions the following of which will ensure that what is said and done is proper, meaningful and so on. Turning to cognitive psychology opens up the discussion to include not only cognitive and linguistic, but also social hinges, norms that have expression only in collective taken-for-granted communal practices. However, the way that hinges influence forms of life, whether universal or local, is unlikely to turn out to be by the exercise of a single directive force.

The first step in getting clear about these matters is to acknowledge the difference between a *proposition expressing a hinge* and a *proposition being a hinge*. To talk about a hinge we must perforce produce propositions, but these may not be hinges themselves. Even if we are using words to bring about conformity to norms, they are rules. And, as such, they are not propositions. For example, inducting a novice into the linguistic practices of *haute couture* one might draw attention to a working distinction in the chief designer's discussion of choice of colours for the fabrics by remarking that 'Cerise is a kind of reddish blue'. This might be meant to be taken as a semantic rule, or it might be offered as a description of a company norm. The second case would fit the situation where the humbler members of the fashion house had previously simply echoed the maitre's choice of words.

Again, enunciating one of the hinges that oil the wheels of social interaction, one might say 'Smile when you want service' and mean this form of words (proposition?) not only to give explicit form to an ethological phenomenon common to higher primates, but to be taken up as a self-instruction by someone who has trouble in shops, encountering only surly assistants. In that role it is not an observation about a practice but an explicit rule, intended to be followed by those who want to create a friendly impression.

Hinges are sources of certainty, of sureness of performance. One can be certain about what one should do as well as about what one should say. The custom that is expressed in 'Congratulate the winner' is a hinge proposition for action. If someone responded to the remark about how to greet the winner, by asking 'Should I?', we would surely wonder what motivated their scruples. If someone says 'I had no parents', we would not at first understand the remark, though we might try to reshape the concept of 'parent' say as 'loving family' to give the remark sense. It would of course be just the right thing with which the first human clone would begin his or her autobiography. Clones *ought* to write in this way.

A sureness in conducting the affairs of life, such as distributing Christmas presents, visiting graves on 'La dia de los muertos' and so on, rather than beliefs as items of knowledge, seems to characterize such hinges as these.

It certainly seems odd to say 'I believe I should visit graves on this day'. All that can mean is that I think people generally think it right so to do. It is not that I cannot be wrong in what I do, but that my practices do not turn on my ascertaining that some hypothesis is correct.

The sureness of the confidence that people have in the affairs of everyday life is not based on the conviction that something they believe is true, an item of well-founded knowledge. There are discourse hinges, that our words have certain meanings; social hinges, that promises will be fulfilled; practical hinges, that the floors will bear one's weight, and even ludic hinges, that winning the next point when one is 40 love up wins a game.

Rules, their uses and their users

The writings of LW2 culminate in the first part of the *Philosophical Investigations*. For the most part philosophers of psychology have drawn on the discussions therein for insights into how psychology might be rescued from the conceptual and methodological problems bequeathed to it under the influence of positivism. For example, the Private Language Argument has been taken to destroy the philosophical underpinnings of Behaviourism (Harré and Tissaw, 2005). Many of those who have opposed the swamping of cognitive psychology by causal hypotheses have used §§179–242 from that work as a guide to setting up an alternative psychology based on the concepts of 'meaning' and 'rule'. There seemed to be no good reason to stray from the orthodox interpretation (Baker and Hacker, 1984), according to which rules are propositional expressions of norms and fit some such general principles as the following:

a. In the end, a cluster of rules is adopted by fiat and grounds a form of life, rather than being based on an indefinite regress of rationalizations.
b. Adopting a rule cannot cause the future to develop in conformity with it. Rather a rule determines what is to count as correct or proper in the future.
c. It makes sense to train people to conform to the local rules, with as little need or reflection as possible.

In conformity with this analysis we should also say that people use rules, are guided by rules and so on, rather than 'rules use people'. The philosophical problem of how to analyse the concept 'being guided by' will not be taken up in this chapter, though it is a natural sequel. At this point it is enough to remark that it will surely turn out to be a word for a field of concepts displaying various family resemblances, as in PI: 172–8.

Already in these sections of the *Investigations* the distinction between following a rule as an instruction and acting in accordance with a rule; that is, acting in a regular and orderly fashion seems to be implicit in some paragraphs. This suggests a close comparison between LW2's use of normative concepts and the use of 'rule', 'schema', 'script' and related concepts as analytical tools in cognitive psychology.

In the social psychology of the 1970s the concept of 'social action as rule-following' was introduced as a thorough going alternative to the causality presumed by most American social psychologists. The 'role-rule' model, popularized by Harré and Secord (1972), was based on the following distinctions in the use of 'rule':

a. Rules as propositions serving as instructions, that is as progenitors of correct practices. For example, at a certain point in a social relationship a Belgian woman who is a family friend might say to a male acquaintance 'We are now at the 3-kisses stage'. In future the man should greet her with a left-right-left sequence of air-kisses.

b. Rules as expressions of sources of correct practices; e.g., scientific reports of seemingly norm-constrained behaviour. These reports may become the grounds for instructions in teaching manuals and so on. For example, studies of everyday rituals in various cultures are customarily written up in terms of sets of rules, without any implication that people ever followed such rules as instructions (Collett ,1977: ch. 1). Training in social behaviour for those devoid of social skills can be accomplished by expressing a regularity in conduct as a rule to be followed as an instruction. For example, to encourage someone to keep talking the listener should lean forward, and to discourage the talker should lean back. This formulation of a customary practice was used to instruct socially isolated people in an Oxford training programme.

c. One of the most important starting points for the move from behaviourism to cognitive psychology was Jerome Bruner's (1986) studies of the role of cognitive schemata in perception. In one experiment, children were asked to match the shape of a coin to a visual image. The children from poor families matched the coin to a 'fatter' image than the children from well-off backgrounds. The relative value of the coins influenced the perception of shape and size. The results reflect the difference between the tacit cognitive schemata involved in these acts of perception through which sensory cues are revised by social meanings. There is no suggestion that the concept of 'rule' should be used in reporting this work. There could be no such thing as a derived instruction to see coins one way or another. The valuations are 'cognitive schemata'.

Non-propositional social hinges are quite subtly related to actual practices; for example, hand-shaking as the hinge on which the Hindu practice of *namasthe* turns. The point of greeting someone by joining one's own hands rather than touching the hand of another to avoid the chance of pollution only makes sense against the background of the 'natural' tendency to shake hands, a tendency amply verified by primate ethologists.

Some light can be thrown on the problem of the status of non-propositional hinges by looking closely at the relative status of laws of nature and causal mechanisms. A law of nature is a proposition, through which the scientific community expresses a belief about the likely regularity of some sequence of observable states of a material system, *ceteris paribus*. Such a law is not just a report of empirical observations but is understood to express a natural necessity. It says what must happen in such a system, all else being equal. However, the natural sciences have evolved by skilful and often successful attempts to discover the causal mechanisms that engender the regularities described in the laws. Thus Boyle's Law, that Pressure varies inversely as the Volume occupied by a gas, is grounded in the molecular nature of gases. If Boyle's Law is a naturally necessary proposition, it expresses discursively the overt manifestations of the working of imperceptible causal mechanisms.

These examples seem to display a precocious shift to something very like a 'hinge'. How far could LW3's shift to the concept of 'hinge' from that of 'rule' be used to illuminate the parallel trend in cognitive psychology?

The rule problem

Coming back to the main thrust of the philosophical analysis, the 'rule problem' presents itself again. Sustaining the non-causal paradigm in psychology can hardly fail to benefit from resolving the problem. It presents at least two versions:

a. What are norms when they are not verbally formulated rules in the imperative mood?
b. What sort of beings could rules express?

Did Wittgenstein really work out the idea of non-propositional hinges? In the first part of *On Certainty* he brings up the possibility of a proposition which 'simply gets assumed as a truism, never called in question, perhaps not even formulated' (OC: 87). This is followed by an even more

explicit reference to unformulated propositions as the bearers of normative constraints, and so, *one presumes, playing the role of hinges*:

> It may be that all enquiry on our part is set so as to exempt certain
> propositions from doubt, if they are ever formulated. They lie apart
> from the route travelled by enquiry.
>
> (OC: 88)

> I believe that I had great-grandparents, that the people who gave them-
> selves out as my parents really were my parents etc. This belief may
> never have been expressed; even the thought that it was so never
> thought.
>
> (OC: 159)

These passages suggest that Wittgenstein is taking 'hidden hinges' to be
unformulated propositions, that is they go with 'belief that ...' as in the
above quotation. Where now is their normative or imperative force?

Baker and Hacker (1984) assume that Wittgenstein admits unformulated rules into his account. Either some rules are not proposition-like,
taking 'proposition' as all three Wittgensteins seem to have intended
it, as a cognitive object subject to assessment for truth and falsity, or we
are being asked to countenance such monsters as 'unformulated rules'.
Moyal-Sharrock says that there are 'pragmatic certainties that can be
verbally rendered for heuristic purposes, and whose conceptual analysis
uncovers their function as unjustifiable rules of grammar' (2004a: 10).
Perhaps 'functioning as unjustifiable rules of grammar' is consistent
with not being rules at all, but serving as normative constraints in some
other way.

Let us try to clarify the problematic status of these 'rules'. Here are
three possibilities:

1. They are denizens of a hidden realm of cognitive objects.
2. They are 'somethings', which, when expressible, are expressed as rules;
   that is, in verbal formulations of a certain kind. (Which kind to be
   addressed!)
3. The usage is metaphorical, drawing our attention to a 'something',
   which is like a rule, in that it exerts a normative influence on the lives
   of the tribe. The formulation is propositional; that is, a putatively
   true description of the custom.

One needs to be particularly wary as to how one expresses oneself in
these discussions. Moyal-Sharrock says in one place that we should think

of 'hinge propositions as expressions of the rules themselves' (2004a: 90). What are these 'rules themselves'? Is an expression of a rule a rule? The exegetical puzzle starts with the way Wittgenstein seems to have opened out the range of linguistic items listed in the *Philosophical Investigations* (PI: 23, 26) that seem to require the replacement of truth-conditions as sources of meaningfulness by felicity conditions, or something like that. In what surely must be a slip of the pen, Moyal-Sharrock seems to suggest a propositional interpretation of 'hinges': 'A hinge is but the artificial formulation of a certainty whose defining feature is ineffability' (2004a: 94). Surely, even though what is formulated is not propositional, the formulation of it is; that is, it truly or falsely reports the nature and existence of a non-propositional hinge.[2]

In this remark a hinge is at least proposition-like. If it is in the imperative, say being used to instruct someone, it has no truth-conditions but it certainly has empirical content and is subject to felicity conditions. The verbal rendition of an 'ineffable' hinge could be used in the imperative as an instruction, and hence as an overt hinge. It could also be used as a report of the existence and content of such a hinge and would then express a proposition in Wittgenstein's strict sense. What, then, is the bearer of the normative constraint? Stroll points to a moment of transition in the text of *On Certainty* at which the idea of hidden hinges as non-propositional somethings appears. I propose using the following terminology:

- '*hinge*' for taken-for-granted sources of order; that is, for normative constraints that are not propositions nor proposition-like;
- '*instructional hinge*' for verbal items that serve as instructions for correct speech, proper conduct and skilful performances;
- '*hinge proposition*' will be reserved for the overt verbal expression of a non-propositional constraint as well as of verbalized instructions.

There can be hinge propositions that express instructional hinges in the very same form of words. The sentence 'Smile when you are happy' may be an instructional hinge, or it may be serving as an expression of a norm, be it functionally propositional or non-propositional; for example, a local ideal. This usage would avoid glossing covert hinges as 'unformulated verbal rules'.

Let us lump together both overt and covert hinges as 'norms in action'. Here are some candidates:

1. Fixed action patterns: 'Smiling when happy': a hinge for the human form of life.

2. Customs: 'Holding the fork in the left hand': a hinge for a tribal form of life.
3. Habits: 'Wearing dark coloured clothes': a hinge for a personal style of life.

What would be the point of giving any of these non-propositional hinges, or for that matter any non-propositional hinge, explicit, discursive; that is, verbal expression? Compare the following rule-like formulations of the above:

1. 'You should smile [to express appreciation].'
2. 'You should hold the fork in your left hand [to conform to European table manners].'
3. 'Choose dark clothes [to maintain an image of seriousness].'

We have created a piece of advice, an item of etiquette and a personal reminder. Note, however, the qualifying phrases in the above. These are all hypothetical imperatives. I could come on as 'Old Grumpy', or as carelessly uncouth, or as driven here and there by the vagaries of fashion.

Why give a hinge propositional expression? The obvious answer in the above is to help regulate the social world, in giving advice, pointing to etiquette or reminding someone of some custom or habit. However, there is another reason, which has played a role in ethnomethodology (Garfinkel: 1967). Rule-expression can be used to emphasize the normative role of hinges in practices – for example, in the giving of accounts – that is, justificatory, sense-making commentaries on whatever seems to have been done. Here we are dealing with hinge propositions not propositional hinges.

Another pass in the same direction

Both Michael Polanyi and Harold Garfinkel realised that there *must* be hinges. The example to follow is taken from conversation with Garfinkel.

What is taken for granted and what is trusted as a matter of course in buying a piece of 'flat-pack' furniture from IKEA? Let us suppose I have purchased a set of book shelves and that these must be assembled from the parts in the box. Eagerly anticipating the pleasure of building the book case I open the package, and look for the Instructions. These are usually lists of things to do, statements in the imperative mood, with accompanying diagrams. I trust them, and do not doubt for a moment that by following them faithfully I will put together the book case *correctly*.

Flat-pack furniture makers do not set about deceiving their customers by putting together impossible sets of rules, and sitting back having a good laugh. However, it soon becomes clear to the homebuilder that not every relevant instruction is written in the brochure. For example, it is part of the Western Form of Life to insert screws clockwise. Here is a non-propositional hinge that sits at the base of innumerable and diverse practices. A little reflection will come up with an open catalogue of tacit norms, even in so simple a procedure as putting together a bookcase.

This point was very fully developed by Polanyi (1966) in a very different context. Every practice, even if it had been reduced to a set of explicit instructions, depends on an indefinitely extended repertoire of skills that Polanyi called 'tacit knowledge'. He applied it particularly to scientific research as a practice. How could one acquire the tacit knowledge necessary to successful (correct) techniques of experimentation? Only by being trained by an expert, in a kind of hands-on way. Even if any such training could be reduced to a rule, there would still be taken-for-granted skills upon which the use of that rule depended.

Parallel errors

When Moore formulated an important manual hinge in the proposition 'I have two hands', he took it that the proposition expressed an item of knowledge. Hence the further step that betrayed his misunderstanding of the place of the hinge in our life form, his declaration 'I know I have two hands', for which the upheld hands were supposed to be evidence. The hinge masqueraded as an empirical fact with truth-conditions that Moore's demonstration appeared to fulfil. When Wittgenstein was learning the clarinet, it surely never struck him that the Boehmer fingering was based on the two handedness of people as a hinge. This norm of human anatomy held firm through various fingering systems. Later, when his brother Paul lost his right hand, and Ravel composed the sonata for the left hand for him, the hinge was no doubt formulated and drifted across the grammatical spectrum to a place where it was correctly judged to be false. This pianist does not have two hands. This story is exemplary of the display of the deep roots of a philosophical error:

a. The propositional expression of a non-propositional hinge is taken to be the hinge itself.
b. The grammar of the hinge proposition is misunderstood.

A similar type of double error is endemic among psychologists. They often mistake the expression of a cognitive or social hinge for the hinge itself, and go on to misread the grammar of the hinge proposition reporting a non-propositional norm as if it were a causal hypothesis. Experiments are then devised to look for evidence for it. For example, there is a non-propositional social hinge, in the taken-for-granted code of manners, that it is rude to disagree with people, unless it is about something of importance. Solomon Asch (1987) became famous for an experimental study of the way a single individual tended to conform to group opinion against his/her better judgement. Turning to the latter part of *On Certainty* would have saved him the trouble.

Modality of hinges

These examples and comparisons make the bald assertion 'Hinges are rules of grammar' very odd. If rules are merely reports of customs, then they lose their normative role and fall within the grammar of truth and falsity. Unless a propositional hinge is a rule in the sense of an instruction, then it can play no role as a source of the maintenance of customs. LW3's discussion in *On Certainty* of the modality of hinge propositions is strongly oriented to the grammar of 'felicity conditions'. In fact, in allowing for hinge propositions that are functionally propositional hinges there is an extension of the range of linguistic proposition-like entities beyond the limits of meaning bound up with truth-conditions.

Those hinge propositions which report hypotheses about implicit norms, such as good habits and the like, are not hinges. They do purport to describe non-propositional hinges. But if we suppose that there is a way of vicariously ascribing modality to the relevant hinges by reference to the modality of their overt expression, in the imperative for example, it cannot be from those which are reports. They must all be in the indicative and, in Wittgensteinian terms, propositions.

There is an alternative in the case of those verbal items I have called 'instructional hinges', which express the normative content *and inherit* the normative force of the non-propositional hinges which they replace. In these cases the reports by a student of etiquette take on a new role as pieces of advice or even mandatory principles of good manners. Here it seems reasonable to ascribe modality to a non-propositional hinge by transference from the modality of the overt expression of the hinge.

Wittgenstein's therapy for social psychologists could turn on relieving them of grammatical illusions that come from misunderstandings of the propositional expression of hinges, as if the hinges were matters of fact. Any programme for defining such a modality that depends in any substantive way on the T/F system, as it appears in the works of Leibniz or Russell, will not do. Reduced to a slogan, the Russell-Leibniz necessity modality comes down to 'Never, Nowhere, Not'. However, it is an important aspect of LW3's account of modality that certain verbal formulations can be transformed from serving as propositional hinges into empirical reports of the way things used to be; that is, as hinge propositions. Both instructional and non-propositional hinges sometimes simply evaporate, no longer either serving as instructions for good practice or reporting what a hinge requires when it is not an instruction. In my youth there was an elaborate etiquette around the raising, doffing and so on of men's hats. I was trained by my mother into always walking on the street side of the pavement when with a lady. I was not aware of this non-propositional hinge among my social resources until rebuked for sexism by a feminist acquaintance, as I changed sides when we were crossing the street.

Kantian synthetic *a priori* propositions express the schematized categories that we use, though not knowingly, to synthesize the sensory flux into the twin domains of the empirical world and the minds of persons. The Kantian categories could not melt away or be replaced by others. Wittgenstein's hinge propositions, in whatever way they are related to the corresponding hinges, are not quite like synthetic *a priori* propositions and the corresponding categories. But they are closer to the synthetic *a priori* than any other historical account of modality.

Being trained in good habits ought to be a clear case of the genesis of a non-propositional hinge. How does a habit exist? Certainly there must have been a change in the neural nets of the brain so that the habit should have the mechanical, unpremeditated spontaneity that it has. However, the habit cannot be the very same entity as the neural structure. The trained neural net has no normative character, and the weights of the connections of a bad habit net would not, in themselves, display the normative difference between good and bad habits, between pulling up the knees of one's trousers when sitting down, and biting one's nails. Something like this appears in LW2's discussion of reading in the *Investigations* (PI: 157): the normative question, 'Can the pupil really read?' is 'independent of ... a mental or any other mechanism'.

In *On Certainty* LW3 is also much taken up with the status of the taken-for-granted ontology of the life world. The thrust of the whole thing is, after all, the critical examination of Moore's refutation of idealism by displaying his hands as paradigmatic material objects. For example, LW3 says: 'Children do not learn that books exist, that armchairs exist etc. etc. etc. They learn to fetch books, sit in armchairs etc. etc.' (OC: 476). In this chapter I have taken for granted that the life world in which people think and act is hung on the materiality of bodies and the flux of events as changes therein. Whatever else serves as a hinge, these must.

Notes

1. As well as *Last Writings on Philosophical Psychology* and *Remarks on Colour* (Moyal-Sharrock 2004a: 1–2).

2. I am grateful to Danièle Moyal-Sharrock for pointing out a remark of Wittgenstein's which exactly catches my unease concerning the reporting of hinges in words: '... the grammatical constructions we call empirical propositions ... have a particular application, a particular use. And a construction may have a superficial resemblance to such an empirical proposition and play a somewhat similar role in a calculus without having an analogous application; and if it hasn't we won't be inclined to call it a proposition' (PG: 127).

7
Dispositions or Capacities? Wittgenstein's Social Philosophy of Mind

Christiane Chauviré

Wittgenstein's contribution to social science is often perceived either through the work of his successors, in particular, Peter Winch (author of the renowned and contested 'Understanding a Primitive Society', and of *The Idea of a Social Science*) or through the anthropology sketched in his own 'Remarks on Frazer's *Golden Bough*' (GB). Often, Wittgenstein's thinking on the social is not distinguished from Kripke's communal interpretation of rule-following, which considers community consensus to be the only (arbitrary) guarantor of correctness in rule-following, hence ensuing in sceptical relativism and making it impossible for Wittgenstein to be the normativist Peter Hacker and Jacques Bouveresse's orthodox interpretations take him to be. In this chapter, I will argue that it is possible to have a social and communal conception of rule-following, as is Wittgenstein's case, without falling into the scepticism attributed to him by Kripke, and without ceasing to be a normativist, though of a different ilk (we shall speak here of a normativity that is *immanent* to behaviour). I will then show that Wittgenstein's social philosophy cannot be reduced to Kripke's view of it, or even to the *community view* reinterpreted in a non-sceptical light; it is richer and more pertinent to the social sciences, particularly in its crucial recourse to the notions – themselves normative – of capacity and know-how; that is, to the mastery of a technique that is learnable and deploys itself in practice.

Wittgenstein does not, for all that, have a dispositionalist conception of the social as does, for instance, Bourdieu, with whom he has otherwise much in common (we need only mention the crucial role accorded to habit in social life and to the inertia of institutions, as well as an anti-intellectualistic philosophy of the social and a holism which precludes any methodological individualism). Wittgenstein is not a dispositionalist – with respect to the mental or the social – because, for him, the idea of a disposition befits only mechanico-causal explanations, and these do not apply to human action. We must therefore circumscribe his critique of dispositional explanation: it targets only the causal version.[1]

There is, in Wittgenstein's social philosophy, a strong pragmatist and anti-intellectualistic component, as well as a methodological holism (if only implicit) that bring him close to Peirce, Dewey and Bourdieu, however different he may otherwise be from these authors. But there is also – and this is the peculiarity in Wittgenstein's philosophy that renders its use by the social sciences so difficult – the grammatical twist which he puts on all these questions, and which is overlooked by exegetes like Kripke. In this chapter, I will urge that we move from Kripke's erroneous reading towards a correct interpretation of Wittgenstein's texts – that is, towards a reasonable normativist conception that would recognize in Wittgenstein a theoretician of the *immanence* of norms in practices and social life (a norm's being immanent does not make it less of a norm!).

We must then seek out Wittgenstein's contribution to thought about the social, where it lives: in his philosophy of mathematics (this is not paradoxical for, in that work, we have constantly to do with, as Victor Descombes ingenuously puts it, rules that I can follow alone, but that I cannot be *alone* to follow (2001: 150, DMS translation) where a social and communal – but not Kripkean or sceptical – conception of rule-following is delineated; in his critique of dispositional or causal explanation aimed at making human action intelligible; and in his philosophy of practice, where know-how and capacities are accorded major importance, thereby granting a central role to what we shall call, though Wittgenstein does not, practical reason. Wittgenstein gives maximum thickness to customs, collective habits, institutionalized regularities, which he takes as always *presupposed* in individual rule-following and its grounding, but we are left to decide which version (causal or not) to give of these omnipresent 'habitus'. It is important, in any case, that we understand the exact sense of Wittgenstein's rejection (limited to a single version) of dispositional explanations that encourage other ways of thinking about the social which perhaps have failed to make a distinction between the grammar of causes and that of reasons.

A heavy dispositionalism: C. S. Peirce

What is a disposition? For example, knowing English. It is not, writes that great theoretician of dispositions, C. S. Peirce – as early as 1873 – the permanent presence of language in an actualized state in the mind of the speaker:

> When I say that I know the French language, I do not mean that as long as I know it I have all the words which compose it in my mind, or a single one of them. But only that when I think of an object, the French word for it will occur to me, and that when a French word is brought to my attention I shall think of the object it signifies.
>
> (1873: 354)

But nor does Peirce want to reduce knowing a language to a series of discrete verbal performances; that is, to the proffering of correct and pertinent sentences. That is a reductionist – Peirce would say: nominalist – mistake which amounts to saying that we know a language only when we are speaking it; intermittently. Whereas in fact our knowledge of English does not vanish between performances:

> ... we do not say that he only knows the language at the moment that the particular words occur to him that he is to say; for in that way he never could be certain of knowing the whole language if he only knew the particular word necessary at the time. So that his knowledge of the thing which exists all the time, exists only by virtue of the fact that when a certain occasion arises a certain idea will come into his mind.
>
> (Peirce, 1873: 3420)

For Peirce, knowing a language is a conditional business: if *I think of an object, the right word comes to mind*. This conditional is a material implication, but Peirce will come to think of this as too nominalistic – that is, as not sufficiently ensuring the reality of the disposition – and he transforms the material implication into a counterfactual conditional, thereby affirming the full reality of potential entities, the *would be's*, and of dispositions in particular: *if I were to think of an object, the right word would come to mind*. The thesis of the reality of dispositions has, then, all to do with the semantics of dispositional utterances that so preoccupied analytic philosophers, from Carnap to Pap to Mellor.

To know a language is to be disposed to utter the right sentence advisedly, without that implying either the permanent presence in the mind of the whole language in an actualized form, or the reduction of the disposition to its occurrences. A disposition does not disappear between two occurrences; indeed, the counterfactual makes it possible to refer to actualizations that are never produced and never will be; it makes clear that the disposition is a permanent potentiality actualizing itself occasionally, in particular situations, or perhaps even never actualizing itself. This would not make the disposition less real – in the sense in which, for Peirce, universals (laws, habits, meanings) are real; that is, they *really* operate in nature. An individual may never suspect she has a certain disposition, much as one may have a talent that was never developed. Analogously, a physical disposition such as the hardness of a diamond may never come to be tested, which does not prevent the diamond from being hard. The paradox of dispositions – their being both permanent and not entirely actual – is attenuated by Peirce's categorial distinction between reality and existence: real entities, such as dispositions, may ultimately never exist: 'It is perfectly conceivable that [a] man should have faculties which are never called forth: in which case the existence of the faculties depends upon a condition which never occurs' (1873: 343).

Clearly, Peircian dispositionalism, just as the Chomskian notion of competence, lies open to Wittgenstein's critique of dispositional explanations whose tenor we shall examine, even if some of Wittgenstein's questions (cf. PI: 20) on the duration of capacities, and their curious presence-absence, seem, unmistakeably, to echo Peirce, at least as regards the phenomenology of dispositions and aptitudes: '... but is this having a mastery [of language] something that *happens* while you are uttering the sentence?' (PI: 20).

Causes, rules and reasons

Wittgenstein is a curious case in the history of twentieth-century philosophy: he could be considered a pragmatist and yet, unlike Peirce, he does not hold a dispositionalist theory of disposition. In short, Wittgenstein is not a dispositionalist in the way Peirce and Bourdieu are. He puts no store in the utility of dispositionalist explanations and is certainly not a dispositional realist in the (ontologically thick) sense in which Peirce is. Strangely enough, Wittgenstein envisages only a mechanistic conception of the disposition, and if he denounces all mention of dispositions in the explanation of human action, it is because he sees in such mentions an appeal to causes, not reasons. Indeed, Wittgenstein, as is well known, was averse to the use of causal explanations in any realm but that of the natural sciences, particularly rejecting a causal approach to human action; emphasizing, rather, in matters relating to philosophy of language, philosophy of mind, anthropology, aesthetics and psychoanalysis, the connection between action and reasons. And, as we shall see, for an agent to invoke a reason for her action often amounts to evoking the rule she has followed and which has orientated her action without, however, restraining it. Moreover, Wittgenstein insists that an explanation by reasons is not reducible to a causal explanation.

Indeed, in the early 1930s, *Voices of Wittgenstein* evokes the case of a driver who is said to stop at a 'Stop' sign and is asked why he has done this (VOW: 111); the driver could certainly reply by giving a neurophysiological explanation – which today we would call naturalist – in terms of reflexes, muscular movements and the nervous system. However, he could also reply by saying that when he was learning to drive he was taught to stop at a 'Stop' sign; and, here, there is no mention of his training as a cause of his action: he does not say that the training created in him a disposition to act thus (causal explanation), but rather indicates the rule that guided his behaviour; in other words, the *reason* for his behaviour, which is of the order of a logical, not of a causal determination (cf. PI: 220). In fact, it could be asked whether it is the same thing that is being explained in both cases: must we not distinguish behaviour as natural phenomenon, explained in terms of causes from intentional action, explained in terms of reasons? But why think of dispositions as causes; that is, as something which, in philosophy, it is useless to evoke to make a human action intelligible? The answer is that Wittgenstein thinks of the disposition as a mechanism meant to automatically produce the agent's every move; a sort of mental machinery, efficacious though immaterial (a mentalist myth, if ever there was one). Recall Wittgenstein's famous corrective in the *Blue Book:* no calculus (in the sense of a hypothetical, and in particular: occult, mental machinery) need be there, present in its entirety, like 'a permanent background to every sentence which we say' (BB: 42). From a Wittgensteinian point of view, writes Jacques Bouveresse, to conceive the mastery of a language in these terms is misguided 'in that it proposes to answer in advance questions that can only remain unanswered in that they exist only in the moment or not at all' (1970: 180, DMS translation). It is this ambition – to have resolved, in advance, a series of problems before they arise – that Wittgenstein stigmatizes via the picture of a machine-disposition, reminiscent of some aspects of Chomsky and his model of linguistic competence. Against such an ambition, Wittgenstein brandishes the idea that a rule 'does not act at a distance' (BB: 14), especially not on the future. Indeed, as we shall see, a rule is not envisaged by Wittgenstein as having force, but authority, or, as he says, a 'majesty' – this is crucial if we are to understand what he takes normativity, both mental and social, to mean.

Rather than work, as Peirce does, with the notion of disposition, Wittgenstein resorts to the lighter notion of capacity. For him, a capacity is, by definition, the mastery of a technique, acquired through instruction and deployed entirely in practice. A capacity is thus a know-how which is simply at the agent's disposal, whereas a disposition is purported to be – at least by a dispositionalist like Peirce – active, operative and tendential. Wittgenstein envisages the disposition exclusively as a mechanism whose action is both causal and utterly constraining, such as Leibniz's necessitating causes. He never thinks to conceive of dispositions on an organic model, as do – with respect to the capacity to speak – Humboldt with his *Sprachform* and Chomsky with his linguistic 'organ'.[2] On Wittgenstein's view, then, dispositional explanation is but a variant of causal-mechanistic explanation; and here we may wonder why commentators, though they have noted it, have never found peculiar this reductionist assimilation of a disposition to a mechanism as if it went without saying; whereas a dispositionalist like Peirce can harbour an organicist conception of disposition: that is, of a disposition acting like a final cause: like a tendency which both directs and determines behaviour.

A mechanistic reduction of dispositions

To think of a disposition as a machine may seem paradoxical, for a disposition is first and foremost a potentiality; a machine is, if anything, actual (even if, in its operation, it produces future applications that turn from possible to actual). To think of a disposition in mechanistic terms compels us to envisage that potentiality in static and actualist terms, whereas Peirce rejected just such a conception of dispositions: 'A man is said to know a foreign language. And what does that mean? Only that if the occasion arises, the words of that language will come into his mind; it does not mean that they are actually in his mind at the time' (1873: 342; cf. vol. 4: 622). In the *Blue Book*, Wittgenstein's comparison of the disposition to a mental reservoir further accentuates this transformation of the proposition into a static, actualized, non-dispositional entity containing the possible in an actualized or quasi-actualized state.

The problem is that it is difficult to think of, or represent, a potentiality other than by appealing to the counterfactual conditional: pictorial representations of it – such as machine or reservoir – tend to rigidify it. So that to represent or describe the disposition without betraying it seems hardly feasible. Language itself is here partly responsible, notes Wittgenstein, because of the ambiguity of the present tense used both in dispositional utterances (recall Quine's example to illustrate the dispositional present tense: 'Tabby eats mice') and in descriptions of states. This encourages us to confuse the mention of a disposition or of a capacity with that of a state of mind or a hypothetical mental machine that would be a model of the mind: 'In these sentences the verb is used in the *present tense*, suggesting that the phrases are descriptions of states which exist at the moment when we speak (*sic*)' (BrB: 117). The machine metaphor cancels the dimension of potentiality, for – in the ordinary use of language and contrary to what is suggested by the mechanistic model of the disposition – in speaking of dispositions we do not mean to say that future applications are already actualized in the machine, but that the machine makes these applications possible in that it will, in functioning, effect them. Likening the disposition to a machine results in a mechanistic reduction of the disposition, as explains Emmanuel Bourdieu:[3]

> A mechanism's action is characteristically conceived of as resulting from the application of calculable rules to an object or an individual; that is, for each 'entry' or problem entered, a finite number of logical 'steps' are taken, which lead – in a blind and automatic way – to an exit or determinate conclusion ... a disposition would then be a machine capable of calculating, according to a certain program, an infinite number of 'outputs' of a certain type (its occurrences), from an infinite number of 'inputs' of another type (its trigger conditions).
>
> (1998b: 176–7, DMS translation)

In the mechanistic reduction described here, the reference to something like a potentiality disappears, except perhaps in the idea that the machine is capable of calculating an infinite number of outputs. In any case, the mechanistic model of the disposition, rightly disparaged by Wittgenstein, makes the disposition seem too 'actualized', even if not in a physical way, for Wittgenstein's mental machine is immaterial or symbolic, and hence as unreal as a Turing machine. E. Bourdieu distinguishes between two versions of the mechanistic reduction of dispositions: one where the machine considered is physically real and operates causally; the other, where the machine operates logically, like a Turing machine (ibid.). But Wittgenstein's machine is neither physical nor logical: it is a model of a physical mechanism that acts causally in an occult sphere, an ethereal milieu about which we know nothing; it is the 'symbol of a machine' meant to model the workings of the mind, but in a pseudo-scientific way. We are therefore not in the presence of a physically real mechanism, nor of a logical machine operating exclusively by virtue of its syntax and unwinding the logical consequences of symbolic expressions, but of a mysterious entity operating in a magical way and capable of performances that no real machine would be capable of: '... the mechanism of the mind, the nature of which, it seems, we don't quite understand, can bring about effects which no material mechanism could' (BB: 3). Clearly, the only reason Wittgenstein adheres to the mechanistic representation of dispositions is so that he can refute dispositional explanation altogether; indeed, he precisely denounces it as neutralizing the possibility of future occurrences by making possibility seem like a weakened reality (cf. PI: 193–6). From a Peircean or Bourdieusian perspective, it may seem a shame that Wittgenstein did not envisage a different, less negative, conception of the disposition, which he might then have endorsed. We shall see, however, that an alternative conception is not open to Wittgenstein inasmuch as he grammaticalizes the question of the not yet actualized.

Dispositions and 'possibility as a shadow of reality'

What is the source in Wittgenstein of this picture of the disposition that evokes both ghosts and machines? Probably the conception he once held in the *Tractatus*, and later rejected, of language as a calculus. The dispositional explanation of linguistic occurrences denounced in the *Blue Book*, *inter alia*, would be a version or a consequence of that conception. In the early thirties, Wittgenstein begins to reconsider one of the master theses of the *Tractatus*, that language is a calculus obeying strict rules and acting automatically without the intervention of the speaker, who in fact plays no role at all in the mechanism of language; a mechanism that operates without his knowledge, its rules acting of their own accord, somewhat like a semantic automaton. Later, Wittgenstein reintroduces the speaker's active participation in the operation of language, which then ceases to be purely calculatory and rigidly mechanistic: language is no longer a vehicle that pilots itself, there is now a pilot at the helm. In the *Blue Book*, for example, to speak a language is no longer to apply a calculus according to very precise rules which the speaker, if he is not totally absent from language (an impression one sometimes gets from reading the *Tractatus*) does not even seem to have implicit knowledge of, or an unconscious capacity to apply them. Moreover, Wittgenstein's disqualification of dispositions is, as we shall see, intrinsically linked to his denunciation of possibility as a 'shadowy reality',[4] in that he sees the notion of a disposition to act as an instance of the misleading image of possibility as a shadow of real action.

Before *Philosophical Investigations* (PI: 194), the best demonstration of the link between Wittgenstein's anti-dispositionalism and his vigorous critique of possibility as an anticipatory 'shadow' of reality is in a text from *Voices of Wittgenstein*.[5] As is well known, the second Wittgenstein put much effort into hunting down the ghostly entities that populate the realm of philosophy, the realm of ghosts *par excellence*. The most prominent of these entities – that have no explanatory use in that they merely push further back the problem they were meant to solve – is the 'possible fact', which anticipates the real fact and is a useless *Doppelgänger* of it, projecting its shadow on the future. In the *Tractatus*, it comes in the shape of the possible fact whose actualization would render the proposition true, and whose non-actualization would make it false. The second Wittgenstein virulently rejects those entities that act as mediators between language and reality, useless duplicates of real entities; and he extends his critique to cover also the shadows that *fore*shadow expectation; hope, desire and other propositional attitudes. The invocation of this kind of entity presupposes that, in some mysterious way, the future is contained in the present, in the name of possibility; that is, of a weakened reality, less real than the real. Dispositions are always denounced for just that reason by Wittgenstein: he sees them as giving a mysterious fore-presence to the agent's future applications, as if they, so to speak, already existed in them.

Capacities versus dispositions

Wittgenstein wants to dissuade us from conceiving capacity as a disposition. So that to know how to follow a rule is a capacity (indeed, the capacity *par excellence*), not a disposition. Moreover, it is a fundamentally practical capacity, a know-how more than a knowing: Wittgenstein extracts from the cognitive realm what philosophers tend to place there and returns it to practice, particularly as regards such excessively intellectualized aptitudes as: playing chess, mental calculation, knowing 12 foreign languages and so on. All of these presuppose rules of which the agent who is following them is not always aware or cognisant ('So how am I to determine the rule according to which he is playing? He does not know it himself' PI: 82); all have a practical basis that is more important than their theoretical dimension. Putnam, for one, doubts that such a practical basis can be made fully explicit in verbal form.

A mental capacity such as understanding is not meant to predetermine future occurrences; it is presented simply as the mastery of a technique; and, in contrast to a mental act such as 'grasping in a flash', it has duration: this is what is revealed by the grammar of the word 'capacity'. It can be said that, for Wittgenstein, capacities are the principle of the intelligibility of action. Capacities are neither reducible to singular applications nor comparable to mysterious mental mechanisms containing their applications in advance. So that knowing a foreign language, knowing how to play bridge, but also knowing *tout court*, understanding, meaning and so on, are capacities that are not reducible to mental occurrences (mental acts, states or processes), though Wittgenstein does not deny that capacities have occurrent states or are accompanied by specific lived experiences. A capacity does not transcend its manifestations as something that permanently stands behind them and prompts them, but nor is it reducible to its manifestations, which are its criteria. The link between a capacity and its occurrences is not a causal, but a criterial – and therefore internal, grammatical – link; whereas the link between the disposition and the acts that emanate from it is purely causal and external. Moreover, when we postulate in an agent a disposition to do something, we are in fact, as in any causal explanation, formulating a hypothesis: a disposition 'is essentially something hypothetical'. 'But of what kind is the hypothesis?' Wittgenstein immediately asks (VOW: 359). Indeed, we do not know which hypothesis, in the scientific sense, we are talking about for we have no way of testing it. We are tempted to say, for example, that the ability (taken in a dispositional sense) is a sort of hypothetical 'reservoir from which the applications flow' (VOW: 359), but machine or reservoir are mere metaphors that tempt us, and not the slightest bit like verifiable scientific hypotheses.

Thus conceived, dispositions summon an image of possibility that is misleading. We can now better understand the reason for Wittgenstein's anti-dispositionalism: 'This disposition is a possibility, and this possibility is conceived now as a shadow of reality' (VOW: 361). To consider a mental capacity such as 'to mean' as a disposition, is to see it as a possibility, a shadow of reality on which all future applications would be projected. An entirely different picture emerges if we consider understanding or meaning as a capacity or an aptitude. The capacity to understand a word or a language is not a possibility, in the sense of a shadow of reality; it has nothing of a mysterious mental mechanism containing or fixing in advance all acts of understanding. Capacity has nothing to do with possibility or with a predetermined future. Rid of all mythology, the notion of capacity has no place in a causal explanation of our performances; contrary to the notion of disposition, heavily causal on Wittgenstein's view, or to the equally mythology-laden notion of competence, in Chomsky's sense.[6] We can say that, for Wittgenstein, capacity is a reason, not a cause, for action; or rather, that it has its place in any explanation by reasons, which liberates it from any mythology of causes.

A mythology of causes

It might be objected, however, that if a capacity is defined as the mastery of a technique, what we have is a circular definition – mastery being itself a capacity. In fact, the key word in this definition is 'technique', which is a purely practical and descriptive notion. But now, does appealing to the notion of capacity give us anything more than would a simple description of regular performances? Is it not redundant in the presence of such a description? No, for the concept of capacity is normative; it implies a reference to notions of success or failure, of the correctness or incorrectness of an application, as well as to the possible reference to a rule as a reason for action. A reason for action can only be given by the agent, in the first person, if she is asked to say why she has acted. A third person or witness, on the other hand, can, by means of hypotheses and induction, find the reason(s) for the other's action and express them objectively in the third person. According to Wittgenstein, the agent can be ignorant of the cause, but not – other than in a psychotherapeutic session aimed precisely at finding it – of the reason for her action. We should note that the grammatical difference between causal explanation and explanation by reasons – which already presupposes a first- and third-person asymmetry – is underpinned by the epistemological difference between the agent's subjective and objective means of access to causes and reasons; indeed, this is the basis of the duality in the realms of nature/humanities research. Moreover, the search for causes is indefinite, whereas that for reasons stops when the agent has given her reason for acting (a good reason is one which the agent gives, and authenticates): 'the chain of reasons has an end' (PI: 326). The capacity for mental calculation, for example, is of the order of *normative* (even if only unconsciously normative) behaviour and not merely *regular* (in the statistical and descriptive sense) behaviour. This is why capacity is not susceptible of the reproach Wittgenstein had levelled at dispositions: giving a verbal or redundant explanation, in the same way that attributing to a calculating machine the disposition of multiplying correctly, is redundant with the simple description of the structure, or of a state, of the machine.

In the Ambrose Lectures, Wittgenstein, honing his critique of dispositionalism, gives as an example the statement 'A loves B'; this, he writes, can be read as

> a dispositional statement that if some process is going on in his mind it will have the consequence that he behaves in such-and-such a way. ... This parallels the description of an idea, which stands either for a mental state, a set of reactions, or a state of a mechanism which has as its consequences both the behaviour and certain feelings.

> (AWL: 91)

Note that, in contrast to dispositionalists, Wittgenstein does not para-phrase 'A loves B' as a counterfactual conditional that attaches to a law:

> But the dispositional statement ..., referring to a mechanism, is not gen-uine. It gives no new meaning. Dispositional statements are always at bottom statements about a mechanism, and have the grammar of state-ments about a mechanism. Language uses the analogy of a machine, which constantly misleads us. In an enormous number of cases our words have the form of dispositional statements referring to a mech-anism whether there is a mechanism or not. In the example about love, nobody has the slightest idea what sort of mechanism is being referred to. The dispositional statement does not tell us anything about the nature of love; it is only a way we describe it. ... It is actu-ally a statement about the grammar of the word 'love'.
>
> (AWL: 91–2)

As in *Voices of Wittgenstein*, in this passage Wittgenstein takes the dispo-sitional statement to be a redundant description that says nothing new about love; a statement merely deploying the grammar of the word 'love' but burdened by a parasitic image: 'what is behind the grammar of that statement is the picture of a mechanism set to react in certain ways' (AWL: 92). The dispositional form of the word 'understand' comprises a misleading reference to an underlying mechanism: 'We think that if only we saw the machinery we should know what understanding is' (AWL: 92). As Bouveresse notes in his gloss on this passage, we tend to look for a mechanism where there is none, to explain the non-mechanical in terms of the mechanical (1995a: 594). But human behaviour does not admit of mechanico-causal explanations; a capacity does not constrain us in any way: we remain free agents. The invocation of a capacity does not serve to predict the recurrence of the agent's performances, nor to state a law concerning it. The notion of capacity is normative, but that is different. A capacity is internally related to its manifestations, and it is from within grammar that the question of the non-causal link between capacity and actions is settled. A capacity is not, as is Bourdieu's *habitus*, the principle of practice of agents, an active capacity; it is a capacity that needs to be activated by the agent in certain circumstances, and in no way infringes on her freedom. As to possibility wrongly conceived as an anticipatory shadow of reality, it, too, is fixed only in grammar: it is grammar that determines possibilities and impossibilities.

We can now highlight yet another way in which Wittgenstein remains original: he nowhere resembles reductionist anti-dispositionalists like

Quine, for whom the dispositional idiom is only provisional, one day to be replaced by the description by science of a molecular or atomic structure. In a sense, both philosophers find redundant the use of dispositional terms, but not for the same reason (in Quine, it is his scientism; in Wittgenstein, his hostility towards mechanistic explanations in realms where they have no business, especially the realm of the mental or that of human action).

Possibility is grammatical

Let us return to Wittgenstein's anti-dispositionalist motivations; that is, to his critique of the idea of possibility as a shadow of reality, which unites in a common error Nietzsche's eternal return (nothing happens but what has already happened) and Frege's reified logico-mathematical facts (possible at best) (cf. VOW: 361). Capacity, we have seen, has nothing to do with possibility or with a potential future. We will not, however, go as far as Ryle and say that to attribute a capacity is nothing more than to indicate a non-impossibility (cf. E. Bourdieu, 1998b: 53): where to know Japanese is to *not be incapable of* speaking it. Such a characterization of capacity is too weak in that it fails to do justice to the ever-mobilizable or available character of capacity. Nor would Wittgenstein have followed Ryle in seeing capacities as weak, non-tendential dispositions: for him, *capacities are categorially distinct from dispositions*. Wittgenstein wants to exclude determinism from the universe of human actions because it is inept to explain them – determinism being in fact nothing but a norm of description of phenomena used in mechanics – and because the question of capacities and possibility is to be settled within grammar. It might be noted that set theory falls into the same trap in its extensive representation of the infinite which also shares in this erroneous conception of the possible because it fails to see that the infinite is a grammatical determination: 'The word "infinite" characterizes a possibility and not a reality' (WVC: 229). Hence 'there can't be possibility and actuality in mathematics. It's all on *one* level. And is, in a certain sense, actual' (PR: p. 164). We are in the presence here of a strong actualism, which tosses anything that is not actualized in the basket of grammar: the modal is grammatical.

As Bouveresse reminds us in *Le réel et son ombre* (*The Real and its Shadow*), one of the fundamental theses of Wittgenstein's philosophy is that possibility is entirely contained in language, and not in a world of possibilities intermediate between language and reality, which is what philosophers tend to believe when they accumulate ghostly entities like possibility, meaning, proposition, and so on. Generally, modalities are in language, not in reality: Wittgenstein saw this in the *Tractatus* with regard to necessity, but not to possibility. At the beginning of the thirties, in the full swing of the grammatical turn, Wittgenstein maintains that grammar does not express what is the case, but what is possible. And so the possible and the impossible are arbitrary in the very sense that grammar is: there are no facts with which we could compare grammar in order to justify it; grammar cannot be subject to the verdict of any reality whatsoever without falling into infinite regression (no description can justify rules without appealing to other rules, and so on *ad infinitum*). This whole analysis must be kept in mind if we are to understand what Wittgenstein finds wrong with dispositional explanations: they mistake grammatical determinations for causal determinations, especially failing to see that possibility is a purely grammatical notion. Whence the need for Wittgenstein to resort to capacities and develop a non-mythological philosophy of capacities.

It becomes increasingly clear that if Wittgenstein assimilates dispositions to underlying mechanisms, it is because of the recurrence of this metaphor in language, particularly as regards mental capacities; and because, if he wants to reject a conception of the possible as predetermined and in some way pre-real, the best representations of such a conception are to be found in the machine (especially the mental one) and in calculus. Perhaps, also, in order to expose the insufficiency and unsuitability of some simplistic behavioural models of behaviour (the 'mechanistic' stimulus–response schema, the 'set-up' of conditioned reflexes) in providing us with an understanding of human action. To break with a mechanico-causal dispositionalism, Wittgenstein turns the question of capacities into a *grammatical* question, independent of the universe of causal explanations; but also into a purely *practical* question, conceptually indissociable from notions of technique and training. Thus does the grammar of capacities free us from the metaphysics of dispositions.

Rule and social constraint

But in Wittgenstein's philosophy, the grammar of capacities can only be deployed against the background of his anthropology, which testifies to a real sense of the social. And we shall see that if in matters relating to the philosophy of mind, Wittgenstein seems estranged from pragmatists and dispositionalists (who are often one and the same, as in the case of Peirce), he is much closer to them in matters of social philosophy, upholding as he does an anti-intellectualistic conception of the practical sphere.

It is clear, also, that the key notions of Wittgenstein's second philosophy – in which everything: language-game, capacity, technique, training, custom, revolves around rule-following – can, once degrammaticalized, make a real contribution to understanding the social game. What especially transpires is that all rules are collective, even social in that they presuppose the social as context or background (to follow a rule is a custom, like orientating oneself from a signpost). Social constraint is something Wittgenstein did not underestimate, particularly the omnipresence of normativity in its different forms, conscious and non-conscious. Making a very diversified use of the notion of rule, Wittgenstein distinguishes implicit from explicit rules; processes that imply rules from processes that are simply in accord with rules; and he anticipates Rawls's and Searle's distinction of constitutive and regulative rules. One does not follow a rule alone; one does not follow a rule only once; private language is conceptually impossible: all of these grammatical remarks can, once transposed, nourish a social philosophy. Even mathematical rules have a social dimension and the price to pay for their transgression is nothing less than exclusion, if not madness: mathematics has a 'civil status'.

Wittgenstein's frequent mention of training, indeed taming, which is itself based on natural regularities, and grounds the concordance of collective practices, further testifies to this. The inculcation of elementary rules in school is constantly evoked by Wittgenstein, who became aware of its importance as a schoolteacher. If rules followed consciously exert no constraint, in the physical sense, on the agent, it seems they nevertheless carry the pressure of society as a whole or, as David Pears (1971) puts it, 'the stabilizing force of social behaviour' – the consequences for refusing to follow logico-mathematical rules being punishment or exclusion. And when the student poor in maths is punished, it is not the rule itself that punishes him, but the person who is responsible for inculcating, and insuring respect for, the rule; that is, the schoolteacher, and through her, society as a coercive milieu. In respecting rules, adults pay allegiance to the authority of the teacher who has taught them these rules and, through her, to society as a whole. Wittgenstein does not always explicitly trace back this articulation of the rule (in itself inefficacious) to the social imposition that renders it efficacious. Peirce, on the other hand, rightly stressed that the law (an entity that is normative, non-causal, ontologically third, and hence distinct from the 'second') needs the 'sheriff's arm' (a causal, ontologically second, entity) to be efficacious; the law and the sheriff's arm being as categorially distinct for Peirce as rule and causal sphere are for Wittgenstein – whence, in both, the irreducibility of the normative to the factual – also categorially distinct.

This is why, for Wittgenstein, even if the rule does not act like a 'driving force' (it has an authority more than a force); that is, even if it is not a cause, it intervenes in the space of causes through the mediation of the coercive social use that is made of it. The social use of rules exerts a constraint on agents that can easily become a physical one in the case of transgression, and acts as a reminder of the classroom origins of rule inculcation, of the training of bodies through punishment that is at times corporeal, a kind of 'embodied sociality' in Bourdieu's sense. This seems to be the reason Wittgenstein always, in the end, evokes training. Whether in speaking of the 'foundation' of mathematics, which is for him a false problem; or of the justification for our following rules, training is always at the end of the chain of reasons; the ultimate reason we can offer for our regulated practices or for 'the hardness of the logical *must*' (RFM: p. 84). In fact, affirms Wittgenstein, it is not the 'must' that is hard; 'it is *we* that are inexorable' (RFM: p. 82); the rule constrains me only in so far as I decide to constrain myself to follow it. And so in the space of causes, taming and drill condition us to follow reasons; but in the space of reasons, the agent is, *vis-à-vis* the rule, in a situation of autonomy, in the Kantian sense of the term (of course Wittgenstein does not speak in these terms): she follows the rule she has freely given herself. This is not to minimize the fact that following rules *presupposes*, Wittgenstein insists, 'as a surrounding particular circumstances, particular forms of life and speech. (As there is no such thing as a facial expression without a face)' (ibid.). 'Following a rule is a particular language-game' (RFM: p. 416) which presupposes the social, with its ways and customs, as well as our form of life. What we see as the inexorability of the mathematico-logical 'must' is in fact 'the expression of an attitude towards a technique of calculation, which comes out everywhere in our life. The emphasis of the *must* corresponds only to the inexorableness of this attitude both to the technique of calculating and to a host of related techniques' (RFM: p. 430). Wittgenstein's mathematical philosophy is the best showcase for his social philosophy, and this should not seem surprising. Mathematics provides an idealized image, or a caricature, of the social; it is in the realm of mathematics that agreement in practice, unanimity in opinion, stability of techniques, and acknowledgement of the rule's sovereign authority are best visible: Wittgenstein stresses that mathematics are the realm *par excellence* where 'disputes do not break out' (PI: 240). It appears then that the criterion of a community's social bond is agreeing on what agreeing is: 'It could be said: that science would not function if we did not agree regarding the idea of agreement' (RFM: p. 197).

Rule and community

The emphasis Wittgenstein places on society as a normative milieu is reminiscent of Durkheim, the difference being in the latter's referring to a transcendence of norms, where Wittgenstein, on our view (cf. D. Pears, 1971), has an immanentist conception of norms, stressing the immanence of most norms in agents' practices. But both authors take collectivity to be the only locus of norms – an individual being unable to produce or follow norms alone, and the adhesion to norms not being the result of accumulated individual decisions (cf. E. Bourdieu, 1998b: 140–1). According to Wittgenstein, an individual can institute nothing at all, not even a ritual as simple as a festival; in *Remarks on Frazer*, he writes:

> ... such festivals are not made up by one person, so to speak, at random, but rather need an infinitely broader basis if they are to be preserved. If I wanted to make up a festival, it would die out very quickly or be modified in such a manner that it corresponds to a general inclination of the people.
>
> (GB: 149)

It should be added that Wittgenstein is not more of a contractualist than Durkheim: agents often follow rules that have never been the object of an explicit convention; it is as if, notes Wittgenstein, a social contract had been passed, though such a contract never existed. The social consensus lies, for him, more at the fundamental level of practices than at the superficial level of opinions. This makes it difficult to agree with such distinguished Wittgenstein commentators as Hacker and Baker in their denial of the existence of a normative behaviour as long as norms are yet to be discovered – that is, as long as agents are not aware of the rules they are following – for, on their view, an unconscious rule cannot have a normative function (so that, on their view, the Nambikwaras would have to have read Lévi-Strauss to have a normative behaviour worthy of the name).

In Wittgenstein's conception of the rule, some 'leeway in practices', as Bourdieu puts it, is tolerated. The rule does not rigidly determine individual acts; it only orientates them, inasmuch as the agent can always choose not to follow a rule, the way a traveller can choose not to follow a signpost (similarly, Bourdieu's *habitus* is supposed to make room for initiative and improvisation). Indeed, Wittgenstein reminds us that the rules of a game (say, tennis) do not determine everything in that game (there are no rules for how high balls can go) – it being in the nature of a game, as Bourdieu rightly understands Wittgenstein to be saying, that part of it remain vague. Moreover, he who does not grasp the point (*Witz*) of the game can follow the rules all he wants, he will not be a good player ...

But we must now say more about Wittgenstein's immanentism with respect to norms. Norms are, in an important sense, internal to practices. Rule-following, says Wittgenstein, is a matter of a community of people who agree in the natural reactions common to humankind, and in basic routines, even prior to agreeing in their opinions; so that norms emanate from practice, and presuppose an agreement in practices that is more fundamental than an agreement in ideas. Wittgenstein is a philosopher of praxis. It can even be said, with David Pears, that the corrective norm is immanent to practices. Granted, Wittgenstein does not offer an explanation as to the emergence of norms in regular practices: he does not say at what point, for an agent, mere regularity becomes a norm. But from what he does say in *On Certainty*, we can infer that, for him, there is the possibility of a passage from regularity in behaviour to norm: some regularities become stable; harden into norms, and regulate behaviour from within. There is in any case, an anchoring of the normative rule in a regularity of nature: we could not, writes Wittgenstein, implement rules if there were not already regularities in nature, such as some 'very general facts of nature' (PI: p. 230): a rule presupposes regularity in nature, a rule is chosen because things always behave in such-and-such a way. Through the choice of rules, nature 'makes herself audible' without, however, completely imposing that choice: a rule does not *only* reflect the nature of things (Z: 364). Indeed – and this is a fundamental thesis since *Philosophical Grammar* – grammar is autonomous; it is not answerable to nature or to facts – though it is undeniable for Wittgenstein that some rules can be chosen under the pressure of facts ('The rule we lay down is the one most strongly suggested by the facts of experience' (AWL: 84)), or for their practical convenience. It may even be that we have certain rules because it has proved to pay, concedes Wittgenstein (cf. OC: 170, 338), but that is not what is essential: what is essential is that the passage to a rule engenders a new order – in the Pascalian sense – which breaks with the natural order; the decision to adopt a rule (and follow it) situates us in an order different from that of natural regularities, and demands therefore an explanation of another type: the logical space where regularities are invoked is that of causal explanations; the space where rules are invoked is that of explanations by reasons – the grammar of the former being different from that of the latter. Nature and norms are intimately linked, though belonging to different orders (ibid.). Wittgenstein refuses to reduce the normative to the factual or to the natural, in the same way he refuses to reduce justification by reasons to causal explanation. To put it in Kantian terms: nature must not be confused with freedom; there is both a point of contact and a breaking-point between natural constraints and the decision to adopt a rule as a norm to which we voluntarily subject ourselves. In his 'Lecture on the Freedom of the Will', Wittgenstein opposes the idea that liberty is an illusion only inasmuch as we are ignorant of the causes that determine us; for him, there is a difference of order between freedom and causality; between our human decisions and the causes that make us act: to someone who would affirm: 'If you understood the working of his mind and understood all the circumstances as well as you understand a piece of machinery you wouldn't hold him responsible for his actions', Wittgenstein would reply: 'how do you know?' (LFW: 436); and, indeed, no one does know.

Praxis versus scepticism

Common obedience to rules completes the soldering together of a collectivity whose practices have already been made regular by the inculcation of routines anchored in our 'form of life'; that is, in an array of natural or instinctive reactions common to humanity. Obedience to norms, and more significantly, the very fact that we give ourselves rules, presuppose not only certain regularities in nature (certain 'very general facts of nature', such as objects staying put or not changing colour from one moment to the next), but also some natural characteristics of our form of life: a whole substratum of spontaneous gestures, reciprocal empathy, recognition of the other as similar to ourselves and so on. Concordance in practices is *presupposed* in language-games that consist in the following of rules. Again, even if on this point Wittgenstein seems close to thinkers who seek to anchor our norms in nature, to give a natural foundation to our rules, particularly the ethical ones, we must recall that for Wittgenstein the grammar of causes is not that of reasons, and that in passing from a consideration of nature to a consideration of norms, we enter a different logical space, that of normative explanations, having left the naturalist-causal one behind. On Wittgenstein's view, seeking to reduce the normative to the factual or to the natural will only make the normative spring back, for it is ineliminable, because internal to grammar and language – a language from which we can no more exit than we could in the *Tractatus*.

This is why Kripke's famous sceptical interpretation of following rules cannot be right, so estranged is it from the spirit in which Wittgenstein conducted his research on normativity. Having completely misread the social theory of rule-following that is Wittgenstein's, Kripke draws the erroneous conclusion that the sole guarantor of an objective correction of rule-following is to be found in the consensus manifested by the community in its application of rules (here, Kripke is close to Pascal: 'Custom is the source of our strongest and most believed proofs' (*Les Pensées*, 1671). The error in this conception is to replace the normative concept of correction, which Wittgenstein does not want to give up, with the statistical concept of the majority use of rules. But it won't do to thus replace the problem of correction with a problem of consensus. For Wittgenstein, there is a categorial difference between correction and consensus; we cannot replace 'This is correct' with 'I agree with you' (though this is Rorty's dream). The consensus that Wittgenstein speaks of is an agreement in practices, deeper than any consensus in opinions or explicit contract; and the norms of correction are, for the most part, immanent to our practices – this escaped Kripke. The constancy of our practices makes the coherence of sceptical doubt impossible. Not that Wittgenstein wants to say, as Hume is at one point tempted to do: 'my practice refutes my doubts'; like Hume, Wittgenstein rejects this solution, he shows rather that there is an incompatibility between the constancy of practices and the language-game of doubt which gives vent to sceptical doubt: the conditions of the language-game of doubt are simply not fulfilled; doubt should therefore not even emerge, and if it does emerge (at PI: 201), it is on the basis of a misunderstanding about rule-following which Wittgenstein quickly dissipates by invoking the irreducibly practical and stable ground of rule-following, as well as the social context it presupposes.

An anti-intellectualistic conception of the social

The primacy of collective practice and the holism of Wittgensteinian language-games seem incompatible with any kind of methodological individualism, as well as with any intellectual voluntarism in social philosophy. As Bouveresse notes: 'For [Wittgenstein], the idea that man can, by dint of free will and invention, as it were, create his language and way of life in a way similar to that by which he can create something within the framework of an accepted language-game and form of life, seems utterly naive and absurd' (1982: 68; DMS translation). Human beings do not select their form of life from a catalogue of anthropological possibles: a form of life is 'what has to be accepted, the given' (PI: p. 226), and the belief that we can change what is prior to all language and thought, and does not initially result from choice, is a typical intellectualistic illusion.

It is only from the inside that we can change language-games into which we are born immersed. For Wittgenstein, it is doubtful that we can change our language at will, by mere dint of a rational decision: such as, for example, replacing our (aptly named) 'natural' languages with Esperanto. The inertia of customs and institutions, the fatality of forms of life seem to him to pre-empt intellectualism as much as individualism. A tradition is not something one can decide to have, just as one cannot believe at will: not to have a tradition is, in a way, irremediable – like unrequited love:

> Tradition is not something a man can learn; not a thread he can pick up when he feels like it; any more than a man can choose his own ancestors.
>
> Someone lacking a tradition who would like to have one is like a man unhappily in love.

(CV: p. 76)

This amounts to recognizing, along with the inertia of social habitus, the relative impotence of the individual to effect change, and the futility of intellectualistic conceptions of the social. The philosopher, notes Wittgenstein, cannot change sartorial fashion with simple words. And he cruelly underlines that the philosopher's warnings always come too late: sound doctrines are useless; it is life one must change (cf. CV: p. 53), and this is hardly feasible by the individual, and rather less so if he is a philosopher.

This is unquestionably a decisive critique of intellectualism (albeit Wittgenstein does not use the word), as understood by James, Merleau-Ponty and Bourdieu. Even if, as we have seen, Wittgenstein proves to be an anti-dispositionalist in the philosophy of mind – preaching, as he does, a philosophy of mental capacities in social philosophy – it would nevertheless not be absurd to attribute to him, if not a dispositionalism *à la* Bourdieu, then an anti-intellectualistic conception of practices and social institutions which gives these maximum texture. Wittgenstein certainly does not see our social 'dispositions' through the eyes of intellectualism, as lucid representations of rules that we follow; nor can we modify them at will as, according to some intellectualistic philosophers of mind, we can 'revise our beliefs'.[7] Moreover, we do not have the language-games we do because we are convinced of their correctness: on the contrary, it is our language-games that determine our judgments of what is correct or not, and they do not therefore offer the intellect a grip for any eventual voluntarist modifications. The resistance of beliefs and customs to the interventions of will and intellect is as much emphasized by Wittgenstein as it was by James in his criticism of Pascal's wager in 'The Will to Believe' (1897) or by P. Bourdieu in *The Logic of Practice* (1990); in this respect, these authors all travel in the same direction.

As regards the revision of beliefs, there is nothing more anti-intellectualistic than Wittgenstein's aphorisms in *On Certainty* on the holistic character of our beliefs, which form a system, and of which some well-grounded ones are only revisable in theory. Indeed, we mustn't underestimate the stability of the system, nor that of 'the inherited background against which I distinguish between true and false' (OC: 94). In this respect, Wittgenstein is very close to the pragmatists, particularly to an anti-intellectualistic pragmatist like James, but also to Peirce, who sees belief as a disposition to action or as a habit, which is something fundamentally practical. According to Peirce, belief cannot be reduced to a mental state, is not necessarily conscious of itself, resists change and seems more difficult to revise than philosophers of mind seem to think, who treat beliefs as representations, pure and simple. Peirce defines belief as a disposition to act in such-and-such a way and in such-and-such circumstances; a belief-habit operating in practice and directing behaviour; in short, a principle of action that will not be easily swayed by doubt. It is because they allow a certain stability to beliefs that Peirce and Wittgenstein both produced a radical critique of doubt, notably of methodical Cartesian doubt. Both maintain that it is doubt, not belief, that must be justified: one needs reasons to doubt, for belief is first, epistemologically, psychologically and, it can be said, grammatically. We could not question all our beliefs; some are not susceptible of doubt, either because they are 'indubitables', fundamental, non-criticizable beliefs (Peirce), or because it would be much too costly in terms of the upheaval of our system of knowledge (Wittgenstein). In *On Certainty*, Wittgenstein attributes a transcendental value to some of our beliefs on which doubt, has no grip and that are like 'hinges' on which our knowledge revolves. Without going as far as Peirce, who develops a dispositional conception of belief, Wittgenstein adopts a practical view of belief in the second part of the *Philosophical Investigations*. Certainly, Peirce goes much further in the theorization of a stable belief which is, so to speak, the mind's natural state, to which it tends to return after the 'irritation' of doubt, and of an active belief, operating in practice. Both agree, at least negatively, in their anti-intellectualistic vision of belief as sufficiently resistant to change not to be mere mental states.

In sum, Wittgenstein, who developed a non-dispositional philosophy of mind and language, has also produced a philosophy of practice and of the social which brings him much closer, in certain aspects, to dispositionalists like Peirce or Bourdieu, not least because of the pragmatism they all share. It is true that, given his mechanistic vision of the disposition, Wittgenstein does not frontally oppose Peirce, who upheld a much more organic and teleological conception of the disposition. We can then discern, amongst these thinkers, pragmatist family resemblances; and Wittgenstein – pragmatist or not – has greatly contributed to the idea of social rules and regulations.

Notes

1. And indeed, there are others; for instance, Peirce's teleological dispositionalism, whose disadvantage is the heavy price it pays to ontology; Bourdieu's dispositionalism (at least in some texts), genuinely causal only in its first, continually retouched, versions of the notion of habitus, and which can rightly be recast in Peircian terms (cf. E. Bourdieu, 1998b).
2. Though Chomsky also conceives of verbal competence on a machine and calculus model.
3. So as not to confuse Emmanuel with Pierre Bourdieu, I shall henceforth refer to the former as E. Bourdieu, and continue referring to Pierre Bourdieu simply as Bourdieu.
4. Cf. VOW: 361; On this subject (cf. Bouveresse, 1988 and 1995b).
5. Cf. both variants of 'Negation' (VOW: 355–65; 365–72).
6. It should be noted that Bouveresse was first, indeed alone, in the 1970s, to critique Chomskyan 'competence' with Wittgensteinian arguments, and that Chomsky ultimately acknowledged Wittgenstein had, so to speak, refuted him by anticipation.
7. This was well shown by E. Bourdieu (1998b).

8
The Myth of the *Outer*: Wittgenstein's Redefinition of Subjectivity

Sandra Laugier

Wittgenstein – it is well known since Jacques Bouveresse's publication of *Le Mythe de l'intériorité* [*The Myth of the Inner*] (1987) – reverses the traditional relation between 'first-person certainty' and 'third-person uncertainty'. It is his treatment of the latter part of the relation, and the questioning of scepticism often associated with it, that have received most attention. Yet, as I shall argue here, Wittgenstein's work in philosophical psychology – particularly his last volume: *Last Writings on the Philosophy of Psychology: The Inner and the Outer* – invites us to shift this focus and attend to his new conception of subjectivity. Not that Wittgenstein reverts to any form of mentalism or psychologism; rather, he is here pursuing the project started in the *Tractatus* of depsychologizing psychological concepts and hence attempting to, as Stanley Cavell memorably puts it, 'undo the psychologizing of psychology'.[1]

In his last works, Wittgenstein seeks to depsychologize subjectivity not by eliminating or 'exteriorizing' it, but by redefining it. Recently, much has been done to stress the importance of subjectivity in Wittgenstein's thought, but the focus has been on so-called grammatical or first-person matters. Here, I shall be looking for that, in his late philosophy, which allows us to redefine the subject – of both language and experience – as no longer the point without extension of the *Tractatus*, or the metaphysical subject, or the subject of psychology.

1 The myth of the outer

Wittgenstein is traditionally read as wanting to deny the inner, or more precisely, to dementalize it; as rejecting the idea that there could be anything at all going on in the 'mind' or the 'soul'. He is seen as challenging the mythology of the 'inner process' – the 'mental' process that allegedly accompanies language:

> Ever and again comes the thought that what we see of a sign is only the outside of something within, in which the real operations of sense and meaning go on.
>
> (Z: 140)

If this idea comes 'ever and again', it is because – like all ideas whose obsessive presence is noted by Wittgenstein – it has its reasons: we 'are inclined to say' that there must be an inner process accompanying speaking because, as Bouveresse remarks, 'we need such a process if the spoken sentence is to be more than a lifeless string of signs' (1987: 60, DMS translation). Indeed, what could *give life* to language if not a deeply seated process? Wittgenstein relentlessly exposes the many problems stemming from the notion of an inner process – what has been called the myth of the inner. But to read this as straightforward criticism or wholesale rejection of the inner and the mental – as is often done in behaviourist interpretations, and today still, in dominant analytic philosophy gone 'mentalist' – is to lose sight of the radicalness of Wittgenstein's thought, which leads him, not to deny the existence of an 'inner', but to rethink inner–outer dualism. When he writes: 'The distinction between "inner" and "outer" does not interest us' (PG: 100), Wittgenstein is not denying the importance of reflecting on the inner and the outer, but what he is interested in is the way inner and outer are, grammatically speaking, *articulated*; that is, the way we speak of an inner only if there is an outer, and vice versa. This, as we shall see, does away with the notion of an inner as something hidden, an inner with no outer, a *private* inner; as also with the notion (which could be attributed to him) of an inner 'on its own'. A passage from the *Remarks on the Philosophy of Psychology* is pertinent here:

> But if we dispose of the inner process in this way, – is the outer one now all that is left? – the language-game of description of the outer process is *not* all that is left: no, there is also the one whose starting point is the expression.
>
> (RPP I: 659)

When Wittgenstein examines the grammar of expressions bearing on the inner and the outer, he is looking to challenge a kind of exaltation we have about the inner life being *private*. This does not amount to his rejecting the idea of an inner life. We know – this is the theme of his discussions on 'private language' – that Wittgenstein contests the idea that we have privileged access to our sensations, and he suggests that we know our own pain no better, perhaps less well, than we know someone else's. But there is something misleading in these familiar, paradoxical affirmations; for, as Cavell recognized, the stake here is not so much evidence of one's access to someone else, as the difficulty (anxiety, even) of accessing one's own inner life. This emerges in the last writings:

> I *can* not observe myself as I do someone else, cannot ask myself 'What is this person likely to do now?' etc.
>
> (LW II: 10)

but was already present in the *Investigations:*

> My own relation to my words is wholly different from other people's. ...
> If I listened to the words of my mouth, I might say that someone else was speaking out of my mouth.
>
> (PI: p. 192)

Wittgenstein, in affirming the other's accessibility – though in an extremely complex way – is led to produce a theory of *inaccessibility*, or at least self-ignorance, which Cavell takes to be the central theme of the *Investigations*; and, in the same breath, to question 'The apparent certainty of the first person, the uncertainty of the third' (LW I: 951). The separation of both questions would in any case only be an artificial one: the question of my own inaccessibility to what is going on in me being also (even if not exactly *the same* as) that of the other's accessibility to himself, as is shown by the following passage:

> The opposite of my uncertainty as to what is going on inside him is not *his* uncertainty. For I *can* be sure of someone else's feelings, but that doesn't make them mine.
>
> (LW I: 963).

It seems as if, towards the end, and after moments (undoubtedly, closer to behaviourism) of radical criticism of the 'self' (BB), Wittgenstein returns to the original question of the *Tractatus* (the self, mysterious), and asks again, though in a new way, the question of the nature of self:

> Thus there really is a sense in which philosophy can talk about the self in a non-psychological way.
> What brings the self into philosophy is the fact that 'the world is my world.'
>
> (TLP: 5.641)

Wittgenstein continues in his attempt to define the non-psychological self, but the question of solipsism disappears; the threat of solipsism gives way (Wittgenstein realizes this later) to that which it masked: the anxiety of the relation to self. Here again, it is tempting to follow Cavell's analysis: the alleged unknowability of the other masks the refusal, or anguish, to know oneself, or rather to *feel* oneself:

> It is as though Wittgenstein felt human beings in jeopardy of losing touch with their inner lives altogether, with the very idea that each person is a center of one, that each *has* a life.
>
> (1979: 91)

What Wittgenstein often says about the confusion inherent in the idea that we have no access to the other and her thoughts has in fact to do with this core anxiety, that of our access to our own sensations and thoughts. Opting for this perspective lets us gauge the full extent of the problematic nature of behaviourist interpretations of Wittgenstein, problematic precisely with respect to the relation to self. Not that someone's examination of their own external reactions is unthinkable, but there is something strange about it, as if it is here precisely that the threat of denial of the inner looms large (sensation of inner 'void'): 'I hear the words coming out of my mouth'.

In the *Investigations*, Wittgenstein repeatedly states that he is not denying the existence of inner processes; for example:

> What gives the impression that we want to deny anything?
>
> (PI: 305)

> Why should I deny that there is a mental process [in remembering]? ...
> To deny the mental process would mean to deny the remembering; to deny that anyone ever remembers anything.
>
> (PI: 306)

Why then, despite such straight-forward affirmations, is Wittgenstein often understood as wanting to reject the inner? A typical remark is the following, familiar one which appears to call for a behaviourist interpretation, and negate the existence of the inner:

> An 'inner process' stands in need of outward criteria.
>
> (PI: 580)

But it can be interpreted differently; witness Cavell:

> The technique in this instance is, roughly, this: The background of the statement, to which it is a response, is that people (philosophers) are led to say that remembering or thinking or meaning, etc. are inner processes, as though that explains something. The message is that until you produce criteria on the basis of which, in a particular case, or count something as an 'inner process', you have said nothing ....
>
> (1979: 96)

The problem is that once the presence of an inner process is made dependent on criteria, nothing is solved; for criteria are outer, not inner. This is a fact of crucial importance for Wittgenstein, but it does not entail that we have no access to the inner. As Cavell then notes:

> But the immediate context of the statement seems to convey this message: Once you produce the criteria, you will see that they are merely outward, and so the very thing they are supposed to show, if you get the criteria correctly in line, is threatened ....
>
> (1979: 96)

That criteria are outer only means that the outer is outside. Remember that Wittgenstein puts the expression 'inner process' in scare quotes. This should move us to be circumspect, and tell ourselves that he does not mean anything as crude as: you can know that something is going on inside you without me knowing it, so that for me to know it you would have to send me signals informing me of it. That is too obvious and uninteresting. On Cavell's view, the question Wittgenstein is really asking himself is the following: when you have sent me your signals so that I am informed of your inner world, do I really *know* that world, or do those signals come from a source which will, to me, always remain unverifiable and private, so that they are the sign of something I can never know? Wittgenstein's answer is not as simple as is generally believed, and it does not consist in negating all inner reality to the benefit of the outer. That the expression 'inner process' is in scare quotes means that what is required are (outward) criteria to *say* that something is (what we call) an inner process. This obviously does not deny the existence of the inner; criteria being, almost by definition, (outward) criteria for the *inner*.

The best way to understand this is through a closer examination of the structure of inner/outer, whose presence is constant in Wittgenstein. It is visible particularly in the original; for in English, *'innere'* and *'seelisch'* are usually translated indiscriminately by 'mental', which is inadequate in both cases. One can get the impression that Wittgenstein is saying that inner and outer belong to two different language games:

> The concept of the 'inner picture' is misleading, for this concept uses the *'outer* picture' as a model; and yet the uses of the words for these concepts are no more like one another than .... .

> (PI: p. 196)

But no: we have here to do only with a critique of the notion of inner *picture,* and what Wittgenstein wants to say regarding duality is much more complex and interesting. 'Inner' means nothing – even if only in terms of spatial localization – independently of 'outer'. First, because of what we saw of the grammatical structure of inner/outer; but it is not only a matter of grammar or rules, we have here to do with a dualism that seeps through all the uses of language, and has therefore a *logical* structure:

> The inner is tied up with the outer not only empirically, but also logically.

> (LW II: 63)

That the duality is a *logical* one means that for Wittgenstein the inner can only be thought (or spoken of) in relation to an outer; that we have here to do with a *structure*; that there is no inner without an outer, and vice versa:

> 'In that case something quite different must be going on in him, something that we are not acquainted with.' – *This shews us* what we go by in determining whether something that takes place 'in another' is different from, or the same, as in ourselves. This shews us *what we go by* in judging inner processes.

> (Z: 340)

We judge the inner by means of the outer; this is a rule, not an empirical fact. It tells us nothing about the empirical relationship between inner and outer:

> There is indeed the case where someone later reveals his inmost heart (*sein Innerstes*) to me by a confession: but that this is so cannot offer me any explanation of outer and inner, for I have to give credence to the confession.
> For confession is of course something exterior.
>
> (Z: 558)

The only access to the inner is outer. Wittgenstein reverses the question of criteria, which leads to scepticism, and suggests a paradox: it comes to the same thing to say something goes on in me and something outside, not because of any (mythical) appropriateness or correspondence between inner and outer, but because that is precisely what we *mean* by *outer* (and *inner*):

> The paradox is this: the *supposition* (*Annahme*) may be expressed as follows: 'Suppose *this* went on inside me and *that* outside' – but the *assertion* (*Behauptung*) that *this* is going on *inside* me asserts: this is going on outside me. As *suppositions* the two propositions about the inside and the outside are quite independent, but not as assertions.
>
> (RPP I: 490)

It is mostly in *Last Writings II* that Wittgenstein develops, in an extremely problematic way, the interdependence of inner and outer:

> 'I see the outer and imagine an inner that fits it.'
> When mien, gesture and circumstances are unambiguous (*eindeutig*), then the inner seems to be an outer; it is only when we cannot read the outer that the inner seems to be hidden behind it.
> There are inner and outer concepts, inner and outer ways of looking at a man. ...
> The inner is tied up with the outer not only empirically, but also logically.
> The inner is tied up with the outer logically, and not just empirically.
>
> (LW II: 63–4)

This passage clearly shows Wittgenstein's deep perplexity, at a time when he is also writing *On Certainty*, about the very nature of this inner/outer relation if it can no longer be conceived, as it was in the *Tractatus*, in terms of *limits*. Here, the question is no longer about the limit between subject and world, or between outer and inner, but about the very nature of a *subject*, which is no longer *between*, but *both* inner and outer. We have now to define this new version – linguistic, not transcendental – of subjectivity.

As noted, Wittgenstein tirelessly repeats that he is not negating the existence of inner processes in the ordinary sense of the term. It is the idea of 'inner processes' (with scare quotes, that of philosophers) that creates the need for outward criteria, and thereby generates the massive problem of scepticism, not only about *other minds*, but – more irksome – *our own* mind. Wittgenstein is not denying the private, but rather the idea (from which philosophy has created the myth of the private) that when we speak of 'our' sensations, thoughts, representations, we are speaking of private and inaccessible *objects*. A classic mistake is to read Wittgenstein as rejecting the idea of an inner when all he is doing is rejecting the idea of conceiving the inner as an object, a private object: the inaccessible 'mental process'. More sensitive interpreters of Wittgenstein, following Cavell (McDowell, Diamond) have therefore found it necessary to reformulate the problem of the 'so-called' private language argument, making sure to eliminate the notion of private object, and to stress that Wittgenstein does not deny the existence of sensations. See, for instance, Diamond's formulation:

> A central insight in the *Investigations* is that, if we take our capacity to talk about and think about our own sensations as a matter of our having, each of us, a private object, then the object thus understood plays no role in our actual language games. Wittgenstein's conclusion is not that there are no sensations, but that our words for sensations do not have their meaning by connecting up with private objects.
>
> (2000: 275)

If there is no private object, what then is the nature of the private? The question is no longer the inappropriate one, of behaviourism, but the following: why should we say of a psychological state or process (thought, pain, expectation, to take familiar Wittgenstein themes) that it is 'inner'? Have we any criteria which allow us to say that a phenomenon is *inner*, and does calling it thus mean anything? Philosophy has the tendency to consider as obvious, as *given*, the difference between inner and outer. But when we think about it, there is nothing obvious about this.

Here, we should note that (as any rapid survey of the occurrences of dualism in the Wittgensteinian corpus will show) most mentions of inner/outer are to be found in the first writings: the *Notebooks* and the *Tractatus*. The logico-transcendental thought of the first Wittgenstein is hinged on the notion of *limits*; this notion being, in an obviously Kantian way, situated between an inner (of language, of the proposition) and an outer. The remainder of Wittgenstein's corpus, after the *Blue Book* transition, goes back to the question, and ponders the nature of the inner. But here again, we would be wrong to think that the *Tractatus* had simply rejected the self or subject. As Hans Sluga, little inclined to Cavellian excess, shows in 'Wittgenstein and the Self', from the *Notebooks* on, Wittgenstein is preoccupied with the self in a way that is clearly linked to the question of the limits of language (cf. also: 'The I, the I is what is deeply mysterious!' (NB: 80)):

> *The limits of my language* mean the limits of my world.
>   There really is only one world soul, which I for preference call *my soul* and as which alone I conceive what I call the souls of others.
>
> (NB: 49)

What emerges in the second and the third Wittgenstein, is a re-examination of the nature of the inner, of the mythology that induces scepticism, as well as of the specificity of the relation to the inner (or to the self) that makes this mythology possible. It is not only a matter of saying that philosophy, in objectifying sensation, withdraws from the language-game that makes it possible for us to speak of sensation. The question, here, is not only a 'grammatical' one. Though it still remains to say exactly what we mean when we speak of ourselves (of the self), and thus to formulate the question of the subject in a new way. The inner is no longer defined as one side of the limit, or as a point without extension. Wittgenstein will ponder the nature of, to use McDowell's term, the inner *given*. Rather than criticize the idea of an inner, he will re-examine our uses and ask himself if, by *inner*, we mean *hidden*. See, for instance, the following remark:

> 'What is *internal* is hidden from us.' – The future is hidden from us.
>
> (PI: p. 223; cf. also LW II: 22)

In what way do we think of the inner as hidden? In *Philosophical Grammar* (p. 104) and in the *Investigations*, Wittgenstein radically opposes the idea that there is in a sentence something hidden that philosophy or analysis has to uncover ('For there isn't anything hidden – don't we see the whole sentence?' (PI: 559):

> For what is hidden, for example, is of no interest to us.
>
> (PI: 126)

This, however, is meant only as a criticism of such philosophical uses or preconceptions that have nothing to do with our ordinary uses, or that detract from them. Wittgenstein is not targeting our ordinary use of the inner which, rather, he seeks to describe. One of our first uses of 'inner' is precisely its association with our inner states, and it can well be asked if the idea of the *hidden* best defines our ordinary use of 'inner'. Wittgenstein makes this important remark in *Philosophical Investigations*:

> That what someone else says to himself is hidden from me is part of the *concept* 'saying inwardly'. Only 'hidden' is the wrong word here ....
> (PI: pp. 220–1)

Hidden is *wrong,* simply because the inner has nothing hidden about it. Cavell asks:

> But why do we think of a state (of mind, say) as *inner*? Why do we think of the meaning of a (some particular) poem as inner? (And mightn't we think of some states of a physical object as inner? Perhaps not its hardness; but its magnetic power? or its radioactivity?) What pertains to the soul is thought of as inner. But why? 'Inner' means, in part, something like inaccessible, hidden (like a room). But it also means *pervasive,* like atmosphere, or the action of the heart. What I have in mind is carried in phrases like 'inner beauty', 'inner conviction', 'inner strength', 'inner calm'. This suggests that the more deeply a characteristic pervades a soul, the more obvious it is. (Cf. envy as a sharp feeling and a state of the soul.)
> (1979: 99)

This ordinary notion of 'inner' refers therefore to both the inaccessible and the manifest. This might well summarize the problem of scepticism. I do not have access to the inner (thought, mind) except via the outer (outward criteria, gestures, speech). But here the question finds a new expression:

> Whatever the criteria tell us by way of identifying the other's state (or process, etc.), they are still *outward*. – Outward as opposed to what? What would an inward criterion be? – Not opposed to an inward *criterion*, maybe; but as opposed to *something* inward. – Name something.
> (Cavell, 1979: 99)

If we examine the external criterion, it will only be that: external. And so it is useless to ask of the external – the criteria – that it give more than it has, or than it is. In other words, the criterion is, by its very nature, disappointing (this is the main thesis of the first part of *The Claim of Reason*), but it is so only inasmuch as we started off with an erroneous interpretation of what the inner is, and what, the outer:

> Silent 'internal' speech is not a half hidden phenomenon which is as it were seen through a veil. It is not hidden *at all*, but the concept may easily confuse us, for it runs over a long stretch cheek by jowl with the concept of an 'outward' process, and yet does not coincide with it.
>
> (PI: p. 220)

What must be done, therefore, is prevent an inadequate overlapping of the uses of both terms, but also, and most importantly, show the impossibility of separating them artificially, of thinking one can function without the other. For such a separation would result in a caricature of both behaviourism (the outer without the inner), and mentalism (the reverse). Wittgenstein's more significant suggestion is that only the outer gives us access to the inner. See Cavell:

> I feel: That 'something or other' is in there is what 'outward' *says*. In itself the word deprives the notion of a criterion of none of its power; and adds none to it. But a false idea of the inward produces a false idea of the outward.
>
> (1979: 99–100)

And so, in the first part of *The Claim of Reason*, Cavell dismantles standard interpretations of Wittgenstein by showing, contra behaviourist and mentalist readings, that nowhere does he uphold the idea of a pure outer: on the contrary, with the indictment of a mythology of the inner, it is the outer that becomes problematic. If criteria cannot refute scepticism, it is because the inner has been displaced. The *Investigations* in various ways explores the idea of a *confinement to the outside* (a confinement not only from the other, but from oneself). The sceptical problem is transformed: no longer a scepticism about *other minds*, or about knowledge of others, but about *access* to others, for which the obstacle is not otherness or privacy, but the impossibility for oneself to access one's self:

> If I take the space I am in to be outer, I have to imagine for the other an inner space which I could not possibly enter. Which *nobody* could possibly enter; for *he* didn't *enter* it.
>
> (Cavell, 1979: 100)

This may sound paradoxical, and yet it is this very idea that seems to pervade the writings on psychology. For Wittgenstein, false conceptions of inner and outer mutually engender and comfort each other. He endeavours, to the end, to correct these conceptions. Cavell notes that 'the correct relation between inner and outer, between the soul and its society, is the theme of the *Investigations* as a whole' (1979: 329). This *corrective* labour gives birth to a new conception of subjectivity, which we shall now attempt to unravel. If the subject is neither within, nor a mere limit, where is it?

2   The subject: expression and inner voice

As we have seen, Wittgenstein throughout his philosophizing remains obsessed with the idea of the self. This is the upshot of the *rapprochement* made by Sluga between the *Notebooks* (NB: 49, quoted above) and the final remarks of *Last Writings*, written a few weeks before Wittgenstein's death:

> (But it is still false to say: Knowing is a different mental state (*Seelenzustand*) from being certain. (I is a different person from L.W.))
>
> (LW II: 88)

Here, Wittgenstein returns to his analysis (in BB) of the difference between the uses of 'I' and 'L.W.', and puts it in a new perspective: as if it were now no longer a question of language-game; as if, more radically, it turned out that the 'I' is indeed 'L.W.'. This moment can be compared to another in the *Investigations*:

> 'I' is not the name of a person, nor 'here' of a place, and 'this' is not a name. But they are connected with names.
>
> (PI: 410)

What, from the *Notebooks* to the *Last Writings*, obsesses Wittgenstein, is precisely this mixture of tautology and difference in use: the idea, both trivial and problematic, that the relation I have to myself is, in some way, not the same as the one I have to others. Here, we see emerging the limits of behaviourism, and of the critique of the myth of the inner. I do not have the same relation to myself as I do to others:

> My own relation to my words is wholly different from other people's.
> I do not listen to them and thereby learn something about myself.
> They have a completely different relation to my actions than to the

actions of others. If I listened to the words of my mouth, I would be able to say that someone else was speaking out of my mouth.

(LW II: 9)

My words and my actions interest me in a completely different way than they do someone else. (My intonation also, for instance.) I do not relate to them as an observer. ...
My words are parallel to *my* actions, his to his.
A different co-ordination.

(LW II: 10)

This is precisely the point at which emerges the peculiar status of subjectivity, defined by the specific interest we have in what we ourselves say or do: the 'coordination', says Wittgenstein, that is 'different' depending on whether it concerns the self and its own words and actions, or the self and the words and actions of others. Here again, it seems that an essential concept of the *Notebooks* and the *Tractatus* is reworked from a different perspective:

But is *language*: the *only* language?
Why should there not be a mode of expression through which I can talk *about* language in such a way that it can appear to me in co-ordination with something else?

(NB: 52; 29 May 1915)

The question – which is the main point of the *Tractatus* – of a coordination between language (what I say) and the world; a coordination which *shows itself* (it can neither be said nor expressed) in language, comes back in the form of a question on the possibility of coordinating the 'I' with what I say or do. As if the question of the subject of language – that, in the *Tractatus*, of a language I alone understand or speak, *die einzige Sprache* (cf. PI: 243) – is no longer exactly the (solipsistic and transcendental) question of the world as *my* world:

Thus there really is a sense in which philosophy can talk about the self in a non-psychological way.
What brings the self into philosophy is the fact that 'the world is my world'.
The philosophical self is not the human being, nor the human body, or the human soul, with which psychology deals, but rather the metaphysical subject, the limit of the world – not a part of it.

(TLP: 5.641)

Wittgenstein's writings on philosophical psychology can be understood as a problematic reworking of this quest for a non-psychological self; not in that he abandoned the idea of the non-psychological nature of the self, but in that he abandoned the idea of the subject as limit, the idea of its non-reality, as it were.

The writings on philosophical psychology seem to be a (sometimes descriptive) elaboration of Wittgenstein's answer to the question of the reality of the subject. The subject was faded out in the *Tractatus* because *language* relates 'the world as I found it' (this is where the subject comes in, says Wittgenstein).

What is, then, this special relationship that Wittgenstein tries to describe between the self and what it says or does? We can begin by saying that it is a linguistic relationship: the subject is a subject of language; here in a trivial and tautological, but also paradoxical way. The subject makes use of a common language, and this use is her own. There is no question here of behaviourism or anti-mentalism: in a way, of course, it goes without saying that 'what goes on' in the mind as the subject is speaking is of no interest to us: everything is in what is said. The problem, as Wittgenstein seems to point out, is that the subjective is also in what is said:

> If someone looking at the model of a cube were to express himself this way: 'Now I see a cube in *this* position – now one in *this*' – he could mean two very different things. Something subjective; or something objective. His words alone do not reveal which.

> (LWI: 447)

Inasmuch, as we saw earlier, as the idea of a purely exterior language (string of words) as well as that of a private language, no longer make sense, we are left with a language that is no longer *private* (for everyone understands it) but *subjective*, albeit in a specific way.

Wittgenstein, as we know, insists on the *public* character of language; and this is of great importance. But another equally important dimension of his work that should not be neglected consists in showing that the publicity of language (its outwardness) is not opposed to its, so to speak, 'intimacy' (a better term is needed here). A language without inwardness would *appear* (outwardly) strange:

> So an uncertainty about the outer corresponds to an uncertainty concerning the inner. ...
> And that does *not* mean that in general the uncertainty about something mental can be expressed as uncertainty about the outer.

> (LW II: 68)

This has nothing to do with behaviourism but, here again, with the structure of the inner/outer. When we do not know what is going on in someone else, our uncertainty, says Wittgenstein, does *not* refer to something going on in the inner (ibid.). The hesitation concerns the *expression* (*Ausdruck*) itself:

> ... the mental finds its expression in the bodily (*im Körperlichen*).
>
> (LW II: 68)

The outer, the *body* is what *gives expression* to the inner. We can see that this conception of expression radicalizes the structure of the inner/outer.

These remarks on expression from *Last Writings* must be correlated with those, written simultaneously, from *On Certainty*. The other's relation to what I am feeling is not an epistemic one – this is the crucial point of *Last Writings II* and the main point of Cavell's interpretation in *The Claim of Reason* – and my relationship to myself is not epistemic either. This is the upshot of Wittgenstein's numerous observations on the status of 'I know' and of certainty. 'I know' is not a description of a state, but an outer expression for which I can neither determine nor feel an inner correlate:

> But don't I use the words 'I know that ...' to say that I am in a certain state ...?
> 'I know' has meaning only when it is uttered by a person.
>
> (OC: 588)

> For how does a man learn to recognize his own state of knowing something?
>
> (OC: 589)

On Certainty therefore seems to explore an aspect of the question of subjectivity (as shown, for example, in the numerous occurrences of the opposition objective/subjective in the work: cf. OC: 179, 194): the incompatibility of certainty (attached to propositions that we cannot doubt) with an inner state. It is noteworthy that the same example as that, quoted above, of *Last Writings*, 'I am called L.W.', recurs obsessively in *On Certainty* (e.g., OC: 470, 515), as an instance of an utterance that cannot be put in question – contrasting the certainty of that ordinary utterance with the indeterminacy and confusion typical of the inner state:

> The 'inner' is a delusion. That is: the whole complex of ideas alluded to by this word is like a painted curtain drawn in front of the scene of the actual word use.
>
> (LW II: 84)

The other aspect of the question of subjectivity is what the writings on psychology are concerned with: the difficulty and confusion in accessing the inner, due not to anything being private, but to the definition of *expression*. Wittgenstein does not deny that when I am in pain, it is *me* who expresses this pain, or who fails to. Nor would he deny that if I do not express my pain, others will know nothing of it. This leads us to think of this situation as one in which I am the only one who knows I am in pain. But – and this is where *On Certainty* and *Last Writings* merge – Wittgenstein denies that we can properly speak of my *knowing* it. We can also relate this to some remarks on the relation to self in *Last Writings II*:

> I do not listen to them and thereby learn something about myself.
>
> (LW II: 9)

> My words and my actions interest me in a completely different way than they do someone else. (My intonation also, for instance.) I do not relate to them as an observer.
>
> (LW II: 10)

It seems then that Wittgenstein does not so much seek to question the private character of the soul as the idea that the private is a matter of knowledge, and therefore of *secrecy*. Recall his criticism of a conception of the self as something hidden *inside*, as if meaning were mythologically hidden in the sentence: there is nothing other than what you see (don't you see the whole sentence?). But just as the sentence *means*, with nothing hidden; is not a string of dead signs; the outer *expresses* without anything being hidden. Recall the passage in which one might listen to the words of one's mouth (LW II: 9; PI: p. 192). That one means what one says; that one has a particular attitude or behaviour towards one's own words (ibid.), is not due to something being hidden. My relation to myself is not one of knowledge, and interpreting it thus leads directly to scepticism. It is not even, as Wittgenstein's vocabulary indicates, a *relation* (this would be highly obscure, if not nonsensical): more an attitude – *Einstellung* , or (in an ordinary, non-technical sense), a disposition.

This notion of attitude, that now supplants the concept of knowledge, emerges in well-known passages of the *Investigations* that can also be misleading:

> My attitude towards him is an attitude towards a soul. I am not of the *opinion* that he has a soul.
>
> (PI: p. 178)

And the following, less familiar, passage:

> Our attitude to what is alive and to what is dead, is not the same. All
> our reactions are different.
>
> (PI: 284)

Here again, it would be misleading to see in Wittgenstein's remarks a
trace of behaviourism: if our reactions are different, it is because we are
dealing with a specific *given* (that of 'forms of life'), not because there is
something hidden, or something that must be in some way *supposed*
(Wittgenstein clearly sets himself against empiricist, Russellian and other
solutions to the problem of other minds). As he reminds us, the inner is
not merely *probable*:

> I do not say that evidence makes the inner *merely* probable. For as far
> as I'm concerned nothing is lacking in the language-game.
>
> (LW II: 40–1).

The notion of the probable (connected with knowing), is inadequate:
nothing is missing; all that is needed can be found in the language-
game. From this point of view, it can be imagined that Wittgenstein does
not so much reject the idea of the private or the inner as that of secrecy.
As Cavell notes: 'his teaching on this point [is] rather that what is accurate
in the philosophical or metaphysical idea of privacy is not captured, or
is made unrecognizable, by the idea of secrecy' (1979: 330). What is private
is not inaccessible: my private life (or a private conversation, or a private
joke) is perfectly accessible to those who I want to give access to it. Let us
now quote the passage in full:

> That what someone else says to himself is hidden from me is part of the
> *concept* 'saying inwardly'. Only 'hidden' is the wrong word here; for if
> it is hidden from me, it ought to be apparent to him, *he* would have
> to *know* it. But he does not 'know' it ... .
>
> (PI: pp. 220-1; cf. LW I: 880).

If he does not know it, it is not because he is not certain of it or because
a doubt subsists, but because here there is no question of knowing at all.
Scepticism would then be less a cognitive problem (the possibility of
knowing the world, or others, or of having access to someone else's inner
self) than a symptom: that of the rejection of expression. The question
of the knowledge of other minds acts like a mirror, or a mask, of my own

accessibility (to the other, to myself). There is no secret, 'nothing is hidden'. Not because everything is outer, but because the only secrets are those we do not want to hear, and the only privacy that which we do not *want* to know, or refuse to give access, or expression (*Aüsserung, Ausdruck*) to.

We conceive of language as the (outer) expression of an (inner) state or thought, and therefore of private language as language that is somehow doomed to remain inside, not exteriorizable. This is what leads philosophers like McDowell, in 'One Strand in the Private Language Argument', to read the Wittgensteinian critique of the private as the first critique of the Myth of the Given (the idea of a pure, inarticulate given to which language would then be applied). Such a critique is indeed a strong component of Wittgenstein's philosophy of psychology, which formally rejects the opposition between an immediate given and its mediatized exteriorization:

> Why shouldn't one say: 'The evidence for the mental in someone else is the outer'?
>
> Well, there is no such thing as outer mediated and inner unmediated evidence for the inner (*Evidenz des Innern*).
>
> (LW II: 67)

But it could just as well be said, following Cavell, that Wittgenstein radically topples the discussion on private language. The problem is not our inability to express or externalize what we have 'inside', to think or feel something without being able to say it (a problem evoked by Wittgenstein in the *Tractatus*: there is the inexpressible, but it cannot be said, thought or even felt); the problem is the reverse: to not *want to say what I am saying*. Here, we might be uncovering one of the sources of the notion of a private language: not a difficulty to know (Wittgenstein insists it is not a question of knowing), but a refusal – perhaps a fear – to want to say, to have access to, or to *expose oneself* to the outside. This would explain the seduction of the idea of secrecy: we would rather believe that our private self is secret than recognize the true nature of that private self, which is that it is entangled in a structure of *expression*. Such is the nature of the outer/inner relation:

> That an actor can represent grief shows the uncertainty of evidence, but that he can represent *grief* also shows the reality of evidence.
>
> (LW II: 67)

This remarkable passage is a quasi-definitive answer to the whole discussion on pretence which runs through the last writings. Cases of pretence or make-believe are put forward to show the inadequacy of outer to inner; whereas, for Wittgenstein, the possibility of pretence shows precisely the *adequacy* – the fact that the outer does indeed express the inner. We can only *simulate* ordinary behaviour; and to simulate means to imitate the inner, in a way just as much as the outer (cf. Z: 340; and RPP I: 607: 'This shews us *what we go by* in judging inner processes'). As Wittgenstein points out:

> Genuineness and falseness are not the only essential characteristics of an expression of feeling.
>
> (LW II: 90)

Again, it is the very possibility of expression (linguistic or other), and even of make-believe, that defines subjectivity. In the *Investigations*, particularly in the remarks on private language, this possibility is envisaged in terms of scepticism, not only with respect to accessing other minds but to accessing oneself. A worry which appears at the various moments in which Wittgenstein is imagining the impossibility, or loss, of speech: is it me speaking with my mouth (or someone else, perhaps many others)?

> What about my own case: how do I myself recognize my own disposition? – Here it will have been necessary for me to take notice of myself as others do, to listen to myself talking, to be able to draw conclusions from what I say!
>
> (PI: p. 192)

Here, the myth of the private gives way to, or perhaps, as Cavell has it, *becomes*, a myth of *inexpressiveness*. The idea of *inexpressiveness* – present in the remarks (PI: 260–1, 270) in which someone is imagined inscribing the sign 'S' for their sensation – turns out to be the very anxiety of expression, the anxiety of the *naturalness* of the passage from inner to outer:

> What reason have we for calling 'S' the sign for a *sensation*? ... – So in the end when one is doing philosophy one gets to the point where one would like just to emit an inarticulate sound.
>
> (PI: 261)

Here, Wittgenstein entertains the temptation (or mythology) not of silence, but of inexpressiveness. As if the passage *outward* were precisely a loss of control of what I *mean to say*, and therefore, as if, ultimately, an inexpressive 'inarticulate sound' were sometimes preferable to a meaning-ful expression:

> So the fantasy of a private language, underlying the wish to deny the publicness of language, turns out, so far, to be a fantasy, or fear, ... of inexpressiveness [of the kind] in which what I express is beyond my control.
>
> (Cavell, 1979: 351)

To accept expression is to accept the reality of the (corporeal) outward-ness of meaning something: 'The human body is the best picture of the human soul' (PI: p. 178); not so much in that it represents the soul (what would that mean?), or possesses it, but in that it gives it expression. This, along with the inner/outer relation thus redefined, is part of our form of life (it is that which is the given), that which must be 'accepted'. To recog-nize this relationship between the inner and the outer,

> ... is equally to acknowledge that your expressions in fact express you, that they are yours, that you are in them. This means allowing yourself to be comprehended, something you can always deny. Not to deny it is, I would like to say, to acknowledge your body, and the body of your expressions, to be yours ... .
>
> (Cavell, 1979: 383)

Such a recognition would be the acceptance of the expression (*Ausdruck*) as identically inner (it expresses me) *and* outer (it exposes me). It is in this final identity, which results from the reworking and radicalization of the grammatical structure of the inner/outer, that the very nature of subject-ivity as reinvented by Wittgenstein is revealed: of course, the subject is a subject of language – Wittgenstein shows it in all possible ways in the *Investigations* – but in the sense in which it is a subject of/subject to expression, both inner and outer. Wittgenstein's remarks on the philoso-phy of psychology, as a whole, give voice to this problematic subject.

Indeed, the subject of language appears (Wittgenstein's style is partly responsible for this) in the form of a *voice*, not of an inwardness. For, is an *inner voice* inside? This is a question raised by many of Wittgenstein's analyses:

> You know that you are lying; if you are lying, you know it. An inner voice, a feeling, tells me? ...
> Does a voice always tell me? And when does it speak? The whole time?
>
> (RPP I: 779).

If there is an inner voice (or inner voices), there will also be an 'inner ear' (cf. also CV: 12):

> You would say that the tune was there, if, say, someone sang it through, or heard it mentally from beginning to end.
>
> (PI: 184)

Of course, it can be objected that the idea of an inner voice is, in its mythological form, also the object of criticism. But Wittgenstein rejects the private only as metaphor; not as the real presence of a 'speaking' voice, a voice which, in a way, is both inner and outer (PI: 232, 233). This inner voice, and the idea of hearkening to it, the idea of an ear attuned to it, also comes up in the *Remarks on the Foundations of Mathematics*:

> Let us imagine a line intimating to me how I am to follow it; that is, as my eye travels along the line a voice within me says: '*This* way!' ...
> It would also be possible to imagine such instruction in a sort of calculating. The children can calculate, each in his own way – as long as they listen to their inner voice and obey it. Calculating in this way would be something like composing.
>
> (RFM: 417–18)

To conclude, it might be supposed that, for Wittgenstein, the subject exists exactly as this voice: in and through language. And what defines this voice is precisely that it is both, identically, inner (I say it) and outer (I hear it). It can be, as Wittgenstein often affirms, the common voice of our agreement (*Übereinstimmung*, PI: 241), of our agreement *in* the language; but it is my voice, or one of my voices, in the trivial (factual) sense that my body is my own. I have towards it 'a different relation' (cf. PI: p. 192).

That it be inseparably inner and outer means that this is not a voice that assures me of my identity, or of my thought, or of anything (inasmuch as it is a voice, it is an expression and escapes me). In other words, there is no *me* to which it speaks. In this light, and in opposition to current preconceptions of Wittgenstein's 'anti-Cartesianism' (or externalism), his presentation of the subject, paradoxically, resembles that of Descartes in its linguistic experience of the *cogito*.[2] To wit, this curious passage where Wittgenstein seems to distinguish speaking *with* oneself from speaking *to* oneself:

> 'Thinking' and 'inward speech' – I do not say '*to* oneself' – are different concepts.
>
> (PI: p. 211; and LW I: 509, LW II: 18)

The subject, thus defined by *voice*, is not a limit or a point, a centre or an interlocutor – to mention a few standard representations – but, suggests Wittgenstein, a 'gappy' space:

> One language-game analogous to a fragment of another. One space projected into a limited extent of another. A 'gappy' space. (For 'inner and outer'.)
>
> (Z: 648)

Thus are Wittgenstein's obscure and confusing texts on the philosophy of psychology an attempt to reply to the question of the *Tractatus*, to the possibility of a non-psychological self: a self defined as a subjectivity without mentality, the subjectivity of the ordinary voice, which is stifled by the conventional definitions of psychology and philosophy, and which Wittgenstein, at times, wants us to hear. As in this bracketed remark:

> (As one can sometimes reproduce music only in one's inward ear, and cannot whistle it, because the whistling drowns out the inner voice, so sometimes the voice of a philosophical thought is so soft that the noise of spoken words is enough to drown it and prevent it from being heard, if one is questioned and has to speak.)
>
> (Z: 453)

Notes

1. Cavell, 1969: 91. See also, in a similar vein, Diamond, 1991.
2. This is Cavell's analysis of it in *The Claim of Reason*.

9
Wittgenstein on 'The Sort of Explanation One Longs For'

Frank Cioffi

The explanations we 'long for' are those in which the state of 'being intrigued and wanting to describe' (LC: 19) finds its proper consummation; or, as Wittgenstein also puts it, which issue in felicitous 'further descriptions' of the experience we were intrigued by. A 'further description' is an account of an experience which specifies what, though perhaps initially unnoticed or unformulated, is nevertheless immanent to the experience and gives it its distinctive character. That the source of your dissatisfaction with a facade was the height of the door is a further description of your impression of the facade; that if the door were altered to take account of your objection the facade would not be so displeasing is an hypothesis. How are these two modes of explaining – further descriptions and hypotheses related? Wittgenstein had two distinct grounds for impugning the relevance of hypotheses in dealing with aesthetic questions. The conceptual objection was that remarks such as those picking out the aspect of a phenomenon felt to be the source of the impression it made were a-causal and not amenable to causal resolution. His non-conceptual objection to hypotheses is that they are not 'what we want'; what we want are similes or some other mode of felicitous reformulation of our experience.

'Being intrigued and wanting to describe': the ineffability problem

Wittgenstein says repeatedly that to resolve our aesthetic (or even psychological) perplexities, what we want are not hypotheses. Yet what he objects to about hypotheses is not just that they can only be resolved by causal enquiry, but that they are not 'developments of the idea with which (the experience) was pregnant' (cf. CV: 69): that they do not 'help formulate what was in your mind' (Rhees, 1971: 23).

G. E. Moore found Wittgenstein's juxtaposition of issues in aesthetics with issues in psychoanalysis puzzling, and wondered how they were related (1966: 305). The connection is that in both these areas we sometimes find ourselves making a demand with respect to the feelings, thoughts and impulses aroused that cannot be met by empirical explanation. What is the nature of this demand?

Some years ago, I consulted a reference work called *The Encyclopaedia of Comedians* (Franklin, 1979), but on perusal found most of the entries disappointing. My reflections on the character of this disappointment illuminated the exegetical puzzle posed by the variety of occasions on which Wittgenstein seems arbitrarily to dismiss the pertinence of empirical enquiry. I understood better his grounds for so doing when I grasped the character of my disappointment with *The Encyclopaedia of Comedians*. When I turned to the entry on the long-forgotten Joe Penner and learned only that he was born in Hungary in 1905 and that, though he became widely known through films, it was on radio that he first achieved celebrity, I felt a vague let-down. Similarly with Zero Mostel. Though it is interesting to learn that he once gave a lecture at Harvard on the philosophy of comedy, nothing is said as to what it was like to watch him perform except that he was 'uproariously funny'. Similarly with Joe E. Brown, Eddie Cantor, Fred Allen, Sid Caesar, Ernie Kovacs. It was not that the entries were too brief or too schematic. The lack lay elsewhere. They were of the wrong genre. They were too discontinuous with what Wittgenstein described as 'the explanation one longs for'. They did not satisfy the craving which leaves us 'intrigued and wanting to describe'. What I was in search of when consulting the entries on my favourite comedians was something which would capture the idiosyncrasies of voice, speech, gesture and the play of facial expression which made each of them so distinctive and memorable a personage. This entry on Billie Gilbert was more like what I had hoped for: 'His trademark was the sneeze – a magnificent production with preparatory heaves, thunderous execution and after the fact embarrassment' (Franklin, 1979,143).

What makes causal hypotheses of our impressions inappropriate on the occasions Wittgenstein has in mind when he speaks of the analysis of impressions is not just what Bouveresse calls the 'palpable [categorial] difference' (1995c: 17) between what explanation can provide and the experience it purports to explain but that our 'longing' is for an evocation or felicitous formulation of our experience rather than an explanation of it.

Wittgenstein's 'strange illusion' and James's 'strange impulse'

In Section 17 of the *Brown Book* Wittgenstein devotes several paragraphs to what he calls 'the analysis of impressions'. The examples he discusses suggest that he had been reading William James who describes 'the analysis of impressions' as 'the most incessantly performed of our mental processes' (1890: 502). In the course of his discussion, Wittgenstein speaks of the 'strange illusion' which may arise with respect to the expression of a face or a tune – that it 'seems to be saying something' and 'it is as though we had to find out what it was saying' (BB: 166). James seems to be referring to the same phenomenon when he speaks in a letter of the 'turmoil of our feelings before ... the wealth of art, the strange impulse to exorcise it by extracting the soul of it and throwing it off in words' (in Perry, 1996: 117).

Let us refer to the issue raised by James and Wittgenstein as the ineffability problem. It is clear that what it calls for is an enhancement of our powers of articulation rather than of discovery. There are occasions when the attempt to produce such articulation defeats us and there are many recorded expressions of the exasperation this induces. A striking instance of the *ineffability predicament* is provided by Robert Blatchford who complained of the 'fatal poverty of language (which) makes us impotent: What can we say of our feelings towards the ocean, the swallow, or the rose? ... The swallow is a wonder and a delight to me ... Times out of number have I stood and watched them dipping and flashing and gliding and wheeling in the sunshine and sweet air, and wondered, What do they mean? What are they?' (n.d.: 152–3). Blatchford's complaint reminds us that the impressions produced by our transactions with the natural world are not always such as to be relieved by the successful consummation of empirical inquiry into its less manifest properties, historical antecedents or causal conditions, but call for something different. But cases like this cannot justify Wittgenstein's more radical anti-explanatory thesis. For he is not merely saying that hypotheses concerning an impression will not relieve our perplexity as to what makes it the impression it is. He is saying that hypotheses concerning it are out of place ('In aesthetic investigation the one thing we are *not* interested in is *causal connections*' (AWL: 38)).

David Pears takes Wittgenstein to hold that if someone says that a facade is displeasing because the door is too high he is not saying anything which experiment could falsify. How is it to be determined whether aesthetic explanations which pick out 'an object of directed attention' like the height of the door – that which gestalt psychologist call 'felt determinants' – imply causal hypotheses? I have argued that it is not its a-causality which marks the difference between an aesthetic explanation and a causal hypothesis, but its *point*. This is to heighten our awareness of what gives the impression its peculiar character and this aim distinguishes it from a straightforward explanation of which we are not entitled to make any such demand. But it does not follow that we may not on occasion ask for an aesthetic explanation that must meet causal criteria. We do so whenever we wonder at the extent of the contribution to the efficacy of a scene in a film of the background music and turn down the sound to see what happens. Let us consider some apparent counter-examples to the a-causality thesis.

Are Mr Spock's ears a-causal *felt determinants*?

I have seen it asserted on several occasions that Mr Spock of *Star Trek* owes his popularity in large measure to the shape of his ears. How are we to determine whether this is so? Is the invocation of Spock's ears as the source of his appeal a hypothesis or is it rather one of Wittgenstein's a-causal further descriptions? Should we permit ourselves to be influenced by what happens to indices of interest and appreciation like pupillary dilatation when Spock's ears are normalized? I think what matters is that though we could experiment we don't, rather than that there is some anomaly in submitting an aesthetic explanation of this kind to experiment.

The remark about Spock's ears has causal implications if those whose interest it arouses treat it as if it had. (This extends to all those remarks which David Pears characterizes as intentionalist and thinks are without causal implications.) We can imagine circumstances in which experimental manipulation of Spock's ears would have been felt appropriate. Imagine Captain Kirk responding to Spock's complaint: 'I am embarrassed by the proposals of marriage and of less mentionable arrangements with which earth women deluge me. It is becoming a nuisance' – 'Lose the ears'. But the remarks as we have them come with no such determinate context and leave us free to imagine circumstances in which manipulation of the ears would be beside the point.

For those for whom experiment does not capture the content of the remark, what then could show the invocation of Spock's ears to be mistaken? If we monitored the unprompted comments of Trekkies and they never mentioned Spock's ears or if they looked nonplussed when the suggestion was put to them, this would certainly incline us to reject the claim about the ears and to consider the invocation of their shape idiosyncratic. What matters for those on the Wittgensteinian side of this argument is what people say when asked what they like most about Spock rather than what happens to the pupils of their eyes or their preference behaviour generally when his ears are humanized. Speaking admiringly of Mr Spock's ears or expatiating on what is so fetching about them can confirm the conjecture as to why he is found appealing without the support of anything like pupillary dilation. Spock's ears and Captain Kirk's are as internally related as the ellipse and the circle in Wittgenstein's analogy, so there are statements about the appeal of Spock's ears which are immune to causal contradiction. But it does not follow that statements which invoke his ears as the source of his appeal are always so immune.

We can easily imagine an a-causal, a-hypothetical transaction with Spock's ears : 'Those ears: wow!' or 'Get those ears!' But we can nevertheless also imagine that someone meant his invocation of Spock's ears as an explanation. The issue would then become one of decorum. Was it appropriate on the occasion in question to introduce causal considerations into the discussion? The source of the inconclusiveness of the question whether we are dealing with an intentionalist-causal hybrid or an a-causal remark is that, as Frank Ramsey said, 'Meaning is mainly potential' and the case of Spock's ears may be one where it is for those who made the remark to explain what they meant by it rather than an occasion for settling the issue by invoking the Great Lexicographer in the Sky.

Spock's ears and David's nose: *further descriptions are not all of one kind*

How context – that is, the use made of the form of words rather than the form of words (LC: 2) – may determine whether we are dealing with an hypothesis or an a-causal further description is illustrated by H.-J. Glock's attempts to accommodate a counter-example to Wittgenstein's thesis of the a-causality of aesthetic explanation (Glock, 1996: 33–4; Cioffi, 1998: 53–4). Glock concedes that the a-causality thesis 'seems to be refuted by stories like that of Soderini, who claimed to be dissatisfied with the nose of the David, but had his qualms dissipated after Michelangelo pretended to have altered it'. However, Glock argues that 'the fact that Soderini's dissatisfaction could be removed without any alteration of the nose no more shows that it was about something other than the nose than the fact that my desire for an apple can be removed without my getting an apple (e.g. by a punch in the stomach) shows that it was something other than an apple that I desired.' No! Soderini's remark that David's nose was too thick cannot be assimilated to statements such as 'I want an apple'. The person who asks for an apple would be disconcerted to be offered a pear (even more so to be punched in the stomach) but Soderini found completely appropriate the steps Michelangelo appeared to take in response to his complaint. Suppose that Soderini learned of the trick Michelangelo had played on him and thereafter, when dining out on the story, said 'I was sure there was something wrong with the nose; apparently I was wrong.' Why are we to say that, in making this concession and permitting a causal fact to contradict his nomination of a felt determinant, Soderini had fallen into conceptual confusion or was violating a linguistic rule? On the other hand suppose that Soderini had conveyed what he felt about the excessive thickness of David's nose with a simile. This would have been immune to any causal fact as to the relation between David's nose and Soderini's dissatisfaction with it. 'Further descriptions' are not all of one kind. Those which identify a felt determinant may imply a causal fact; those that evince an experience via a simile, even one based on a misapprehension, do not.

In the case of felt determinants like Spock's ears or David's nose the speaker may have discretion as to whether his remark is to be taken causally or a-causally. The utterances in dispute may have no analysis independent of his say-so. (This is sometimes Wittgenstein's own view.) Furthermore, the very request for a clarification of the epistemic status of the utterance may be itself a violation of decorum. Our interlocutor's response to the question whether he intended his remarks apodictically or hypothetically might be neither 'Experiment might show me to be wrong' nor 'Experiment is irrelevant' but more like – 'Give us a break'. But there are occasions when an exasperated response to a request for clarification would be unjustified. Wittgenstein does not confine his rejection of causal enquiry to aesthetics, but extends it to the conditions addressed by psychoanalysis. Freud, too, is charged with raising questions whose conceptual character precludes the proffering of causal hypotheses as their solution since what is called for is rather clarifying what was at the back of the patient's mind or as Glock puts it, articulating his worries (1996: 111).

Effie Gray's pubic hair as *cause* and as *felt determinant*

The problem of the relation of further descriptions to hypotheses, of the nomination of felt determinants to causal facts, is raised by the familiar, though speculative, account of a Victorian *cause célèbre*, John Ruskin's failure to consummate his marriage and its consequent annulment. This is an example particularly well suited to bring out the pragmatic dimensions of intentional object remarks. How is the cause of Ruskin's reluctance or inability to make love to Effie Gray related to the reason he might have given if asked? This is a particularly pertinent example of Wittgenstein's distinction between explaining and 'getting clear' – the one served by the advancing of hypotheses and the other by 'further descriptions' – and of the problems of determining their epistemic relation to each other, their respective appropriateness and their relative value.

In 1854 Effie Gray wrote an account of the non-consummation of her marriage to Ruskin: '... finally he told me his true reason ... that he had imagined women were quite different from what he saw I was and that the reason he did not make me his wife was because he was disgusted with my person that first evening' (Hilton, 1985: 118). Ruskin's own account runs: '... though her face was beautiful her person was not formed to excite passion. On the contrary there were certain circumstances in her person which completely checked it' (ibid.). To see why Wittgenstein does not wish to assimilate felt determinants to hypotheses we need only ask: when Effie wondered why Ruskin didn't make love to her that 'first evening' what was she wondering about? Was she canvassing hypotheses or was she speculating as to the 'target' of his repugnance? That is, how is what she wondered Ruskin was 'disgusted with' related to 'the certain circumstances in her person' that Ruskin held back from delicacy but could have communicated had he been intent on candour? Would the speculation she entertained be something that Ruskin's view of the matter could contradict or was it similar to the kind of speculation Wittgenstein felt was out of order in an aesthetic investigation – a hypothetical, causal speculation like that of an ethologist who explains the failure of a male stickleback to go into his courtship dance in terms of the female's abdomen being insufficiently protuberant and rounded?

It has been suggested that the reason Ruskin found Effie Grey's person 'not formed to excite passion', the 'certain circumstances ... which completely checked it', but which he was loathe to speak explicitly of, was her unanticipated possession of pubic hair. 'Unanticipated' due to Ruskin's having derived his notion of the female form from its representations in Greek and Roman classical sculpture whose realism was limited in this regard. In consequence Ruskin responded to Effie Grey's body as if she were a classical Venus on which someone had stuck pubic hair the way vandals draw moustaches on the Mona Lisa. Had Ruskin concurred with this account it would have answered to Wittgenstein's 'further description'. The actual state of Effie Grey's genital area would be related to the idealized version which was presented by classical statuary as the ellipse to the circle in Wittgenstein's analogy. Ruskin could only explain how he felt about one by referring to the other, and hypotheses wouldn't come into it.

Now suppose a conventional psychoanalytic account of Ruskin's dismay, to the effect that what unconsciously appalled him about Effie was her lack of a penis and that his notion that it was her pubic hair which had put him off was a symbolic displacement of the real cause – her castrated state. This would be a typical psychoanalytic hypothesis. How is Ruskin's further description of his experience related to that feature of her person which – on a Freudian view – was the cause; that is, that but for which Ruskin would not have experienced the aversion which he imputed to the hirsuteness of her genital area? I think they are incompatible unless a special context is created for them in which Ruskin's account is pulled in the direction of a protocol statement – a statement shorn of its normal force and restricted to what he felt at the time.

What is correct in Wittgenstein's resistance to assimilating intentional object remarks to causal hypotheses is its implication that the subject's view of the matter is normally a necessary ingredient in such remarks ('You have to give the explanation that is accepted. That is the whole point of the explanation' (LC: 18)) Our curiosity as to Ruskin's honeymoon night is not like that of an ethologist as to the role of the contours of female stickleback's abdomen to the male stickleback's courtship dance, though segments of our culture may be inclined to pull it in that direction. But for most of us it is natural to construe a non-psychoanalytic, pubic hair conjecture as not just a causal hypothesis but as an attempt at a reconstruction of Ruskin's internal soliloquy. We would not be entertaining the causal hypothesis independently of the internal soliloquy. We would be considering possibilities like Ruskin reflecting 'When I looked at Effie an image of the Venus de Milo came into my head and I thought, how different! How appallingly different!' We would not just be entertaining the counterfactual 'If Effie Grey had shaved her pubic area Ruskin would not have been unmanned' even if we believe this to follow from our reconstruction of the internal soliloquy. To reduce our reconstruction to a bald counterfactual would be to treat a conjecture as to the truth of the pubic hair account as if it were epistemically indistinguishable from the ethologist's speculation as to role of the female stickleback's swollen belly and so to misconstrue it.

I think it was considerations such as these which impelled Wittgenstein to say that the game played with the conscious motive is 'quite different' from that played with the unconscious motive. But though the hypothesis game and the 'object of directed attention', 'felt determinant' game, are different, it does not follow that they are completely insulated from each other. The occasion of Ruskin's incapacitation was a causal episode with a causal structure to be investigated even if it also had an expressiveness to be articulated. But suppose Ruskin used Freud's equation of the Medusa's snaky locks and female pubic hair (Freud, 1922: 273–4) to evince his feelings of repugnance at the hirsuteness of Effie's 'person'. We might then feel that this had an independence of causal enquiry which Wittgenstein mistakenly extended to the identification of the intentional object. If 'Medusa' was 'the word that sums it up' for Ruskin, then this is something causal enquiry cannot impugn, but it does not follow that his singling out her pubic hair as the source of his disinclination or incapacitation to consummate was also something that causal enquiry could not impugn. Ruskin could not attest with the same degree of authority to the causal influence of Effie's hirsuteness on his incapacitation as he could to the felicity of the simile 'like a vandalized Venus'. The correct explanation is not the one accepted; only the correct simile is.

Further description versus *hypothesis* in dream interpretation: the branch, the phallus and the lily stalk

In the third of the lectures on aesthetics and psychology, Wittgenstein says: 'Freud does something which seems to me immensely wrong. He gives what he calls an interpretation of dreams ... A patient, after saying that she had had a beautiful dream, described a dream in which she descended from a height, saw flowers and shrubs, broke off the branch of a tree etc. Freud shows what he calls the "meaning" of the dream. ... He shows relations between the dream images and certain objects of a sexual nature' (LC: 23). What was 'immensely wrong' with Freud's interpretation of the flowery dream? Wittgenstein's objection has the same underlying structure as his remarks on causal explanation in aesthetics. Both devalue empirical enquiry since its outcome can have no bearing on what is really of interest to us – our impressions and how to evince and evoke them more adequately.

Wittgenstein does not, in these remarks, explicitly advert to his a-causal thesis. He does not say that there is something conceptually confused about suggesting that certain earlier mental transactions of the dreamer with the idea of a celebrated courtesan, certain associations with menstruation and camellias, and certain thoughts and/or desires about phalluses played a role in producing the flowering branch episode of the flowery dream. This is not what Freud's confusion of cause and reason comes to here. The reason Freud's 'bawdy' interpretation constituted cheating for Wittgenstein was not due to any causal inexplicability of the dream image of the flowering branch, but because the unconscious phallic associations invoked were not at 'the back of her mind' among her 'crush of thoughts', were not 'developments of the idea with which the dream was pregnant' (cf. CV: 69).

Though the psychoanalyst Charles Hanly does raise one pertinent objection to Wittgenstein's dealing with the flowery dream, he also displays a profound misunderstanding of the character of Wittgenstein's objection. This is what Hanly says: 'Wittgenstein felt compelled to come to the rescue of beautiful dreams and the innocence of hysterical women' (1972: 86) To grasp the character of Hanly's mistake, imagine an alternative interpretation in which the flowery dreamer felt a vague repulsion at the sight of the withered camellias, their colour in particular inspiring distaste, and then on reflection produced the simile 'like menstrual blood' and that it was Freud who introduced, on circumstantial grounds, the theme of the Angel of the Annunciation with the lily stalk. Under these circumstances Wittgenstein would have found that it was the imposition of the aspect suggested by the Angel's lily that constituted 'cheating'. So Wittgenstein's objection had nothing to do with coming 'to the rescue of beautiful dreams' but in insisting on the discussion taking the route of further description rather than hypotheses.

When should we seek a *further description* of an experience rather than an *explanation* of it?

There is nevertheless a remaining objection of Hanly's which must be addressed once his misunderstanding has been cleared up. What grounds can be given for preferring a discourse constituted of further descriptions to one made up of hypotheses? The reason that it is no mistake to attempt to determine whether it was the vicissitudes of the flowery dreamer's sexual desires and fantasies which explained the presence in the flowery dream of an upheld branch sprouting camellias and dismiss her own attempts at articulation of the felt significance of these images is that she was a patient, and so it was the diagnostic significance of her dream that was the proper focus of interest. We need only imagine that she suffered from a functional dysmenorrhoea, say, for the repressed ideational material responsible for her symptoms, and discernible via her dreams, to take centre stage and to pre-empt any previous interest we had in developing the ideas with which her dream was 'pregnant'.

Wittgenstein had grounds for feeling that the flowery dreamer had been cheated other than her having been proffered a hypothesis when she ought to have been helped to formulate what was in her mind. It was

Freud's assumption that the correctness of his interpretation impugned her own view that the dream was 'beautiful'. Wittgenstein finds this as unwarranted as the conclusion that because an enchanting scent was made from materials having 'intolerable smells', the scent itself was repellent. But does the dream impression stand to its interpretation in as comparable a relation of invulnerability to information as the scent? Was the flowery dreamer allowing herself to be cheated by Freud when she ceased to take pleasure in her dream as a result of his having persuaded her that there was a causal relationship between her shameful sexual desires and her sense of exaltation at the beauty of her dream? Wasn't her response a natural one? The doctor-poet Dannie Abse wrote: 'I know the colour rose and it is lovely,/ but not when it ripens in a tumour' ('The Pathology of Colour', 1977). Was Abse cheating himself or can causal truths exercise a legitimate sway over the aspect presented by an impression? If they can, why should Freud's implication that his 'bawdy' interpretation of the flowery dream dispelled its beauty constitute a cheating of the dreamer? Can discovering the causal role of what Hanly calls 'the disordered impulses' be as inert in its influence on the impression made by the dream as learning of the repellent ingredients required for manufacturing a perfume on its scent?

Did Freud 'cheat' the flowery dreamer? The bearing of *information* on aspect

Disputes as to the bearing of information on aspect are not uncommon. A familiar example is the occasion reported by John Stuart Mill in which he was reproached by his friend Roebuck for admiring the beauty of sun-touched clouds:

> It was in vain I urged on [Roebuck] that the imaginative emotion which an idea, when vividly conceived, excites in us, is not an illusion but a fact, as real as any of the other qualities of objects. ... The intensest feeling of the beauty of a cloud lighted by the setting sun, is no hindrance to my knowing that the cloud is vapour of water, subject to all the laws of vapours in a state of suspension.
>
> (1958: 128–9)

In his remarks on the flowery dream, is Hanly playing Roebuck to Wittgenstein's Mill? Shall we say that Freud was wrong to imply that the beauty of the flowery dream was an illusion just because it was the 'cover for an unhealthy sexuality'? The problem of what bearing our knowledge of the causal conditions of a phenomenon should be permitted to have on the impression it makes has a peculiar pertinence to our mental lives, where there is an obvious strain in considering a phenomenon both from a symptomatic, diagnostic and a purely appreciative point of view. If compassion can be a reaction formation against sadism, as Freud maintains, can we regard it in the same light as compassion which isn't? A Freudian account of reaction formation asks us to believe that in the unconscious background of the animal rights activist's outrage at the mistreatment of animals are unconscious fantasies of inflicting agony on them. Doesn't this fact put his compassionate activities in a different light? His case is not like that of Franz Kafka who abstained from eating meat because his grandfather had been a kosher butcher and Kafka was determined to spare as many animals through his abstention as his grandfather had killed in the course of his ritual activities. Kafka's motive doesn't alter aspect; unconscious sadistic fantasies do. Why then should the fact that the flowery dreamer felt differently about her dream in the light of Freud's 'bawdy' explanation of it have constituted a 'cheating' of her?

Though there is something mildly repellent about Freud's self-congratulatory tone ('The dreamer quite lost her liking for this pretty dream after it had been interpreted' (1900: 347)), making him rather like Hofrat Behrens in *The Magic Mountain* showing Hans Castorp an X-ray of his mistress's arm and commenting, 'That's what they put round you when they make love you know', this is nevertheless not sufficient to warrant Wittgenstein's charge of cheating. Wittgenstein himself, in another connection, produces an example where information is felt quite licitly to alter aspect. In the *Philosophical Investigations,* we are asked to consider how a smiling face changes its aspect depending on what we imagine it is smiling at, whether children at play or the suffering of an enemy (PI: 539). It thus seems to me that the flowery dreamer was manifesting no idiosyncratic susceptibility to aspect change when, as Freud said, she lost her liking for her dream in consequence of his 'bawdy' interpretation.

More on the rivalry between *further description* and *hypothesis*: Shelley and Kirilov

In Aldous Huxley's *After Many a Summer,* a hard-boiled medical materialist describes a character who suffers from melancholia as 'a pharmacological tragedy', and goes on to apply this characterization to Shelley: 'Has it ever struck you … what a lot of the finest romantic literature is the result of bad doctoring? Shelley for example: "I could lie down like a tired child/ and weep away this life of care." Lovely! But if they'd known how to clear up poor old Shelley's chronic tuberculous pleurisy it would never have been written. Lying down like a tired child and weeping life away happens to be one of the most characteristic symptoms of chronic tubercular pleurisy' (1976: 192). In Dostoevsky's *The Devils*, the mystic-nihilist Kirilov describes his 'moments of eternal harmony' to his friend Shatov: 'There are seconds – they come five or six at a time – when you suddenly feel the presence of eternal harmony in all its fullness'; Shatov warns: 'Take care Kirilov. I've heard that's just how an epileptic fit begins. An epileptic described to me exactly that preliminary sensation before a fit, exactly as you've done ... Be careful, Kirilov – it's epilepsy!' (1972: 586–7).

The question these cases raise is at what point the content of a mental state becomes interesting enough in its own right to warrant its clarification or elaboration rather than scrutiny of its causal-diagnostic implications. Instead of writing 'Stanzas of Dejection before Naples', Shelley could have pondered the causes of the depression he evinced in it, as Shatov in Dostoevsky's *The Devils* thought the epileptic, Kirilov, ought to have pondered the symptomatic significance of his 'moments of harmony'. What counts against this assimilation?

The situations do not differ conceptually due to the impertinence of causal enquiry, but only pragmatically. We have only to imagine that Shelley's unawareness of the symptomatic nature of the state which impelled him to create his poem could have been fatal to him, for us to see grounds for his aborting composition of the poem and inquiring into the sources of his melancholy instead. Nor would we permit the satisfaction Kirilov might take in a felicitous commentary on his 'moments of harmony' to count as a demonstration that investigation of the electrical activity of his brain was less eligible than a further description, however 'cheated' Kirilov might have felt by this account. It is the character of our interest and not the conceptual character of the explanation which differentiates these cases. In the case of Shelley's poem our interest is confined to its internal relations – that unarticulated hinterland which makes the experience of reading it the experience that it is.

By contrast, here is an example of Wittgenstein illustrating not only the perfect propriety of contradicting a subject's presumably authoritative account of his mental state, but impugning its pertinence in the way that analysts impugn pertinence of the manifest content of a dream:

A student in a mood of deep depression, for which he felt that Wittgenstein's philosophy was in some way responsible, went to Wittgenstein and explained: 'Life seems to me pretty pointless and futile. In a few years I shall have ceased to exist. And it's no consolation that human life will go on ... in time the sun will cool down, life will become extinct, and it will all be as if life had never been.' Wittgenstein replied: 'Suppose you were sitting in a room, facing a door which was completely black. You sit and stare fixedly at it, saying over and over again, "That door is black! That door is black!" After a bit you could easily begin to feel miserable about it, and to feel that it was the blackness of the door that was the melancholy fact which had produced your gloom.'

(Gasking and Jackson, 1951)

In this story Wittgenstein was taking a view of his student's depression rather like that of Shatov towards Kirilov's 'moments of harmony' and like Freud and Hanly towards the beauty of the flowery dream.

Rival conceptual analyses or rival modes of life?

When is it a mistake to introduce causal considerations into the discussion of experiences which may have internal relations to be articulated as well as causal conditions to be uncovered? Of course the flowery dreamer might have profited enormously from having her thoughts and feelings directed to matters on which she was authoritative, her sexual life and her married life in particular. But this would leave whatever symptoms she manifested to be explained by another method – one adapted to uncover causes.

Much more influential than a disagreement over the a-causality of certain explanations is a disagreement as to whether the discussion should be taken in the direction of causal enquiry or not. Conceptual considerations do not seem to be at the heart of such disputes. These illustrate rather the way in which non-conceptual considerations determine the direction taken. The scientific explanations Ziff looks forward to, even if conceptually eligible, would have no relevance to the matters which interest Wittgenstein. At the end of his criticism of Wittgenstein's rejection of a scientific aesthetics, Ziff (1981) invokes an example which can be used to bring this out. 'Looking at an unsigned drawing I say "That strikes me as a Klee" Why does it give me that impression? I say "Look at the lines!" But what about the lines?' And Ziff goes on to speak of the advances in our understanding of the visual brain which might answer this question. But there are those who would not feel that the natural sequel to their self-addressed question 'What is it about the lines that makes them Klee-like?' was a speculation concerning the functioning of the visual brain. The explanation they long for would answer rather to the account

William James gives in the case of 'judgments made intuitively': 'the desire strains and presses in a direction which it feels to be right but towards a point which it is unable to see ... the gap becomes not just a void but an aching void ... To fill it up is our thought's destiny' (1890: 584). And this preference cannot be impugned by the eligibility of scientific explanation. Thus what is at issue is not competing conceptual analyses of the nature of aesthetic explanation but competing directions of interest, themselves the manifestation of competing forms of life.

What would bring peace to the love-troubled?

Wittgenstein wrote: 'Every explanation is an hypothesis. But for someone broken up by love an explanatory hypothesis will not help much – it will not bring peace (*beruhigen*)' (GB: 3). What did Wittgenstein mean by this? If we are to adjudicate the rival interests for us of explanation and self-clarification, of hypotheses and further descriptions, we must consider more carefully the kind of explanation on offer and the kind of peace intended.

Yvor Winters said of some poems he admired, 'They offer no solace unless clear understanding be solace.' If it is this kind of peace of which Wittgenstein is speaking – an epistemic peace – then it must be asked why explanation is precluded from supplying it. What would Wittgenstein have the love-troubled one do if not to seek for an explanation of his condition? Rush Rhees expresses doubts about the pertinence of explanation comparable to those of Wittgenstein. This is when he dismisses the bearing of a reconstruction of infantile life on the predicament of someone 'bewildered at the sort of person he finds himself to be', since such a person may be 'concerned at what he *is*; not at conflict and frustration among his wishes' (Rhees, 1971: 25). It is difficult to say whether Rhees is right in his insistence that the question he raises is out of reach of explanation because it is not clear what Rhees's question is. Just what was it about the person he found himself to be that bewildered him? In a notebook entry of 1930 Wittgenstein resorts to a telling device for getting someone who mechanically demands an explanation to realize that he has no clear conception of what he is asking for. Wittgenstein writes out the statement 'the growth of a great style depends on ...?', and follows it with blanks. He then asks 'Could we name anything for the blanks?' (Rhees, 1974: 161). This suggests a general device for getting someone to recognize that he has no clear conception of what a satisfactory outcome to his explanatory efforts would consist in. Suppose for 'a great style' we substitute the thraldom of Wittgenstein's love-troubled one.

Don't we have a comparable difficulty in filling in the blanks? It isn't clear what would confer perspicuity on thraldom as insult and injury confer it on resentment and vengefulness. Similarly with a person's bewilderment 'at the sort of person he finds himself to be'. But it may not be just the failure to specify more precisely what it is we want to know that hinders the explanatory enterprise, but the realization that something other than explanation is wanted.

'I am unhappy and I do not know why' (Mikhail Zoshchenko)

No one had greater hopes of the explanatory prospects of anamnestic enquiry than Mikhail Zoshchenko, or was more convinced that the success of his aetiological project would bring him not only understanding but happiness. Before he undertook his aetiological project, Zoshchenko was convinced that he knew why he was unhappy and imputed his 'melancholy and causeless anguish' to his 'higher consciousness' ('The world is horrible. People are cheap and vulgar' (1974: 10)). In time, however, he came to develop a suspicion of the cogency of this view which he had formerly bolstered with quotations from fellow sufferers such as Sophocles, Schopenhauer, Flaubert, Gogol, Poe, Tolstoy et al. All these testified, so he had thought, to the legitimacy of his despairing response to life. Having then decided that this explanation of his melancholy was mistaken, he sought for an alternative and determined to go in search of 'the unfortunate accident' beyond the reach of his current memory ('beyond sunrise') that must have been responsible. The reasoning with which Zoshchenko justifies his abandonment of the view that he and his fellow sufferers were just responding to the nature of things, warrants quotation: 'Side by side with the great people I have listed, I found no fewer great people who had experienced no depression at all, although their consciousness was equally high ... And so I decided to recall my life in order to discover the reason for my misfortune ... to find the incident or series of incidents that had affected me adversely and made me an unfortunate particle of dust to be blown about by every gust of wind' (1974: 18). Zoshchenko retrieves a series of traumatic memories from his childhood but dismisses the explanatory adequacy of each of them:

> Not in a single episode could I find the unfortunate experience which had ruined my life; which had given birth to my melancholy and despair ... Of course certain scenes are extremely sad, but not sadder than what usually takes place. Everyone's father dies; everyone sees

his mother in tears; everyone has disappointments in school, hurt feelings, anxious moments, deceptions ... No! not in a single episode could I find the unfortunate experience which had ruined my life.

(1974: 149–50)

He then decides, under the influence of Freud's writings, that the most promising place to look is in 'the world of the infant ... that world of oblivion where our miseries sometime have their source' (ibid.: 173). But Zoshchenko never does find an infantile trauma which is not open to the same objection as those he had previously rejected and so is compelled to invoke his 'sensitive psyche', which he could have invoked at any stage during his aetiological quest or even before he had begun it.

What account shall we give of the failure of Zoshchenko's aetiological enterprise? What episode could possibly have 'filled in the blanks' of his 'melancholy and despair'. Isn't the moral of Zoshchenko's failure that we sometimes find ourselves asking for explanation when we have no grasp of what would constitute one? And that this may be because the request for an explanation isn't the appropriate expression of what we long for?

The past as influence and as metaphor

I have suggested that what may make empirical enquiry inappropriate is not the failure of articulation between the question and the proposed answer, but the failure of the question to adequately express the craving which prompted it. Reflection may then persuade us that explanation will not meet our needs, but another genre of epistemic achievement – a succinct graspable expression of our predicament, a 'synoptic view' of it – might.

When Rush Rhees speaks of someone's bewilderment at 'the sort of person he finds himself to be (1971: 25), the kind of bewilderment he has in mind involves an internal relation between our sense of self and our characterological aspirations or expectations, and so its eligibility for self-clarification is obvious. In terms of Wittgenstein's analogy, you may feel yourself to be an ellipse and it may be necessary for you to speak of a circle to convey what it is that you failed to become, but it doesn't follow that you originated as a circle and were squashed into ellipticality. There is thus a distinctive non-empirical, but nonetheless epistemic, preoccupation with the self: the self as an object of scrutiny presenting a multiplicity of aspects and thus posing the problem, akin to an aesthetic one, of articulating more clearly which aspects are felt to be more and which less constitutive of its nature. A Wittgensteinian overview of these aspects would facilitate self-understanding.

Wittgenstein's solution to Empson's paradox

The literary critic, William Empson gives an apparently paradoxical account of his procedure when analysing poetic effects, which illustrates the way in which the introduction of external relations into a discourse has a value independent of their veridicality and serves the purpose of bringing to a sharper focus the immanent internal features of an experience:

> Continually in order to paraphrase a piece of verse, it is necessary to drag in some quite irrelevant conceptions; thus I have often been puzzled by finding it necessary to go and look things up in order to find machinery to express distinctions which were already in my mind; indeed, this is involved in the very notion of the activity, for how else would one know what to look up? ... so that many of my explanations may be demonstrably wrong and yet efficient for their purpose and vice versa.
>
> (1949: 253)

If we adapt Wittgenstein's remark on 'developmental hypotheses' to the case of psychological aetiologies ('a development hypothesis as a disguise for a formal relation'), we have what might be called Wittgenstein's solution to Empson's paradox. Wittgenstein is saying that we sometimes speculate as to the causal origin of a phenomenon in the same spirit in which Empson went in search of his 'quite irrelevant conceptions' – in order to better evince and convey his experience of a poem – and so the failure in historicity of a speculation is consistent with its clarificatory power.

When does anachronism matter?

One test of whether a claim concerning the relation of an earlier to a later state is genuinely causal is that when our attention is called to the anachronistic character of the relation, we may feel that its literal falsity is irrelevant to its purpose, which was to convey the character of the later experience rather than to explain it. Sometimes this is clear from the start, as when Herbert Pocket in *Great Expectations* says: 'I think I must have committed a felony and forgotten the details of it. I feel so miserable and guilty.' It does not matter whether there was such a felonious occasion in Herbert's previous life or not. When Santayana attempts to account for the childhood exaltation he felt at the spectacle of the festival of Corpus Christi, he invokes an essay of Alain's only encountered years later; and yet this arouses no misgivings in us. On the other hand we would naturally share Wittgenstein's reservations about the reminiscences of the deaf mute Mr Ballard, who remembered distinctly a period when he was 'tossed to and fro like a shuttlecock' by his perplexed musings as to the origin of the world, at a time before he had mastered the vocabulary which would appear necessary for such matters to be raised. Wittgenstein imagines posing Ballard the question: 'Are you sure ... that this is the correct translation of your wordless thought into words?' But sees no way of resolving it. 'Do I want to say that the writer's memory deceives him? – I don't even know if I should say *that*. These recollections are a queer memory phenomenon, – and I do not know what conclusions one can draw from them about the past of the man who recounts them' (PI: 342; the Ballard example is taken from James's *Principles of Psychology*).

The same irrelevance of anachronism is illustrated by a reminiscence of Stendhal who attempted to evince a bereavement he suffered in childhood by invoking a later experience: 'The same part of my heart is moved by certain of Mozart's accompaniments in *Don Giovanni'* (*The Life of Henri Brulard*, 1900: 43). Stendhal's predicament is like the one Wittgenstein evinces in his relation to the music of Brahms. The 'certain accompaniments' in Don Giovanni performed, for Stendhal, the function that the analogy with the prose style of Gottfried Keller performed for Wittgenstein in enabling him to express what he felt about Brahms. 'The correct explanation is the explanation that is accepted' (LC: 18).

In his book on autobiography, Roy Pascal makes it an objection to the historicity of Richard Church's account of his childhood that since Church himself acknowledges that 'in recording these scenes I am translating them into the language and concerns of adult life', 'embellishment had usurped translation' (1960: 165). But Church's account may deserve the same kind of indulgence Wittgenstein extended to the Ballard reminiscence. Why is it any more a retrospective 'embellishment' in the case of a childhood memory, where the literal occurrence of the thought or image invoked would involve anachronism, than where we retrospectively describe a state of gloom as like 'the descent of a permanent cloud' or accept a lengthy paraphrase of a joke in spite of the fact that it cannot have literally been in mind?

Proust's narrator uses his own childhood trauma at being denied his mother's customary goodnight kiss to evoke another character's anguish at the pain caused him by his rupture with a lover (Swann and Odette). Here there can be no possibility of a causal construal of the relation between the experiences brought into apposite conjunction since they were the experiences of distinct persons. Thus Marcel's mother's goodnight kiss is in this instance an epistemically unambiguous 'formal relation' or 'psychological fixed stars'. Contrast this with Marcel's assimilation of his disappointment on the occasion his mother failed to give him his goodnight kiss to his feelings of desolation when parting with his lover, Albertine, where a causal construal is open to us. But even if Marcel's feelings for Albertine would have been what they were without the causal influence exerted by his childhood distress, this distress might still be his best means of elucidating the nature of his dependence on Albertine and the significance of her parting kisses. (Marcel is sometimes explicitly a-causal in his account of the nature of Albertine's goodnight kiss: 'what I at once call to mind in comparison is … the night on which my father sent Mama to sleep in the little bed by the side of my own.'; and he goes on to speak of 'the identity of the grace bestowed' (Proust, 1968: 2). This comparison is several times resorted to: 'a soothing power the like of which I had not known since the evening at Combray when my mother stooping over my bed, brought me repose in a kiss', and 'almost as precious as when my mother in the evening at Combray used to press her lips upon my brow' (ibid.: 94, 96). These remarks are all 'further descriptions' rather then hypotheses.

What does 'bewilderment at the sort of person one finds oneself to be' call for?

One more turn of the screw. When someone decides to abandon an aetiological enterprise of the kind Zoshchenko envisaged, he may proceed in either of two directions, even if these are distinct might not be immediately apparent. There are two distinct grounds for the insufficiency or irrelevance of empirical explanation. One that it fails to clarify our feelings; the other that it fails to relieve them. But this latter desire may remain ungratified even when we have succeeded in producing an orderly arrangement of what was already known.

It may misrepresent the nature of our situation if we assume that all that we needed was a synoptic grasp of our predicament. Some of those who come to realize that they had misguidedly sought explanation when what they wanted was self-clarification may, when they have achieved self-clarification, still feel that something they had vaguely hoped for was lacking – exoneration perhaps or reconciliation. They may then express this in epistemic idioms, as did Rush Rhees, and speak of their continued 'bewilderment' at the person they are and look forward to some epistemic dissipation of this bewilderment, whereas what is called for is something non-epistemic – not relief of bewilderment but attenuation of dismay. And even if this attenuation is not achievable, at least it would be clearer to them that what they are condemned to is not ignorance but torment.

In J. C. Powys's *Autobiography* there is some pertinent counsel (probably inspired by William James's thesis in his discussion of self-esteem that 'Our self-feeling is in our power' (James, 1890: 310–11)). Powys applies this formula to someone's realization that he is 'a cowardly, blundering, incompetent worm': 'Very good. So be it. But it is in my power to be a worm with a deep calm, resolute cheerfulness' (1934: 627). A comparable sentiment was expressed by a character in a thriller I once read, who reflects upon realizing that he is a fool: 'I'm all I've got.' Though simple explanation may not by itself succeed in bringing about this enviable *rapprochement*, since disquietude as to our foolishness may survive the discovery as to whether we were born foolish or gradually became so, neither is closure guaranteed by a synoptic grasp of the variety of ways in which this foolishness manifested itself (though this has its music too). What is rather longed for is attainment of a Parolles-like resilience: 'Simply the thing I am/ shall make me live'. It only generates confusion to treat learning to bear one's cross as an epistemic achievement.

Neither explanation nor self-clarification, but peace

To sum up: we begin with a strong desire for some explanatory resolution of the perplexities provoked by the person we have become and thus of dissipating the problematicality which attaches to our particular mode of being. At a later stage (or in a contrasting mood) it is all one to us whether we jumped, fell or were pushed. It is a clearer view of our obscure intimations on these matters that we may want – a sounder grasp of our candidates for blame, say, rather than knowledge of which one was actually to blame. But this synoptic achievement may no more meet the need which incited our search than explanation had. What we really longed for was neither the discourse which explains nor that which clarifies. What we longed for was peace.

10
Patterns in the Weave of Life: Wittgenstein's *Lebensmuster*

Jean-Jacques Rosat

> So we are talking about patterns in the weave of life.
>
> (LW II: 42)

In his last writings, Wittgenstein sometimes compares life to a carpet or a weave, on which emerge, in intertwined patterns, the feelings and behaviours that make up human life: pain, joy, grief, hope, but also – this must be stressed from the outset – *simulated* pain or joy. ' "Grief" describes a pattern (*Muster*) which recurs in the weave of our life (*Lebensteppich*)' (LW I: 406); and in a passage about the simulation of pain, he writes: 'Pretence is a (certain) pattern within the weave of life' (LW I: 862).

Comparison is a tool that enables us to see things with the help of a picture: to make an unprecedented comparison is to generate a new picture that will train and re-educate our philosophical eyes, help us relinquish our routine ways of seeing, and teach us to see that to which we had been blind although it was always before us. We constantly, and without thinking, compare the soul (or the mind) to a box of secrets whose contents are accessible only to its owner: this *spatial* comparison makes us see the soul through a *picture of interiority* (an *inner* space). Almost as unreflective is the *optical*, indeed *cinematographic,* comparison of the soul (or the mind) to a roll of film unwinding before the light of a projector: here, the soul is seen through the *picture of a stream of thought* (stream of consciousness). An important part of Wittgenstein's work in philosophical psychology is to reveal the conceptual ruts these pictures relentlessly drag us back to.

In *Remarks on Colour*, we find this aphorism: 'The wrong picture confuses, the right picture helps' (RC III: 20; 26 March 1950). The purpose of this chapter is to answer the following question: *in what way is the picture of 'patterns in a carpet' a good picture*, or at least a more correct (*richtig*) picture than that of the box of secrets or of the roll of film? What will we see if we train ourselves to look at the phenomena we call 'psychological' through *this* picture; or, more precisely, if we use this picture to describe our uses of 'psychological' concepts?

'A purely geometric way of looking at things' (LW II: 40)

The carpet in question can be described as an interweaving of numerous, multicoloured threads; that is, human life with its innumerable experiences, facts, words and gestures. From this intricate background emerge diverse *patterns* (Wittgenstein uses the German word *Muster*, which can be translated both as *model* or *pattern*), such as pain, joy or hope. Each of these patterns is a motif that recurs more or less regularly, though never in exactly the same way, for a multitude of tiny variations allow it to vary infinitely: each of our joyful moments differs according to the circumstances, and may manifest itself in a different facial expression. Some of the patterns in the carpet are more, others less, complex, and the more complicated ones borrow some of their elements from the simpler ones. The simulation of joy is therefore a more complex pattern than sincere joy, but it borrows some of the latter's traits. Finally, these patterns are so intertwined that a single thread can belong to different patterns, or be seen, at one time, as belonging to the background from which a pattern emerges; at another, as part of another pattern. Indeed, the innumerable *Muster* do not only emerge from the background, they *are* the background; they are the carpet, human life itself. Wittgenstein calls them *Lebensmuster* – patterns of life.

The point of this new comparison is clear. On a carpet all is, in principle, visible, open to view. If a pattern is not visible to me, this is not because it is covered, hidden or disguised, but because I cannot discern it; perhaps it is too enmeshed with others or too complex to detach itself distinctly from the background; or perhaps it is a variant too unlike the typical pattern for me to correctly identify it.

In a novella by Henry James, *The Figure in the Carpet*, a famous writer informs a young critic that a unique idea runs through all his work, which no critic has ever discerned though it is everywhere manifest and 'as concrete ... as a bird in a cage, a bait on a hook, a piece of cheese in a mouse-trap. ... It governs every line, it chooses every word, it dots every i, it places every comma' (1896: 157). It is 'something like a complex figure in a Persian carpet', ventures the critic; to which the author replies: 'It's the very string that my pearls are strung on!' (ibid.: 162)

Like Wittgenstein, Henry James resorts to the picture of a figure in the carpet because it is a fitting illustration of the idea that for a thing to be hidden, there is no need for it to be under lock and key; it is enough that it be open to view in circumstances where no one is looking. When we do not understand someone, says Wittgenstein, when we cannot 'find our feet with them' (Z: 390), we should refrain from assuming that it is because there is 'in his head' something inaccessible and incommunicable, but think rather that we are unable, for one reason or another, to grasp what his words and deeds lay open to view. Therefore, what distinguishes a simulated feeling from a sincere one is not the absence, in the box of secrets or in the light of the projector, of something that is purportedly the feeling itself. The sincere and the simulated feeling are better compared to two different patterns where the first is the simpler; the latter, the more complex one which borrows some of its elements from the first. The simulated feeling should not be seen as an 'embarrassing appendage' which is a mere 'disruption' of the initial organization of the pattern (the feeling) it imitates, but as constituting an altogether new pattern – with characteristic context, behaviour and intentions – even if a naive onlooker may not be able to discern it as that.

To expose Tartuffe,[1] Dorine, the maid, does not, as it were, trespass into his inner self to insure that no feeling of piety is to be found there. Rather, she immediately recognizes posturing and ostentation in the religious zeal that Orgon mistakes for an expression of exceptional devotion. And in Tartuffe's marked attention to Orgon, which the latter reads as an expression of deep affection, she immediately detects a series of manoeuvres designed to win over his daughter and appropriate his fortune:

> ... you can portray a pretender on the stage. So there is such a thing as an appearance (*Erscheinung*) of pretence, and it is much more complicated than the appearance of suffering, for instance. Otherwise pretence could never be exposed.

> (LW I: 863)

Simulated piety has distinct characteristics that make it a more complex pattern than that of genuine piety, though related to it. If Orgon is deceived, it is because he is blind to these characteristics and to that complexity. He sees the impostor's behaviour as much too elementary a pattern.

I will not further discuss Wittgenstein's analysis of pretence as this would require a chapter in its own right.[2] What matters here is that the picture of patterns in a carpet enables Wittgenstein to juxtapose both genuine and simulated feeling on the same level, thereby treating the difference between them as one not in kind, but in degree of complexity. This 'way of looking at things', affirms Wittgenstein, is 'not ... common'; he characterizes it as 'a purely geometric way of looking at things' in that 'cause and effect do not enter [into it]' (LW II: p. 40). Here, 'purely geometric' means purely descriptive, as opposed to causal, explanatory and theoretical – a point on which we will have more to say.

Patterns organize the stream of life

The picture of patterns in a carpet clearly brings out the idea that psychological phenomena, such as emotions and some feelings – particularly those, like pain, which are inseparable from characteristic bodily experiences – have a typical *physiognomy*: in ordinary and simple cases, we identify them immediately. Just as we see a pattern detach itself from its background, we can, in most cases, see the joy or sadness in someone's face; we do not conjecture it from preliminary observation and identification of some physical traits:

> 'We *see* emotion,' – As opposed to what? – We do not see facial contortions and *make the inference* that he is feeling joy, grief, boredom. We describe a face immediately as sad, radiant, bored, even when we are unable to give any other description of the features. – Grief, one would like to say, is personified in the face. This is essential to what we call 'emotion'.
>
> (RPP II: 570)

But the physiognomy characteristic of each emotion should not be seen solely as a synchronic organization of gestures and bodily posture; it is also a diachronic organization of the individual's general behaviour. Each emotion has a dynamics typical of it which deploys itself according to a characteristic, indeed a *constitutive*, rhythm and *tempo*.

Sadness, for instance, says Wittgenstein, follows a course (*Verlauf*) which is typical of it. It is a phenomenon that has, one might say, an autonomous life: it appears, evolves and expires according to modalities that are different from those of fear or anger. Its unfolding is not mechanical, discontinuous or repetitive: 'If a man's bodily expressions of sorrow and joy alternated, say with the ticking of a metronome, then this would not result in the pattern of sorrow or of joy' (LW I: 406). A pattern, in Wittgenstein's sense, is also a *temporal form of organization*: it connects the moments of our life to one another, and structures them.

Indeed, Wittgenstein sometimes suggests, in contrast to all forms of dualism or functionalism, that we would be less prone to error in our descriptions of mental phenomena if, rather than consider them as states, activities or functions of some 'soul', 'mind' or 'psyche', we saw them as modes of temporal organization and structuring of our ways of acting; as bodily or existential rhythms:

> Comparison of bodily processes (*Vorgängen*) and states, like digestion, breathing, etc. with mental ones, like thinking, feeling, wanting, etc. What I want to stress is precisely the incomparability. Rather, I should like to say, the comparable bodily states would be *quickness* of breath, *irregularity* of heart-beat, *soundness* of digestion and the like. And of course all these things could be said to characterize the behaviour of the body.
>
> (RPP I: 661)

In MS 124,[3] dated 1944, Wittgenstein considers fear or hope as 'techniques of thinking' (*Denktechnik*) or 'habits' (*Gepflogenheit*); that is, as articulated forms of behaviour, or what, four years later, he will call 'patterns': 'To hope, believe, fear or expect that this or that will ... happen etc., is to move within a technique of thinking, outside of which – and thus, outside of habit – there is no thinking; no more than there can be speaking outside a language.' Of course, someone – call her, for short, the philosopher of introspection – intent on seeing fear or hope as something qualitatively unique felt by an individual may protest:

> But I do know immediately, it is immediately clear to me, that I can (for example) hope for something independently of whether I have hoped for it or thought about it in the past. It is clear to me that the act of hoping can exist separately, in itself, logically independently from anything preceding or following it.

But how could a feeling be seen as an isolated 'mental act'? Hope has a history and can only occur within a history. To describe my experience of expecting, my lived expectation – my impatient waiting for someone whose arrival I long for – is to describe what I say (including what I might say to myself) and what I do, and the manner in which I do it: it is to recount my acts, my words and my thoughts:

> I hoped that he would visit me this afternoon and bring me money. This had a prehistory. – I stayed home in the afternoon, got this or that ready for him; thought of him frequently; if I heard the front door open, I paid attention, asked who had arrived, etc. I did, interpreted,

thought and said various things and my mood changed in definite ways. That is the picture, the phenomenon, of hope in this circumstance. The connection of all this with that man is an historical one.

Fixated on the identification of psychical phenomena with something felt, we are inclined to believe that a sliced-off minute of this hope is still hope, as long as in that minute we feel 'what it is like' to hope: 'If I am sitting in my room, hoping that N.N. arrives with money, and a minute of that hope could be cut off and isolated, what went on in that minute, would that not be hope?' To which Wittgenstein replies: 'But all connections (*Verbindungen*) are cut off, and all the signs used during that minute have lost their meaning.' In a minute of hope that is bracketed, arrested in immobilized and decontextualized time, I could not hope, for all connection with the flow of my life would have vanished. The philosopher of introspection protests: 'But your conception of things seems to remove from the spiritual process – from hoping, wishing etc. – its force and meaning (*Bedeutung*) during the time it takes hold of my mind.' But here, she treats the force and meaning of hope as identical to the intensity and direction of a feeling that takes hold of her and which she experiences in her inner self. To which Wittgenstein responds: 'What then do the force and meaning of hope reside in? Is it not in the manner in which they manifest themselves in the life of the person who hopes? Hope as "guiding star".'

It is noteworthy that precisely at this point in the manuscript, Wittgenstein explicitly refers to William James and stream of consciousness theory, highlighting both what is right and what misleading about it. The picture of a stream, directed against psychical atomism, rightly illustrates that psychological phenomena must be considered in terms of their characteristic deployment and duration; it is, however, misleading in that if hope does have a course, it is not like the unwinding of a film of lived moments in the projector's light of consciousness. The course of hope is indissociable from the course of our life, on which it imprints its ups and downs: 'What goes on within also has meaning only in the stream of life' (LW II: 30).

We can then consider the picture of patterns in a weave as both stemming from and correcting the picture of stream of consciousness. Like James, Wittgenstein is well aware that each mental episode derives its meaning only in connection with what precedes, accompanies and follows it; but contrary to him, he does not see this context as a purely mental context; for Wittgenstein, the context is not only the stream of thought, but the stream of life.

Background and infinite variation through repetition

'We judge an action according to its background within human life' (RPP II: 624), and 'the background against which we see an action' is '[n]ot what *one* man is doing *now'*, but the stream, or as Wittgenstein also puts it, 'the whole hurly-burly' of human actions and passions (RPP II: 629). So that when we attribute a feeling or emotion to someone, it is the connection between what he does and what he says at a given moment, *as well as* this background that 'determines our judgment, our concepts, and our reactions' (ibid.). For example, when I say that A is really sad or that B's anger is feigned, my reaction and judgment here are due to the ability I have acquired in the course of my own life to identify the pattern of sadness and that of anger – two of the recurrent patterns in the carpet of human life.

In what terms can this background be described? What characterizes it? First, it is not an undifferentiated background, but is constituted by the interweaving of innumerable patterns, themselves infinitely repeated. The course of human life is made up of the interweaving of our feelings and ways of acting – pains, joys, hopes, ploys and so on – and consists of nothing but their infinite repetition. This means that in order to rest assured in our judgments, we have at our disposal no support or reference other than this perpetually moving background, which obeys no general plan nor is determined by some global order. The manner in which human actions and passions are intertwined is more like something resembling chaos or hurly-burly: 'How could human behaviour be described? Surely only by showing the actions of a variety of humans, as they are all mixed up together' (RPP II: 629).

Second, this background is not, for all that, pure diversity; regularities are also present. The actions and passions that make up the stream of life are always present in certain forms, in certain constantly recurring patterns. Indeed, the background has something of a mechanism: 'The background is the bustle (*Getriebe*[4]) of life' (RPP II: 625). Without this repetition, this mechanism, our concepts would have no grip: 'And our concept points to something within *this* bustle' (ibid.). That – to use current terminology – successive *tokens* of action (or passion) are organized according to a same *type* (a same pattern) and are subsumed under this same type (or pattern) does not mean that they are strictly identical to each other; on the contrary – and this is the third feature of the background – each *type* or pattern admits of a limitless variability of *tokens*. Variability in the expression of any feeling is essential to that feeling in that it is a human feeling: 'Variability itself is a characteristic of behaviour without which behaviour would be to us as something completely different. (The facial features characteristic of grief, for instance, are not more meaningful than their mobility.)' (RPP II: 627). Sadness, like any other emotion, has characteristic facial, bodily and verbal expressions without which we could not identify it as sadness; but neither could we attribute sadness to a face if that face were only capable of displaying stereotypical and rigid expressions, jumping, as it were, from one to the other as in a mediocre cartoon. Both mobility of facial features (or bodily postures) and continuity in the diverse successive expressions of the same feeling contribute to the identity of that feeling. And so, '[a] facial expression that was completely fixed couldn't be a friendly one. Variability and irregularity are essential to a friendly expression. Irregularity is part of its physiognomy' (RPP II: 615). Conversely, if I try to imagine circumstances in which I would be inclined to say of a human body that it had no soul, '[t]he *only* thing I can imagine in that case is that this human body acts like an automaton' (LW II: 66) – that is to say, it would be a body which lacked the permanent variability and mobility of expression.

Third, the concept of irregularity (*Unregelmässigkeit*) must be understood in the strict sense of absence of rules. The diverse *tokens* of a *type* (or pattern) are not related to each other, or to the type, by any rule; nor is there, for each *type* of emotion or feeling, a delimited set of expressive characteristics to be found in each of its occurrences. The variability of each type (or pattern) is therefore unlimited. The pattern does not exist in advance, or independently, of its repetition, and has therefore no strict delimitation or essence. It is the repetition of analogous (or seen as analogous) configurations that engenders the pattern; however, what repeats itself has, as such, no beginning or end; an analogous or neighbouring configuration can always be found going up- or downstream: 'For a bustle comes about only through constant repetition. And there is no definite starting point for "constant repetition"', writes Wittgenstein (RPP II: 626). In its indefinite repetition, a pattern has, as it were, no fixed edges and is always susceptible of new metamorphoses. (Here, a *rapprochement* might be made – though Wittgenstein does not, to my knowledge, make it – with the principle of musical variation, where a theme's repeated variation makes it unrecognizable, or even metamorphosed into another theme – as, for instance, Diabelli's waltz, which Beethoven varies to the point where it becomes a melody by Leporello in Mozart's *Don Giovanni*.)

The picture of patterns and the indeterminacy of the mental

What can we gather from this description of the carpet of human life as a *background*? Certainly, a form of organization can be discerned, but which is not the product of a law that determines each of its applications. When order emerges from obstinate, but constantly varied, repetition, it necessarily leaves room within itself for a good deal of irreducible indeterminacy. Peter Hacker rightly speaks, in this regard, of the *indeterminacy of the mental* (1993: 136–41). To help us understand the nature of this indeterminacy, Wittgenstein uses a picture not unlike that of the carpet, which seems but a more elementary variation of it: that of a strip of paper on which a stencilled pattern (*Schablone*) regularly recurs:

> 'If a concept refers to a certain pattern of life (*Lebensschablone*) then it has to contain a degree of indefiniteness.' I am thinking of something like this: On a strip of paper we have a continuous and regular pattern of bands. This pattern of bands forms the background for an irregular drawing or painting, which we describe in relation to the pattern, since this relation is what matters to us. If the pattern were to run: a b c a b c a b c etc., I would have a special concept, for example, for something red that is on a *c*, and something green that appears on the following *b*.
>
> Now once anomalies occur in the pattern I will be in doubt as to which judgment ought to be made. But couldn't my instruction have provided for this? Or *do I simply assume* that in being instructed in the use of the concept, that particular pattern was just taken for granted, but was never itself described?
>
> (LW I: 206)

How are we to understand this slightly complicated comparison? There is, in human life, a repertory of feelings and ways of acting which we use to identify and characterize a particular action or attribute a particular feeling to someone (just as we can identify different shades from a colour sample card). But there can be anomalies. Upon being told of the death of a loved one, some people, rather than break down in tears, remain impassive; not because they feel nothing, but because their pain is so deep that it finds, at that moment, no appropriate form of bodily or verbal expression. The pattern of affliction or of great moral suffering admits of this extreme variation whose manifestation is diametrically opposed to its more common manifestations, and strangely resembles the manifestation of indifference or of Spartan-like self-controlled emotion. How then do we settle on what is being manifested? The pattern of affliction is in fact so complex and variable that, as Wittgenstein says, it has never been described to us. We have learned to use it through a kind of *training* set up by education on the basis of our primitive emotions and reactions. But it does constitute a background, something presupposed. In ordinary cases, we can rely on it, but in certain situations, we are bereft of all criteria and know not what to think. We might, writes Wittgenstein, picture the background 'as a very complicated filigree pattern, which, to be sure, we can't copy, but which we can recognize from the general impression it makes' (RPP II: 624).

The same comparison to a recurrent motif on a strip of paper occurs in another context where, this time, the discussion concerns the possibility of distinguishing between patterns of genuine and simulated pain. Pretence is a pattern in its own right, with characteristic circumstances and external signs; and there are clear cases of genuine pain and clear cases of simulated pain. The problem is, as previously, that we cannot draw an exhaustive list of traits belonging to genuine pain that would distinguish it from its simulated counterpart. There are cases, then, where I will be hesitant to declare whether the pain I am witnessing someone as having is real or not; and even cases that are undecidable – cases where the authenticity/pretence alternative is not pertinent at all:

> Imagine it were really a case of patterns on a long ribbon.
>
> The ribbon moves past me and now I say 'This is the pattern S', now 'This is the pattern V'. Sometimes for a period of time I do not know which it is; sometimes I say at the end 'It was neither'.
>
> How could I be taught to recognize these patterns? I am shown simple examples, and then complicated ones of both kinds. It is almost the way I learn to distinguish the styles of two composers.
>
> (LW II: 42–3)

I have learned to recognize these two patterns, but not by applying rules transmitted to me in advance. A music lover who knows nothing of the rudiments of music can, upon hearing the first bars of a piece he has never previously heard, recognize its composer from habit: generally, a phrase from Schumann does not have the same physiognomy or atmosphere as one from Chopin. The music lover may have created his own musical sample-card. In his case, recognition will often be immediate, although he may be incapable of justifying his conviction by a technical enumeration of the precise characteristics that enabled his identification of the piece, and which would give others reasons to share his judgment. What we have here is evidence that is not based on rules, or what Wittgenstein often calls *imponderable evidence* (cf. PI: p. 228). Yet, of course there are cases where the absence of rules leaves us undecided, or even cases where a person is left undecided while another is absolutely certain.

Under pressure from the inner/outer picture, we are generally tempted to see such perplexing or undecidable cases as indicative of the metaphysical inaccessibility of others' mental states. The advantage of the 'patterns in a carpet' picture is that it allows us to say instead that these are simply situations in which *we do not see* the pattern. Either because the variation we are witnessing is too unlike that of the common model (as in the case of deep, silent pain); or because the figure (or motif) we encounter is particularly ambiguous and can be seen as one pattern or another (either as genuine pain or as simulated pain); or, finally, because we have here to do with a figure that cannot be related to any pattern at all in our usual repertoire without being seriously falsified or deformed. Indeed, there are cases in which it simply makes no sense to ask if a person is sincere or not:

> Just think of how often we can't say: someone is honest or dishonest, sincere or insincere. (A politician, for example.) Well-meaning or the opposite. How many foolish questions get asked here! How often *the concepts don't fit!'*

> (RPP II: 713)

The inappropriateness of these questions and concepts is *not* due to an unbridgeable gap between the multiform irregularity of psychical phenomena and the regulated uniformity that would be required for a meaningful use of the concepts. To suggest that would be to echo James's and Bergson's complaint about the poverty and rigidity of our language, supposed incapable of rendering the richness and fluidity of experience and life. Rather, the inappropriateness is due to an incompleteness inherent in the language-game itself.

Indeed, it would be an illusion to think that because we have discerned the occurrence of a pattern, all the traits that can be linked to that pattern *must* be there; and that, if we do not see them, it is because they are hidden in an 'inner' or an 'unconscious'. On the contrary, the very principle of the 'patterns in a carpet' picture – that of infinite repetition by variation – guarantees that no single occurrence of simulated hope or joy presents all the characteristics of simulated hope or joy. Each *token* is necessarily incomplete. But, because we subsume all occurrences of a single pattern under the same concept, we tend to believe that simulated hope or joy *must* include the same characteristics in each of their occurrences. This tendency to want to complete what 'mere' description seems to leave incomplete is at the heart of the *illusion of theory* that Wittgenstein relentlessly seeks to root out:

> Seeing life as a weave, this pattern (pretence, say) is not always complete and is varied in a multiplicity of ways. But we, in our conceptual

world, keep on seeing the same, recurring with variations. That is how our concepts take it. For concepts are not for use on a *single* occasion.

(RPP II: 672)

'Here *is* the whole. (If you complete it, you falsify it.)' (RPP I: 257)

In his *Lectures on Philosophical Psychology, 1946–47*, Wittgenstein asks us to imagine that we are the masters of a tribe of slaves who have no soul, but to whom we want to teach the use of our psychological vocabulary; for, in order to have the slaves execute tasks, we need them to tell us about their aptitude to work, whether they are not feeling well and the like. In other words, we want to teach them to signal through 'I am in pain' that they are in pain so we can fetch the doctor, or to signal through 'I am depressed' that they are lacking in stamina so we can have someone replace them at their job. And because we are to suppose them as having no 'inner', the only way we can teach them these signals is on the basis of their behaviour. So now we are faced with people who have a whole gamut of bodily behaviour – they groan, cry, stamp their feet – but nothing *a priori* compels us to group certain moves as typical manifestations of pain or depression:

> If we see people groaning, crying, etc., what says how we are to group together phenomena of pain? We distinguish moaning with pain from moaning without pain by various criteria, e.g. whether the man has hurt himself. But need we group phenomena that way? ... With the slaves, we are interested only in their behaviour as regards their work. But why should I take notice when a slave scratches or shrieks? Why should I group together a facial expression of cheerfulness and an expression of cheerfulness in bodily movements?
>
> (LPP: 38)

Groupings necessarily have something arbitrary about them: depending on our needs and interests, we bring together under a single pattern traits that are, at first glance, unrelated, and we attribute to different patterns apparently similar traits:

> For a purpose, I group behaviour which offhand differs; and I distinguish behaviour which offhand looks alike. Off-hand one wouldn't group together drumming on the chest and bared teeth, but both are danger signals. Again, a grin of friendship grin of rage may be visually

similar, but the consequences are different. You go by what follows,
e.g. he bares his teeth in rage; in friendship; to clean them.

(LPP: 281 and 39)[5]

This brief exercise in fictional anthropology allows us to see that our concepts of 'joy' or 'pain' do not refer so much to simple and quantitatively
unique experiences as to groupings we effect, arbitrarily or in any case
according to our interests, of compound and heterogeneous traits. And so
the pattern of pain is constituted of at least five different types of elements:

> (1) primitive pain-expression, crying, writhing, etc., (2) causes of pain,
> etc., burning, cutting, etc., (3) things to relieve pain, (4) emotional reac-
> tion to pain, (5) effects of pain – e.g. I should not trust a workman if
> he were in pain.

(LPP: 38)

Note that in characteristic features of physical pain, Wittgenstein unhesi-
tatingly includes causes as well as our own reactions to another's pain,
which – but I cannot here further elaborate this important point – belong
to our criteria for the use of the concept of pain.

In *Remarks on the Philosophy of Psychology*, Wittgenstein takes a slightly
less speculative example – that of the *sly idiot*. We might happen to call
someone *sly* without alluding to the presence in his mind at a given
moment of an intention to deceive – perhaps because knowing the person's limited capacities, we would judge such a mental representation
too complex for him. The utterance 'he is sly' would not therefore point
to the presence 'in the agent's mind' of any particular thought, but to a
number of expressive and contextual characteristics of his behaviour,
which we identified as belonging to the motif of slyness:

> An idiot could behave slyly, for that's what we'd call it, but we wouldn't
> think him capable of *planning* anything. If we're asked 'What's going
> on inside him?' we say, 'Surely very little goes on inside him.' But
> what do we know about it?! We construct a picture of it according to
> his behaviour, his utterances, his ability to think.

(RPP II: 650)

And Wittgenstein then adds, in a slightly elliptical manner: 'The picture
of the inner completes the Gestalt' (RPP II: 651). How should we
understand this?

To realize that the idiot is sly, I need not – this is what the example
shows – conjecture that he, at any time, contrived a plot. My consideration

of the idiot as sly occurs immediately in my identification of his *behaviour* as sly; that is, as having the pattern of slyness. I spot his slyness in his very words and deeds. In such conditions, if the picture of the inner intervenes, it does so after the fact, as it were, so as to suggest either that, in his deeper self, the idiot *must after all have* contrived some kind of plot; or, failing this, that some unconscious mechanism *must after all have* pushed him to behave as he did. This amounts both to reducing the slyness to an episode that took place, consciously or not, in the mind of the agent; and to seeing, in that postulated mental episode, the explanation of that individual's behaviour. But to thus complete the description is to falsify it by introducing a putative explanation:

> Mere description is so difficult because one believes that one needs to fill out the facts in order to understand them. It is as if one saw a screen with scattered colour-patches, and said: the way they are here, they are unintelligible; they only make sense when one completes them into a shape (*Gestalt*). – Whereas I want to say: Here *is* the whole. (If you complete it, you falsify it.)
>
> (RPP I: 257)

Someone who thinks that the pattern of slyness remains incomplete as long as it is not connected to a hypothetical inner episode is like the viewer of an abstract painting who, not content to see, as Maurice Denis famously put it, only 'a flat surface filled with colours put together in a particular order', tries to complete it until he sees what he is irresistibly inclined to look for: 'a horse, a naked woman, an anecdote' (1890: 51). In its strict sense, the question: 'What took place *in the mind* of the idiot?' has no more pertinence than the question that might be asked when viewing an abstract painting: 'What does it represent?' The illusion is the same: we believe that, in order to recognize and identify what lies plainly in view, we must look for something that is behind or beyond. Unsatisfied by the colour lines and spots that are there on the flat surface of the painting, I look behind this surface, in the depth of a third dimension, for the horse or nude whose existence would allow me, or so I believe, to both describe differently these lines and spots, and explain their presence. Not satisfied with a person's apparent anger or sadness, I feel bound to conjecture the existence, in the backstage of her mind, of states and processes which would constitute both the true reality of her anger or sadness and the explanation of their nature.

Wittgenstein in no way contests the legitimacy of our looking for explanations for someone's anger or sadness, no more than we would contest someone's right to look for explanations of an abstract painting. Viewing a *Composition* or an *Improvisation* by Kandinsky, I might want to know the reasons that motivated the artist to paint it, what techniques he employed or what optical laws he used to produce that particular contrast or effect; and I would then obtain explanations of various kinds. But to want, at all costs, to see in the painting the picture of a horse or a naked woman, as if this were a Rorschach test, will take me nowhere. Even if, through a kind of psychological projection, I did succeed in seeing a woman or a horse, not only would this fail to provide me with an explanation of anything, but more importantly, I will have contrived a superfluous, and particularly cumbersome picture which will thereafter prevent me from simply seeing what is before my eyes. Analogously, I can certainly ponder the reasons for someone's anger or research the physiological processes of anger, but if I contend that the truth or reality of the anger consists in a mental state or process belonging to an *inner space*, not only will I have found no explanation for the anger, but I will have fabricated a theoretical representation of a psychological phenomena that will prevent me from seeing what anger is – that is, how it differs from pain or hope.

In the *Lectures on Philosophical Psychology*, Wittgenstein notes that once we consider pain, depression or anger as psychological phenomena, and once we treat sentences such as 'He has pain', 'He is depressed', 'He is in rage' as descriptions of states or processes that occur in the head or in an inner, we tend to make them all comparable, put them all on the same plane, and thus neglect their differences:

> Originally [in the fable of the soulless tribe] we did not speak of psychological phenomena. But now we do. We introduce a picture of the phenomenon he now observes. The picture has an equalizing influence. ... At first when we treated them as signals, there seemed to be no comparison between them at all. What the equalization does is to conceal the uniqueness of each of these.
>
> (LPP: 164)

'Uniqueness' does not here refer to a qualitatively unique experience, but to the fact that each type of signal (or verbal expression) has a meaning only if it occurs in determinate circumstances with determinate consequences. Imagine that we had taught our imagined soulless slaves the use of four signals:

(i) The pain signal: it generally goes with the name of a part of the body, or a gesture. The name of the part of the body is generally used when hurt there. Also, this has various consequences. (ii) Another signal – the depression signal; in this case, there is no injury. It is something completely different. Even if he wipes away tears, I do not do anything to his eyes. (iii) Want signal: the slave utters a word for some food or fruit. (iv) Another signal: 'I'm going to do that.' Of these we can say: (a) These may be important. (b) The slave gives them without observing himself. (c) Usually, we can rely on what follows. (d) The signals need not to be of comparable use to me.

(LPP: 163)

What happens if we now treat pain, depression, desire and intention as psychological phenomena, as states of things of an inner world?

Suppose someone says – he is having an experience in all the cases. What does it matter? There is nothing common among them. They do not suggest even anything comparable going on anywhere. ... The psychological concepts are not comparable in the way in which James thinks.

(LPP: 163)

What Wittgenstein has in mind here is the James-Lange theory of emotions, which identifies the emotions with generalized bodily sensations[6] – sensations produced by our body's reactions to certain situations, whether we are conscious of it or not. The James-Lange theory is typical of a theory that completes the pattern. All emotion is said to be diffuse bodily sensations and if, as in the case of depression, we are not aware of them, *they must nevertheless necessarily* exist. The tendency to complete the pattern with a picture of the inner is what makes us slide from the rough ground of description towards pseudo-theoretical constructions with scientific pretensions, what Wittgenstein calls *metaphysics*.

It can now be seen how radically different Wittgenstein's use of the metaphor of patterns in a carpet is from that of Henry James's. Certainly, in both cases, grasp of a pattern symbolizes access to a synoptic view, an *übersichtliche Darstellung*, of either the writer's entire *oeuvre*, or the grammar of psychological concepts. But, for Henry James, to see an *oeuvre* through a single pattern would be to have gained access to the single perspective from which its perfect unity and utter completion would be revealed. That perspective, if it existed, would give absolute understanding and total satisfaction. For Wittgenstein, on the other hand, to see human life as a multiplicity of infinitely varied patterns, is to free oneself from the obsession of reducing all of it to an idea, a principle, a system.

Giving up the idea of a total or unifying picture can be frustrating, but the synoptic view sought by Wittgenstein is one that will make us pay attention to the irreducible heterogeneity of psychological phenomena, and of psychological concepts and their uses. It appears, then, that the picture of 'patterns in a carpet' was indeed a successful *guiding picture*: it gave the phenomenological research that the later Wittgenstein was engaged in, the right direction.

Notes

1. The impostor in Molière's *Tartuffe*.
2. Cf., in any case, John V. Canfield's 'Pretence and the Inner', in Moyal-Sharrock (2004b), 145–58.
3. All quotations in the next two paragraphs are extracted from MS 124: pp. 228–35; translated from the German by DMS.
4. The French translation renders *Getriebe* as 'mécanisme'; the English as 'bustle'. 'Bustle' does not sufficiently evoke the notions of a mechanism and of repetition, essential to Wittgenstein's point, which he explicitly makes: 'And it is the very concept 'bustle' (*Getriebe*') that brings about this indefiniteness. For a bustle comes about only through constant repetition. And there is no definite starting point for "constant repetition" ' (RPP II: 626). On the other hand, 'mécanisme' fails to render the indefiniteness also essential to the kind of repetition in question: one embedded in life. Having contemplated alternatives, such as 'movement', 'drive', 'bustle' still strikes me as the best translation in that it does convey something of a repeated movement, whilst retaining indefiniteness.
5. Here, sentences borrowed from Jackson's and from Geach's accounts are intermingled.
6. Wittgenstein: 'There was a theory (James-Lange) that an emotion is a generalized bodily feeling. "A man is sad because he cries," said James; he meant that part of your sadness is *feeling* yourself cry' (LPP: 39).

11
Wittgenstein on Psychological Certainty

Danièle Moyal-Sharrock

> Subjective and objective certainty.
> Why do I want to say '2 × 2 = 4' is objectively certain, and
> 'This man is in pain' only subjectively?
>
> (LW II: 23)

Wittgenstein gives approximately 300 examples of basic certainties in *On Certainty*, and we are well aware that these are but an infinitesimal sample of the innumerable basic certainties that underpin our everyday acting, thinking and speaking in the world. Examples of these are: 'My name is such and such' (OC: 571), 'The person opposite me is my old friend so and so' (OC: 613), 'I have never been on the moon' (OC: 218), 'Cats don't grow on trees' (OC: 282), ''I have a body' (OC: 244), 'Here is a hand' (OC: 9), 'My hands don't disappear when I'm not paying attention to them' (OC: 153), 'I am a human being' (OC: 4), 'The words composing this sentence are English' (OC: 158). There is, however, a specific subgroup of basic certainties – or what we might call 'hinge certainties'[1] – that is hardly mentioned in *On Certainty*: these are *psychological* certainties.[2] These, Wittgenstein largely addresses in his writings and lectures on philosophical psychology, the last of which – *Last Writings on the Philosophy of Psychology, Volume II* – is contemporaneous with the notes that make up *On Certainty*. The aim of this chapter is to follow the *third* Wittgenstein – that is the post-*Investigations*, Part I Wittgenstein[3] – in his attempt to grasp the nature of our psychological certainty. But note that the certainty in question here is psychological not in its nature, but in its objects: it is a certainty regarding things psychological. Indeed, I will argue that, on Wittgenstein's view, some *psychological* certainties – both first- and third-person – have a *logical* status.

As is well known, Wittgenstein pointed out an asymmetry between first- and third-person psychological statements:[4] the latter, unlike the former, involve observation or a claim to knowledge,[5] and are therefore *constitutionally* open to uncertainty. In this chapter, I challenge this asymmetry by challenging the *constitutional* uncertainty of third-person psychological sentences, and argue that Wittgenstein ultimately also did.

I begin by suggesting that, on Wittgenstein's view, most of our *third-person* psychological statements are noncognitive; they stem from a *subjective* certainty which, though not the result of an epistemic process such as inference, is not invulnerable to error in that it is a kind of *assumption*. I then go on to show that, following relentless questioning and wavering, Wittgenstein concedes that some third-person psychological certainties are not merely subjective but (what he calls) objective; that is, they are logically indubitable (of the same order as 'I am in pain' or '$2 \times 2 = 4$'; cf. epigraph above). This puts in question Wittgenstein's affirmation of a first-/third-person asymmetry, but it also positively reinforces his rebuttal of other mind scepticism. I conclude with a response to objections about the legitimacy of calling an assurance that is *logical* (i.e., that does not have uncertainty or doubt on its flipside) a 'certainty', by suggesting that the flipside is to be found in pathological cases. I focus here on cases of *dyssemia* – a disability affecting non-verbal communication, whereby individuals cannot properly interpret the meaning of, and/or express meaning through, facial expressions, tone of voice, body movements, posture, gestures and so on. Such pathological cases constitute a foil to the default objective certainty with which we ordinarily grasp and express basic expressions.

1   Wittgenstein's objective ('hinge') certainty

> Need I be less certain that someone is suffering pain than that $12 \times 12 = 144$?
>
> (LW II: p. 92)

In *Last Writings* II, Wittgenstein himself marks a distinction between subjective and objective certainty (cf. introductory epigraph). But what Wittgenstein calls 'objective certainty' differs from what is usually understood by 'objective certainty': it is neither a certainty *à la* Nagel grounded on mind- or human-independent objectivity, nor a certainty based on 'compelling grounds' (OC: 270), and therefore indistinguishable from knowledge. What Wittgenstein understands by *objective certainty* is *not* to be confused with knowledge;[6] it is a certainty in which mistake is 'logically', not *rationally*, excluded:

> With the word 'certain' we express complete conviction, the total absence of doubt, and thereby we seek to convince other people. That

is *subjective* certainty. But when is something objectively certain? When a mistake is not possible. But what kind of possibility is that? Mustn't mistake be *logically* excluded?

(OC: 194)

I now briefly describe the nature of that objective or logical certainty which characterizes our basic certainties,[7] before going on to address its psychological variety. On Wittgenstein's view, our basic certainties are not falsifiable propositions but unhesitating *attitudes* or *ways of acting*[8] that are reflex-like and that only show themselves, *qua* certainties, *in* what we do and *in* what we say. So, for instance, our certainty that newborns cannot care for themselves shows itself in our feeding and clothing them, and in our saying such things as 'I need a babysitter for tonight'. We sometimes formulate our basic certainties (e.g., the sentences: 'Human beings think', 'Newborns cannot pretend', 'We cannot feel another's pain'), but such *sentences* do not, *qua* basic certainties, constitute propositions or thoughts; they are mere formulations – mostly for heuristic reasons, such as philosophical analysis or pedagogical instruction – of certainties that are nothing but natural reflexes (e.g., 'I have a body') or acquired automatisms (e.g., 'This is (what we call) a hand'). What makes these *objective* (or *hinge*) is that unlike *subjective* certainties, they *logically* underpin our epistemic enquiries; which means, as Wittgenstein makes clear, that someone seriously purporting to 'doubt' them could only (1) be prey to a psychological disorder:

'If someone said to me that he doubted whether he had a body, I should take him to be a half-wit.'

(OC: 257)

'If Moore were to pronounce the opposite of those propositions which he declares certain, we should not just share his opinion: we should regard him as demented.'

(OC: 155)

or (2) not be engaged in *real* doubt, but only in the behaviour of doubt:[9]

Doubting has certain characteristic manifestations, but they are only characteristic of it in particular circumstances. If someone said that he doubted the existence of his hands, kept looking at them from all sides, tried to make sure it wasn't 'all done by mirrors', etc., we should not be sure whether we ought to call that doubting. We might describe his way of behaving as like the behaviour of doubt, but his game would not be ours.

(OC: 255)

or (3) be prey to a linguistic misunderstanding:

If someone were to look at an English pillar-box and say 'I am sure that it's red', we should have to suppose that he was colour-blind or believe he had no mastery of English and knew the correct name for the colour in some other language.

(OC: 526)

2   The pull in two directions

Before we begin investigating the nature of specifically psychological certainties, I would like to suggest the existence, throughout Wittgenstein's philosophizing, of a persistent pull in two directions: on one hand, his *reactive* and *revolutionary* resistance to sharp boundaries and closed concepts, to Platonic essences or Kantian schemata – a resistance that gives rise to family resemblance concepts, highlights the positive importance of indeterminacy of sense, and appeals to the notion of *imponderable* evidence – the stress being on 'imponderable' (cf. LW I: 920–4). Pulling against this reactive and revolutionary tendency, however, is a *reactionary* one which I want to draw attention to particularly because it is not sufficiently recognized; indeed, the slightest allusion to any such tendency is rejected by many Wittgensteinians, especially those of Therapeutic, or New Wittgensteinian persuasion.[10] This reactionary pull is a constant gravitating back, on Wittgenstein's part, towards regularity, predictability, fixity, and indubitability. It translates itself in the work as an urge to draw limits (e.g., to thought or sense, as in the *Tractatus*; cf. Preface); as a repeated appeal to *frames of reference*;[11] an acknowledgement of *foundations* (even 'unmoving' ones) – those of our language-games (e.g., OC: 403), or of thought and action (e.g., OC: 411), *scaffoldings* (of the world: TLP: 6.124, or of our thoughts: OC: 211), and *hard substrata* (of our concepts: RPP I: 600, or of all our enquiring and asserting: OC: 162); a growing commitment to the idea that for the door of inquiry to turn, its hinges must *stay put* (OC: 343); and a relentless urge to find that *stopping* place of inquiry, where one's justifications are exhausted, and where one's spade is turned (PI: 217). This tendency is certainly not limited to *On Certainty* – indeed, the drawing of limits to thought or sense is from the *Tractatus*, and the 'turned spade' image comes from the *Investigations*.

It is also blatantly visible in the philosophy of psychology: in Wittgenstein's repeated and explicit attempts to *classify* psychological concepts (cf. RPP II: 148) and to trace *patterns* of life (LW I: 211);[12] in his reminders that, though psychological judgment is by no means an exact science, *Menschenerkenntnis* can be learned from someone more 'expert' than oneself, and improved through experience;[13] and in the stress he also puts on *evidence* in 'imponderable evidence'. Two directions, then: one away from regularity and fixity; the other towards it. So that this same philosopher can say both that 'the application of a word is not everywhere bounded by rules' (PI: 84) and that '[t]he rule-governed nature of our language permeates our life' (RC III: 303).

The pull both ways is particularly noticeable throughout the third Wittgenstein's questionings on psychological certainty. There is a constant vacillation and struggle between two imperatives that is well encapsulated in the notion of 'imponderable evidence': acknowledging and formulating the buzzing indeterminacy, spontaneity and irreducibility of human life,[14] whilst perspicuously assessing its basic regularity and predictability, as well as the certainty on which it is all hinged. For, that is what Wittgenstein – as he is unravelling the hurly-burly of our actions – keeps bumping into again and again: a fundamental, reliably human, 'constant repetition' (RPP II: 626); and a certainty which, without reason or justification, lies there as the given and necessary bedrock on which our uncertainties can battle. The pull both ways is then symptomatic of the *difficulty* Wittgenstein is experiencing in his attempts to describe our ways of thinking and acting, as well as of the *nature* of what he is attempting to describe. For, as Jean-Jacques Rosat puts it (p. 200), in his chapter in this volume:

> The course of human life is made up of the interweaving of our feelings and ways of acting – pains, joys, hopes, ploys and so on – and consists of nothing but their infinite repetition. This means that in order to rest assured in our judgments, we have at our disposal no support or reference other than this perpetually moving background, which obeys no general plan nor is determined by some global order. The manner in which human actions and passions are intertwined is more like something resembling chaos or hurly-burly. ... [Yet] this background is not, for all that, pure diversity; regularities are also present. The actions and passions that make up the stream of life are always present in certain forms, in certain constantly recurring patterns. ... Without this repetition, this mechanism, our concepts would have no grip.

There is an *indefiniteness* or *indeterminacy* essential to the kind of *repetition* in question; for it is a repetition that is embedded in life. And yet, as Wittgenstein takes the plunge, for philosophy, from the static, abstract, sovereign regularity of third realms into the stream of life, he realizes that the stream could not be one if it had no bedrock. But let us first see how Wittgenstein deals with the indeterminacy.

3 *Logical* indeterminacy and *constitutional* uncertainty

For Wittgenstein, the background of psychological judgements is a pattern in highly complicated filigree (RPP II: 642). Human behaviour is not everywhere uniform or predictable, and so the concepts that capture that behaviour are accordingly indeterminate. This indeterminacy shows itself above all 'in two prominent aspects of human life: (i) the irregularity of human physiognomy; (ii) the unpredictability of human behaviour' (ter Hark, 1990: 149). Our form of life is such that there is not only one, or even a handful of 'occasions' that we might call 'grief', but innumerable ones that are interwoven with a thousand other patterns (cf. LW I: 966). And this is so for *all* our psychological concepts, because the 'natural foundation' for the way they are formed 'is the complex nature and the variety of human contingencies' (RPP II: 614). As a result the concepts themselves lack determinacy and have a kind of elasticity. Where Wittgenstein's agenda is to capture the natural indeterminacy in our psychological concepts and judgments – 'I do not want to reduce unsharpness to sharpness; but to capture unsharpness conceptually' (MS 1367: 64) – most philosophers attempt to tame or reduce the indeterminacy; that is, to simplify, formalize or schematize it.[15] But, as Wittgenstein suggests, any attempt to give our psychological concepts fixed limits, to reduce or restrain the variety, would not be an attempt to draw *our* concepts (cf. RPP II: 615). It is, then, to be expected that such indeterminacy of sense should result in uncertainty of judgment:

> Concepts with fixed limits would demand a uniformity of behaviour. But what happens is that where I am *certain*, someone else is uncertain. And that is a fact of nature.
>
> (RPP II: 683)

Still, Wittgenstein cautions us against seeing the uncertainty in our psychological judgments as the inevitable result of the *hidden nature of mind* or of a temporary blindness due to our not (yet) having the right epistemic tools at our disposal; rather, he says, it is an *objective* uncertainty, and he calls it (or rather, he calls the certainty regarding this uncertainty) *constitutional*:[16]

> 'To be sure, this uncertainty isn't always subjective, but sometimes *objective*.' (But what does that mean?)
>
> (LW I: 887)

> 'Objective uncertainty' is an indefiniteness *in the nature of the game,* in the admissible evidence.
>
> (LW I: 888; my emphasis)

> The uncertainty of the ascription 'He's got a pain' might be called a constitutional certainty.
>
> (RPP I: 141)[17]

Our psychological judgments are uncertain or indeterminate because our psychological concepts are indeterminate; and our psychological concepts are indeterminate because human behaviour is indeterminate. So that, unlike *subjective* uncertainty, *objective* uncertainty, is *not* due to an epistemic shortcoming that can be remedied, say, by getting closer to the evidence; it is an *essential* feature of our psychological concepts.[18] This means that, unlike most of our physical concepts, our psychological ones could seek precision only at the cost of betraying the very nature of their object: 'unforeseeability must be *an* essential property of the mental. Just like the endless multiplicity of expression' (LW II: 65).

Wittgenstein does not view psychological indeterminacy as a vice of psychological concepts, but nor does he see it as pervasive or all-prevailing:

> We are playing with elastic, indeed even flexible concepts. But this does not mean that they can be deformed *at will* and without offering resistance, and are therefore *unusable*.
>
> (LW II: p. 24)

For, though our psychological language-games are elastic, they are not so elastic as to lack a hard core, or what ter Hark calls 'a solid centre of meaning'. In his analysis of individual psychological concepts, such as 'willing' or 'expecting', ter Hark writes:

> ... Wittgenstein, as a philosopher, does draw sharp lines and boundaries. In this way he shows that psychological concepts within language-games have a solid centre of meaning. Although he is convinced that

these concepts too show a certain elasticity at their edges, since they are embedded in forms of life, this does not mean that their meaning cannot be clearly defined within certain limits.

(1990: 153)

Indeed, both Rosat and ter Hark find that Wittgenstein's depiction of psychological indeterminacy is everywhere bounded – not by rules, but by certain *regularities*.[19] As Rosat makes clear, an 'order' emerges from obstinate, though constantly varied, repetition; the evidence has telltale *characteristics*, our feelings and behaviours are informed by *patterns*; *typical physiognomies*, indeed a *constitutive* rhythm and tempo (see p. 197). Also, as Wittgenstein notes, 'here there are simple and more complicated cases; and that is important for the concept' (LWI: 967) – indeed, for it is the simple cases that give the concept its solid centre, its unambiguous core. Though the margin is elastic, though '[s]ufficient evidence passes over into insufficient without a borderline' (RPP II: 614), there is a core of sufficient evidence provided by the simple cases; so that where the evidence for real laughter is insufficient, it is not so insufficient as to be evidence for the opposite.[20] Similarly, if '[s]omebody gets burned and cries out; only in very rare circumstances would his behaviour be called "pretence"' (LWI: 967).

And so our uncertainty, however *objective* or *constitutional*, turns out, for all that, not to be pervasive. Because of the overlapping of our concepts, our judgment often 'fluctuates' (LW I: 953); but not always:

'The *uncertainty* whether someone else ... is an (essential) trait of all these language-games. But this does not mean that everyone is hopelessly in doubt about what other people feel.'

(LW I: 877)

Recognizing the extent of 'psychological indeterminacy' does not blind Wittgenstein to the possibility of psychological certainty. Although he admits that '[t]here is no clear border separating sufficient from insufficient evidence', he goes on to say: 'And yet, there is evidence here' (LW I: 952). He calls this evidence *imponderable* (LW I: 921). It is evidence that does not have the character of proof such as might be presented in a court of law, but that includes such things as 'subtleties of tone, of glance, of gesture' (LW I: 936). Still, the indeterminate nature of the evidence does not preclude it from being evidence:

That an actor can represent grief shows the uncertainty of evidence, but that he can represent *grief* also shows the reality of evidence.

(LW II: p. 67)

That *an actor* can represent grief shows that we can be tricked into believing that someone is grieving when they are in fact not grieving; but that he *can* do this; that he knows what gestures, what posture, what tone to adopt in order for us to believe he (his character) is grieving – indeed, to the extent that some of us shed tears of compassion for him – shows the *reality* of the evidence. As Wittgenstein writes: '"That seems genuine" only makes sense if there is a "That is genuine"' (LW II: 86). Our emotionally engaging in something that is not real but only pretence or 'make-believe' is due precisely to the fact that there is something that we consider 'the real thing' that can be imitated. And it is, as Wittgenstein affirms, only in the power of great art to capture it:

I can recognize a genuine loving look, distinguish it from a pretended one. And yet there is no way in which I can describe it to someone else. If we had a great painter here, he might conceivably represent a genuine and a simulated look in pictures … .

(LWI: 937)

And here, it is important to distinguish, with Wittgenstein, between our *right* to treat something as evidence, and our inability to spell out (to more than 'full detail') the evidence that it is:

Haven't I the *right* to be convinced that he is not pretending to me? – And can't I convince someone else of my right?

(RPP II: 589)

If I tell him in full detail how my friend behaved, will he have any reasonable doubt as to the genuineness of my friend's feelings?
Does anyone doubt the genuineness of Lear's feelings?

(RPP II: 590)

That the evidence is not clear-cut (that the reasons for the certainty cannot be specified (cf. RPP II: 654)) does not make it less compelling:

If it is said, 'Evidence can only make it probable that expressions of emotions are genuine', this does *not* mean that instead of complete certainty we have just a more or less confident conjecture.

(RPP II: 684)

That the evidence is indeterminate does not make the certainty half-hearted; indeed, affirms Wittgenstein, imponderable evidence is sufficient to make one *completely certain*. But what does Wittgenstein mean here by 'complete certainty'? Are we in the realm of *subjective* certainty, where we might be *completely certain* – that is, convinced – and still be wrong? Or have we moved to the realm of *objective* certainty, where indubitability is not psychological or epistemic, but *logical*? Put another way, have we moved from asking: '*Does* anyone doubt the genuineness of Lear's feelings?' to: '*Can* anyone doubt the genuineness of Lear's feelings?' If we have, then Wittgenstein must have given up the idea of a *constitutional* uncertainty as regards third-person psychological judgments.

4　Kinds of psychological certainty

> And everything descriptive of a language-game is part of logic.
>
> (OC: 56)

4.1　Kinds of *objective* psychological certainty

In Table 11.1, I have listed the different kinds of psychological certainties that I take Wittgenstein to treat as *objective*. I will consider unproblematic the inclusion here of (C): sentences that resemble empirical descriptions or generalizations, but are in fact grammatical elucidations, either of (i) individual psychological concepts – what Wittgenstein also calls 'conceptual stipulations'[21] – of say, being grateful, regretting, pretending; or of (ii), what look more like anthropological generalizations, but are in fact also grammatical.[22] I will also consider unproblematic the inclusion of (A): first-person psychological certainties that are not descriptions.[23] But what about the inclusion of (B): some third-person psychological certainties? If, as I will suggest, this should also be seen as unproblematic, there must be less asymmetry between first- and third-person psychological ascriptions than Wittgenstein originally believed.

4.2　Third-person *subjective* psychological certainty

We grasp psychological phenomena, in most cases, without inference or indeed with no cognitive process taking place at all – immediately:

> ... We do not see facial contortions and *make the inference* that he is feeling joy, grief, boredom. We describe a face immediately as sad, radiant, bored, even when we are unable to give any other description of the features. – Grief, one would like to say, is personified in the face. This is essential to what we call 'emotion'.
>
> (RPP II:570)

Table 11.1 Kinds of objective psychological certainties

'And everything descriptive of a language-game is part of logic' (OC: 56)

(A) First-Person	(B) Third-Person	(C) Conceptual Elucidations	
		(i) Of Individual Concepts/verbs	(ii) Anthropo-logical …
			'The basic concepts are interwoven so closely with what is most fundamental in our way of living that they are therefore unassailable' (LW II: 43–4).
		EXAMPLES	
'I am in pain'	'He is in pain' (e.g. about someone falling into the flames and crying out (LPE: 287), or someone badly wounded and in dreadful pain (LW I: 964))	'We cannot feel another's pain' (LPP: 155) 'A man can pretend to be unconscious; but conscious?' (RPP I: 931)	'Human beings feel pain' 'Human beings sometimes think' (RPP II: 29) 'We can't talk about the joy and sorrow, etc. of fish' (RPP II: 29)
'I am a human being/ I have a mind'	'He is a human being' (about someone towards whom we have 'eine Einstellung zur Seele' – an attitude towards a soul (PI: p. 178))	'Neither is the newborn child capable of being malicious, friendly, or thankful. Thankfulness is only possible if there is already a complicated pattern of behaviour' (LW I: 942) 'A child learns to walk, to crawl, to play. It does not learn to play voluntarily and involuntarily' (RPP II: 269) 'Anyone who regrets something thinks about it' (RPP II: 306)	'… a table or a stone don't have any motives' (RPP I: 631) 'We don't say of a table and chair that they think; neither do we say this of a plant, a fish, and hardly of a dog; only of human beings. And not even of all human beings' (RPP II: 192) 'An animal cannot point to a thing that interests it' (LW II: 41)

In most cases, we do not infer from someone's behaviour that he is sad or angry. We will not ask ourselves whether a driver shouting insults in the direction of a car that is blocking traffic, repeatedly pounding on his horn, eyes glaring and nose flaring, is sad or angry. We *assume* he is angry and either stay out of his way or try to calm him down. In most cases, we *read* or *see*[24] the emotion in someone's behaviour or expression; we do not *infer* it.[25] Inasmuch as no cognitive process is taking place, the assumption is not a case of knowing, but of noncognitive certainty. In reaction to his objector's claim that we can never be certain about what someone else is feeling (because it is hidden from us), Wittgenstein often insists that in fact, we *are* certain:

> Every day we hear one man saying of another that he is in pain, is sad, is merry, etc. without a trace of doubt, and we relatively seldom hear that he does not know what is going on in the other. In this way, then, the uncertainty is not so bad.
>
> (RPP I: 138)

But this uncertainty – that is 'not so bad' – makes room for a *subjective*, not an *objective* certainty. Granted, there is, in ordinary and simple cases, no *trace* of doubt, but this does not mean that doubt is logically excluded. Unlike the case of first-person certainties, here 'know' does *not* mean that the expression of uncertainty is senseless (cf. PI: 247). We may be certain that someone is happy, sad or bored, but in some cases, we could be wrong; in many cases, the certainty is subjective; it is a mere *assumption*.[26]

4.3   Third-person *objective* psychological certainty

Note here, with Rosat, that the reason we can be mistaken in the *subjective* cases is not necessarily because there has been dissimulation, and certainly not because emotions are inner and therefore hidden, but simply because we are not always able to discern what is in front of our eyes; perhaps an emotion is too enmeshed with other emotions or too complex to detach itself distinctly from the background; or perhaps it is a variant too unlike the typical pattern for us to correctly identify it.[27] But of course there is also the possibility that the person is simulating an emotion. Indeed, the nature of the beast is such that we *are* capable of dissembling. Yet, what Wittgenstein also says (contra Descartes) is that we can't always be had, precisely because dissembling is *not* always a possibility. To the question: 'Is it thoughtlessness not to keep the *possibility* of pretence in mind?' (RPP II: 591), Wittgenstein's answer is clear:

Dissimulation is *nothing* but a particular case; we can regard behaviour as dissimulation only under particular circumstances.

(LW I: 252)

The concept 'dissimulation' has to do with the cases of dissimulation; therefore with very specific occurrences and specific situations in human life. And here I mean external occurrences, not inner ones, etc.

Therefore it isn't possible for all behaviour, under all circumstances, to be dissimulation.

(LW I: 253)

If dissimulation is not a universal or systematic possibility, nor can doubt be universal or systematic.[28] It is at this conceptual point that Wittgenstein passes from subjective to objective certainty – to cases, where we *could not* be mistaken because there is no *logical* room for mistake, even in the case of third-person psychological certainties:

If we see someone falling into the flames and crying out, do we say to ourselves: 'there are of course two cases: ...?' Or if I see you here before me do I distinguish? Do you? *You can't!* That we do in certain cases, doesn't show that we do in all cases.

(LPE: 287; my emphasis)

Just try – in a real case – to doubt someone else's fear or pain.

(PI: 303)

If I see someone writhing in pain with evident cause I do not think, all the same, his feelings are hidden from me.

(LW II: 22)

'I can only guess at someone else's feelings' – does that really make sense when you see him badly wounded, for instance, and in dreadful pain?

(LW I: 964)

'I am *certain* that he's in pain.' – What does that mean? How does one use it? What is the expression of certainty in behaviour, what *makes* us certain?

Not a proof. That is, what makes me certain doesn't make someone else certain. *But the discrepancy has its limits.*

(LW II: 21; last emphasis mine)

If the discrepancy has its limits, this means that there *are* cases where what makes me certain *does* also make someone else certain. In *Last Writings, Volume II*, Wittgenstein is making his way from believing that 'There is no such agreement over the question whether an expression of feeling is simulated or genuine' (LW II: 24) to believing the opposite:

> In an extremely complicated way the outer signs sometimes mean *unambiguously*, sometimes without certainty: pain, pretence and several other things.   ·
>
> (LW II: 59; my emphasis)

And, moreover, to believing that the certainty is of a logical kind:

> There is an *unmistakable* expression of joy and its opposite.
>   Under these circumstances one *knows*[29] that he is in pain, or that he isn't; under those, one is uncertain.
>
> (LW II: 32; emphasis in the original)

> Yet there *are* cases where only a lunatic could take the expression of pain, for instance, as sham.
>
> (LW II: 33; emphasis in the original)

> In the first place, 'I cannot know (*wissen*) his feelings' does *not* mean: ... as opposed to *mine*. In the second place, it does not mean: I can never be completely sure (*ganz sicher*) of his feelings.
>
> (LW II: p. 89; emphasis in the original)

The last passage indicates that the problem is now no longer to determine whether or not certainty can be objective – it *can* be – but to stress that objective certainty should not be confused with knowing. Here, in the penultimate passage of *Last Writings II*, Wittgenstein distinguishes between the logical (and physical) impossibility of *knowing* what is going on in someone's mind, and the fact that we *can be*, and indeed often are, *certain* about what is going on in someone's mind:

> Is[30] the impossibility of knowing (*wissen*) what goes on in someone else physical or logical? ...
>   The logical impossibility lies in the lack of exact rules of evidence. (Therefore we sometimes express ourselves in this way: 'We may always be wrong; we can never be certain; what we observe can *still* be pretence.' ...) ...

> But of course it isn't true that we are never certain [*sicher*] about the
> mental processes in someone else. In countless cases we are.
>
> (LW II: 94; my emphasis of last two sentences)

It is impossible to *know* what goes on in someone else for knowledge
requires justification, and here there are no 'exact rules of evidence' – the
only 'evidence' is *imponderable*. But that there is no exact evidence does
not mean that we cannot be *certain* about what is going on in someone
else – and 'in countless cases we are'.[31] Knowledge, no; certainty, yes.
That Wittgenstein isn't here alluding to mere *subjective* certainty is made
clear by the sentence being a direct response to his objector's allusion to
the ever-lurking possibility of error: 'We may *always* be wrong; we can
never be certain'. It would seem, then, that at the close of his last writings on philosophical psychology – and we should note here that the
passage is dated 'April 15 1951', and that the last dated passage of *On
Certainty* is '27 April 1951' – Wittgenstein is no longer saying that uncertainty is a *constitutional* or *essential* trait of our psychological ascriptions.
He has come to see that, in some cases, we *are* as *objectively* certain about
'He is in pain' as about 'I am in pain'.

5   *Einstellung zur Seele*: objective certainty as an attitude

> I want to say: it's not that on some points men know the truth
> with perfect certainty. No: perfect certainty is only a matter of
> their attitude (*Einstellung*).
>
> (OC: 404)

Our certainty about people around us being human beings, capable of
thinking, suffering, pretending, is not subjective, but objective. And on
a more individual level, doubting whether my neighbour of ten years is
a human being, or whether the retired businessman I have just had a
conversation with on the train has a mind, would not result in any suspicion about them, but only about my sanity. As mentioned earlier, objective certainty is not the product of an attentive or conscious attitude
towards a hypothesis, but manifests itself as an unhesitating attitude –
an *Einstellung*.[32] And, indeed, this non-intellectual certainty, this *Einstellung*, is best seen in our treatment of 'other minds':

> My attitude towards him is an attitude towards a soul (*eine Einstellung
> zur Seele*). I am not of the *opinion* that he has a soul.
>
> (PI: p.178)

As Wittgenstein uses *'Einstellung'*, writes Peter Winch:

> There is no question here of an attitude which I can adopt or abandon at will. My *Einstellung* ... is a condition I am in vis-à-vis other human beings without choosing to be so.
>
> (1980–81: 149–50)

And Winch goes on to say that, by using this expression, Wittgenstein 'is obviously emphasizing the *instinctive* character of the phenomena he is interested in' (ibid.: 150), and its not involving having certain quasi-theoretical beliefs about other people (ibid.: 147). Like that of instinctive and habitual actions, the manifestation of this certainty involves no degree of choice, but also no degree of attention. On the contrary, the presence of attention would be a sure sign that the certainty in question is not a hinge certainty.

It might be objected, then, that the logical nature of this certainty should preclude it from being called a certainty at all. That is, it would only make sense to speak of behaviour as non-doubting or certain if that behaviour could conceivably be replaced by a doubt or an expression of uncertainty. This is a valid objection – precisely the kind of objection made by Wittgenstein to our claiming to 'know' in cases where we couldn't *not* know: 'I can't be said to know that I have toothache if I can't be said not to know that I have toothache' (LPE: 287). Similarly here, can I be said to be 'certain' if I can't be said not to be certain?

6   Can we speak of certainty here at all?

> The language-game allows for senseless utterances – even though not for 'false' ones. [var. 'even though not for error'].
>
> (LW I: 187)

Where indubitability is, as in the case of objective certainty, logical – that is, where it is *not* the result of verification, but stems from something's not being susceptible of doubt (and therefore of verification and falsification) *at all*, is it not idle to speak of certainty? Olli Lagerspetz refuses to call something 'certainty' that does not admit of the logical possibility of the absence of that certainty; for certainty to be worthy of the name, there must coexist the possibility of doubting.[33] On his view, to call 'certainty' something that is logically impervious to uncertainty must be *tautologous* (cf. Lagerspetz ,1998: 161). This, of course, does not mean that being *actually* certain requires envisaging the possibility of not being certain or doubting; all that is required, says Lagerspetz, is an 'outside' perspective from which one can imaginably suggest uncertainty or doubt (ibid.: 133).

This 'outside perspective' is, I suggest, provided by pathological cases. Where Lagerspetz speaks of the breakdown of the natural order as *unimaginable*, and that therefore to speak of *trusting* it (or being certain of it) would be superfluous or 'tautologous', he fails to envisage cases where the natural order, or the normal order, *does* break down. So that the obverse of objective or logical 'certainty' would not be a logical uncertainty or doubt, but lies in the absence or breakdown of objective certainty – that is, as Wittgenstein repeatedly points out, in pathology, aberration, dementia, alienation (e.g., OC: 71, 155, 257, 281, 674).

Where, in normal cases, human beings are objectively – that is, effortlessly, non-inferentially and indubitably – certain of themselves and others having a mind, some autistic individuals are unable to intuitively attribute mental states to self and others;[34] they suffer from what psychologists call an impaired 'Theory of Mind' – or what is also called 'mind-blindness' (Frith and Happé, 1999: 1, 7). An autistic child, for example, must be explicitly trained into what others intuitively possess or unproblematically acquire, like the use of the self-referential pronouns 'I' and 'me', and the attribution of emotions or sensations, even pain, to other than themselves. Unlike normal individuals, autistic individuals must *work at* such things as self-consciousness, introspection and belief attribution; what is ordinarily automatic and thoughtless requires from them thought, anticipation, considered effort and explicit training. This effort is most apparent in individuals with high-functioning autism or Asperger's syndrome who manage to arrive at belief attribution and self-consciousness, but only by 'a slow and painstaking learning process (ibid.: 2). And in spite of all effort, the understanding of mental states developed by these individuals remains rather different from the effortless, automatic, intuitive grasp of the normal preschooler (ibid.: 7). This 'mind-blindness' betrays a psychological *struggling* about many aspects of self and others, where normally there is a comfortable *certainty*. Accounts from patients of Asperger's syndrome invariably relate the difficulty of what normally *comes naturally*:

Autism makes me hear other people's words but be unable to know what the words mean. Or autism lets me speak my own words without knowing what I am saying or even thinking.

(Frith and Happé, 1999: 15)

It was ages before I realized that people speaking might be demanding my attention ... you have to work so hard in order to understand
speech ... trying to speak is quite an effort.

(Frith and Happé, 1999: 15)

In many delusional beliefs also, we find the pathological exceptions
that confirm the rule: for instance, the conviction that thoughts are
constantly being inserted into our brain (psychiatrically identified as the
Delusion of Thought Insertion), or that we are dead (the Cotard Delusion).[35] Normal, ineffable, recessive certainty about our fellow humans
having thoughts, feelings, desires, beliefs; about our being alive and not
dead, *can* and *does* break down, or can be altogether absent. There *is* an
'outside' possibility of the absence, betrayal or breakdown of objective
certainty, and so objective certainty *does*, however recessively, deserve
its name.

Delusional beliefs and autistic behaviour attest, then, to the breakdown or absence of some first-person and third-person basic certainties,
but there exists a less familiar disability that has struck me as particularly apposite here. It is called *dyssemia,* a term coined in 1992 by psy-
chopathologists, Stephen Nowicki and Marshall Duke, to refer to a 'non-
verbal social communication deficit', which manifests itself as a 'difficulty
(*dys*) in using nonverbal signs or signals (*semes*)' (1992: 18), and:

> By nonverbal signs we mean all human responses that are not words
> (either spoken or written) but convey meaning, especially emotional
> meaning. Nonverbal behaviours include facial expressions, tone and
> inflection of voice (paralanguage), body movements and posture (some-
> times called kinesics), gestures and touching, use of personal space
> (proxemics), and rhythm and use of time (chronemics).

(2002: 5)

In much the same way that dyslexics have difficulty with the written
word, *dyssemics* 'cannot understand or 'read' the quieter messages of
others' (Nowicki and Duke, 2002: 19). For example, a dyssemic child will
misread a happy face as an angry one and as a result will return a smile
with a frown or glare. Reading faces accurately is only half the story; if
the child is affected with *expressive* as well as *receptive* dyssemia, she will
also be unable to produce facial expressions that reveal her true feelings:
she will unknowingly put on an angry face where she means to smile;
or, indeed, have a 'negative resting face' – our resting face being the

expression we show when we are emotionally in neutral – so that the child looks permanently *intensely* angry. The problem may also be one of *modulation*: a person may be unable to smile in moderation; if he tries to smile, he has to laugh out loud (ibid.: 88). Duke and Nowicki photographed dyssemic children who had been asked to make facial expressions reflecting *various feelings*; all the photographs turned out to look essentially *the same*. The children were unaware of it, but they were using *the same facial expressions* to communicate *different emotions* (ibid.: 87).

Besides *facial* dyssemias, there are *gestural* and *postural dyssemias*, where for example words are paired with a gesture of opposite meaning, or a slouching resting posture is adopted though the person is highly interested in what is being said. Or *spatial or territorial dyssemias*, where individuals unknowingly infringe or violate other people's space; for example, a dyssemic individual will move up to an inch of another person's nose to speak to them; or choose the seat next to the only other person in an empty theatre, or get into an elevator last and stand facing and looking straight at the people already there, rather than, say, turn around to face the door, or look at the changing floor numbers.

One easily imagines the reactions to these socially inept behaviours: a dyssemic girl who looks angry when she thinks she looks happy will prompt a negative response. And of course these predictable reactions only highlight the existence of solid and unmistakable norms or expectations. That, as the authors write: 'other children *cannot help but* respond to her as if she were upset' (Nowicki and Marshall Duke, 2002: 12; my emphasis) says as much about the pathology as about the normality. The majority of normal children, when presented with clear-cut, basic, unambiguous (cf. LW II: 59) samples of facial expressions – what Wittgenstein would call the 'simple cases' (LW I: 967) – and asked to identify them, have no trouble doing so.[36] So that Nowicki and Duke are convinced that 'although the grammar of the nonverbal language is unwritten, there are still rules for its use': '*residual rules*' – these are the non-verbal rules for any given situation, and they are only noticed when they are broken.[37] Dyssemia, then, provides us with the pathological flipside to an otherwise default certainty regarding *basic* facial expressions, gestures, postures and so on.

The point here is not to eradicate indeterminacy, but to recognize that there are *basic* regularities in the 'hurly burly of human action' (Z: 567), and that these are what shape our psychological bedrock or psychological grammar. This, without losing sight of the fact that 'simple language-games ...

are *poles* of a description, not the ground-floor of a theory' (RPP I: 633; my emphasis). So that, *pace* Lagerspetz, we, as philosophers and psychologists, do have a need for 'the language of certainty'. The concept of objective certainty is needed for when the 'residual rules' are violated, to explain the exceptional, cases.[38] As Wittgenstein writes:

> After all, there could be someone who had serious, hopeless doubts about others. But how would he act? (Like a lunatic.)
>
> (LW I: 248)

7 Scepticism about other minds

Whereas in *On Certainty*, Wittgenstein defeats external world scepticism,[39] in his philosophical psychology, he can be said to rebut scepticism about other minds. In both cases, Wittgenstein rebuts the sceptic by showing that, inasmuch as it addresses knowledge, her objection fails to address our primitive certainty. Knowledge is our secondary, not our primary, assurance; and it vitally rests on a pre-epistemic certainty that is *logically* invulnerable to doubt. This gives us a version of Wittgenstein's rebuttal of other mind scepticism that is more robust than Michel ter Hark's. As ter Hark sees it, first-/third-person asymmetry allows us to confound the sceptic's *comparative* argument that first-person knowledge is superior to, because more immediate than, third-person knowledge by replying that there is no question of knowledge *at all* in the first person: we do not 'know' ourselves directly or indirectly,[40] and therefore the comparison is otiose (cf. 1990: 129). What I am suggesting is a stronger, more positive, rebuttal of scepticism, resulting from Wittgenstein's realization that some third-person psychological certainties are as *logical* or *indubitable* as some first-person certainties; that I *am* as objectively certain of others having a mind as I am of having a mind myself. Our certainty about other minds is an *Einstellung zur Seele*. Not a *knowing* at all, but a condition for knowledge; or as Winch says, a *condition* I am in *vis-à-vis* other human beings.

There are (fictional or pathological) contexts in which a human being comes to know that others have minds, but in normal circumstances, we do not come to know such things. Our belief in other minds is not a hypothetical belief, but an instinctive, non-epistemic attitude; not resulting from inference, it is not open to falsity or mistake. It may be open to pathological failure, but then this, as we have seen, is only the exception that confirms the rule.

Notes

1. On the strength of a well-known metaphor used by Wittgenstein: 'That is to say, the questions that we raise and our *doubts* depend on the fact that some propositions are exempt from doubt, are as it were like hinges on which those turn' (OC: 341). Though, as I argue elsewhere, on Wittgenstein's view, these *Sätze* are in fact not propositions at all, and so the term 'hinge propositions' is erroneous; one should speak of 'hinge beliefs' or 'hinge certainties'; or simply 'basic beliefs' or 'basic certainties' (cf. Moyal-Sharrock, 2004a: ch. 2).

2. The only mentions of what can be called psychological certainties, are to our *basic* reliance on/certainty about our memory (cf. OC: 66, 201, 337, 345, 346, 416, 419, 497, 506, 632); to one's certainty of being in pain as the benchmark for basic, noncognitive certainty (cf. OC: 41, 178, 504); and to one's claim that someone else is in pain as cognitive (OC: 555) or perhaps not (OC: 563).

3. The writings focused on here are PI, Part II; RPP I and II; LPP; LW I and II. For a discussion of the existence of a 'third' Wittgenstein, cf. Moyal-Sharrock (2004b).

4. Cf. 'The salient thing [about the psychological verb] is the asymmetry; "I think", unlike "he thinks", has no verification' (LPP: 49); 'The truth is: it makes sense to say about other people that they doubt whether I am in pain; but not to say it about myself' (PI: 246).

5. '[The] characteristic [of psychological verbs] is this, that their third person but not their first person is stated on grounds of observation' (RPP I: 836); cf. also RPP II: 63.

6. 'I should like to say: Moore does not *know* what he asserts he knows, but it stands fast for him, as also for me; regarding it as absolutely solid is part of our method of doubt and inquiry' (OC: 151; my emphasis); 'For when Moore says "I know that that's..." I want to reply "you don't know anything!" – and yet I would not say that to anyone who was speaking without philosophical intention. That is, I feel (rightly?) that these two mean to say something different' (OC: 407). Knowledge requires justification, and so cannot be the kind of assurance Wittgenstein is looking for here: 'Whether I *know* something depends on whether the evidence backs me up or contradicts me. For to say one knows one has a pain means nothing' (OC: 504; my emphasis); 'If "I know ..." means: I can convince someone else if he believes my evidence, then one can say: I may well be as certain about his mood as about the truth of a mathematical proposition, but it is still false to say that I *know* his mood. ... That is: 'knowing' is a psychological concept of a different kind from 'being certain', 'being convinced', 'believing', 'surmising', etc. The evidence for knowing is of a different kind' (LW II: 88; original emphasis). For a more sustained discussion, cf. Moyal-Sharrock (2004a), ch. 1: 'Objective Certainty vs. Knowledge'.

7. Note the attitude (act)/object ambiguity here. Although Wittgenstein does not explicitly distinguish between the two, he is in fact describing two things in *On Certainty*: objective *certainty* (the attitude) and objective *certainties* (the objects of that attitude).

8. 'As if giving grounds did not come to an end sometime. But the end is not an ungrounded presupposition: it is an ungrounded *way of acting*' (OC: 110; my emphasis); 'I want to say: it's not that on some points men know the truth with perfect certainty. No: perfect certainty is only a matter of their *attitude*' (OC: 404; my emphasis). But if certainty is a way of acting, should we call it

certainty? At some point, Wittgenstein's answer would have been negative: 'There isn't any question of certainty or uncertainty yet in their language-game. Remember: they are learning to *do* something' (Z: 416); but at that point he hadn't yet firmly come to the notion of a non-epistemic certainty, of a certainty *in deed*, that he will come to later, particularly in *On Certainty* (cf. OC: 342).

9. Doubt-behaviour is not the same as pretending to doubt; in the former case, the person may well believe they are doubting (indeed, this is the case of most philosophers who purport to have doubts about the existence of other minds etc.), but the doubt here does not translate itself in practice; it is, as Wittgenstein puts it, only that 'they talk rather more about certain things than the rest of us' (OC: 338). And, again: 'So how does the doubt get expressed? That is: in a language-game, and not merely in certain *phrases*' (RPP II: 342; original emphasis).

10. Cf. *The New Wittgenstein* (ed. A. Crary and R. Read; Routledge, 2000). Of course, no one would want to deny the 'therapeutic' element in Wittgenstein's philosophy; the particularity of Therapeutes or New Wittgensteinians is their *reducing* Wittgenstein's thought to therapy, thereby minimizing or altogether ignoring the substantial problem-solving and thematic contributions Wittgenstein makes to philosophy.

11. For example, 'The frame of reference to which we fasten these words is ordinary human behaviour. The further away a human being is from this the less we could know how to teach him' (LPP: 158–9); and: 'Again, having been taught, the child must use the word in a normal way. There will be exceptions, but the centre of reference is ordinary human life, and the further we go from ordinary human life the less meaning we can give such expressions' (LPP: 37).

12. On these two subjects, see respectively Chauvier's and Rosat's contributions in this volume.

13. 'Is there such a thing as "expert judgment" about the genuineness of expressions of feeling? – Even here, there are those whose judgment is "better" and those whose judgment is "worse"./ Correcter prognoses will generally issue from the judgments of those with better knowledge of mankind./ Can one learn this knowledge? Yes; some can. Not, however, by taking a course in it, but through "experience". – Can someone else be a man's teacher in this? Certainly. From time to time he gives him the right tip. – This is what "learning" and "teaching" are like here. – What one acquires here is not a technique; one learns correct judgments. There are also rules, but they do not form a system, and only experienced people can apply them right. Unlike calculating-rules' (PI: p. 227); 'To be sure, there is this: acquiring a knowledge of human nature; it is also possible to help someone with this, to give lessons, as it were, but one only points to cases, refers to certain traits, gives no hard and fast rules' (RPP II: 607).

14. 'What is ... difficult here is to put this indefiniteness, correctly and unfalsified, into words' (PI: p. 227).

15. This is characteristic of logical positivists who attempted to eradicate this indeterminacy of sense by translating ordinary psychological language into a more precise language, with the help of (different versions of) 'protocol sentences'. See ter Hark (2004: 126) on Carnap's treatment of indeterminacy of sense as a defect that has to be repaired by replacing psychological language with a language suitable for use in rigorous (physical) science.

16. Though elsewhere, he does call the *uncertainty* constitutional: cf. RPP II: 657.
17. Cf. also: '"But you can't recognize pain with *certainty* just from externals." – The *only* way of recognizing it is by externals, and the uncertainty is constitutional. It is not a shortcoming.// It resides in our concept that this uncertainty exists, in our instrument. Whether this concept is practical or impractical is really not the question' (RPP II: 657).
18. Ter Hark sees here 'a categorial difference between psychological concepts and concepts for the description of all sorts of physical facts' (2004: 142).
19. Here, we might speak, with Gordon Bearn of a 'Superficial Essentialism' (Bearn, 1997: 110), as does Jeff Coulter: '"Essence", a term that Wittgenstein uses at several junctures in his later writings, has taken on a new significance. ... In his mature work, for Wittgenstein, it no longer means (as it had for generations before him) a hidden, unitary core or commonality across instances, revealed as such only by philosophical analysis and abstraction, but rather, 'essence' now encompasses those myriad cases of the use of a word which perspicuously exhibits its grammar of use, the ways in which it can (and contrastively, cannot) be used intelligibly, thus constituting what concept it expresses. In Bearn's helpful phrase, "grammatical investigations would uncover superficial essences" – i.e., what constitutes the intelligibility of a concept is to be discovered by laying out many richly-detailed examples of the roles it plays in the weave of our lives as we observably live them (including, of course, in the weave of our discursive actions and interactions)' (Coulter, 1999: 150–1).
20. Cf. ter Hark, 1990: 151.
21. '"One can't pretend like that." – This may be a matter of experience – namely that no one who behaves like that will later behave in such-and-such a way; but it also may be a conceptual stipulation ("That wouldn't still be pretence"); and the two may be connected./ That can no longer be called "pretence"' (Z: 570).
22. '"Human beings think, grasshoppers don't." ... one could impart this to a person who doesn't understand the English word "thinking" and perhaps believes erroneously that it refers to something grasshoppers do' (RPP II: 23). Cf. also: 'Could a legislator abolish the concept of pain?/ The basic concepts are interwoven so closely with what is most fundamental in our way of living that they are therefore unassailable' (LW II: 43–4).
23. For not all first-person psychological statements are nondescriptive: 'Surely one doesn't normally say "I wish ..." on grounds of self-observation (*Selbstbeobachtung*), for this is merely an expression (*Äusserung*) of a wish. Nevertheless, you can sometimes perceive or discover a wish by observing your own reactions' (RPP II: 3). For a discussion of Wittgenstein's 'thesis of asymmetry', see Stéphane Chauvier's chapter in this volume.
24. 'In general I do not surmise fear in him – I *see* it. I do not feel that I am deducing the probable existence of something inside from something outside; rather it is as if the human face were in a way translucent and that I were seeing it not in reflected light but rather in its own' (RPP II: 170).
25. In *most* cases, not *all*, as Peter Winch reminds us: 'That is not to deny that often our reactions are based on reflections about others' states of mind, or probable future behaviour. The point is, first that it is not always so; and second, that our *un*reflective reactions are part of the primitive material out of which our concept of a human person is formed and which makes such more sophisticated reflections possible' (1980–81: 147).

26. Which, however, is not to be confused with a tacit presupposition (cf. PI: pp. 179–80), or with what Wittgenstein calls an 'intuitive conviction', which manifests itself as follows: 'I am sure, *sure*, that he isn't pretending; but someone else isn't. Can I convince him? And if not – do I say that he [the person who can't see it] can't think? (The conviction could be called "intuitive.")' (RPP II: 688).

27. Or as ter Hark puts it: 'If the inner seems concealed, this is not because it is hidden by the outer, but because the *outer* is hidden' (1990: 144).

28. Although this of course does not prevent uncertainty from being 'hopeless' in particular cases: 'And then there is what I should like to call the case of hopeless doubt. When I say, "I have no idea what he is really thinking –". He's a closed book to me. When the only way to understand someone else would be to go through the same upbringing as his – which is impossible' (RPP II: 568). Indeed, such a possibility constitutes a foil against which we measure our ordinary unproblematic grasp: 'It is important for our view of things that someone may feel concerning certain people that their inner life will always be a mystery to him. That he will never understand them. (Englishwomen in the eyes of Europeans.)' (CV: p. 74).

29. In *On Certainty* and works contemporaneous with it, one must be wary of Wittgenstein's use of 'know', particularly when it appears in italics or scare quotes. In such cases, Wittgenstein is not referring to knowing as he understands it (i.e. as justified true belief; cf. *inter alia* OC: 91, 504), but to the objective, noncognitive certainty that is mistaken for knowledge (by philosophers like Moore, or in ordinary language): 'I should like to say: Moore does not *know* what he asserts he knows, but it stands fast for him, as also for me; regarding it as absolutely solid is part of our *method* of doubt and inquiry' (OC: 151). I discuss this in more detail in Moyal-Sharrock (2004a), 25–7.

30. Date 'April 15<51>'. Recall that the dated parts of OC were written between 23 September 1950 and 27 April 1951.

31. Cf. also LW II: p. 85.

32. E.g. my objective certainty that someone lying there with a gaping wound is in pain manifests itself in my spontaneous, unhesitating *treating* him as such, my *tending* to him, and my informing someone on the telephone that a person is lying next to me in great pain, and asking how I can alleviate it.

33. Cf. particularly Lagerspetz (1998), 32–3. Elsewhere (Moyal-Sharrock, 2004a: 191–8), I have addressed Lagerspetz's objections to calling primary trust a 'trust'; here, I shall be applying these objections to the legitimacy of calling primitive or objective certainty a 'certainty'.

34. See Frith and Happé (1999), but also Toichi et al. 'A Lack of Self-Consciousness in Autism' *Am J Psychiatry* 159 (2002), 1422–4, and R. P. Hobson, and J. A. Meyer, 'Foundations for Self and Other: A Study in Autism' *Developmental Science* 8:6 (2006), 481–91.

35. For an explanation of these, cf. Davies and Coltheart (2000).

36. (1992: 86). Also, 'the average fifth-grader can recognize twenty-nine out of a possible thirty-two facial expressions correctly' (1992: 136).

37. 'They are residual because they would be the "rules" left over after we hypothetically write down all of the official and formal rules of society that are codified by our systems of etiquette and justice. Examples of residual rules are plentiful because their number is nearly infinite. One rule, for instance,

says that when we are sitting in a room, involved in almost any activity, we do not touch anyone else. We know that this is a rule, because if we break it, we ask forgiveness from those we've offended by saying, "Oh I am so sorry, pardon me".' The term 'residual rules' is Thomas Scheff's (2002: 17)

38. And, less seriously, as Wittgenstein suggests, where we would need to explain our form of life to aliens: 'I meet someone from Mars and he asks me "How many toes have human beings got?" – I say "Ten. I'll shew you", and take my shoes off. Suppose he was surprised that I knew with such certainty, although I hadn't looked at my toes – ought I to say "We humans know how many toes we have whether we can see them or not"?' (OC: 430).

39. For a discussion of this, cf. Moyal-Sharrock (2004a), ch. 8: 'Objective Certainty vs. Scepticism'.

40. Of course, there is a sense in which we do 'know' ourselves, and can therefore predict our behaviour – e.g., 'I know myself, I won't be able to hide my feelings from her'. But this is not the knowledge arising from the fundamental, epistemic, indubitable and exclusive acquaintance with, or introspection of, our own mind that is put forward as a benchmark by the sceptic.

12
Criteria and Defeasibility: When Good Evidence is Not Good Enough

Eric J. Loomis

Wittgenstein held that a certain type of non-inductive evidence, which he sometimes labelled 'criteria', serves as evidence for the applicability of certain concepts or the truth statements containing those concepts, while at the same time being partially or wholly constitutive of the meaning of those concepts for which it is evidence. Articulating a defensible notion of criterial evidence for third-person attributions of psychological concepts that meets these conditions has proven to be difficult. The central difficulty concerns how to give an account of the defeasible nature of such evidence while simultaneously preserving the idea that the evidence plays a role in meaning constitution. A promising candidate, that of 'necessarily' or 'grammatically' good evidence that is nonetheless defeasible, has been intermittently defended over several decades.[1] I will argue, however, that the notion of grammatically good evidence is beset with serious problems, and that attempts to render it coherent have failed. If I am correct, then the challenge of providing an account of non-inductive evidence that preserves its role in meaning constitution remains an open one. Yet providing such an account is important to our appraisal of Wittgenstein's work in the philosophy of psychology. For if the notion of non-inductive evidence as he used it is indefensible, then many of his remarks on the philosophy of mind and language are undercut, since they require acknowledging a distinction between inductive correlations and meaning-constituting, non-inductive evidence (cf. PI: 353; PG: 219f; BB: 24–5; LW II: 87).

I will argue that we ought to understand the relation between non-inductive evidence and those propositions for which it serves as evidence in terms of truth-conditions, and specifically in terms of a logical entailment. I will maintain that the holding of non-inductive evidence forms a necessary part of a logically sufficient condition for the truth of certain empirical statements.[2] When conjoined with a fallibilist theory of knowledge, this account will be shown to accommodate the problematic epistemological feature of non-inductive evidence, namely its defeasibility. In defending this position, I will argue that we have good reason to endorse a real distinction between the meaning conditions for a statement, and the conditions required for being justified in believing it.

Non-inductive evidence and defining criteria

Many of Wittgenstein's comments on the philosophy of mind and language require that in some cases there be a relation between the meaning of a concept, φ, and the criterial evidence justifying the assertion that an individual *A* is φ. For example, part of what it means to assert that someone is in the state of having an opinion is, Wittgenstein tells us, determined by the criteria for his having reached an opinion or altered that opinion (PI: 573). Similarly for someone's having mastered an arithmetical technique (PI: 692). This has the consequence that the relation between a criterion and the concept for which it is a criterion is a 'grammatical' one in Wittgenstein's sense of the term:

> It is part of the grammar of the word 'chair' that *this* is what we call 'to sit on a chair', and it is part of the grammar of the word 'meaning' that *this* is what we call 'explanation of meaning'; in the same way to explain my criterion for another person's having a toothache is to give a grammatical explanation about the word 'toothache' and, in this sense, an explanation concerning the meaning of the word 'toothache'.
>
> (BB: 24, cf. ibid. 57; PI: 322, 371)

As I will understand it, calling the explanation 'grammatical' here means that *c*'s being evidence for φ is, or is akin to, a definitional truth or a rule of language. To borrow another term of Wittgenstein's, the relation is 'internal': φ would not be the concept that it is if *c* were not evidence for the truth of some statements involving it, such '*A* is φ' (cf. PG: 152; PI: p. 212). Here *c* functions as evidence in virtue of giving grounds by which one recognizes something, like a state (RPP II: 44). I'll call evidence that exhibits a grammatical or internal relation to the truth of certain statements 'non-inductive evidence'. What have commonly been called 'criteria' by Wittgenstein and others are a species of non-inductive evidence. I prefer here to speak of 'non-inductive evidence' instead of 'criteria', both because it is arguable that there are other forms of evidence that are non-inductive and yet not commonly recognized as criterial, and because I wish to by-pass the complicated issue of whether we should have a 'theory of criteria'. Whether or not there should be a theory of criteria, I think we can investigate the relation between non-inductive evidence and that for which it serves.

The central difficulty which the notion of non-inductive evidence faces is the defeasibility of such evidence, particularly in cases involving third-person attributions of mental or psychological predicates like 'pain' or 'opinion'. In many contexts, there seems to be the open possibility of further evidence appearing which would defeat the attribution of an empirical predicate governed by non-inductive evidence.[3] It was this feature which led Malcolm, among others, to acknowledge that the propositions that describe the criterion of someone's being in pain typically do not logically imply that he is in pain, since someone's pain-behaviour could, for example, be faked (Malcolm 1963: 113). This result led many to reject the idea that criteria could be invoked against scepticism, as Malcolm had tried to do.[4]

Despite this difficulty, the notion of non-inductive evidence has been regarded as relatively unproblematic in cases where we have a simple, and usually single, 'defining criterion' for something, such as Wittgenstein's angina example (BB: 25), or the example of being a chess grandmaster. Having a score of at least 2500 according to the *Fédération Internationale des Échecs* defines, in part, the meaning of 'chess grandmaster'. Here the meaning-constitutive role of non-inductive evidence is transparent: it is simply a part of what it *means to be* a chess grandmaster that one have a score of at least 2500, and evidence that someone has this score is evidence that they are a chess grandmaster. I wish, first, to consider such relatively uncontroversial defining criterion cases of non-inductive evidence. In an important respect, defining criterion cases have a greater kinship with the more problematic cases of non-inductive evidence, such as third-person pain ascriptions, than is usually recognized.

Suppose that we have evidence that a person, B, has an FIDE score of 2501. Does this evidence entail that they are a grandmaster? It does not, for it is possible that the *evidence* is defective in some way, for instance, because B's score came about through deception, or a miscalculation. Indeed, with a bit of imagination it seems that any given bit of evidence that B has a score over 2499 can, in principle, be defeated. Yet the defeasibility of our evidence that B is a grandmaster does not undercut the claim that having an FIDE score of at least 2500 entails that one is a grandmaster. To the extent that one is willing to grant that there are defining criteria at all, the proper response to the defeasibility of our evidence in these cases is that the defining criterion functions in effect as a conditional: necessarily, *if* the evidence that B has a score of at least 2500 is not defective, *then* B is a grandmaster. The point can be put as follows: the grammar of 'chess grandmaster' is fixed, in this case by the FIDE. It specifies an entailment from the obtaining of a condition to someone's being a grandmaster. It is a further, *epistemic* question whether we know, or are justified in believing, that the condition holds in a given case. It would be a mistake to suppose that the possibility that any given evidence that someone is a grandmaster is defective shows that the evidence isn't logically decisive when it isn't defective. In some sense, yet to be explored, it seems correct to say that the *undefeated* evidence that B has a score over 2499 entails that B is a grandmaster.

The grandmaster example reveals that the possibility of doubting that a given bit of evidence obtains is perfectly compatible with the existence of an entailment from that evidence to the truth of some statement.[5] A common response to these sorts of defining criterion examples has been to grant that, while non-inductive evidence can be an entailment in some simple cases like 'grandmaster', it cannot be one in more complex cases, such as evidence for the ascription of third-person psychological states like pains, opinions and toothaches. For instance, Philip Bennett has claimed that 'Some concepts are governed by defining criteria. Many more are not', and cites the grandmaster case as an example of the former, and the toothache case as an example of the latter (1978: 381). Peter Hacker has likewise insisted that 'it is not possible to give a uniform account of [Wittgenstein's] notion of a criterion. In some contexts a criterion amounts to a sufficient condition, whereas in others it constitutes grammatically determined presumptive grounds' (1993: 251). I am not here going to try to answer the question of whether Wittgenstein meant to include something like 'grammatically determined presumptive grounds' within his notion of a criterion, other than to note that it is hardly obvious that he did.[6] I will, however, investigate the reasons that Bennett, Hacker and others have offered for seeing a difference in the grammar of defining criterion cases of non-inductive evidence compared with other, more difficult cases, such as third-person ascriptions of opinions, pains, toothaches and other psychological states.

The entailment view

As noted, the undefeated evidence that B has an FIDE score over 2499 entails that B is a grandmaster. Contra Hacker, it is certainly possible to generalize this example to give a uniform account of non-inductive evidence. Consider the following generalization. Let S be some contingent statement asserting that a concept ϕ is true of some individual A, where φ is governed by non-inductive evidence; that is, there is a grammatical or internal relation between the evidence and φ. Let c be that non-inductive evidence for S, and let C be a report which states that c holds. There may be several bits of non-inductive evidence for S, and in such cases we can begin by supposing that C is a conjunction of all such Cs.[7] So in the context of Wittgenstein's *Blue Book* example, φ might be the concept of *having a toothache*, c_1 might be evidence that an individual, A, *is holding his jaw* and c_2 might be evidence that *A is moaning*, S might be the statement that *A has a toothache*, and C might be the conjunction: *A is holding his jaw and moaning*. Finally, suppose that d is some further bit of evidence that would defeat c as evidence for S in some way. So d could be evidence that *A is faking jaw-pain*, and D a statement reporting this evidence. Since there might be many such bits of defeating evidence, let D be the disjunction of all such statements of evidence that would defeat c's being evidence for S (for every c). Then the *entailment view* claims that ($\sim D$ & C) entails S, for any S governed by non-inductive evidence; that is, for any S for which there is evidence that stands in an internal relation to S itself. I have already said that, if there are cases of defining criteria at all, then ($\sim D$ & C) entails S in those cases (for suitable values of 'D,' 'C' and 'S'). I'm going to argue that this same general schema offers us our best hope of making sense of the notion of non-inductive evidence in general.

What is gained by trying to understand such cases in terms of an entailment? The answer is that it gives a clear account of how non-inductive evidence can be partially constitutive of the meaning of certain concepts in the way that Wittgenstein claimed (cf. BB: 24, 57; RFM: 319; PI: 353, 572). If one understands how a defining criterion partially constitutes the meaning of a statement by entailing it in the absence of a defeater, as in the grandmaster case, then since the generalization to *all* cases of non-inductive evidence shares the same general structure, one ought to grant that one also understands how non-inductive evidence can partially constitute the meaning of an expression or statement in all cases which exhibit this structure. That is, regarding the relation between non-inductive evidence and that for which it serves as an entailment in the absence of a defeater makes clear how such evidence can stand in a 'grammatical' or 'internal' relation to a concept.

The grammatically good evidence view

An alternative view has been proposed for explicating third-person psychological ascriptions in terms of non-inductive evidence while withholding the attribution of an entailment from the undefeated evidence to the truth of a statement. This view rests on the idea that non-inductive evidence is conceptually or grammatically tied to that for which it serves in virtue of being 'necessarily good' and thereby partially meaning constituting. Nonetheless, such evidence is held to always be defeasible in principle, since it's only good or presumptive evidence, not evidence that would entail the truth of a contingent statement under any circumstances. I'll call this view the 'Grammatically Good Evidence' (GGE) view.

The GGE view has several variants. The first and original variant proposes that c's being non-inductive evidence for S means only that it is a necessary truth that c is evidence for S (Shoemaker, 1963: 3–4; cf. also Kenny, 1967; Lycan, 1971; Hacker, 1993). This variant simply proposes a new category of evidence, without attempting to explicate it by rejecting traditional semantic assumptions, or rejecting a standard monotonic logic for empirical concepts. A second variant of the GGE view combines the postulation of GGE with the replacement of a 'truth-conditional' theory of meaning with a 'constructivist' (Baker, 1974) or 'assertion-condition' (Wright, 1982) theory.[8] A third, more recent variant proposes treating the logic governing non-inductive evidence as non-monotonic (and thereby defeasible) while nonetheless attempting to distinguish that evidence in terms of its having a distinctive role in warranting assertions and in burden-of-proof shifting in dialogue (Tomassi, 2001). All of these alternative proposals to the entailment view share, however, a desire to ensure that non-inductive evidence can be both partially meaning constituting and an evidential basis for knowledge (cf. Baker, 1974: 156; Hacker, 1993: 259; Tomassi, 2001: 46).

I will argue that all three variants of the GGE view have problems accounting for meaning constitution and knowledge in contexts involving concepts governed by non-inductive evidence. I will label the objections to the GGE view the 'semantic objection' and the 'epistemic objection'.

The semantic objection

Advocates of the GGE view claim that non-inductive evidence can be at least partially constitutive of meaning in virtue of its being 'necessarily good' evidence or 'grammatically determined presumptive grounds'. Yet on the view, GGE is nonetheless always in-principle defeasible; it's only *prima facie* or presumptive evidence, not evidence that would entail the truth of a contingent statement under any circumstances. This latter qualifier is important, for advocates of the GGE view insist that the defeasibility of non-inductive evidence is a *conceptual* or *grammatical* matter, so that it is part of the grammar of the relevant concepts that the evidence for them is always defeasible. This commitment is expressed by the claim, made by advocates of the GGE view, that there simply are no entailment conditions in such cases.[9]

GGE is thus supposed to be less than logically decisive in any circumstances, but nonetheless partially constitutive of meaning in virtue of being grammatically good. On pain of losing the alleged distinctiveness of GGE, the defender of such evidence must thus oppose the entailment view and affirm that the negation of every defeater for non-inductive evidence c, conjoined with the presence of that evidence, is always compatible with the falsity of any statement for which c serves as evidence; that is, that '$(\sim D \ \& \ C) \ \& \ \sim S$' is always possibly true, for any D, C, and contingent S governed by the non-inductive, grammatically good evidence C. To deny this possibility is to abandon the GGE view for the entailment view.

I think to the contrary that it is not possible to coherently assert the conjunction of $(\sim D \ \& \ C) \ \& \ \sim S$. For the statement that $\sim S$ has as a precondition of its truth that S be meaningful. However, the joint assertion of $(\sim D \ \& \ C) \ \& \ \sim S$ insures that S is not meaningful. This is because the joint assertion of $(\sim D \ \& \ C) \ \& \ \sim S$ undercuts the relevant evidentiary connection that S is supposed to have to C, in virtue of which S is, in part, meaningful.[10] This claim is closely akin to an argument that has been advanced by John Canfield. Canfield has also argued that the non-inductive evidence view is incoherent.[11] His argument seems to me to be sound, and my claim that $\sim D \ \& \ C$ are incompatible with $\sim S$ reaches a similar conclusion. Philosophers who deny this refuse to grant that where non-inductive evidence C is partially constitutive of the meaning of S, $\sim D \ \& \ C$ are logically sufficient for S.[12] The problem in doing so is that any case in which $\sim D \ \& \ C$ is true is a case in which $\sim S$ is devoid of meaning, and such meaning is a necessary condition of its being intelligibly false. Since, furthermore, the conditions for S's having meaning include that condition that the evidence for S's truth obtain, and that evidence *does* obtain (since it's present and undefeated), S must be true.

This is, in a nutshell, the conceptual difficulty involved in rendering coherent the notion that all relevant non-inductive evidence for S can be present and undefeated and yet S false. Seeing how this difficulty undercuts the GGE view's ability to make sense of example cases of non-inductive evidence requires a clearer specification of what kinds of things count as defeaters for evidence. I will here give such a specification of evidence and defeaters, and then use it to provide a strong intuitive argument against the GGE view's ability to coherently assert the conjunction of $(\sim D \ \& \ C) \ \& \ \sim S$ in an example case, despite the view's being committed to the coherence of this conjunction.

Evidence and defeaters

Assume that *e* is some evidence, of any type, for some statement *S*, and let *E* be a statement which reports that *e* obtains. Then *d* is a *defeater of e for S* iff *e* fails to be evidence for *S* in the presence of *d*.[13] Thus, where *D* is the statement reporting that a defeater *d* obtains, *D* & *E* fails to be reason for holding that *S*, although *E* was such a reason by itself. This characterization of defeaters makes determining what counts as a defeater a function of *e*'s being evidence for *S*.[14]

What then is evidence? As I will use the notion, saying that *e is evidence for S* is to be understood as saying that, according to the rules of evidentiary support or confirmation, were *e* available to some person *B*, and were *B* both aware of that evidence and reasoning in accord with the rules of evidentiary support or confirmation, then *B* would have some degree of warrant for holding that *S*. In this subjunctive characterization of evidence, it is not required that *e* actually be available to some *B* in order for it to be evidence for *S*. Nor is it required that *B* actually notices *e*. It is enough that were *B* to notice *e*, then *B* would, if she is reasoning in accord with the rules of evidentiary support, have some degree of warrant for holding that *S*. I think that this characterization of 'evidence' is consonant with our ordinary use of the word, for we are generally willing to grant that there can be evidence for something that is nonetheless not currently available to anyone. Note that a defeater *d* of evidence *e* for *S* is itself evidence, and might be of any kind. Before proceeding, it is necessary to note several features of this characterization of defeaters.

First, we should not regard the contradictory of *S* as itself a defeater for *e* (where *e* is evidence for *S*). The reason is that it is generally not the case that a statement, such as ~*S*, is *evidence* for its own truth or falsity.[15] In general, if something is a defeater of evidence for *S*, then it is a reason relevant to our holding to the truth or falsity of *S* in virtue of being a part of a chain, with at least one member, of evidence for *S*. If we included ~*S* among the defeaters for the truth of *S*, we would be including ~*S* in the evidentiary chain relevant to belief in the truth or falsity of *S*. Of course it is true that, if someone is justified in believing that ~*S*, then they are justified in believing that ~*S*, but it does not follow that ~*S itself* justifies one in believing that ~*S*. To suppose otherwise would be to allow a species of question-begging argument as a justification for belief, and question-begging arguments, while valid, are not cogent precisely because justification does not transmit from premises to conclusion. Thus the contradictory of *S* should not be included as a defeater for the evidence for *S*.

The contradictory of *E*, however, *is* a defeater for the evidence *e*. This might not at first be obvious, for, since (*E* & ~*E*) entails *S*, it might appear as if ~*E* does not defeat evidence for *S* but in fact insures that *S*. However, as we have just observed above, the evidentiary relation is not the relation of logical implication. If Mr *X* tells me that *E*, but Ms *Y* tells me that ~*E*, I do not thereby have justification for *S*. If I believe myself to be in possession of *e*, then evidence that ~*E* defeats *e* as evidence for *S*.

The *contraries* of *E* and *S* are also defeaters for *e*. That *an evil deceiver is causing me to falsely believe that A has a toothache* is a contrary of the claim that *A* has a toothache, and it is thus a possible defeater of *A*'s moaning and holding his jaw as evidence that *A* has a toothache.[16] This contrary of *E* is also a possible defeater for *S* itself, the claim that *A has a toothache*. This may seem to be at odds with my assertion above that the contradictory of *S* is not a defeater for *e*. That an evil deceiver is causing me to falsely believe that *A* has a toothache implies that *A* does not have one; that is, that ~*S*. So why should this contrary be a defeater for *e*, when the contradictory of *S* is not? The answer is that the evil deceiver causes me to believe that *S* by means of defective evidence. I *think* that *A*'s moaning and jaw-holding is evidence that *A* is in pain, but it is not because the evidence is defective; I am the victim of an Evil Deceiver.[17] In this respect, that *there is an Evil Deceiver causing me falsely to believe that S*, which is a contrary of *S*, is a possible defeater for *e* in the same way that the non-contrary thesis that *there is an Evil Deceiver* is a possible defeater for *e*. Both work by undercutting one's grounds for holding that *e* is evidence for *S*, since if one has some justification for supposing that either of these defeaters obtain, then even if one sees *A* holding his jaw and moaning, one has no good reason for thinking that he has a toothache.

With this account of evidence and defeaters, we can return to the semantic objection to the GGE view, and explore its plausibility with an example. Suppose that we observe that *A* is moaning and holding his jaw, say, and in this simplified example we consider this type of behaviour to be non-inductive evidence (*C*) for *A*'s having a toothache. That *A is faking toothache behaviour* is a defeater for *C*, and so it is in ~*D* and is false. This is because *A*'s faking toothache behaviour is not a contradictory of *A*'s having a toothache; one can have a pain or a toothache and yet still fake pain or toothache behaviour, as children frequently demonstrate when a minor injury results in a dramatic display of pain in front of sympathetic viewers. Likewise, that *there is an Evil Genius causing observers to falsely believe that A is holding his jaw and moaning* is a contrary of *C*, and so like all of *C*'s contraries is in ~*D* and is false; so too for any other possible deceptive mechanism. That *A disavows having a toothache* is also an obvious defeater for *C*, and so is false (I consider such cases further below). Similarly, every other bit of defeating evidence for *C* does not obtain – this is the content of saying that ~*D* is true.

In such circumstances it is evident that no content has been given to the claim that ~*S* is possibly true. For example, the question 'Why could *S* be false?' has no answer. The GGE view itself requires that *S* have a semantic connection to *C*, so it is not enough to say in this case that we are not *warranted* in asserting that ~*S*, for this observation, while true, fails to provide content to ~*S* itself.[18] Likewise, to ask us to 'imagine a possible world' in which (~*D* & *C*) and ~*S* are all true is to assume that ~*S* is meaningful independently of *S*'s internal relation to *C*. In other words, it is to implicitly deny an internal relation between them. Absent an appeal to intrinsically private evidence (imagining to oneself that '*A* doesn't have *this*' when mentally focusing on one's own toothache), there is nothing for us to conceive or imagine here; the non-inductive evidence is present, and there is *ex hypothesi* nothing that would defeat it.[19] It is unlikely that defenders of GGE wish to rest their view upon the possibility of private evidence, but without it there is no reason to block the conclusion that conjunction of ~*D* with *C* makes ~*S* empty of semantic content by denying it a grammatical connection with *C*.

Seeking a law in the way a word is used

I have noted that seeing a kinship between 'defining criteria' and other cases involving non-inductive evidence, like third-person ascriptions of psychological predicates, makes perspicuous how such evidence can be meaning constituting. This fact forms the basis for my reply to an anticipated objection to my characterization of such evidence using the notion of entailment. The objection holds that seeing an entailment in all cases of non-inductive evidence is a 'conceptual prejudice'. Thus, citing Wittgenstein's remark that 'in general we don't use language according to strict rules', Bennett has claimed that we look at language as if it were a calculus if we seek 'defining criteria of a precise and logically compelling sort', while failing to heed Wittgenstein's injunction (at BB: 27) not to always seek a 'law in the way a word is used' (Bennett, 1978: 58–9). Baker (1974: 165–6), and Hacker (1993: 259) have raised similar objections. Although I am not giving a theory of criteria *per se*, my view that undefeated non-inductive evidence ought to be understood as a logically sufficient condition for the truth of some contingent statements presumably falls within the intended scope of this objection.

The objection rests, however, on a misconception of the nature of Wittgenstein's observation that there is not always a law in the way a word is used. Consider two different positions, *P* and *Q*, on the nature of the evidence for word *w* in cases where it seems like some evidence *e* may be non-inductive:

> *P*: There is no law in the way a word is used because it has simply not been settled how a given bit of evidence *e* is actually being used (i.e., whether *e* is being used as non-inductive evidence for the application of *w* or as inductive evidence).
>
> *Q*: There is no law in the way a word is used because there simply is no difference, actually or in principle, between using a given bit of evidence *e* as non-inductive evidence for *w* and using it as inductive evidence for *w*.

P is consistent with the claim that non-inductive evidence really is a distinctive form of evidence in any case in which it is present, while *Q* is not. The entailment view is compatible with *P*, but not with *Q*. It is compatible with *P* because it does not require that there always be a definitive answer to the question of whether, in a given case, *e* is functioning as non-inductive evidence. In this respect, the entailment view can allow that our use of words might be indefinite, while nonetheless holding to the conditional claim that, if a given bit of evidence is non-inductive, then it involves an entailment to the truth of a statement in the absence of a defeater. Indefinite cases involve an oscillation between various possible ways of treating certain evidence; a feature that Wittgenstein himself identified:

> Nothing is commoner than for the meaning of an expression to oscillate, for a phenomenon to be regarded as sometimes a symptom, sometimes a criterion, or a state of affairs. And mostly in such a case the shift of meaning is not noted.
>
> (Z: 438; cf. PI: 354; RPP I: 649)

Indeed, the very *Blue Book* passage that Bennett cites suggests a similar point:

> It appears we don't know what ['knowledge'] means, and that therefore, perhaps, we have no right to use it. We should reply: 'There is no one exact usage of the word "knowledge"; but we can make up several such usages, which will more or less agree with the ways the word is actually used.'
>
> (BB: 27)

To see Wittgenstein's remarks about there being no law in the use of a word as constituting an objection to the claim that non-inductive evidence is defining or decisive, Bennett and others need to see it as making a claim stronger than *P*. They need *Q*, or something close to it. But *Q* is little more than an outright denial that there is anything distinctive about non-inductive evidence at all, it least in those cases where it isn't a species of defining criteria. *Q* is the kind of claim that we expect to find in philosophers such as Quine and his defenders: it amounts to simply refusing to grant anything distinctive about non-inductive evidence when it isn't obviously defining. Yet Wittgenstein clearly did not intend his comments to advance the Quinean claim that evidence for empirical statements can exhibit no differences in kind – to the contrary, Wittgenstein saw a difference where Quine saw none.

Nonetheless, Wittgenstein's observations that ordinary language isn't strictly rule bound may still appear to clash with the claim that we ought to characterize non-inductive evidence in terms of an entailment relation. For if the actual use of a word fails to require distinguishing between a bit of associated evidence being inductive, versus its being non-inductive, then users of that word are not committed to the existence of an entailment, but only to an ambiguity. Does not the assertion that non-inductive evidence forms a necessary part of a sufficient condition therefore constitute a simplification of the actual use of language in such cases?

It does. But the reasons for making this simplification reflect Wittgenstein's philosophical method, for they stem not from an attempt to get 'behind' the use of language to reveal the operation of a hidden calculus, but from an attempt to render perspicuous how grammatical relations function in the context of many empirical statements. Wittgenstein's observation of the oscillation apparent in the use of words did not lead him to refuse attempting to render certain uses of language more perspicuous in terms of comparisons to simpler, more easily understood examples. Quite to the contrary, he emphasized the importance of inventing new cases in order to command a clear view of the use of our words (PI: 122). This is evident from the simplified, constructed examples of the opening passages of the *Investigations*, as well as in Wittgenstein's frequent insistence that the philosophical task of clarification is distinct from the empirical study of language (PI: 109), or the exact cataloguing of grammar (Z: 464). As he put it apropos of psychological concepts:

> And here what is in question is not symptoms but logical criteria. That these are not always sharply differentiated does not prevent them from being differentiated.

Our investigation does not try to *find* the real, exact meaning of words; though we do often *give* words exact meanings in the course of our investigation.

(Z: 466–7)

Seeing a commonality between relatively simple cases of non-inductive evidence, such as the chess grandmaster case, and less simple ones, such as ascriptions of pain or toothache, by seeing in both the presence of an entailment in the absence of a defeater, helps to render perspicuous how it is that non-inductive evidence can play a distinctive role. It does so, as I noted, by making clear the meaning-constituting role of that evidence.

Entailment conditions

The entailment view has been criticized for assuming that there exists a definitely circumscribable list of conditions for the entailment. Hacker, for instance, writes that it:

presupposes that there is a definitely circumscribable list of conditions (both positive and negative) which is such that if it is satisfied, then it *must* be the case that the person is, say, in pain, sad, thinking, or whatever. But the range of defeating conditions is arguably indefinite, and the defeating conditions themselves are defeasible.

(1993: 258; cf. also Baker, 1974: 161).

Malcolm has advanced a similar objection:

It is quite impossible to list six or nine such circumstances and then to say 'that is all of them; no other circumstances can be imagined that would count against his being in pain.' The list of circumstances has no 'all' in that sense; the list is, not infinite, but *indefinite*. Therefore, entailment-conditions cannot be formulated; there are none.

(1963: 114)

These criticisms rest on several misconceptions.

First, recognizing an entailment from the undefeated non-inductive evidence for S to S itself is compatible with the possibility that non-inductive evidence may take a wide variety of forms, such as its being part of a 'cluster concept', its appearing only in virtue of a family resemblance to other things, or its appearing as evidence only to members of a community that share possession of a certain technique, 'know-how', or an ability to recognize important similarities or regularities (cf. PI: 325). These latter conditions may not be expressible in a demonstrative-free language, and in such cases, we should recognize that the reports of evidence are meaningful only to those who share mastery of the relevant techniques or abilities. Much of what we count as evidence, including much of our non-inductive evidence for pain and toothache ascriptions, exhibits such features. For instance, toothache ascriptions likely presuppose an ability to recognize a family resemblance between a certain ostended example behaviour ('*That* person has a toothache', said perhaps to a child), and other cases. Here the success of the explanation presupposes a considerable 'background' of appropriate circumstances and suitably prepared learners (cf. PG: 88; BB: 12). Moreover, we may not be in a position to enumerate what we count as non-inductive evidence in many such cases. For instance, it is unlikely that we can state what evidence is necessary for an ascription of pain, and we don't expect competent language-users to be able to do so. Indeed, we may not use *any* statements of conditions in teaching, explaining or justifying pain-ascriptions. We seem simply to learn that certain behaviour is distinctively pain behaviour, and expect competent language users to be able to identify characteristic pain behaviours.

These considerations may appear to render untenable the claim that there is an entailment between undefeated reports of non-inductive evidence and the truth of certain statements. For it may be thought that if we cannot enumerate the conditions required for the entailment, then there cannot be an entailment at all. But this does not follow. The fact that we cannot state necessary and sufficient conditions on something's being φ does not mean that there are no conditions on being φ. It may mean rather that what conditions there are can only be given in other ways, as with Wittgenstein's observation that what one knows of the concept 'game' could be 'completely expressed' only by 'describing examples of various kinds of game; shewing how all sorts of other games can be constructed on the analogy of these; saying that I should scarcely include this or this among games; and so on' (PI: 75). That we may only be able to express conditions for being a game in these ways doesn't mean that there are no conditions. Indeed, Wittgenstein's observation is perfectly consistent with the possibility that there is an *entailment* from something's being such-and-such, or its relevantly resembling such-and-so, to its being a game. It is an illusion to suppose that there can be an entailment only if we can state the conditions required for it. What is required is that we be able to recognize what counts as a condition, even if the recognition cannot be replaced with a list, or expressed in a demonstrative-free language.

Nor should the fact that we may not be able to give a demonstrative-free expression of the evidence required to say that someone is in pain, say, be confused with the claim that it is not possible to report evidence when we do recognize it. The fact that we may be unable to articulate how X resembles Y does not mean that we cannot report *that X resembles Y*. Hence, although examples such as Wittgenstein's toothache example may be simplified, they aren't *simplistic* in a way that blocks relevant generalizations to more complex cases, and the entailment view can allow for considerable latitude in what counts as evidence in particular cases.[20]

A second and related misunderstanding involves the assumption, evident in Malcolm's above-quoted remark, that the entailment view requires that we be able to list or formulate the defeating conditions. The assumption is again mistaken. Entailment conditions require only an ability to recognize and adjudicate among relevant defeaters, not an actual enumeration of them. For instance, it's not a condition on the intelligibility of calling a statement true that we be able to enumerate every defeater for that statement. Consider that for a given statement S, the truth of any contrary of S would be a defeater for S. In most cases, we cannot enumerate even every contrary of S. But we nonetheless acknowledge that the truth of S has as a necessary condition the falsity of every contrary. For example, if S is the statement 'L is in Mobile, Alabama at time t', then the truth of S entails the falsity of every contrary of the form: 'L is in Blois, France at t', 'L is in the lunar crater Petzval at t', and so on for every possible location. We cannot enumerate every such location. But that does not block us from recognizing an entailment from the truth of S to the falsity of every contrary of S. If true, S entails the falsity of every contrary, and if any contrary is true, that defeats our judgment that S is true, regardless of whether or not we can enumerate the contraries.

A related complexity introduced by third-person ascriptions concerns the 'overlap' of the grounds for such ascriptions with first-person avowals in some cases. Thus both A's holding his jaw and moaning, and his avowing that he has a toothache, may be grounds for saying that he has one. My position is compatible with this possibility, for it requires only that $\sim D$ & C be jointly sufficient for the truth of S. It does not require that C be necessary for S. A's avowing that he has a toothache is grounds for saying he has one, even if jaw-holding and moaning are not present. C's meaning-constitutive role with respect to S is preserved as long as a competent speaker must recognize C as evidence for S; she need not recognize *only* C as evidence.

These remarks might in turn seem to raise the possibility of a conflict between third- and first-person pain ascriptions, but, barring an implicit appeal to intrinsically private 'evidence', they do not. If *A* is holding his jaw and moaning, then in the above simplified example, he has a toothache in the absence of any defeater. If *A* were to confess to someone that he does not have a toothache, then that is evidence which, were it available, would defeat the claim that he does – this would be a situation in which ~*D* would be false. My characterization of evidence does not require the actual availability of such evidence, nor should it; here again a comparison with the grandmaster case is helpful. The undefeated evidence that some-one has an FIDE score over 2499 entails that the person is a grandmaster, whether or not we know that there is no defeater, or even in the complete absence of the relevant evidence. If all chess records were destroyed, there wouldn't cease to be an entailment, although we would be prevented from justifiably asserting that anyone is a grandmaster.

However, my general characterization leaves open the possibility that the claim that there is an entailment in all cases involving non-induc-tive evidence might collapse into a trivial truth in some cases. This is because ~*D* & *C* might entail *S* in a 'narrow' logical sense if *S* is logically derivable from ~*D* & *C* by the consequence relation of a standard system of logic.[21] I see no way to prove that this could never happen. If it did, then in such cases my claim that there is an entailment from ~*D* & *C* to *S* would appear trivial, since *S*'s truth would just be a narrow logical conse-quence of making what turned out to be an unexpectedly strong assumption. In the face of such possible cases, the entailment view can avoid triviality by being made stronger. It can assert that, besides the narrow logical entailment to *S*, there is a 'broader' entailment such that there is some collection of statements of evidence E_1, E_2, ... E_n, which jointly do not entail *S* in the narrow logical sense, but which *do* entail *S* when conjoined with ~*D*. Thus, in claiming that there is an entailment from ~*D* & *C* to *S*, for contingent statements *D*, *C*, and *S*, I am stating, in part, that there is a 'definitional' or 'tautological' statement of the form 'If ~*D* & (E_1 and E_2 and ... E_n), then *S*'.[22]

The epistemic objection

As I indicated above, there is another serious problem with the GGE view, one suggested by McDowell (1982). The GGE view, which McDowell labels the 'criteria' view, requires that non-inductive evidence always be defeas-ible in such a way that under no circumstances can it constitute an entail-ment relation. But an epistemic problem arises here, since the GGE view's assumption that a given criterially governed judgment is always defeasible has the consequence that it is always logically possible for that statement to be false, even in cases that are completely indistinguishable from those in which it is true (McDowell, 1982: 457). As McDowell puts it:

> Consider a pair of cases, in both of which someone competent in the use of some claim experiences the satisfaction of (undefeated) 'criteria' for it, but in only one of which the claim is true. According to the suggestion we are considering, the subject would in the latter case know that things are as the claim would represent them as being; the subject in the former case does not. … However, the story is that the scope of experience is the same in each case: the fact itself is outside the reach of experience.
>
> (1982: 459)

McDowell is imagining epistemically identical situations, situations in which all possible evidence is the same. The GGE view must countenance as coherent the possibility that in one of those situations a claim is true, and in the other it is false.

If this is possible, then when is a competent language user ever justified in saying that they *know* that S? McDowell's thought experiment reveals that, on the GGE view, a situation in which S is true can be epistemically identical in every way with one in which S is false. Such a result invites an extreme form of scepticism. If nothing available as possible evidence marks a difference between cases in which S is true and those in which it is false, then a claim that S is true is never fully justified and is in fact always open to doubt – and this as a matter of *grammar*. Importantly, this defect is not shared by the entailment view, by which the obtaining of the undefeated non-inductive evidence for S logically entails that S is true.

Knowing that S

Nonetheless, the entailment view might itself appear to be vulnerable to the charge that it sets the bar too high to allow us to have knowledge of the truth of statements governed by non-inductive evidence. For in characterizing non-inductive evidence as a necessary part of a sufficient condition, I have appealed to a totality of defeaters D for the non-inductive evidence for some statement S. Yet in actual cases we are in no position to know that these defeaters do not obtain. And if we cannot know that there is no defeater for the evidence for S, then it may seem that we cannot know that S is true on the basis of the non-inductive evidence for it.

In fact, the entailment view is compatible with *fallibilist* accounts of knowledge, for fallibilism does not require that, in order to justifiably claim to know that S (or be justified in believing it), one must have evidence which entails S.[23] Rather, fallibilists allow that one can justifiably claim to know that S on the basis of evidence e even though there are alternatives to S that are also compatible with e. As a result, fallibilist accounts of knowledge and justification tend to recognize, I think correctly, a distinction between the conditions required for S to be true and the conditions required for someone's belief that S to be justified. Fallibilism thus allows us to preserve the intuition that there are important differences between the meaning conditions for S and the conditions for the justified belief that S. Where S is governed by non-inductive evidence, the meaning conditions for S include, but aren't necessarily limited to, the entailment from ($\sim D$ & C) to S. On the other hand, the conditions for a person B's justified belief that S are importantly different. They allow that, where S is contingent, B can be justified in believing that S without having evidence which entails S.

This latter is an eminently reasonable qualification. For requiring that B be justified in believing that S only if B has evidence that logically entails S would have the consequence that we are justified in believing very few things indeed.[24] In so far as we cannot in practice exclude every possible defeater, we would never or almost never have knowledge in ordinary contexts. Indeed, we would almost never have knowledge even in extraordinary contexts where we were being epistemically very cautious. For consider again the kinds of things that can count as defeaters for our evidence e for a given empirical statement S. They include at least every contrary of S. Suppose, for instance, that I claim to know that *today is New Year's Day* on the basis of various forms of evidence that I have accumulated, such as checking calendars, public broadcasts of the date, asking other people and so forth. A contrary of the statement that today is New Year's Day is the statement that *I have been the victim of a successful and massive deception aimed at getting me to falsely believe that today is New Year's Day*. If I have not secured that this contrary (and every other possible defeater) is false, then I don't have evidence that entails that today is New Year's Day. And if knowledge of a contingent statement S requires evidence that entails S, then I don't know that today is New Year's Day. Yet this is highly implausible. For while it is always possible for a sceptic to hold our knowledge claims to an incredibly high standard like the possession of logically entailing evidence, doing so has little to do with our ordinary standards of knowledge ascriptions in normal contexts.

Thus, the entailment view can appeal to fallibilism to avoid sceptical consequences. Nonetheless, it may be thought that on the entailment view, even if B's being justified in believing that S does not require that

B have evidence which entails *S*, *B* cannot *know* that *S* if *B* isn't antecedently justified in believing that there is no defeater for the evidence for *S*; that is, in believing that ~*D*. For if *B* knows that *S*, then *S* is true. *S*'s truth is governed by non-inductive evidence *C*, since this entails *S* if ~*D*. So at a minimum, if *S* is true then so is *C*, and hence ~*D* must be true. But this then seems to make *B*'s having evidence for ~*D* a precondition of *B*'s knowing that *S* after all.

It does not do so, however, for just as it is implausible to require that *B* have evidence that entails *S* in order for *B* to be justified in believing that *S*, it is implausible to require as a precondition of *B*'s claiming to know that *S* that *B* know that ~*D*. Indeed, if the entailment view is correct, then requiring that *B* knows that *S* only if *B* knows that ~*D* has as a consequence precisely the unacceptable requirement that *B* have evidence that entails *S* in order to be justified in claiming to know it. For on the entailment view, if ~*D* is true, then *C* is true, for every *C* in C. The reason for this is that, as I noted above, the contradictory of evidence *E* for *S* is a defeater, and *C* is evidence for *S*. Hence its contradictory, ~*C*, is in *D*, and so *C* is in the conjunction ~*D*, which trivially entails *C*. Since (~*D* & *C*) entails *S*, requiring as a precondition of knowing that *S* that one knows that ~*D* reduces again to the implausible requirement that the justification required to know that *S* is that one have evidence that entails *S*.[25][26]

Conclusion

A fallibilist conception of knowledge attributions allows us to see how they are compatible with the existence of an entailment between the undefeated obtaining of the non-inductive evidence for *S* and *S*'s truth. And analysing non-inductive evidence in terms of an entailment offers us our only clear model of how such evidence can have a distinctive role in meaning constitution. Resistance to the entailment view has been found to stem from misunderstandings of the conditions required for an entailment, or from a distorted conception of how philosophical clarification is achieved.

Notes

1. Variants of this position can be found in Shoemaker (1963); Kenny (1967); Lycan (1971); Baker (1974); Wright (1982); Hacker (1993); and Tomassi (2001) among others.
2. My own position is close to that advocated by Canfield in his *Wittgenstein: Language and World* (1981). Canfield is hesitant to speak of what he calls the

'criterial relation' as an entailment, although he concedes that on his view, 'the relationship is close enough to an entailment that we might as well call it that' (1981: 87). Understanding non-inductive evidence on the model of an entailment was also defended by Malcolm (1963) and Albritton (1959), although Albritton (1966) later abandoned the entailment view. McDowell has also suggested something close to an entailment view, arguing that epistemological considerations imply 'an indefeasible connection between the actual, as opposed to apparent, satisfaction of a criterion and the associated knowledge' (1982: 470).

3. As Wittgenstein noted (cf. LW I: 964; LW II: 79 and *passim*), there do seem to be some contexts in which the possibility of the subsequent defeat of a pain attribution, e.g., cannot be conceived of without undermining the coherence of the concept *pain*. I'm indebted to Danièle Moyal-Sharrock for emphasizing this point to me.

4. Cf. Kenny (1967); Cavell (1979); McDowell (1982); McGinn (1998). I agree with these commentators that the notion of non-inductive evidence ought not to be regarded as a guarantee of *certain* (infallible) knowledge, although I argue below that it allows the justified attribution of knowledge in many ordinary contexts.

5. Pollock and Cruz deny this, claiming that 'The only kinds of reasons that can be derived from entailment relations are reasons that are themselves entailments – conclusive reasons' (1999: 145). This is clearly incorrect. A concept like 'grandmaster' can derive its content from entailment relations even though our reasons for the belief that someone is a grandmaster are defeasible and so not 'conclusive'.

6. For a defence of the claim that Wittgenstein regarded all criteria as akin to defining criteria, see Canfield, 1981: 35–51. For a criticism of the attempt to read the notion of defeasible evidence into Wittgenstein, see McDowell, 1982: 462–6.

7. This is a simplification for, as I note below, the non-inductive evidence *C* need not always form a conjunction in order to be a necessary part of a sufficient condition.

8. Wright (1982) develops such a possibility without endorsing it. Baker later moved away from his more 'constructivist' inclinations, but continued to endorse a version of the GGE view; cf. Baker and Hacker, 1985: 678.

9. Cf. Lycan, 1971: 110; Baker, 1974: 161; Hacker, 1993: 258. Tomassi (2001: 47) expresses a similar idea by claiming that the logic of criterial concepts is non-monotonic, thereby ensuring that any inference made on the basis of non-inductive evidence remains open to defeat.

10. In saying this, I am here committing myself to a further assumption, namely that in order for a contingent proposition *S* to be meaningful, there must be some relevant grounds for its assertion or denial. This commitment is made by defenders of GGE as well; see, for instance, Hacker, 1993: 258.

11. Canfield, 1981: 79–91. Note that Canfield uses the term 'non-inductive evidence' to refer to what I call the 'GGE view'.

12. As I observe in my remarks on evidence below, there are additional conditions on something's counting as evidence, such as community standards for warrant. I'm assuming in this discussion that such conditions are met; i.e., that we are in the presence of a community of language users with some standards for counting things as evidence.

13. My account here derives from Klein (1981). I'm also indebted to Kevin Meeker for numerous helpful suggestions.

14. I am by-passing here the problem of 'defective defeaters', or evidence that appears to defeat some other evidence, but does not do so. For discussions, see Klein (1981); Pollock and Cruz (1999).

15. Some foundationalists think that some statements can justify themselves as well as other statements, hence my qualifier 'generally'. Even if there are self-justifying statements, however; statements governed by non-inductive evidence are not among them.

16. This is only to say that were evidence that there is an evil deceiver available to some person B, then B would have reasons that defeat A's having a toothache. It is not to say that the mere possibility of there being an evil deceiver is defeating evidence.

17. A *prima facie* counter-example case might be one in which the Evil Deceiver just 'puts the thought in my mind' that A has a toothache, despite A's not having one. In this case, however, A's not having a toothache is not a defeater for my *evidence* that he has one, for in this case I don't believe that A has one on the basis of evidence.

18. Lest an 'assertion condition' semanticist be tempted to object that our not being warranted *does* provide content to ~S, on the grounds that they recognize no difference between warranted assertability conditions and semantic content, I note the following. First, the identification of semantic content with assertion conditions by itself does not establish that '~S' has content in cases such as the above, in which none of the conditions for the warranted assertion of '~S' obtain, while those for 'S' do. To block an entailment from ($\sim D$ & C) to S, one must demonstrate that ~S can have content despite the truth of ($\sim D$ & C). If anything, tying semantic content to assertion conditions would seem to further erode any hope of such a demonstration. Second, it's mistaken to argue, as Baker has in defence of his broadly assertion-condition account of criteria, that any appearance of incoherence in the GGE account of non-inductive evidence stems solely from a further commitment to a network of 'classical' semantic and epistemological theses that his theory can reject (1974: 164–5, 176–7). The arguments advanced by both Canfield and myself against GGE require no such 'classical' commitments. Rather, they rely only on premises that Baker explicitly accepts himself, namely that criteria partially determine the meaning of concepts and that *all* criterial support for S is defeasible while not-S is true (cf. 1974: 161–2).

19. Here my position differs from that of Tomassi (2001: 47), who holds instead that ~S is conceivable in the undefeated presence of C, and only its assertion is unwarranted.

20. Saying that $\sim D$ & C entail S is also consistent with the existence of empirical statements for which there is no non-inductive evidence, such as judgments of sameness (cf. RFM VII: 40; PI: 377), some first-person judgments (PI: 377), and avowals (PI: 253, and p. 189).

21. I'm indebted to Cory Juhl for emphasizing to me the importance of this point.

22. Recall Wittgenstein's remark that ' "A man has angina if this bacillus is found in him" is a tautology' (BB: 25).

23. My account is also compatible with thinking that some apparently empirical statements that are *not* governed by criteria might be known, and known with

certainty. I have in mind cases such as those that Wittgenstein considers, such as the belief that I am in my room, where the possibility of being mistaken seems logically excluded (cf. OC: 194–5, 67–74, and *passim*).

24. I'm supposing, roughly, that B *has* evidence e if B either: (1) actually *subscribes to* or accepts that E, at least in the sense of being disposed to assert that E in appropriate circumstances; or (2) has E *available* because E is a part of some chain of propositions that have their origin in some proposition that B actually subscribes to. This chain is one in which each proposition justifies the following one, and B is able to recognize this.

25. This has the result that the bare absence of any defeater of the criteria for S entails that S is true. This may appear to make the non-inductive evidence irrelevant, but it does not, for we get this entailment from $\sim D$ to C only because we have used C to determine the content of D, as when we allowed that since '$\sim C$' is a contradictory of C, it is in D.

26. There is a further issue here that concerns whether the set of propositions known by B is closed under entailment, such that it be true that if B knows that S, and B knows that S entails R, then B knows that R. This *closure principle* is weaker than the requirement that B knows that S only if B has evidence that logically entails S, since the set of statements entailed *by* S is a subset of the set of statements that entail S. Yet if the closure principle is true, then it seems that in order to know that S, one must know the falsity of every contrary of S, since these are all entailed by S. The closure principle is arguably false. Even if it is true, however, there are a variety of ways of maintaining a fallibilist account of knowledge in the face of it – see for instance Klein (1981), and Cohen (2000).

13

'Tennis Without a Ball': Wittgenstein on *Secondary Sense*

Michel ter Hark

It is fundamental to our idea of language that words are applied to things that somehow are the same. In their attempt to provide a justificatory explanation of language and knowledge, philosophers have often claimed that there must be a unity underlying the diversity of objects to which a certain word applies if the use of words is not to break up into semantic anarchy. As is well known, Wittgenstein has challenged this philosophical explanation. In his famous discussion of the meaning of 'game', he has argued that there is no need to postulate an underlying unity of this kind. The concept of game may be held together by a network of 'similarities overlapping and criss-crossing'. With this and other examples, Wittgenstein was primarily thinking of concepts used within their normal home bases. But there are classes of cases where the meaning of words is extended to include objects and features outside their home bases. A notorious example is the use of 'fat' and 'lean' to describe days of the week:

> Given the two ideas 'fat' and 'lean', would you be rather inclined to say that Wednesday was fat and Tuesday lean, or the other way round? (I am definitely inclined towards the former).'
>
> (PI: p. 216; also BB: 137)

Such uses of words, Wittgenstein says, might be described as 'secondary', relative to their ordinary familiar uses.

Wittgenstein's explicit remarks about secondary sense are sparse and his examples often highly idiosyncratic. But at least a few authors have noticed that Wittgenstein introduced these examples to throw light on issues of deep philosophical importance. In the main they have concentrated on the relevance of secondary sense for aesthetics. B. R. Tilghman (1984) and Oswald Hanfling (1991), for instance, have argued that the question how we can experience and describe works of art as we do the emotional life of human beings cannot be answered by displacing the emotional character of a work of art to the feelings of the artist or the audience, but by conceiving the language of emotion here in a secondary sense. From a slightly different angle, Cora Diamond (1966–67) has sought to illuminate what Wittgenstein meant by ethical and religious expressions in an 'absolute sense' by drawing on certain logical resemblances with words used in a secondary sense. What has been much less appreciated is the relation between Wittgenstein's discussion of secondary sense and his philosophy of psychology. This neglect is remarkable because immediately following 'fat Wednesday' and 'lean Tuesday', Wittgenstein discusses calculating in the head as another example of a secondary use of words. Other references to calculating in the head are to be found in *Philosophical Investigations* (PI: 364–6) and in *Remarks on the Philosophy of Psychology*, but the most comprehensive account is in *Wittgenstein's Lectures on Philosophical Psychology, 1946–1947*. What emerges from these discussions is that 'calculating in the head', despite its regular use in education and the market, is as much a secondary use of words as 'fat Wednesday' and that the reluctance to accept this fact comes from our being naturally disposed to misunderstand and oversimplify our own concepts. Calculating in the head therefore contains all the ingredients of a Wittgensteinian drama.

In what follows I will first interpret the idea of secondary sense drawing on as many sources in Wittgenstein's work as possible. Then I will focus on calculating in the head. What I hope this discussion will make clear is that Wittgenstein's probing questions and examples are not isolated insights, but are directly related to his more general account of philosophical error. At the close of the chapter I will show that this kind of philosophical error holds in its grip the contemporary debate in developmental psychology on child's pretend play.

Secondary sense

Wittgenstein introduces the topic of secondary sense by drawing attention to the phenomenon of experiencing the meaning of a word. It would be better to speak of the phenomena of experiencing the meaning of words because this term covers a huge variety of cases ranging from idiosyncratic associations to finding the apt word for a feeling. Frege (1962) relegated these phenomena to the 'tone' of words thereby distinguishing rigorously between the objective sense of words and private, subjective associations or mental images. For Frege this distinction was one with that between respectively fact-stating language having determinate truth-conditions and other forms of language like the expressive, performative or evocative use of words lacking such conditions. On the other hand, Frege considered the tone of words part of the notion of meaning and since meaning is communicable, his explanation in terms of private mental images was contradictory. Much of the later philosophy of ordinary language was a corrective of this Fregean contemptuous treatment of forms of language other than assertions, but it was only Wittgenstein who focused on the tone or colouring of words in the strict sense of these terms. His discussion of proper names is exemplary in this respect. Prosaically speaking, a proper name is a label which is tagged on to us at birth, its meaning being a kind of gesture toward us. But apart from identifying its bearer, a name can also be used in a different way, on account of an autonomous secret concealed in it: the name itself seems to have absorbed the qualities of its bearer and is replete with meaning. This aspect becomes clear by comparing, for instance, the statement 'Beethoven was born in Bonn in 1770' with the cry 'Beethoven!' on recognition of his music. In the latter case the name has become the bearer of a significant tone or aura, and this tone is heard in it. Not only words but also vowels possess this kind of secret: 'For me the vowel *e* is yellow' (PI: p. 216). The example is rather like Rimbaud's vowel symbolism: 'A noir, E blanc, I rouge, U vert, O bleu; voyelles.' The importance Wittgenstein attaches to this phenomenon is that it evidently provides a counter-example to his claim in PI: 43 that the meaning of a word is its use in the language. But there he had already made a restriction by saying that it was valid for a large class of cases, not for all. And he had also restricted it in another way in *Philosophical Investigations*, which is pertinent to secondary meaning:[1]

> But when one says 'I *hope* he'll come' – doesn't the feeling give the word 'hope' its meaning? (And what about the sentence 'I do *not* hope for his coming any longer?') The feeling does perhaps give the word 'hope' its special ring; that is, it is expressed in that ring. – If the feeling gives the word its meaning, then here 'meaning' means *point*. But why is the feeling the point?
>
> Is hope a feeling? (Characteristic marks.)

(PI: 545)

In Manuscript 180b, discussing the experience of meaning, Wittgenstein seems to come back to this restriction when he writes: 'And if one wants to speak of meaning here, it does not consist in the use of words' (Ms 180b: p. 6); 'The meaning or a word, I said, is its use. But an important addition has to be made to this' (ibid.: p. 8).

What would you be missing if you did not experience the meaning of a word, Wittgenstein asks? He compares a person who fails to experience the meaning of a word with one who is unable to hear or see something in a certain way, as opposed to somebody who has a musical ear or a painter's eye, and he speaks of 'meaning-blindness' just as he speaks of 'aspect-blindness'. What is somebody missing who can only use proper names as labels? And what about somebody who has no sense of how a word loses all meaning and becomes purely acoustic when he utters it a number of times in succession? At first sight this kind of person would not seem to be missing a great deal. It is a plain fact that, in everyday communication, proper names function as labels rather than as symbolic experiences. One takes as little interest in such experiences as in other people's dreams. At any rate it does not matter so much, or at all, whether my neighbour, in hating me, experiences the meaning of my name. But if one takes a different angle from that of ordinary communication, then experiencing the meaning of a word has far more than a subsidiary role. Wittgenstein already suggests this by pointing out that secondary meanings and aspects are pre-eminently exploited in an aesthetic context. In fact, in aesthetics the world seems turned upside down: there, secondary meanings and aspects are of *primary* importance. But on Wittgenstein's view, aesthetics is not a separate world, independent of a more pragmatic context. On the contrary, he is convinced of the kinship between aesthetic phenomena and language: 'Why should I say at all what meaning is? Why should I not say: Language, music and much that we call similar to language is meaningful?' (Ms 180b: p. 6). The characteristic feature of the phenomenon of experiencing the meaning of a word, Wittgenstein goes on, is that: 'in *this* situation we use this expression: we say we pronounced the word with *this* meaning and take this expression over from that other language-game' (PI: p. 216). A different, yet related, example illustrates this point very well:

The feeling of the unreality of one's surroundings. This feeling I have had once, and many have it before the onset of mental illness. Everything seems somehow not *real*; but not as if one *saw* things unclear or blurred; everything looks quite as usual .... But why do I choose precisely the word 'unreality' to express it? Surely not because of its sound. (A word of very like sound but different meaning would not do.) I choose it because of its meaning. But I surely did not learn to use the word to mean: *a feeling.* No; but I learned how to use it with a particular meaning and now I use it spontaneously like *this* ...

(RPP I: 125)

Here we are not dealing with experiencing the meaning of a word, but with using a word in giving expression to a feeling. The word 'unreality' is spontaneously chosen because of the meaning it has in its home base, even though we have not learned to use it to express a feeling. Extending the meaning of a word seems not to go together with shifting meaning. Indeed, it seems essential for the experience at hand that the meaning of the word 'unreal' has not changed. And yet something has changed, in that a word, formerly used to describe aspects of facts and things has now come to express feelings. To deal with this conceptual complexity, Wittgenstein introduces his distinction between the primary and secondary sense of words.

Reflecting upon his inclination to call Wednesday 'fat' and Tuesday 'lean', he asks whether 'fat' and 'lean' have some different meaning here from their usual one.[2] Again the suggestion is that words used in a secondary sense do not differ in meaning from their primary meaning. So that, if asked what other meaning 'fat' as applied to days of the week has, one could not say. This is why Wittgenstein notes: 'I could only explain the meanings in the usual way. I could *not* point to the examples of Tuesday and Wednesday' (PI: p. 216).[3] One might object that in this game the word does change its meaning after all because one can hardly say that Wednesday weighs more than Tuesday. The proper response is that this objection fails to recognize the point of this game, which is to say that Wednesday *is* fat rather than taking account of all the conceptual relations 'fat' has in the primary game. On the other hand, children 'pitying' their dolls often transfer a whole package of concepts, 'speaking' to their dolls and 'treating' their 'painful' limbs. Because no shift in meaning is involved, secondary sense is not the same as non-univocal meaning of words; 'bank' does change its meaning when taken in one sense and another. Wittgenstein goes on in the same fragment:

> They have a different use. – So ought I really to have used different words? Certainly not that. I want to use *these* words (with their familiar meanings) *here*.
>
> (PI: p. 216; LW II: 795)

Metaphorical use equally involves transferring words from their home base to another context, but Wittgenstein emphatically denies that secondary use is metaphorical:

> If I say 'For me the vowel *e* is yellow' I do not mean: 'yellow' in a metaphorical sense, – for I could not express what I want to say in any other way than by means of the word 'yellow'.
>
> (PI: p. 216)

Metaphors can be paraphrased and depend on the apprehension of likenesses or analogies of one sort or another. But if someone would say ' "e" is like yellow' would we understand him? 'Isn't the point of the game precisely that we express ourselves by saying *e is* yellow?' (LW II: 59). It is also unclear how similarities should be established. It is instructive to take notice of Wittgenstein's earlier discussion of this theme in *The Brown Book*. Why do we speak, he asks, of mental strain just as we speak of physical strain? (BB: 132). The answer that forces itself upon us is that they must have something in common, for otherwise we would not be using the same term. But asked to specify this similarity any further we feel that we are either simply repeating the same expression in different words (e.g., 'tension') or appealing to facts that were not part of the original experience (e.g., we might realize that our biceps contract each time we talk about mental strain). For if there were no similarity, why should we call them both 'strain'? In the manuscript sources of this part of *The Brown Book*, Wittgenstein replies: 'But can't the similarity just consist in this that you are inclined to use in both cases the same metaphor, the same expression?' (Ms 150: p. 15). Likewise, one cannot say or explain how 'Beethoven' fits the man's music without repeating and expressing the name 'Beethoven.' The 'similarity' therefore logically cannot be described or established without using the familiar word in its secondary sense; that is, in its new situation. With straightforward metaphors, by contrast, it is possible to establish the similarities and analogies one wishes to highlight independently of the metaphorical language in question. For instance, we can say in what respect the human mind is a computer without using the word 'computer'. We also come to learn this metaphor by rationally assessing the similarities and differences between minds and computers. But we cannot say how the vowel *e* is yellow without repeating the word 'yellow'. Neither do we have a rational explanation for using this word in this new way. Yet it is essential for the experience at hand that we use 'yellow' in its familiar meaning here. This means that only those who understand the primary meaning of 'yellow' can use it in a secondary sense and have the relevant experience. This is why Wittgenstein says about the relation between the primary and secondary sense of words: 'In both cases the explanation of the word is that of its primary meaning. It can only have a secondary meaning for someone if he knows its primary meaning' (LW II: 797; cf. PI: p. 216).

   The role *similarity* plays in metaphorical language also implies another difference from secondary sense. Metaphors are chosen because of a similarity in certain respects, but not in others, between two domains of language (e.g., man is a wolf). Therefore, the shift of words from one area to another is accompanied by a shift in meaning. The secondary sense of a word is also a new use of language, but here the word is not used to refer to *something* new. Rather what is new is the situation in which it is used. Explaining the difference between the primary and secondary sense of a word in terms of different objects referred to therefore rests on a confusion between secondary sense and metaphorical language.

Speaking of a 'secondary' use has had some unfortunate effects in the literature. 'Secondary' may mean of minor or subsidiary importance and the examples of 'fat Wednesday' and 'lean Tuesday' have only reinforced this impression, but immediately following these curious examples Wittgenstein mentions calculating in the head as another case of secondary use. Unlike attributing colours to vowels, calculating in the head is a well-established language-game and not easy to dispense with. Hence, even words used quite naturally may still have a secondary sense. The philosophical importance of this is not to be underestimated. Being embedded in a stable and reliable practice, calculating in the head may seem as 'normal' a concept as calculating on paper. And yet, precisely by juxtaposing the curiously idiosyncratic examples of fat and lean days of the week and the pedestrian calculating in the head, Wittgenstein seeks to draw our attention to the fact that the latter is a new use of language with respect to the concept of overt calculating. At the same time, this shows that secondary sense plays a larger and more important role in our lives than some have wanted to believe.

Indeed, some of the commentators who have pondered Wittgenstein's brief remarks about calculating in the head have failed to see this point. Thus Robert Fogelin observes that fat Wednesday is too exotic to illuminate calculating in the head (1976: 180). Likewise, Hanfling notes that calculating in the head does not fit into the context of fat and lean because it is obvious that the former, unlike the adjacent examples, is not an idiosyncratic use of language (2002: 160). But although the examples differ in semantic respectability, logically they are in the same boat: both are forms of what Wittgenstein calls secondary sense. Granted, this is also how Fogelin and Hanfling classify calculating in the head, but precisely by failing to take the analogy with more idiosyncratic examples seriously, they have explained it in such a way that it can no longer be recognized as a secondary meaning of 'to calculate'.

Calculating in the head

> Only if you have learnt to calculate – on paper or out loud – can you be made to grasp, by means of this concept, what calculating in the head is.
>
> (PI: p. 216)

The analogy with fat Wednesday so far is (merely) that only those for whom the word 'calculate' has the normal sense of doing sums overtly can use it in the sense of 'calculating in the head'. The meaningful use of 'calculate' in the latter context depends on the command and use of its occurrence in the former context. 'Can', to be sure, has to be taken logically which means that somebody unfamiliar with the concept of calculating out loud or on paper would not be able to use or understand the concept of calculating in the head. But who apart from a behaviourist would say that calculating is not the sort of thing we 'think' of as being a process in the head, just as to speak of 'fat Wednesday' may seem to one an aberrant use of the word 'fat'? Furthermore, although there seems to be no reason for predicating 'fat' of Wednesday and 'lean' of Tuesday, there seem to be respectable reasons for saying that a person has performed a calculation in the head. Indeed, according to Fogelin, calculating in the head 'looks like' calculating on paper and it is this similarity that would justify our extending the latter concept to include the former. He compares the relation between the primary and secondary sense of a word with the relation between the game of patience and an (existing) game of double solitaire. 'It is not hard to see why this game is still called solitaire: it *looks like* solitaire', writes Fogelin (1986: 180).

It is doubtful whether this analogy sheds any light on the notion of secondary sense. Let us examine it more closely. Double patience is a competitive version of Klondike patience (solitaire). Each player deals a layout, as in Klondike: 28 cards in seven piles, each with the top card face up and the rest face down. The left-hand pile has just one card, the second two, and so on. Each player begins with a stack of 24 face-down cards. The player with the lower value card on her one-pile starts. On your turn, you can make a series of moves, just as in Klondike. You place your cards on your own layout, and on the foundation piles when they fit, and move cards from your discard pile to your layout or the foundations. You are not allowed to play on, or use, your opponent's layout or discard pile. To end your turn – when you cannot, or choose not to, make any other moves – you turn over the top card of your face-down stack, and place it on your face-up discard pile. The game ends when one of the players has played all the cards in the foundation piles, or when both players are blocked. As this description makes clear, we would not say of a person that he could not be playing double solitaire if he were unfamiliar with solitaire. Double solitaire is like solitaire in many respects, it is a game of the same kind and can be explained independently of one's knowledge of, or expertise in, solitaire. The command of solitaire is not therefore a logical prerequisite for being able to play double solitaire, hence the latter is not a secondary sense of the former.

What the card example particularly reveals is an unreflective use of the word 'kind'. Double solitaire is a different version of solitaire, but for Wittgenstein the meaning of 'version' and 'kind' is precisely what is at issue here. Consider what he says a few remarks later: ' "Talking" (whether loud or silently) and "thinking" are not concepts of the same kind; even though they are in closest connexion' (PI: p. 217). At first sight it is unclear who would be the target of this remark because most philosophers and psychologists would in fact deny that thinking and talking are of the same kind, but the issue can be cleared up by asking further in what sense they are not of the same kind. The natural answer – that the one is a different kind of activity from the other (just as a number is often thought to be a different kind of object from a numeral) – is what Wittgenstein believes is confusing. As he puts it in a different context in *The Blue Book*: 'They think they are making such a statement as "A railway train, a railway station, and a railway car are different kinds of objects", whereas their statement is analogous to "A railway train, a railway accident, and a railway law are different kinds of objects" ' (BB: 64). The linguistic picture operative here is that the difference between concepts is to be explained in terms of the different subject matters talked about. The rudimentary mistake, owing to our concentrating on a hopelessly narrow range of examples, is to suppose they are talked about in the same way: in both areas the concept's function is to name and describe the relevant subject-matter. The temptation to subsume the concepts of 'talking to oneself' and 'talking loudly' ('calculating in the head' and 'calculating on paper') under the single paradigm of concepts for describing processes and activities is especially strong because they are as a matter of fact in 'closest connexion'. The relation of 'being in closest connection yet not of the same kind' is of crucial importance in coming to understand Wittgenstein's thought. Unfortunately it has hardly received any attention,[4] although it is not limited to calculating in the head and is quite prominently at work in his extensive treatment of the relation between the concepts of seeing and imaging. Thus he writes: 'The *tie-up* between imaging and seeing is close; but there is no *similarity*' (RPP II: 70; Z: 625); 'The language-games employing both these concepts are radically different – but hang together' (RPP II: 71; Z: 625).

A game analogy that would better fulfil the purpose of illuminating how calculating in the head is related to overt calculating, then, would be one in which two different games, for instance variants of chess and draughts, made use of the same board and the same pieces, but with similar pieces performing different functions. Fogelin's and Hanfling's description of mental calculating, on the other hand, focuses merely on the similarity of the 'states' and 'processes' involved and by-passes the differences. According to Hanfling, there is no difference at all because mental and physical steps alike can be seen as phases of the same calculation (2002: 161). Consider now Fogelin's description:

> Usually enough of the standard surroundings of calculating are present to make this transition natural. I am dealing with a person who has had our regular school training; he is given a problem that falls within his normal competence; he does not produce an answer at once, instead he falls silent for a moment (or perhaps mumbles to himself) and comes up with an answer; if I ask him how he got the answer so quickly, he may say that he used the trick of dividing by eight and moving the decimal point instead of multiplying directly by one-hundred and twenty-five, etc.
>
> (1976: 181)

To be sure, Fogelin goes on, the person has not produced overtly the characteristic patterns of symbols that we recognize as essential to calculation in its original form, but the new domain of application preserves so much of the 'look' of calculating that the transition is made without much difficulty. But so what if the person did not produce a pattern of symbols in his mind? Would it make Fogelin and Hanfling suspend their judgement that the person had calculated? Following mental steps just as one follows steps on paper is on their view essential to calculating in the head, and the only difference seems to be that in the one case the steps are visible or audible whereas in the other they are not. Wittgenstein challenges precisely the assumption that the difference between mental and overt calculating can be explained in terms of a distinction between inner processes and overt behaviour. On his view, calculating in the head is not a phenomenon partly withdrawn from view by the epistemic limits set to introspection or by the external façade of behaviour: '… it is not hidden *at all* but the concept is confusing' (LW II: 852). Ironically, the concept is confusing precisely because it parallels overt calculating and overt speaking so much. Like overt calculating, mental calculating takes a period of time and seems to be divisible into a series of steps. And, like overt calculating, it is a process taking in numbers and reaching, after following a mathematical or methodical route, a certain result. In virtue of these similarities philosophers and psychologists are inclined to construe mental calculating on the conceptual model of overt calculating: a concept referring to internal activities and processes.

On Wittgenstein's view, conceptually coming to terms with the concept of calculating in the head is hampered by the tendency to inflate the similarities with normal calculating. This, I believe, is the reason why he invents the curious game of 'tennis without a ball'. This game is almost indiscernible from real tennis, yet it is fundamentally a different game:

> Imagine *this* game – I call it 'tennis without a ball'; The players move around on a tennis court just as in tennis, and they even have rackets, but no ball. Each one reacts to his partner's stroke as if, or more or less as if, a ball had caused his reaction. (Manoeuvres.) The umpire, who must have an 'eye' for the game, decides in questionable cases whether a ball has gone into the net, etc., etc. This game is obviously quite similar to tennis and yet, on the other hand, it is *fundamentally* different.
>
> (LW II: 854)

We would call it tennis (without a ball) because it has all the gestures, setting, score-keeping of tennis. At the same time we do not fail to see the difference with real tennis, which is as fundamental as, for instance, the difference between imagining and seeing.[5] The analogy therefore is meant to show how one game may look like another, yet not coincide with it conceptually. Likewise, Wittgenstein wants to say, the concept of calculating in the head looks similar to the concept of overt calculating, yet is as closely related and as disparately separate as the concepts of a cardinal number and a rational number (LW II: 857; cf. PI: p. 220).

There are many linguistic analogies which may make us think that the concepts are similar and of the same kind, just as a pain and a tickle can be subsumed under the same genus of concepts of experience. Thus we say as easily 'I calculated in my head' as 'I did that sum in Room 23,' thereby suggesting that there is a place in our head where numbers are counted and divided (LPP: 251). Wittgenstein seems to challenge this view on introspective grounds: can one really say more when asked what one has been doing when pondering silently than just 'I have calculated in my head?' (LPP: 28). But his point is logical. When we think we can answer the question, we are taken in by misleading analogies. Suppose, he says, there is some impenetrable country (LPP: 130–1). A traveller going there does not know the way. There is only one road. Yet the traveller arrives at his destination and so he must have followed the road. This situation seems analogous to reaching a multiplication result in one's head, but the difference is that the road the traveller took can be described; that is, it makes sense to suppose this. On the other hand, it makes no sense to describe how we came, in our head, from the multiplication problem to the result.

Another reason for taking the talk of place in a literal (and hence primary sense) is that the assumption that science will discover physiological processes or even 'modules' in the brain underlying our calculating procedures looks plausible. To this Wittgenstein responds that 'even the scientists don't know, and you certainly don't know, and you once used the phrase without knowing anything of what the scientists might know' (LPP: 269). Put otherwise, physiological hypotheses are of no help because they could solve the problem only under different circumstances, namely those in which physiological talk is used by the people themselves to describe what goes on when they calculate. Concepts that are not acknowledged and conceded by actors themselves are powerless to function as genuine criteria.

In the *Lectures on Philosophical Psychology*, Wittgenstein describes a number of thought experiments to show that calculating processes similar to writing down columns of numbers or typing in numbers on a display are not a necessary condition for our speaking of calculating in the head. For instance, he imagines a person who is given a multiplication to do but does not calculate and, if asked what he is doing, says that he is not calculating but doing something else. He writes the alphabet on paper and claims that this somehow connects with the multiplication. Of course we are surprised to hear this and perhaps inclined to say that he has gone mad, but then he translates the series of letters in numbers and gives the correct result. Now we would no longer hesitate to call this calculating, even though it is completely clear that his 'activities' bear no resemblance whatsoever with what we think of as mental calculating.

Closer to home, take calculating geniuses. The American psychiatrist Benjamin Rush described as early as 1789 the lightning-quick calculating ability of Thomas Fuller, who understood little maths more complex than counting. When Fuller was asked how many seconds a man had lived by the time he was 70 years, 17 days and 12 hours old, he gave the correct answer of 2,21,500,800, one minute and a half later.[6] The important thing to note is that here too we speak of calculating, even though no process has taken place analogous to what we would recognize as such.

But there are other analogies underlying the claim that calculating in the head is a process resembling overt calculating. A particularly powerful analogy, also operative in other areas, is what Wittgenstein refers to as the distinction between a direct and an indirect description. Compared with a description like 'John is typing in numbers on his hand-held calculator and waiting for the result', the sentence 'John is calculating in his head' may look like an indirect description of the process of calculating. Mental calculating – and here is an analogy with the discussion about the relation between seeing and imaging – seems like a weak or vague copy of the visible and audible signs used when doing sums in the classroom. Conceived this way the difference between both forms of calculating becomes merely gradual, just as the difference between mental images and impressions was once conceived as a matter of degree, of force or vivacity. Wittgenstein takes seriously the fact that we are inclined to explain the difference this way. The inclination may be as strong as representing dreams in films in blue and never in red (LPP: 129). Conceding this inclination the question can still be raised, what is meant by 'weaker'? Has it really to be taken as a difference in degree much as when we say that '2 + 2 = 4' on dirty paper is a vague copy of '2 + 2 = 4' on the display screen of a calculator? On Wittgenstein's view, this would amount to confusing different language-games, and I take this to be the point of his discussion of the pair 'direct–indirect'. This contrast is applicable in certain regions of our language and the mistake is that we transfer it to other areas where it logically does not apply.

Wittgenstein's example in the *Lectures* is 'Mr Smith is hanging on the wall; not himself but his portrait.' Someone who said 'Mr Smith is hanging on the wall in my room', and who, upon noticing the oddity of what he said, might correct himself by adding: 'Not he himself but his portrait', could point to the portrait but also to Mr Smith *in vivo*. Hence there is a direct and an indirect representation of the person:

> The procedure is: Not that but something else. But (and this is obvious) in that case I show Smith as well as the picture, and in the calculating case I cannot direct my attention away from the paperwork to something else I can show.
>
> (LPP: 269)

What else he did (other than writing down a number in his mind) cannot be specified or described without using the concept of overt calculating. 'In the head' suggests a place where processes or activities take place, but the point is that we cannot but describe these processes 'by analogy' with processes and activities not taking place in the head. The analogy is not an analogy or metaphor that can be paraphrased or explained in terms of similarities that can be identified without using the concept of overt calculating. It is precisely in this resistance to being reduced to metaphors that can be paraphrased that 'calculating in the head' is a secondary use of the words 'to calculate'. Wittgenstein's reminder that one teaches someone to calculate in his head by ordering him to *calculate* is meant to make us aware of this secondary use and to guard us against assuming that the concept, to be meaningful at all, must refer to an activity or process just as overt calculating does. For it is this assumption that lies at the bottom of a variety of ontological and epistemological debates in psychology and the philosophy of mind.

The distinction between the primary and secondary sense of words is not meant to defend the meaningfulness of certain idiosyncratic forms of speech nor to contribute to a theory of aesthetics as some have supposed. Neither is it Wittgenstein's aim to explain by means of the notion of secondary sense how psychological concepts are meaningfully ascribed to organisms other than human beings, or to lifeless things. The general aim of the distinction is in fact a variation on the basic theme of the *Philosophical Investigations*: to correct a mistaken, but tempting interpretation of language and so to preclude certain philosophical and foundational problems from arising. The view that naming and referring present the fundamental paradigms of how words have meaning is one that philosophers and psychologists have often uncritically adopted in areas where it does not apply. In the area of talk about the mental this view has led to the idea that mental terms get their meanings through referring to hidden mental states and processes. In his attempt to break the spell of this way of viewing mental talk, Wittgenstein has sometimes been taken as denying that people have an inner life, feel pain or remember, whereas in fact he has also shown that behaviourism is another side of the same semantic coin; for rather than having mental terms stand for *inner* states and processes the behaviourist has simply shifted the reference to *outer* states and processes. By noting similarities to certain non-referential uses of language, like gestures, cries of pain or signals, Wittgenstein has sought to break the spell of a fixed way of looking at things common to both dualism or mentalism and behaviourism. His discussion of secondary sense fits squarely within this general therapeutic approach to foundational problems in psychology. The natural or traditional way of dealing with such concepts as calculating in the head and reading silently, is to explain their meaning in terms of other facts or experiences they would refer to when used in their linguistic home bases. That is, they are being treated as if of the same kind as concepts referring to physical activities. But this is to confuse what is in fact a secondary sense of words with a primary sense of words. This confusion is deeply rooted in the language used in speaking about mental 'activities'. Contrary to these deeply rooted linguistic analogies, mental calculating and speaking in the imagination are fundamentally different from their overt counterparts. Perhaps they exemplify the most dramatic shortcoming of what Wittgenstein calls the Augustinian picture of language. For in that picture, the only way to stand by one's conviction that the meaning of a word is the object it stands for is to assume a similarity of one sort or another between mental 'activities' and their physical counterparts. But if Wittgenstein is right, it makes no sense to speak of similarity here, and thinking it does is to confuse secondary sense and metaphorical language.

Confusing secondary sense with primary sense lies at the root of philosophical and foundational debates in psychology. Indeed, to ignore the logical dependency of the secondary sense of a word on its primary sense and to see the former, much as the latter, as language referring to objects and facts may just as easily lead one to behaviourism as to mentalism or dualism. But when calculating in the head is a secondary use of words rather than a primary one, it cannot be dealt with in the same way we deal with language describing overt calculating. Yet this is precisely what seems to happen. Denying that calculating in the head refers to anything in the head means to treat this concept on a par with concepts describing facts (e.g., typing numbers in on a calculator) and then to conclude that whereas the latter expression refers to an observable phenomenon, the former does not, and hence is meaningless. Likewise, casting about for another object guaranteeing that the expression 'calculating in the head' has meaning is also to treat this concept as a concept referring to activities and processes, and to conclude that the semantic difference can be explained only by assuming that the former concept refers to another sort of activity than the latter. Calculating in the head is fundamentally different from, yet dependent on, overt calculating. Wittgenstein's usual way of explaining differences is to point to criteria for using the concepts. Although he is not explicit on this point, the criteria for saying of someone that he multiplied in his head are similar to what he says about dream reports and confessing what one thought: 'The criteria for the truth of the *confession* that I thought such-and-such are not the criteria for a true *description* of a process' (PI: p. 222). The truth of a confession, like that of a dream report, 'is guaranteed by the special criteria of *truthfulness*' (ibid.).[7] The criteria for a true description of a process imply that the description can be compared with what is being described and checked by others for its accuracy. When we accept a person's answer that he did the multiplication in his head or that he took such-and -such steps we have no way of comparing it with the facts. On Wittgenstein's account, this should not be seen as an epistemic defect but as a sign that the criteria for the truth of saying what one thought are that the person speaks truthfully. On the other hand, we would never accept his answer had he been unable to calculate in writing or orally.

Conclusion: pretend play

In order to show that in criticizing the idea of confusing a secondary sense and a primary sense of words Wittgenstein is not flogging a dead horse, I turn to a recent discussion in developmental psychology. In the last two decades there has been an explosion of research investigating pretend play or pretence. The term 'pretence' is used here not as a form of deception, but primarily to refer to a child's pretend play. In pretend play, children treat objects or events in some respects as if they were other objects or events, or as if they had properties other than the properties they actually have, without any intent to deceive. As noted in the introduction to this essay, Wittgenstein himself makes a link between pretend play and secondary sense. In his *Last Writings on the Philosophy of Psychology*, he states even more explicitly in which respect in pretend play concepts are used in a secondary sense: 'Only children who know about real trains are said to be playing trains. And the word trains in the expression "playing trains" is not used figuratively, nor in a metaphorical sense.' (LW II: 800).

The psychologist Alan Leslie (1987) has developed a theory of pretend play which is explicitly pitched at the information-processing level, according to which the mind/brain manipulates all sorts of mental representations. His work marked the beginning of a flood of publications concerned with the child's 'fictive mental processes'.[8] In pretend play, the pretender has 'double knowledge', which is explained by Leslie as involving the presence, at the moment of pretence, of two simultaneous mental representations, one for how the situation is actually taken, the other representing what the pretence is. His problem in explaining pretence is in fact in explaining how real and pretend mental representations interact.

Pretence, Leslie emphasizes, ought to strike the cognitive psychologist as a curious phenomenon. Pretence flies in the face of the evolutionarily grounded principle that perception and thinking ought to get things right. In pretence we deliberately distort reality. How is it possible for a child to think about a banana as if it were a telephone? 'If a representational system is developing, how can its semantic relations tolerate distortions in these more or less arbitrary ways? ... Why does pretending not undermine their representational system and bring it crashing down?' (Leslie, 1987: 412). Leslie calls this the problem of representational abuse. His suggestion is not that it does arise, but that it would arise when the child's epistemic predicament would be such that both literal and pretend representations would be primary representations:

> If both representations are *primary* ..., then both have a literal meaning. And because the pretense relates to the same actual situation in the serious cognition, both representations have to be representations of the same situation. But typically the pretense representation contradicts the primary representation. Consequently, something has to give here.
>
> (Leslie, 1987: 415)

To forestall the danger of representational abuse the child, according to Leslie, develops another type of representational system for use in pretend play. The products of this system are secondary representations, or representations of representations. Pretence representations are produced by copying primary representations on to a meta-representational context. This second-order context gives a report or a quotation of the first-order expression. In this way, it makes opaque the expression that was previously transparent. For example, when the child represents the world seriously or in reality-oriented play it may have the representation *The cup is full of water*. But in pretending that the cup is full of water, its representation will have the content *I pretend 'the cup is full of water'*. The quotation marks indicate that the expression contained in them is decoupled from its primary context, thereby suspending its normal semantics. Secondary representations are freed from their usual meanings, from their normal input–output relations, so that one object can substitute for a different object without the child confusing actual semantic relations.

There is much in Leslie's theory that would deserve critical discussion, such as his endorsement of the language of thought hypothesis and his quotation theory of intentionality, but for reasons of space I have to bypass these issues. Instead, I focus on his more important first steps. It is noteworthy that the problem of representational abuse is not an empirical problem. Consider for instance this observation by a child psychologist now almost forgotten, but one of the most prominent European psychologists before the Second World War, and a precursor of Jean Piaget: Karl Bühler. Typical of *illusory games*, as he called pretend play, is that the child is completely absorbed by them, yet the distinction between play and reality is firmly rooted in the background of his mind (Bühler, 1930: 331). Or take his contemporary, the philosopher and psychologist, Alexius Meinong. Meinong introduced a new category of psychological phenomena, *assumptions*, to deal adequately with a number of psychological facts among which: pretend play. But note his description of pretend play:

> ... that the child at play really is in a state of delusion during its play, i.e., that a chair which it has harnessed to the table as a horse to a wagon really is taken by the child to be a horse and that the table really is taken to be a wagon ... any person who has had the opportunity to observe children is far more likely to have had occasion to wonder at the sureness with which children even at an early age know how to distinguish between play and reality, than to find them confusing such situations.
>
> (Meinong, 1983: 83)

Precisely because the child does *not* confuse play and reality, pretend play cannot be classified in terms of one of the two traditional psychological categories of judgement and idea or representation. The threat of representational abuse therefore is a conceptual issue. The problem arises because concepts get mixed up. From the outset, Leslie assimilates the language of pretence to language for describing reality reliably. Indeed, only by initially conceiving of the language of pretence as a primary representation having the same literal meaning as non-pretend language can he conclude that it is logically aberrant, deviant and a form of misrepresentation. But if pretend concepts have a secondary sense, they are neither primary representations having literal meaning nor non-primary representations having derivative meaning.

His solution of the problem of representational abuse in terms of secondary representations is equally logically flawed. A secondary representation is like a primary representation – it is a copy – but without the normal 'input–output relations' of the latter. But what does that mean? That the child when pretending that its banana is a telephone suspends its judgement when asked what it means by 'banana'? Or that it can give no answer to the question whether bananas are yellow and taste sweet? Is it supposed to explain the meaning of 'banana' by referring to a telephone? The absurdity of these questions shows that what Leslie calls a secondary representation is not what we mean by pretend play. The ability to use a word in a pretend context depends upon understanding how to use the word in its primary sense, and hence implies distinguishing the different uses.

Leslie's refusal to recognize pretend play as an autonomous yet logically dependent language-game is further illustrated by his proposal to explain the logic of pretence in terms of the logic of other psychological concepts, in particular the so-called propositional attitudes. According to the 'quotational' approach, initially defended by Rudolf Carnap and later by Jerry Fodor, the intentionality of propositional attitudes can be explained in terms of sentences enclosed within quotation marks. Thus, in the report: John said 'The king of France is bald', 'the quotation marks the embedded expression as toothless, suspending its normal service' (Leslie, 1987: 417). Likewise, in a pretence context, a primary representation, for instance the perceptual report that this is a banana, is decoupled to 'this is a banana', thereby suspending its normal semantics. The expression can be manipulated freely without fear of abusing the normal representational system existing outside this context.

The implication of this conceptual assimilation is that pretence situations are epistemologically defective. But this is clearly absurd. Is a child that acts as if a wooden block is a train in the same (opaque) situation as Oedipus who took his mother for his lover? For Oedipus the situation was referentially opaque because he didn't know that the reference of 'Iocaste' was identical with the reference of 'mother of Oedipus', but the child playing trains with wooden blocks does not mistake the former for the latter. Were it to mistake blocks for trains, it would not be playing a secondary language-game but making a wrong move in a primary language game. In a primary language-game the child's mistakes could be rectified, but what would rectification in a secondary context look like? Should one ask the child to take her doll to the hospital in order to determine whether it really has pain? In the secondary language-game referential mistakes are not at issue because in this fictive use of language the child is simply not committed to the truth of what it says and does. Hence there are no criteria for determining truth-conditions in this language-game, as there are in the primary game, and this makes it a different kind of game.

Notes

1. I thank Danièle Moyal-Sharrock for pointing this out to me.
2. Instead of 'usual' Wittgenstein also speaks of 'familiar' or 'primary', but no deep theoretical sense has to be given to these terms. 'Primary' is used in a loose sense covering the standard use of words in standard situations or language-games.
3. As Cora Diamond (1991: 228) observes, the point is not that in some cases one cannot use another word, but that this word will involve a similar shift from the primary use ('Wednesday is corpulent').
4. For an early account see ter Hark (1990), chs 6 and 7.

5. Although Wittgenstein has taken great pains to combat the Humean idea, there is only a gradual difference between imaging and seeing; cf. RPP II: 63ff.
6. Darold A. Treffert and Gregory L. Wallace, 'Islands of Genius', *Scientific American* 14 (2004): 16.
7. I am indebted to Moyal-Sharrock for this point.
8. For a series of contributions to the debate, see, for instance, Martin Davies and Tony Stone (eds), *Mental Simulation* (Oxford: Blackwell, 1995).

14
The Cradle of Language: Making Sense of Bodily Connexions

Stephen J. Cowley

Introduction

Much is rotten in the 'sciences' of language and cognition. To those familiar with Wittgenstein's work this is apparent in, for example, the gulf that separates investigations of mind from those of language. Equally, it appears in how empirical work tends to skate over conceptual issues while theories of discourse proceed with disregard for causal processes. Taking another direction, I invoke 'natural history' in asking new questions about the origins of minded and discursive behaviour.[1] In this context, I use 'micro-investigations' to demonstrate how a single interaction can be used to throw light on human development. Rather than argue for the proposed ascriptions, my aim is to show the power of the method by exploring a moment when 'understanding dawns'.

Specifically, I scrutinize an event involving a 9-month-old baby. Micro-investigation serves to trace why the baby comes to *feel like* fetching a block. Having shown how neural capacities use bodily connexions with his mother's body, I defend two claims. First, the baby develops by virtue of bio-behavioural events that index social norms. Specifically, these prompt his proto-thinking and, as a result, he has an experience of *authoring* his fetching.[2] Second, the method shows that Wittgenstein's conceptual clarifications can be used for the real-time investigation of human biomechanics. By considering how reactive-responsive bodies use culturally based expectations, we can generate empirical hypotheses. While concerning 'mental' events, these invoke – not inner minds – but bodily connexions. In cases like the one described, the challenge is to clarify how the neural control of behaviour links events to customs which are historically aligned with the 'word' *fetch*.

Natural history and its developmental setting

For those sympathetic to Wittgenstein, Canfield's (1993; 1995) sketches of development are both apt and illuminating. Scrupulously avoiding cognitivism, he presents a 'purely descriptive anthropological study' (1993: 166) of how infants find a way into language-games. Below, emphasizing cognitive issues, I use this both in orienting the reader and sketching its limits. Specifically, I show how empirical work can generate hypotheses about how, why and what *develops*.

Focusing on what Wittgenstein calls 'word-language' (PI: 494), Canfield treats this as 'a set of customs in which words play a role' (1993: 185). Turning to the natural history of such events, he seeks out 'the bedrock of the development of speech' (1993: 166). In so doing he focuses on how 'proto-language games' give rise to prelinguistic expression or conventional gestures that undergird our modes of life. Across time, each stage reflects 'steady ways of living, regular ways of acting' (CE: 397) where the conventional and verbal ('language use') function to meet our social needs. Speech extends 'the certain action patterns that underlie its earliest uses' (1995: 197). Indeed, Canfield thinks that, as a cultural extension of pre-existing interaction, early language requires little learning. Given the child's dispositions, she 'naturally takes part in relevant action patterns' (1995: 197) and, thus, comes to 'command various convention governed ways of acting' (1993: 173). Since she can recognize her mother, it is enough that, when together, she responds to the effects of parental alertness (1995: 198). Chimpanzees play similar proto-language-games when, for example, they present a bodily area to be groomed. This constitutes a generalizable request akin to a child's special wiggle that shows she wants to get out of her chair (1993: 174). Although humans and chimps invent similar 'projects', their lives soon diverge. For Canfield, humans alone rely on stylization (1995: 202) as a basis for conventional or prelinguistic gestures (e.g., pointing). Later, drawing on animal nature, they extend these actions to verbal signs.

With verbalization, a child becomes a cultural creature. Without leaving a framework of interaction and gesture, she employs words 'from a common vocabulary' (1993: 177). 'One fine day', Wittgenstein (RPP II: 171) notes, she steps into language. Around their first birthday, children use words to make requests. For Canfield, it is 'brute fact' that we make, comply with and describe wants (1993: 178). Resembling as it does the gestural expression of prelinguistic games, there is no deep puzzle about this new word-language. The indeterminacy of translation is a non-issue because, in time, one way of acting replaces another. Looking across cultures,

Canfield (1993) provides a tentative classification of language-games into types: (1a) making requests; (1b) responding to requests; (2a) making intention-utterances; (2b) responding to intention utterances; (3a) uttering prohibitions; (3b) responding to prohibitions; (4) greeting; and (5) mere naming. By the end of the second year, though, cultures and groups diverge. For example, in one setting a child proceeds by saying things like 'Climbing chair' or 'Duck, frog downstairs'. Early intention-utterances begin to morph into announcements of plans, and then branch around words like 'then' (e.g., 'Jump first, then shirt'). In later months, verbal fillings allow forward projection of action (e.g., 'eat later'), decision making ('I'll be there at 3 o'clock') and, eventually, promising ('I *will* be there at 3 o'clock').

An anthropological perspective brings much of value to conceptualizing how language influences development. By stressing that talk is fundamental in shaping how they act, Canfield shows that, early on, infants do not *learn* language. Accepting Wittgenstein's view that language is an extension of action (1976: 740), he takes the view that children – not brains – learn to participate in talk. In this way, he avoids many discussions that bedevil linguistics. His approach sidesteps debates between rationalists and empiricists as well as arguments about which aspects of word-language are 'learned' outside-in and which grow inside-out. Emphasis on how children find a way into talk makes it necessary to posit neither that brains are general learning mechanisms nor that they run language-ready programs.[3] What matters, then, is how a baby comes to use utterances to act, understand and mean.

Anthropological distance makes the model simple. Above all, it distinguishes the 'natural processes' of the first months from the natural-cultural events that are made possible by conventions. With the rise of hybrid processes at the end of the first year, the infant's activity meshes with word-language. So far, so good. Not only does this fit current views of human development but it provides rich description of how children use 'universal language customs'. However, given his reliance on diary records of Z's doings, Canfield is bound to emphasize speech and the speaker. Developmental effects are conflated with evolved biases and, given his method, understanding falls out of the picture. In emphasizing that children *share* adult perspectives, he underplays both the non-conventional ('Everything has a shadow except ants') and the particularity of dialogue. This happens, above all, because examining how speech can be described requires him to emphasise what is universal. The diary method also requires Canfield to play down the adult's role and, by extension, the effects of action-around-speech. As a consequence, he says little about the child's agency or when and why development occurs. As with all stage theories, he obscures why infants come to modify how they act. In line with the critique of such models by Elman and colleagues (1997), little is said about how changes arise, why or when they occur and, especially, what it is that changes.

Given his anthropological approach, Canfield addresses neither the details of real-time events nor the non-linear course of ontogenesis. By focusing on games that engage children, he can avoid questions about how children influence adults or, for that matter, when and how they come to take adult-like perspectives. By focusing on what children say, he can leave out the caregiver reinforcement and, by extension, the affective dynamics of early life. This, in turn, enables him to regard the movements and sounds of 'infant-directed speech' as a matter of *convention*. Further, it enables him to avoid dealing with those aspects of behaviour that instantiate what Wittgenstein refers to as the 'new (spontaneous, specific)' (PI: p. 224).[4] Similarly, while steadfast in eschewing the Inner, Canfield overlooks both what adults attribute to infants and how their behaviour draws on *practical* understanding. By treating practices as communal, he tends to write as if conflict were minimal and 'the child's' development arose from matching habits to adult expectations. Focusing on what makes us *human*, he writes as if bodies could attune to conventions.

While Canfield's approach helps understand how we become human, he has little to say about cognitive and causal processes. To bring such events into focus is, of course, to ask why and how development occurs. This requires one, first, to address how understanding and action mesh neural processes, affect, experience and behaviour by others. Second, we must move beyond the observation that while small infants or bonobos try things out, later progress is channelled by social norms and conventions. Instead, we can ask about what motivates the child, caregivers' prompts, and real-time interaction. In asymmetrical events each party assesses and manages the other such that the infant gradually becomes an adaptive and flexible decision maker. Further, if language-games emerge from what is spontaneous and, for the child, novel, the affect-based coupling of bodily and facial expression is the only possible basis for later action. In dealing with requests, for example, we need to investigate how, across time, children comply with, refuse and propose what adults 'require'. Equally, while projects like tearing a toilet roll into pieces (Canfield, 1993: 180) seem distinctly human, we will ask why. Unlike language-using bonobos, it seems, children like to draw attention to both themselves and their worlds. For example, struck by a red Santa Claus on a newly decorated

Christmas tree, our son was moved to 'tell' what he could see. He pointed and, with deliberation, said 'owl'.

It is only by shifting our emphasis from what is human to individual *history* that we can examine developmental processes. Until this is done, we cannot explain either how or why human activity changes, and thus remain blind to what it is that develops. Given his focus on speech, Canfield has little to say about such questions and feels able to ignore relationships, action, content and timing. Equally, he leaves out adult beliefs, attitudes and actions or why, at specific moments, we treat children as having mental states. He fails to ask how events between people impact on understanding or how a child's later imaginings draw on the world of vocal and visual dynamics (or images). Identifying language with word 'use' implies that surface grammar (which is opaque to the child) is implicit in visible expression and vocal sound. Strikingly, little is said about how these dynamics help make the child – not just a sentient creature – but a human being who can, among other things, hope and grieve. Canfield, indeed, takes higher-order language (its verbal features) more seriously than the sound and movement that spur early understanding. In addressing cognitive issues, I emphasise the constructive nature of intelligent action. Specifically, I use micro-investigation to show how, for one baby, sound and movement enact a request. As the infant shows, human development bases rule-following on agreements in judgment. Expanding the anthropological view, I show how the infant falls under the sway of custom. Gradually, a baby becomes a hearer-seer-actor who uses biomechanics together with culture to grasp what is wanted. In life, we say, 'He *really* understands his mother'.

The cradle of thought

Within developmental psychology, most agree *when* babies begin to use 'proto-thinking'. As Canfield implies, this arises with a cultural influence that already complements natural behaviour in the second half of the first year.[5] In this period which Hobson (2000) calls the 'the cradle of thought', children use motivated pointing as well as 'social referencing' (Campos and Sternberg, 1981; Striano and Rochat, 2000). For example, in laboratory experiments, a visual 'cliff' (a special Perspex-induced perceptual effect) can elicit complex 'triadic' behaviour (Sorce, Emde, Campos and Klinnert, 1985). In well-replicated work, infants do not use convention to deal with the apparent danger. Rather, while younger infants baulk at the visual cliff, at around 9 months events come under the influence of norms that shape social signalling. When caregivers are anxious, infants

Figure 14.1   Triadic behaviour

hang back but, if visibly encouraged, they may crawl forwards. The mother's dynamic image influences how a child integrates experience with perceptions and actions. Like other child–caregiver–object activity, social referencing links two humans with an aspect of the world. While the origin of triadic behaviour is debated, its importance is endorsed by all. For Tomasello (1999), indeed, it distinguishes normal children from both their autistic counterparts and chimpanzees. To get its general flavour we can consider the events behind the following stills.

In interaction between 9-months-old Luke and his mother Sheila (Figure 14.1), the first frame shows the baby inadvertently letting go of a block. In the second, Sheila tries to get him to fetch it and, in the third, 9 seconds later, the infant (finally) moves off to get the block. The advantage of micro-investigation is that it can help us grasp how, why and when the baby comes to do what is wanted. Next, therefore, I put the events against a theoretical frame before using the micro-investigations to develop Canfield's insights.

Theorizing triadic behaviour

While some invoke mental representations to explain triadic behaviour, such theories no longer dominate the field. Leaving internalist models aside, therefore, I sketch three views that, in different ways, treat word-language as a set of customs. For each model, therefore, the events contribute to the causal processes of *understanding*. The child's relevant capacities are taken to develop because, in our species, bodies and culture are mutually adapted. However, while Shotter (2003) appeals to experience of a body-in-the world, Tomasello (1999) and Dennett (1991) take the view that culture has adapted to fit the peculiar nature of human brains.[6]

Although Shotter's recent work aims at characterizing conscious adults, the same model can be applied to what Luke does. This is because, avoiding the inner, he invokes two factors. First, humans are reactive-responsive beings whose 'attitudes' allow bodies to serve as mirrors of the soul. Emphasizing this, Shotter (1980) already takes the view that our humanity is based in 'joint action'. This is in accordance with the stills where, plainly, each responds to the other's responding. Second, drawing on Merleau-Ponty, Shotter (2003) now proposes that 'going on' derives from 'chiasmic change'. Just as vision gives us a sense of depth, Shotter claims, we experience the 'meaning' of social events. Using responsive bodies, life history makes us into meaning detectors. Applied to Luke, chiasmic change opens him to the meaning of 'fetch'. Using felt experience that is shaped by social perception, Luke grasps what Sheila's action means. Since he detects an abstract quality, he uses perceived reality and, for Shotter, fetches quite unlike a dog.

While I apply Shotter's theory to an example, he aspires to develop a general model of how shared realities arise. Many, therefore, might object at the fact that, given phenomenological grounding, it is ungrounded by neuro-behavioural events. Dennett, for example, would challenge its first-person basis by suggesting that the posited 'meaning' is a fiction based on verbal *reports*.[7] Given the baby's inability to understand even 'oops', Dennett would stress that it lacks adult-like phenomenology. In doing what his mother wants, therefore, the child is still a Skinnerian creature. Given lack of language, he would not be seen as undertaking anything spontaneous or new. Presumably, then, Dennett would trace the events to learning based in previous episodes of, among other things, joint attention, social play and crawling-to-fetch. On such a view, Luke's behaviour derives from general or ABC learning that, for this reason, resembles the fetching of a dog. To dig deeper, it would seem, we need models that throw light on neurobiological change.

In place of chiasmic change or ABC learning, Tomasello (1999) asserts that a special competence drives the 'nine-month revolution'. Agreeing that training is insufficient, like Dennett, he highlights changes *within* the baby. At the same time, with Shotter, he emphasizes triadic action and, implicitly, contrasts the baby with a dog. This is the keystone of his theory: intention recognition is possible, he posits, because human brains have a 'socio-cognitive adaptation'. Literally, the child 'sees' his mother's perspective between the second and third frames. Over-riding scepticism about the causal powers of inner intentions, he might claim that this indicates infant recognition of what its mother wants (why else would it smile *before* getting the block?). Such a view, moreover, fits with the fact that, between Frames 1 and 3, the mother says 'Do you want to fetch that?' Not only does she report what she wants but, idiomatically, the child 'understands'. While using reactive-responsive bodies and ABC learning, Tomasello claims that humans have a special neural device. In spite of philosophical arguments, a baby has a private neural system that allows it to *recognize* what another person intends.[8]

How do we go on?

In grasping what his mother wants, Luke does something remarkable. Although lying between the 'natural' and the 'conventional', this way of describing what happens shows nothing about why he decides to get the block. Theory tempts us to deal with this either by invoking phenomenology or appealing to a hidden process. Empirically, of course, invocation of first-person accounts is even less attractive than appeal to an inner 'competence'. This is because while appeal to hidden processes invites questions about the mechanisms of learning and evolution, phenomenology is inimical to empirical study. Accordingly, neither method can be used to deal with the *desiderata* of clarifying why, how and what develops. Equally, Wittgenstein believes, the alternatives are confused. Rather than conceptualize what is unknown as inner, we can examine the view that mental states arise 'via behaviour'. How is this to be interpreted? Must we take it on trust? Alternatively, can it be treated as an empirical claim about the natural history of what we call 'mind' and 'language'?

Below I use micro-investigations to scrutinize the events that constitute this moment in Luke's natural history. My case is that the method is powerful enough to open up new kinds of empirical enquiry. In other words, using video and audio technologies, it is possible to use observations to explore the no-man's land between the empirical and the conceptual. A person 'observes':

> Roughly, when he puts himself in a favourable position to receive sense-impressions in order (for example) to describe what they tell him.

(PI: p. 187)

Using sense impressions, observational evidence can be teased apart from observational acts. Physical features of events can thus be used to develop descriptions that parallel how events are conceptualized. In scrutinizing physical acts, therefore, attention can be given to what those familiar with the relevant customs perceive in the recordings. Although sense impressions connect an observer's natural history to his command of a word-language, the resulting descriptions are not subjective. Rather, to the extent that observational acts draw on shared customs, they can be used in tracing how minded activity arises from behaviour. Emphasizing connexions independent of word-language, helps bring to light how conceptualizations of the inner distort our understanding of vocal and visible events. We come to ascribe mental capacities to others, it seems, through the ways in which behaviour is distributed in time.

Micro-investigations: the power of observation

'Nothing is hidden' (PI: 435) can be used as a principle for asking about the rise of minded behaviour.[9] Hypothetically, given a record of every movement that influences a child, observations might help clarify what makes us human. In taking this view, however, it must be stressed that events use – not just experiential time – but relationships, interactions and, above all, vocal and visible gesture. Accordingly, to give a sense of these complex dynamics, I develop a thick description of events by using both the video-frames shown and others from the same sequence.

The first two frames (Figure 14.2) set the scene. As Luke sucks on the block, he finds his mother pulling at his attention. Over the long sucking time (3080 ms), Sheila distracts him by trying to set up a giving game. To this end she uses movements, gaze and accompanying vocalization.[10] The first frame (340 ms after sucking begins) shows that Luke's gaze is already being drawn to his mother's. By the second (2740 ms later), Sheila has repositioned the block so that it sits on 'top' of her right hand. To adult eyes, the slow and deliberate movements make it 'obvious' that she is offering

Figure 14.2   Setting the scene: Frame 1 and Frame 2

the block. Strikingly, as the second frame makes clear, Luke grasps this too: he gazes at her intensely while, broadly, matching her expression.

Luke is not simply reacting. Rather, he uses maternal movements and gaze to orient to *what she is doing*. Already, (in Frame 2) he is anticipating a giving game as is shown by his hands that move towards the proffered block. In these circumstances, this has unforeseen consequences. As can be seen above the box (in Frame 2), the block he was sucking falls. As it happens, the next few seconds of human interaction come to be organized around this unexpected event.

The third and fourth frames (Figure 14.3) show Sheila changing her agenda. While her gaze reacts to the falling block in micro-time (200 ms), the hand movements are slower. Thus, in Frame 3 (540 ms after Frame 2 in Figure 14.2) she is still placing the block between the fingers above Luke's left hand. Her change of mind, it seems, has been triggered by her gaze-system's reaction. By Frame 4 (after another 400 ms), however, she has ceased to look at either the baby or the block she was holding. Instead, she is uttering a salient high-pitched 'whoops'.[11] Since this can be used to comment on errors, observers hear Sheila as taking Luke's perspective. The baby, however, is deaf and blind to this subtlety. His body, in Frame 4, still shows readiness for the giving game. From Sheila's perspective, he 'hasn't understood'. He is disoriented in the sense that he doesn't grasp what she means. Seeking to remedy this, she slips the green block out of sight and remains in the crawling posture that she has adopted. In orientating to the block (off camera in the bottom left), she sets a new agenda.

In Frame 5 (700 ms later) Luke grasps what this is about (Figure 14.4). Not having responded to 'whoops' or bodily movements, a high-pitched 'oooh' acts as a precursor to Luke's gaze following. However, in looking where his mother looks, Luke has taken nine times longer to reorient than

Figure 14.3   Changing the agenda: Frame 3 and Frame 4

Figure 14.4   It's about the block: Frame 5

she did. While meeting her goal, he draws on her vocalization, movement and gaze. By Frame 5, then, positioned arms show that she now aims – not to get the block – but to engage the baby in a project. In part, Luke understands, in that he gazes at the block. In spite of this, Luke fails to understand the block's importance. Although looking at the block, his arms are relaxed and there is no sign of motor movement: he does not grasp her intent. (Surprisingly, he has no need to look back at it in the next 2300 ms). Picking up on the point of contact, Sheila builds the object of shared attention into their subsequent activity.

It is hard to communicate at 9 months: for Luke seeing the block means little. Indeed Frame 6 represents a moment 1280 ms after Frame 5 and a period of a further 1040 milliseconds is covered by Frames 7, 8, and 9 (Figure 14.5). Over this time, Sheila not only suggests fetching the block twice but looks from block to baby twice before, in Frame 9, resting her gaze on the block. As before, gaze drives the interaction as she takes Luke's perspective with the words 'Do you want to fetch that?' (using 'that' to refer to the gazed at object in Frame 6). Although he does not understand

Figure 14.5 Luke's proto-thinking: Frames 6, 7, 8 and 9

what she intends, he realizes that she wants them to do something together. Thus, Luke looks back. Then, in Frame 7, building on mutual gaze, Sheila varies the theme. Making a conversational move, his mother breaks gaze, looks at the block and says 'Go fetch it'. In Frame 8, she repeats her attempt at communication but, again varying the theme, silently rests her gaze on the block. Her 'meaningful' look lasts almost as long as the others put together.[12]

Luke's face features complex expressive dynamics. In Frame 6, looking into her eyes without understanding, his lowered eyebrows hint (to her) that he expects a reaction. This impression is enhanced by the fact that, in Frame 7, he starts to close his mouth. Strikingly, when Sheila looks away, the dominant right eyebrow rises into a knitted expression that might, in an adult, be said to express 'what do you want?'. Yet, when his mother returns to Luke's line of sight, in Frame 8, his gaze focuses, his eyebrows relax and, it seems, he shows the shadow of a smile. By the end of her meaningful look, in Frame 9, she too is smiling and, like Luke, she is relaxed. The baby, though, still does not grasp her intent. Intriguingly,

Figure 14.6   Understanding dawns: Frame 10

Figure 14.7   I'll get the block: Frame 11

however, Luke's eyebrows rise as, in Frame 9, his smile brightens, his expression seems 'intelligent'.

In Frame 10 (840 ms later), as his mother's gaze returns, Luke is beaming Figure 14.6). His smile has full Duchenne features that depend on a full rise of the eyebrows that, in this case, make even his tongue visible.[13] Given the slow pace of this beam (earlier, Sheila looked from block to baby and back in 340 ms), this is plainly an *action*. Indeed, there is nothing public to which Luke could be reacting. After their joint effort, Luke *experiences* how to 'go on'. Assuming that this does not come out *ex nihilo*, I describe Luke's visible expressions in Frames 6–9 as 'proto-thinking'.

In Frame 11 (400 ms later), Luke sets out to pick up the block (Figure 14.7). Strikingly, moving into crawling happens twice as quickly as his smile. This hedonic event marks that the child is about to accomplish a social goal. While Luke works out how to act, this is prompted by Sheila's movements and vocalizations. Using her dynamic image, he appropriately solves the perennial social problem of 'What should I do now?' Without words, he responds sensibly to 'Do you want to go and fetch that?' He acts within customs where, with seeming transparency, word-language makes sense. Since his smile occurs *before* fetching, it gives hedonic value to 'knowing how to go on'.

The power of proto-thinking

In aligning to 'Do you want to fetch the block?', Luke enacts precisely the kind of event that theories of triadic behaviour seek to explain. Next, therefore, I use their strengths and weaknesses in considering Luke's role in 'reinventing' a custom. In so doing, I use a pared down view of the events:[14]

- In Frames 1–4, Luke does *not* pick up on his mother's change of project.
- In Frames 5–9, he holds in mind that the goings-on concern the block (after looking at it, evocative facial expressions fade into a beaming smile).
- In Frames 10 and 11, he grasps what his mother wants, smiles and moves off. (We lack clear evidence about what prompts the 'decision'.)

Luke's doings cannot be explained by ABC learning because his understanding depends, overwhelmingly, on real-time events. He uses his mother's movements which are, indisputably, dynamic attempts to get Luke to modify how he acts. In everyday terms, while using his brain to hold the brick in mind and anticipate reward, Sheila prompts him to *grasp* what she wants. The timing of Luke's perspective taking shows that he is only partly dependent on brain-side processes. Far from seeing meanings, recognizing intentions or relying on ABC learning, he picks up on the sense of Sheila's behaviour. Given social experience, each reactive-responsive body prompts the other to act. Not only does this shape what accompanies proto-thinking (Frames 5–9) but, somehow, it triggers Luke's understanding (Frames 10 and 11). In deciding *how to go on* the baby shows exquisite sensitivity to affectively charged action. Given powers of gaze-following, inhibiting alternative actions, and keeping to the topic, this need be complemented by little more than well-timed felt action. Whether or not the biases have a genetic basis, some (perhaps all) internal change fits Dennettian logic. Using ABC learning, Luke meshes what comes automatically with behaviour that, in the circumstances, enacts what his mother wants.

In a case like this public events are of paramount importance. What Luke does, therefore, is incompatible with an inner-process view of understanding. The incident thus jars with both Tomasello's inner competence and the chiasmic change that Shotter posits as motivating what Luke does. The events depend on, not just Luke's brain, but also on how joint action is *distributed in time*. The 9 seconds taken to grasp what his mother wants show that, biomechanically, grasping how to go on is difficult. Indeed, the pace of events itself speaks powerfully against any model based in phenomenology or intention recognition. Second, because of the slow pace, we can trace how he draws on neural abilities for not forgetting, following gaze, inhibiting action and so on. In spite of his brain work, however, Luke fetches under *social* influence. Unlike a dog, he uses his mother's dynamics and, by extension, needs no fetching inclination (see Frames 5–9), no orienting excitement, and no canine quickness. In contrast to a Skinnerian creature, Luke uses Sheila's *belief* (namely that Luke may be able to fetch the block). While training, reinforcement and imitation contribute to the experience, Luke is sensitive to social norms that influence what his mother does. Fine control enables him to integrate events as disparate as Sheila's expression, the brick, and feedback from his smile. Far from needing to see meanings or recognize intentions, brain-based learning allows events to be concurrently controlled by both parties. Just as a small baby can use its mother's manifest wishes in learning when to fall silent (cf. Cowley et al., 2004), *fetching* arises as, in a familiar social setting, two brains exert dual control.

Luke's beaming smile goes some way towards explaining what we might call 'mind-reading'. This arises because, given slow emergence, it prompts and rewards both parties. For Sheila, smiling prior to movement shows *real* understanding and, for the baby, it gives a sense of authorship.[15] It is, I believe, highly significant that she rewards Luke's previous (in)action before he gets the block. Leaving much aside, its timing shows, first, that Luke's action arises from integrating proto-thinking with maternal movements. Second, inter-individual coupling prompts Luke to *feel* when to exploit how Sheila enacts a want. Development thus co-occurs in three domains. It changes the baby's brain and body, shapes what is likely in a relationship and, crucially, alters Sheila's beliefs. Indeed, this is what spurs her to act in ways that make proto-thinking a prelude to a reward. Using world-side events, the baby smiles and, at once, enacts his understanding. Whatever the neural basis of the events in Frames 10 and 11, Luke *wants* to get the block. For the baby, the feeling is spontaneous.

Since much occurs world-side, spontaneity must be distinguished from novelty. First, all Luke's actions are singular in spite of the fact that he relies on practised routines. The novelty of his action, then, arises from connecting with his mother's doings. It takes on a value as, in real time, he aligns to what she says and does. In contrast to spontaneity, novelty is thus rooted in culture. By linking these with what the baby does, *Sheila* makes it seem that Luke 'really' understands. If she accepts this, it becomes reasonable to test it (and train Luke) by setting up new 'fetching' opportunities.[16]

While spontaneity is jointly constructed, it is experienced individually. The hedonic property of the act is experienced by the baby (through the beaming smile). even though, as micro-observation shows, its causal basis lies partly in a set of customs. Without the cultural context, Luke would be unable to align his behaviour to what is actually said. He exploits not just dynamic attunement but, above all, how Sheila acts in getting Luke to fetch the block. The social event thus depends on close-coupling between intentional movements and the baby's growing sensitivity to norm-based caregiver doings. Remarkably, this shapes an event whose novelty and spontaneity put Luke on the edge of language. Bio-behaviourally, changes in his repertoire are based in how he times his part in joint action. While *fetching* is easy for a crawling, grasping baby, the event's coherence depends on Sheila. Remarkably, she enables the baby to align its behaviour with the grammar of 'fetch'. Using culture, Sheila helps Luke attune to a bundle of local customs.

Since development integrates world-side and neural events, the process can be seen as based in mutual *gearing*. Using both micro-movements and longer lasting 'actions' each party adapts to the doings of the other. Thanks to this gearing, future interactions come under the influence of both true and false beliefs. In this case, Sheila's perception of Luke's pleasure makes her likely to encourage fetching games because, as she might say, 'he understands what to do'. As Luke becomes skilled in grasping where 'fetch' serves his interests, he learns about 'requests'. Mutual gearing can produce such outcomes because it is based on bodily action where adults use cultural constraints (expressed by the words actually spoken). Luke can adapt to these by using both extant skills and his sense of authorship. Further, in that causal chains reach beyond the skull, Luke and Sheila develop ways of playing based on joint control. In short, natural history can draw on bio-behavioural events in a cultural setting. The example clarifies how requests arise from brute facts (Canfield, 1993: 179). Given cultural constraints, decisions about action use brain-side processes that prompt bodies to gear to each other while setting off neural events that drive joint activity and, at the same time, affective experience.

Connexions before language

Many concur with Bennett and Hacker (2003) that scientific enquiry cannot be used to investigate mental phenomena. In their view this is because, as Wittgenstein shows, it is mistaken to regard the relevant predicates as naming properties of minds (or brains). Thanks to a Cartesian and empiricist heritage, such misconceptions dominate everyday psychology and, if used in science, they argue, can only compound confusion. This happens, above all, if we conceptualize the mental as private, as available to introspection and as constituted by inner systems that correspond to named mental entities. For Bennett and Hacker, such views constitute an important 'misconception of the logical nature of experience and its ascription' (2003: 85). To avoid the error, we must distinguish two forms of enquiry: either we must investigate logical relations or, if we wish to pursue empirical work, we should investigate the nervous system. When science seeks to clarify our mental concepts, it seems that we are bound to fall into conceptual confusion.

Must the scientist leave the mental to philosophy? Does minded behaviour fall outside empirical enquiry? While some may take this view, Canfield opposes any such interpretation. Rather, he thinks that reducing Wittgenstein's work to arguments about concepts can produce superficial readings. To establish when his remarks are correct, Canfield suggests, 'what one must do is look below the surface' (1975: 153). This, presumably, is why he scrutinizes how children engage with customs in which words play a part. Breaking with Wittgenstein's precedent of 'inventing' natural history, Canfield's anthropology has an empirical base. Further, as shown above, he *establishes new facts bearing on the social basis of mind and language.* The spirit, moreover, is consistent with, for example, Wittgenstein's forthright statement that philosophical analysis does not preclude investigation of 'the possible causes of the formation of concepts' (PI: p. 230).[17] This, of course, is the common goal of Canfield's work and my micro-investigation of how Luke gains practical understanding of *fetch*. Conceptually, both approaches remain, in one sense, Wittgensteinian. This is because, unlike Dennett and Tomasello, we reject pure third-person accounts while, challenging Shotter, we ascribe no causal powers to detected meanings. Micro-investigation of Luke's fetching goes beyond such perspectives by stressing his mother's *second*-person activity. Luke experiences *fetching* because of Sheila's beliefs and how she interprets what he does. Of course, this is possible only because of how his body (and brain) respond to events, giving him – above all – a feeling of what happens. Folk views of 'understanding' cannot therefore illuminate how such a concept develops. This indeed is why learning to fetch – and learning to talk – arise from mutual gearing. Much mental life arises as babies show sensitivity to behaviour while using neural tricks that, for example, allow them to follow gaze, hold an object in mind, and feel like authors of actions.

Micro-investigation sustains the gearing *hypothesis*. This is, for current purposes, sufficient: my current goal is merely to show how empirical work can draw on Wittgenstein's conceptual clarifications to develop new perspectives on the rise of mind and language. As independently observable phenomena, simple concepts are grounded in behaviour. What Luke shows, from this perspective, is why we must reject both the individualism of mainstream cognitive psychology as well as conceptual constructs that give coherence to mental talk. Even if this leads us to see human subjects as bodies who, immersed in culture, develop a range of potentialities (2003: 52), I doubt that Bennett and Hacker would approve of the conceptual implications of this work. This is because, if some concepts arise as bodies gear to each other, this contradicts our everyday views of 'understanding'. While consistent with the claim that neither minds nor brains function causally, learning to fetch – and other practical knowledge – requires special brain mechanisms. It implies that social events depend on neural processes that exploit intricate dual control.

Minded behaviour emerges because of how changing brains exploit events in a micro-world. Mind and language exploit connexions between bodies that are, traditionally, overlooked by common sense and cognitive science. In natural history, asymmetries between baby and caregiver play important developmental roles. Indeed, it is difficult to see how a baby could gear to conceptually based expectations without special predispositions. Further, while a baby learns conventions, these are of less intrinsic interest than the modicum of control they provide. Through mutual gearing, using biomechanics, Luke becomes a player of intentional games. This, moreover, is compatible with the developmentalist's finding that qualitative change co-occurs with the emergence of triadic activity. What micro-investigations add is a method that, in this case, serves to generate hypotheses about how babies use two brains to develop new forms of control. Although proto-thinking allows Luke to experience 'how to go on', his feeling arises as his brain prompts him to co-ordinate with his mother's culturally constrained dynamics. He uses how her 'want' shapes her looking, moving and vocalizing to create opportunities for action that impacts on his development. Given such findings, one must contest models where development is confined to the organism. In the rise of triadic behaviour, no causal powers need emanate from either a socio-cognitive device or a first-person phenomenology.

Fetching links biomechanics, maternal beliefs and a set of customs. It is part of a developmental process that depends on how a child's body can use caregiver activity to, among other things, produce a sense of agency. Indeed, Luke's doings seem to be highly consistent with what Wegner (2003) calls the 'illusion of conscious will'. Grasping when to get a block is a form of affective experience that gives Luke a sense of authorship and, where similar events recur, this will help him to anticipate the right thing to do. Far from seeking to pursue such empirical hypotheses, however, my goal is to show that, drawing on Wittgenstein's conceptual work, we can examine natural history by micro-investigations. In some cases at least, minded behaviour arises as maternal beliefs prompt a baby to discover how sense making can derive from bodily connexions.

A set of customs

Everything about Luke fits the view that language is a set of customs in which words play a part. Early on, word-language can only function by virtue of how it is embedded in behaviour. By implication, models where learning to talk is conceptualized in terms of learning or acquiring word-forms are misguided. Rather, much early development proceeds as bodies act to establish agreement in judgments. In the example, Luke and his mother need merely concur, in practice, that *this* affords fetching a block. That is all. The baby's ability to *go on* integrates biomechanics, proto-thinking and beliefs based in a set of customs. By mutual gearing, Luke and his mother each prompt *de facto* judgments. Rather than appeal to stylization, speech and the individual speaker, the example sketches how, given culture, biomechanically mediated events give rise to mind and language.

Once Sheila believes that her baby understands *fetching*, she will encourage such activity. Indeed, this strange capacity can shape much of our natural history. Exotic beliefs can be used to train infants by getting them to gear to our manifest expectations. This is brought out in how Sheila persists in getting Luke to fetch the block until, after a full 9 seconds, the baby meets her expectation. Mutual gearing not only shapes their joint action but, remarkably, enables Luke's brain to mark the event as future relevant. Far from needing word-language, affect enables him to experience *fetching* as spontaneous, novel, appropriate and rewarding. Similar gearing will, at other times, give rise to other joint practices. Without needing conceptual knowledge, a baby can rely on how other persons exploit word-language. Far from using inner understanding, biomechanical and affective tricks enable Luke to align his actions in events that can elicit detailed word-based descriptions (e.g., fetch, block). His decision making uses Sheila's manifest thinking: his categories derive from *actions based on a history of dual control*. Given his mother's view of their agreements in judgment, mutual gearing can lead to the (re-)invention of intentional games. As Luke becomes a person, he will hone many skills. Just as gearing can promote fetching, other settings can give rise to capacities useful in practices as diverse as word-language, fighting, singing and dancing.

Notes

1. Wittgenstein puts it that 'the facts of our natural history that throw light on our problem are difficult for us to find out, for our talk passes them by' (RPPI: 73). To surmount this I use micro-investigations as a form of 'measuring' where descriptions of variable activities make them intelligible (cf. RPPI: 1109).
2. The phrase applies to some of a baby's expressive moves in a fetching game. My aim is not to delve into how the biomechanical connects with the social but, echoing Wittgenstein, of 'noting' what happens (PI: 654–5). Of course, appeal to proto-thinking parallels Canfield's (1993: 173) invocation of 'proto-language'.
3. Pinker (1994) and Sampson (1996) debate rationalism and empiricism (for another view, see Cowley (1997)). Hirsh-Pasek and Golinkoff (2000) discuss language acquisition by contrasting outside-in and inside-out models.
4. Canfield uses this quotation (1995, 2003) to consider the rise of complex language-games. In contrast, I focus on how a child can author behaviour that is *felt* to have these properties.
5. Elsewhere I use micro-investigation to show signs of culture in a child of three months (see Cowley, Moodley and Fiori-Cowley, 2004).
6. Dennett writes little about development and, like Tomasello, underestimates the role of human bodies. Shotter, by contrast, ignores the brain. This is in line with the brain–body dualism noted by Bennett and Hacker (2003).
7. Irrespective of views on Dennett's hetero-phenomenological method, the claim that first-person reports are, in part, fictional fits with biophysics. Thus, in work on how we see a sequence of images as a moving film, Kolers and von Grunau (1976) report experiments on the phi phenomenon. Subjects consistently report seeing a red light that, at a determinate place, becomes green. Physically, however, a red light flashes (completely) before a green one does so. The impression and reports arise because the flashes are only a few milliseconds apart. For Dennett, even first-person perceptual 'reports' are fictional (see Cowley and Love, forthcoming).
8. While never invoking Augustine's 'natural language of mankind', this too requires a brain that shows us the intentions of others. For critique of Tomasello's theory, see Cowley, Moodley and Fiori-Cowley (2004).
9. Wittgenstein uses 'nothing is hidden' to suggest that how sentences represent meaning is open to view. Using micro-investigations, I apply the same insight to action (cf. PI: 126). Even if a full bio-behavioural theory would depend on

using standard empirical methods, micro-investigations are needed to counter folk beliefs and, by so doing, ground plausible hypotheses.

10. She seems to say, softly, 'go on my baby love'.
11. At this level, people cease to be unitary: gaze, hand movement, and vocalization seem partly autonomous.
12. The durations are 340, 720 and 1040 milliseconds respectively.
13. In 1862, Duchenne pointed out that while half-hearted smiles involved only muscles of the mouth, the sweet emotions of the soul also activate the *pars lateralis* muscles around the eyes. For a recent neurally informed view, see Soussignan (2002).
14. This is necessary in events that ground agreement in judgements. Since these warrant many ascriptions, it is easy to get bogged down. I hope readers will agree that the 'pared down' account is broadly correct.
15. While the smile might show that Luke recognizes an intention (or sees a meaning), this is doubtful. First, recognition is passive and – typically – does not produce smiling. Second, Luke gives a full Duchenne smile. Third, this ascribes causal power to inner intentions. Fourth, since getting blocks (unlike, say, bones for a dog), is not intrinsically pleasurable, the smile is more likely to be a consequence of coming up with a way to act.
16. Although this is probably not the first instance of such fetching, Luke is not yet skilled in the activity. For expository purposes, therefore, I regard it legitimate to write as if this were a 'first'.
17. One rather striking implication of this chapter is that mothers, too, invent natural histories for their babies just as, later, children narrate their life histories.

15
Getting Clear about Perspicuous Representations: Wittgenstein, Baker and Fodor

Daniel D. Hutto

> A main source of our failure to understand is that we do not *command a clear view of the use of our words* – Our grammar is lacking in this sort of perspicuity. A perspicuous representation produces just that understanding which consists in 'seeing connexions'. Hence the importance of finding and inventing *intermediate cases.*
>
> *The concept of a perspicuous representation is of fundamental significance for us. It earmarks the form of account we give, the way we look at things. (Is this a 'Weltanschauung?')*
>
> (PI: 122)

1 Introduction

Deciding what role perspicuous representations play in Wittgenstein's philosophy matters, not only for determining what one thinks of the contributions of this great figure of twentieth-century philosophy but also for recognizing the 'live options' for conducting philosophical enquiries, full stop. It is not surprising, given this importance, that perspicuous representations is the topic of the opening chapter of Gordon Baker's posthumous collection of essays on philosophical method. In that contribution he offers grounds for thinking that the relevant passage in which the notion is explicitly mentioned (cited above) should be read as promoting a strongly therapeutic approach to philosophy: he exposes 'this possibility' in the modest hope of persuading receptive readers to explore it further for themselves (see Baker, 2004: 46). I endorse some of Baker's central insights about understanding and use of perspicuous representations, but I firmly reject his conclusions about the end of philosophy.

Specifically, I agree with him that Wittgenstein set his face against the very idea of philosophical 'theorizing', but I deny that this led him (or ought to lead anyone) to promote a *purely* therapeutic philosophy. In the first three sections, I supply reasons for preferring an account of Wittgenstein's approach to philosophy that emphasizes its clarificatory ambitions. In doing so, I say something about: (i) what I take perspicuous representations to be and how they function; (ii) what motivates Baker's reading and its implications; and (iii) how perspicuous and other forms of representations have been misused in attempts at so-called philosophical theorizing. I conclude by proposing that in steering clear of both theory and extreme therapy, it is possible to prosecute a positive philosophy – one that employs perspicuous representations to bring 'relevant connections' to light for the purposes of enabling us to understand and reflect on aspects of various domains of human being.

2   The nature of perspicuous representations

Philosophical Investigations §122 tolerates more than one coherent interpretation. Its message is not only complex, it is also highly condensed. And for all its fundamental importance, Wittgenstein cites no example to aid our understanding of it. Indeed, as Baker observes, the colour-octahedron, found in *Philosophical Remarks* §§51–2, is the one and *only* named instance of a perspicuous representation supplied in the whole of his corpus. Focusing on its properties encourages the idea that all perspicuous representations have certain identifying features in common. Using the colour-octahedron as the guiding exemplar, it appears to distil a complex set of rules into a single, concrete picture – literally embodying them as it were. Such a totem would seem to be of great use to the philosopher because it captures, without remainder or ambiguity, the full range of possibilities relating to a particular grammatical domain – in this case, that of colour space. Generalizing from this case, it seems that all perspicuous representations should have the dual properties of being both *complete* with respect to their proprietary domain and they should be easily *surveyable* – that is, in leaving nothing out they present the *relevant* possibilities in such a way that they can be immediately 'read off', without confusion. The colour-octahedron reveals immediately what can and cannot be said, thought or done with colours. In crystallizing and encapsulating these possibilities within a single image, this icon has obvious advantages over an ungainly compendium of rules that might, or so we might imagine, descriptively state the very same possibilities, only using discursive as opposed to imagistic means (cf. Baker, 2004: 35). In contrast, the colour-octahedron appears to 'condense something complex into a simple and manageable symbol'; and 'this seems to be the defining characteristic of what Wittgenstein called a "perspicuous representation"' (ibid.: 23).

With this in mind we might be led to think that it is the philosopher's job to find, or better, construct such illustrative devices – ones with the peculiar properties just mentioned. These could then be used for the purpose of revealing the relevant *a priori* possibilities in particular domains. And it is easy to see how in doing so these devices would be the primary tools for a philosophy that only aimed to clarify our understanding of a given domain – a philosophy shorn of any 'explanatory' ambitions. Even so, such a philosophy would not be rightly characterized as *merely* descriptive – for it would not proceed by fixing on just *any* feature in a given domain nor would it seek to describe *every* feature of such a domain. For the fact is that perspicuous representations, even as just imagined, could only be used to highlight *certain* illuminating aspects of a domain and they could not do so in an interest-neutral way; rather they would only be useful relative to certain purposes.

Perspicuous representations so used would be, in one sense, like maps: they make evident *certain* features of a particular domain for the purposes of navigating it successfully – only philosophically as opposed to physically. Like good maps, they do not represent just *any* feature or features of their target terrain nor do they represent *all* its features, describing it completely or even accurately in every respect. Such devices highlight illuminating features as an aid to getting to grips with a particular domain and this is done for certain, clearly defined purposes. They function like Harry Beck's renowned 1933 map of the London Underground. His famous 'tube map', inspired by circuit diagrams, displays the certain features of the underground network in a revealing way – just the ones relevant to serve the needs of its daily users (see Figure 15.1 below). It is not an accurate or complete representation of all aspects of the network nor is it meant to be (e.g., it does not show the distances between stations accurately or to scale). Indeed, its usefulness precludes it being such. What shows – so successfully and quite literally – are the 'relevant connections' in a single surveyable design. For the *purpose of travelling by tube* it is both clear and comprehensive (and has become more so over time, with modifications).

If perspicuous representations are understood in this way, they would be limited in the scope and nature of their application. Like the tube map, they would only illuminate specific aspects of a particular domain because in doing so they answer to a specific need.

For this reason, it is a mistake to think that many such devices operating in conjunction could 'be employed to clarify sizeable domains of grammar

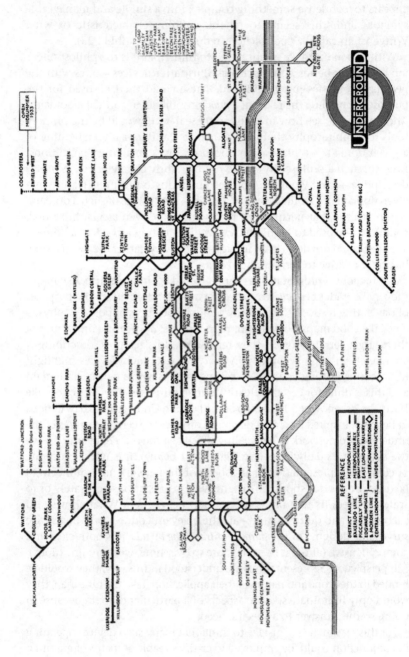

Figure 15.1 Beck's original London Underground map

and ... dissolve many different philosophical problems all at once' (Baker, 2004: 26). That is, it is a mistake to suppose that the philosopher's job is a kind of global logical cartography, for not all perspicuous representations function in the same way. Inasmuch as perspicuous representations are not mere descriptions of particular domains, there is no prospect of collecting them together in order to 'reveal the working of the whole of grammar'. This is not because all the relevant possibilities could not be revealed at once, or because they are not fixed, or because our ways of being in the world are complex and the features of each domain vary significantly. All of this is true of course, but the primary reason perspicuous representations cannot be cobbled together to form a single overarching representation is that although like maps, they are *not* like ordinance survey maps – they do not all do the same thing *in the same way*. Thus it makes no sense to think that collectively they could chart all of grammar at once, so it could be viewed from on high. Baker calls this the Bird's-Eye View Model and argues that it completely misrepresents Wittgenstein's intended use of perspicuous representations in nearly every respect (ibid.: 26, 41). But, as the example above hopefully makes clear, we need not subscribe to it when making sense of the proper use of perspicuous representations in clarificatory projects. Philosophical investigations must be prosecuted in a piecemeal way. In conducting them, we *make* our way through a particular landscape – driven by certain needs. Perspicuous representations are *used* in this process in just the way commuters use Beck's map to get from A to Z. This requires being clear about what one is hoping to achieve, for to be confused on this score might otherwise result in a hopeless activity such as that akin to attempting to use the tube map to determine the distances between London landmarks.

Although the analogy with Beck's map helps, the fact is that we need not understand perspicuous representations as specially designed symbols at all. I agree with Baker in thinking that what makes a remark a perspicuous representation 'is not its intrinsic features, but its function'; that is, in providing some sort of landmarks, patterns, analogies, pictures, etc. which enable us to find our way about' (2004: 41). Hence, there is 'no general restriction on what form a perspicuous representation may take' (ibid.: 31). This significantly widens the scope of the kinds of things that could play such a role – and once we understand this, it becomes clear that Wittgenstein's writings are in fact replete with perspicuous representations. His language-games are, on this reading, prime examples: 'The language games are rather set up as objects of comparison which are meant to throw light on the facts of our language by way not only of similarities, but also of dissimilarities' (PI: 130). Indeed, Wittgenstein makes the stronger claim that 'Nothing is more important for teaching us to understand the concepts we have than constructing fictitious ones' (CV: 74).

Clarifying our understanding of the roles that certain responses or activities play in our lives, say, for example 'pain' or 'thinking' is achieved by imagining other possible reactions and practices that they might have sponsored or which might have surrounded them. Achieving this does not require precise or complete detailing of *all* aspects of what this would look like. It is enough that we can shed light on these by means of targeted comparison with the roles they could have played in the lives of 'others' – real or imagined. By proceeding in this way, we are at once broken of the idea that an illuminating understanding could be had by investigating these 'phenomena' objectively or scientifically. At the same time we are also reminded of their place and point in our lives.

Although I have said philosophizing in this way is not *merely* descriptive, it is descriptive nonetheless. Perspicuous representations do – in one sense – reveal the *inherent* order in various domains – they *exhibit* possibilities without imposing or altering them. They selectively bring out what is there in the space of possibilities. This is not to be confused with a notion of what is 'there in reality' as it might be understood by devotees of 'crude realism'. Perspicuous representations no more attempt this than Beck's map attempts to be an accurate model of the physical layout of the London Underground as-it-is-in-reality: both highlight certain features of certain domains in order to serve as useful devices for navigating them. It helps to remember that it is possible to conduct philosophical investigations free of worries about *how* the possibilities in question came to be as they are or *whether* they will stay so. This point will become important again shortly.

This way of understanding the role and function of perspicuous representations fits with Wittgenstein's insistence that 'Philosophy simply puts everything before us, and neither explains nor deduces anything. – Since everything lies open to view there is nothing to explain. For what is hidden, for example, is no interest to us' (PI: 126). For, on the above model, finding or creating perspicuous representations does not involve making new theoretical discoveries or the advancing of any claims about the state of the world; rather it involves using tools for prosecuting a clarificatory philosophy. If handled with care, perspicuous representations can be used as the basis for positive philosophical investigations. Hence, I take issue with Baker's claim that they have *only* a therapeutic use. In order to make an effective stand against this view, it is important to understand what encourages him to think this.

3   Seeing aspects, therapy and relativism

In taking issue with the Bird's-Eye View Model, Baker also rejects the idea 'that Wittgenstein left room for a positive role for philosophy which stands in contrast to and supplements its predominantly negative or therapeutic task' (2004: 26).[1] His reason for thinking that we should eschew any kind of positive approach, presumably even the kind described in the previous section, is that there simply can be no reading off of *intrinsic* possibilities in any given domain. It seems that he thinks any elucidatory philosophy must be committed to a crude kind of 'objective determinism', necessarily – why else would one talk of uncovering the inherent limits in various grammar domains as opposed to merely revealing open-ended possibilities? (see also Read, 2004: 94). Thus, the reasoning goes: since it would be a mistake to think that an independent 'reality' as-it-is-in-itself somehow *fixes* the grammatical possibilities *a priori*, we must accept that our grammar has no interesting constraints. This is one way of reading the following:

> We say grammar determines which combinations of words have sense and which do not; but on the other hand also, that grammar is not answerable to any reality, that it is in a certain sense arbitrary. Hence if a rule forbids me to construct a certain combination of words, then I have only to abrogate this rule ...
>
> (VOW: 39; cf. also 381).

Some strength is lent by Baker to this interpretation given that Wittgenstein cites the colour-octahedron as an example of perspicuous representation in his middle period writings. For it is interesting that the passage above is swiftly followed by a discussion of the notorious case of the seeming impossibility of our saying of an object that it is both (simultaneously) red and green all over (VOW: 199, 401). Although our first reaction is to judge any such statement to be nonsense on the grounds that it apparently violates the law of non-contradiction, it is always possible for us to alter our meanings and revise this ruling – the grammatical possibilities are not, as it were, written in stone. Of course, there would be consequences. Taking this line would necessarily break faith with and threaten to undermine some of our familiar practices (this explains why we may be initially unable to 'make sense' of this kind of 'arbitrary' ruling, and indeed why it may *never* be generally accepted at all: it may fail to have any wider point or purpose, given the sort of beings we are (and which we are likely to continue to be)). And here we see that the stability of our grammatical tendencies need not rest on there being an *a priori* order of things that is somehow 'independent' of us. Crucially, it is possible to reveal both the nature of such rules and the important role they have in our practices without endorsing the simplistic idea that there exists an underlying, pre-given 'external' reality that fixes the bounds of possibility. One can adopt the kind of 'navigational' account of the use of perspicuous representations I sketched in the previous section while rejecting crude objectivism about the status of rules of grammar. Holding both positions is perfectly consistent.

Equally, there is no reason to object to philosophical attempts to reveal the structure of colour space by means of perspicuous representations on the grounds that the grammar of this domain may change in ways we simply cannot anticipate. Once it is made evident that the job of perspicuous representations is not to reveal an absolutely *fixed* order of things, it is easy to see that they can be adapted if a domain changes in unexpected ways. Why shouldn't perspicuous representations be able to keep pace with such change in much the same way that the tube map has been updated when certain stations or routes are added and others become defunct? Even if things are open to change, there would still be a point in highlighting certain features of specific domains *just as they stand*, for particular current purposes that is.[2]

In taking these worries too seriously Baker, like certain New Wittgensteinians, was persuaded to think that perspicuous representations can only play a more limited role in philosophy – that is, helping to reveal *other* equally legitimate aspects or ways of looking at the domain in question. So understood, their role would be to 'make visible' what might otherwise be obscured by a one-sided diet of examples. Since there is no prospect of doing anything more positive, breaking the spell cast by dogmatic thinking is philosophy's one and *only* purpose. Its job is to show that there are more possibilities than certain philosophers have dreamt of. For this reason:

> The unity of method turns on the application to grammar and language of the concept of an aspect (and of the related concepts of seeing an aspect and being blind to an aspect).
>
> (Baker, 2004: 33; see also 35)

Accordingly, the task of philosophy – it turns out – is not that of clarifying our thinking on certain fundamental topics but that of freeing philosophers from their one-sided visions. The function of philosophical dialogue is to get one to recognize that there are *always* other possibilities: there are no '*musts*' in philosophy. Perspicuous representations are the tools used for achieving this; they can do nothing more.

Baker's therapeutic vision of philosophy looks to have been inspired by certain remarks that resulted from the Waismann and Wittgenstein collaboration which took place between 1928 and 1939 (this interaction was the result of Waismann's attempts, under Schlick's direction, to make Wittgenstein's thinking more accessible).[3] The following are examples of some of the methodological advice found therein:

> We have no system. That is, there is no possibility of another's agreeing or disagreeing with us; for we really indicate only a method.
>
> (VOW: 289)

> Our task is to lay down distinctions and not to make assertions ....
>
> (VOW: 109)

Baker's driving thought is that it is simply not possible to advance genuine philosophical theses or hypotheses. And seeing no other possible non-theoretical use of perspicuous representations, he is compelled to adopt a maximum strength therapeutic philosophy. Highlighting one example, Baker insists it 'betokens a grave misunderstanding of the spirit of the *Investigations* to treat Augustine's picture as a theory which is the least common denominator of a wide range of theories of meaning and to interpret his critical exploration of it as wholesale *reduction ad absurdum* of these theories (Frege's philosophy of language, the logical atomism of Russell and the *Tractatus*, etc.)' (Baker, 2004: 39). Since there are no genuine theories in philosophy, it follows the above cannot be examples of 'false theories'. Hence, for Baker, they are understood as merely other 'forms of representation' (ibid.). Accordingly, it turns out that Augustine's conception of language – the general formula that the meaning of a word is fixed by the object for which it stands – is a legitimate, if limited way of representing language (ibid.: 42). It is just one amongst many equally good second-order ways of representing language. Augustine's only mistake is to promote its virtues to the exclusion of all others. Thus, we are told:

> It is not a theory which excludes anything or which could be held to misdescribe (or describe!) anything. Nothing defies being cast into this pattern, though there may be much more difficulty with some words rather than others. Augustine's picture of language can be seen as a dogma that controls the expression of all description of the uses of words and sentences.
>
> (Baker, 2004: 39)

On Baker's view, Augustine *could* not have been advancing a refutable philosophical theory, 'position' or 'view' for the simple reason that there can be no such animals. Rather, Augustine presents us with a way of representing our grammar which, while not being 'mistaken' in itself – for it is no better or worse than any other – is wrongly promoted as all inclusive. It is obsessive, singular attachment to certain pictures that must be avoided; philosophy's work is to cure us of such tendencies (Baker, 2004: 39–40). The crux is that on this construal all 'forms of representation' are of equally good standing. In line with this, in using perspicuous representations to deliver a course of philosophical therapy, one's job is to make visible as many alternative forms of representation as possible. For, seeing the full range of possible ways of representing a particular domain acts as a kind of prophylactic, keeping us from falling into dogmatism. Likewise the 'cure' to thinking that things *must* be a certain way involves coming to acknowledge that there are other legitimate possibilities (ibid.: 34). Effecting such cures is all that philosophy can do.

There are resounding relativistic implications of this strong therapeutic proposal. Baker is quite open about this. He writes: 'Wittgenstein seems to have been explicitly subscribing to a form of relativism which most of his would-be followers reject' (Baker, 2004: 43).[4] Also, for this sort of reason, he holds that

> it seems doubtful whether we can legitimately contrast Wittgenstein's investigation of 'psychological concepts' (or his treatment of mathematics) with standard philosophical positions (behaviourism, Cartesian dualism, etc., or Platonism, intuitionism, etc.) by claiming that he merely described 'the uses of words' whereas other philosophers looked at grammar through distorting spectacles of particular conceptual schemes or metaphysical prejudices.
>
> (Baker, 2004: 43).

Seeing Wittgenstein's approach as inherently relativistic is merely the flipside of thinking that the contributions of other philosophers merely emphasize other equally legitimate aspects – different ways of seeing a given domain that do not add up to genuine, but mistaken, theories. And certainly Wittgenstein was not offering his own rival 'theory' by way of response. By implication, all philosophical contributions can be laid alongside each other (Wittgenstein's own attempts included) without competing.

I agree that there can be no genuine 'philosophical' theories, but it hardly follows from this that we should endorse Baker's relativistic therapeutic proposal about how to interpret Wittgenstein and, even more crucially, what we can hope for from philosophy. It is wrong to think that Wittgenstein's sole philosophical aim was to expose and eradicate certain one-sided tendencies in our thinking – that is, that his *only* criticism of those who are under the sway of certain 'pictures' is that they had failed to see other possibilities. For, typically, such 'dogmatism' is driven by an explanatory agenda – one driven by the idea that the job of philosophy is to produce theories. Hence, it is not *just* that they are in the grip of a single 'form of representation' – capable of seeing only one aspect – it is rather that in their explanatory zeal they are inclined to focus on misleading analogies and to 'impose' these where they do not belong. It is not the case that the products of so-called philosophical speculation are flawed *only* in that they tend to blind philosophers to the true range of possibilities. And it is precisely because the source of this kind of disquiet is much more complex than Baker makes out that it is also much harder to 'cure' than he suggests.

4 Rational theory construction in philosophy

It is instructive to consider how well Baker's 'blinded by a single aspect' diagnosis fares when it comes to dealing with some real cases – that is, contemporary offerings of those philosophers who promote the idea that philosophy really is just a kind of theorizing. For, looked at up close, it is not very plausible to claim that the *only* mistake that they make is to dogmatically promote a single way of seeing. This neither captures the complexity and depth, nor the precise *nature* of their problems.

To demonstrate this, I focus on just one such theoretical proposal: the Language of Thought Hypothesis advanced by Jerry Fodor. I do not claim that all the attempted products of philosophical theorizing share its features – far from it; each has its own peculiar characteristics and complexities. Consequently, no sweeping statement about what goes wrong when one tries to produce such 'theories' will do. Nevertheless, examination of this representative of the species suffices to remind us of the salient features of its kith and kin. Indeed, it proves an ideal test case for our purposes for several reasons:

1. it is self-consciously advanced as an empirical hypothesis taking the form of a philosophical theory;
2. its core thesis non-accidentally resurrects Augustine's model of language;
3. the 'arguments' for believing its truth are in fact logical demands (they are not empirically based); they are not only dogmatic but possibly

circular because they depend on characterizing the domain in question in line with the demands of the 'theory' itself.

I discuss the ways in which the language of thought hypothesis exhibits all of these features before returning in the final section to say why Baker's proposed therapeutic method is either inadequate (as presented) or seriously underdescribed. Either way, a more detailed analysis of the way 'forms of representations' are typically misused in so-called philosophical theorizing throws light on how they might be properly used, when suitably understood, in clarificatory pursuits.

Even if there are no genuine philosophical theories, many imagine that such things exist. Indeed, the dominant trend in analytic philosophy is to suppose that *all* philosophizing really is *nothing but* theorizing. Fodor's approach of advancing the language of thought hypothesis as an empirical hypothesis enshrines the spirit of much post-Quinean philosophy. In so doing, he self-consciously and *directly* opposes Wittgenstein. Speaking for the tradition, he disparages Wittgenstein's reasons for rejecting philosophical theorizing. The following remark captures their deep disagreement over method:

> I would have thought that explaining the empirical data by postulating processes whose nature is left for later investigation is a characteristic of rational theory construction. Isn't that exactly what Newton did about gravity? Is it psychology that Wittgenstein doesn't like, or is it science as such?
>
> (Fodor, 2003: 11 n. 4)[5]

This remark epitomizes the received view of Wittgenstein's philosophy as being retrograde and anti-scientific.[6] But, to put the record straight, it was never unpolluted psychological theorizing *per se* (nor the scientific contributions of Newton) to which Wittgenstein objected – he only ever rejected the idea that *philosophy* could be prosecuted in a scientific manner – that is, that its problems could be resolved by making new discoveries about the operations of the 'mind', to stick with the example. In complete opposition to this, Fodor, like many others today, regards philosophy as nothing other than rational theory construction – theory construction of the sort that takes its lead directly from science.[7]

What precisely does this involve? What does it look like? Let us consider how the language of thought hypothesis (or LOTH) was forged. The core features of Mentalese, its syntax and semantics, are modelled on those of public language sentences. The analogy is not perfect. On the one hand,

Mentalese lacks some properties that natural languages have – for example, its sentences lack phonological properties. Mental sentences are therefore only envisioned to have formal properties akin to *written* linguistic signs. Yet, unlike the inscriptions of public language, the manipulation of sentences in the language of thought (or LOT) leaves no physical trail, trace or record in the world – not even at the neurological level. On the other hand, Mentalese is thought to have additional features that natural languages lack – its sentences are utterly well-formed, perfectly unambiguous constructions. The LOT is an *ideal* language. Its sentences are therefore only *partially* modelled on natural language sentences. The ways in which they are, and are not, are provided by the above 'commentary' on the 'model' (Sellars, 1956/1997: 103–4).

It is common scientific practice to begin theorizing by using metaphors and, modifying and developing these until the core constructs can be explicated in more abstract terms (McMullin, 1984: 33; Brown, 1986: 295). The LOTH is a good example of how 'philosophical theorizing' tries to follow a similar pattern. In constructing a philosophical theory, one typically: (i) focuses on some salient features of a given domain (in this case features of natural language sentences) for inspiration; (ii) decides which features of the model are to be retained and which altered in order that it can perform its role in supplying the requisite explanations. After that, one tries to test the worth of the model by abductive comparison with its rivals; by its capacity to deal with counter-examples; by demonstrating its success in providing satisfying 'explanations'; and/or by appeal to logical argument. This sort of practice is rife in contemporary philosophy.

It is worth focusing on step (ii), in which the theorist decides which features of the original to retain and which to modify. In Fodor's case, the development of the 'model' is driven by a particular *explanatory* need. Thus the LOT is just the kind of thing one would postulate if one tried to make good on the Augustinian account of language acquisition.[8] Early on in the *Investigations*, Wittgenstein writes 'Augustine describes the learning of human language as if the child came into a strange country and did not understand the language of the country; that is, as if it had already had a language, only not this one. Or again: as if the child could already think, only not yet speak' (PI: 32; BB: 41). And, as he writes elsewhere, 'We often think as if our thinking were founded on a thought-schema; as if we were translating from a more primitive mode of thought into ours' (PI: 597).[9]

A major weakness of this 'theory' is that it gets *all* of its life from the analogy with natural language and the self-protecting adjustments that convert it in an 'ideal' language. For example, we are never told *how* the LOT came into existence or *how* it could have come to have had its special properties. Yet one thing is clear: the account of the peculiar properties of the syntax and semantics of 'mental' symbols must be entirely different from that of public languages. This follows from the fact that according to the LOTH, public languages derive their compositionality and meaning from the structured representations of Mentalese. But if so, how then did those symbols become structured? How do they acquire content? The spotlight worry is that credible answers to these questions are not forthcoming. Certainly, the offerings to date have not been encouraging.

The truth is that the defenders of the LOT hypothesis have no workable theory of content that could support the claims of semantic supremacy which they make on behalf of Mentalese. There are intractable difficulties in providing one along causal-informational lines. Nor is the gravity of the situation lost on the LOTH's most prominent supporters. It is admitted that 'The hardness of understanding intentionality and thought isn't, these days, as widely advertised as the hardness of understanding consciousness, but it's quite hard enough to be getting on with' (Fodor, 2003: 22). It might be thought that it is unreasonable to reject the 'theory' on these grounds. The LOTH, we are told, is after all still developing – it is still in its infancy. Its lack of a well-worked out psychosemantics should not therefore be a basis for condemning it prematurely; it is rather that this lack of a semantic theory must be a major agenda item. The hope is that an explanation will come, in time. Since we currently have no adequate account of Mentalese semantics, we must reserve final judgement on the Mentalese proposal until one is developed. Yet, even if we accept this, it is important to correctly understand the true situation. It is not as if there were an existing theory of content which is in good basic order and which merely requires further adjustment – it is rather that the theories of naturalized semantics that have been offered to date are beset by *fundamental* logical difficulties – difficulties of the kind that should make us doubt that *any* possible psychosemantic account will work (Hutto, 1999: chs 2 and 3; Putnam, 1990, 1988). At root, the problem is that the very idea of 'content' – as something given in perceptual encounters and manipulated in other sub-personal cognitive processing – rests on a confused use of the 'carrying information' metaphor (see Hutto, 2006a). But even if we withhold final judgement, we must realize that, as things currently stand, the LOTH gets *all* of its strength on the semantic front *from* the analogy with public language. Any other is illusionary and stems solely from the fact that its proponents are prepared to write bold promissory notes.

The situation is even worse (or, rather, more obvious) when it comes to Mentalese syntax. For, as yet, there simply has been no attempt to account for the ontogenesis of formal features of the LOT *at all* – not even inadequate ones. The existence of appropriately structured symbols is just presupposed. To see why this matters it helps to make a comparison with natural language inscriptions. If I write 'I will not speak ill of the Language of Thought' a hundred times on a chalk board – the words in the first and last sentences will no doubt look considerably different, due to my tired hand. But, in truth, none of the resulting token linguistic signs comprising any of the other sentences will look *exactly* the same on close inspection. To the trained eye they are easily recognizable as being composed of the same words and letters – and we can see this because each adheres to its own common template (making allowances for illegibility). Each letter and each whole word are produced in line with normative standards for their formation: years of painstaking training pay off. Even if I wrote the sentences in an alien alphabet, the marks in question ought to be recognizable to a non-native speaker, one who knew nothing of their meaning. They would still discern the similarity between the repeated forms. That letters and words have specified shapes and sounds rests on certain public conventions surrounding their formation and combination and certain capacities of human language users to recognize and follow these[10] – public norms, such as the rules of spelling, govern such practices. These practices were instrumental to the original forging of 'symbols' and their subsequent maintenance. Linguistic symbols and their formal features are cultural artefacts with a history; they are not natural kinds.

What equivalent story can LOT theorists tell about the ontogenesis of Mentalese symbols? How do LOT symbols acquire their syntactic shapes – shapes that putatively allow them to serve, in effect, as Fregean 'modes of presentation' in private mental languages (see Fodor, 1994)? Obviously, there can be no appeal to cultural practices to explain this. Hence, if the very existence of modes of presentation depends on the existence of certain public norms, practices and conventions, for example, the use of pseudonyms, then LOT theorists are in trouble. The point is that we have yet to be offered an account of *how* or *why* formal Mentalese symbols – posited to be distinctively 'shaped', pre-labelled, mental tags – came into existence. This represents a very serious lacuna for LOT theorists.

To be sure, philosophers are not typically interested in such matters. But *scientific* theories are assessed by their progress in answering such questions and the same criteria of adequacy would apply to philosophical theories that tried to do the same – if we imagine there to be any.[11] Why then, if not for its empirical credentials, is the LOT hypothesis so attractive to certain philosophers? I suggest it is because – given their grounding assumptions – they cannot help but think it *must* be true. It looks to them as if it is the *only* possible way to explain certain otherwise perplexing phenomena – such as our capacities to learn a language, to reason logically and to communicate with sense. Certainly, the preceding discussion brings out the fact that, advertisements to the contrary, philosophical 'theories' like the LOTH are quite unlike any ordinary scientific or empirical theories.

In this light it is interesting to note that the LOT is only *allegedly* defended by an inference to the best explanation. But there are precisely *no* worthy rivals, or so it is claimed: no other remotely credible explanations of the relevant phenomena against which to compare it. Hence, it putatively earns the accolade of being the *best* explanation by default. As Fodor acknowledges, 'arguments to the best explanation can be pretty persuasive; especially when the explanation that they claim is "best" is *de facto*, the only one that anybody has been able to think of' (2003: 102). Masquerading as an 'argument from an inference to the best explanation', what we have is really an 'argument from an inference to the *only* explanation': the truth of the LOTH is *guaranteed* (at least as things stand, for presumably other explanations are logically possible, it just so happens that there are none). If this appraisal were correct, we would have no choice but to postulate the LOT. It is not correct, thankfully. There are other options: so perhaps the method is better described as 'an inference from lack of imagination'. But I do not want to discuss the alternatives here; instead I want to focus on the lessons to be learned about philosophical methodology. For one might wonder what an inference to best explanation comes to when there really are no other possibilities!

Despite what 'philosophical theorists' like to claim, in the end, it is logical arguments and not empirical evidence that do the heavy lifting in convincing us to endorse their proposals. Typically, arguments are offered which are designed to show that we simply have *no option* but to accept the theory in question (given, of course, a few crucial background assumptions, which – as we shall see – are typically fuelled by adherence to the picture itself). These *demonstrations* usually depend upon accepting certain widely held, but eminently questionable assumptions. And in some prominent cases these assumptions are themselves supported by a tendency to understand the phenomena in question in a one-sided way.

For example, Fodor's notorious Ur-argument about what is required in order to learn a language putatively demonstrates that we *must* accept the existence of the LOT. The claim is that unless we postulate pre-existing linguaform representations with precisely the same expressive power as any 'learned' concepts (or words), we would not be able to explain how we acquire such concepts or first languages at all. His argument rests on the idea that without postulating a LOT we would be unable to explain the formation of the hypotheses needed to fuel the learning processes. He has been rehearsing this line of argument, virtually unchanged, since 1975.[12] To learn a concept (or local linguistic label for one) one must *already* be able to think about its extension. Thus, to learn the concept (or local label for) X entails having the prior capacity to *think* about Xs 'as such'.[13] This argument only works, however, if we accept certain assumptions – specifically certain intellectualist assumptions about how concepts/language *must* be learnt. The key premise is that new learners must form full-fledged hypotheses about the meaning of the words or concepts and that these are tested out during the learning process. Since formation of such hypotheses *must* precede the learning of public language, they cannot be couched in public language; hence the resources of a language of thought are required. To be convincing this argument must deny that there could be any serious proposal about this learning process which avoids the questionable intellectualist assumption. And, unfortunately for LOT theorists, there are other credible accounts (see Hutto, 2007); but, yet again, here I simply want to focus on the self-protecting character of this kind of 'argument'.

Fodor's other arguments have much the same form. Taking just one more example: he has recently defended the language of thought hypothesis on the grounds that *only* thoughts and not public language sentences exhibit the kind of determinacy needed to explain semantic compositionality. As a result, *only* thought constituents could possibly serve as the fully determinate semantic atoms needed to explain the generative and productive features of propositional thinking:

> Here's the argument: If, as between thought and language, only one of them can plausibly be supposed to be compositional, then that is, *ipso facto*, the one that comes first in the order of the explanation of content; the other has only such secondary content as it 'derives' from the first. But, as a matter of empirical fact, language is pretty clearly not compositional; so it can't have content in the first instance. Q.E.D.
>
> (Fodor, 2001: 10–11).

The pivotal claim is that only determinate thoughts – not indeterminate natural language sentences – are in a position to explain compositionality. Compositionality requires the existence of stable building blocks that can play recurring roles across contexts. Since natural language expressions are not in position to supply such building blocks, then to the extent that natural language expressions exhibit compositionality this is only something they inherit from the underlying Mentalese thoughts (as Fodor would have it, like their semantics properties quite generally). If it is true that only Mentalese sentences explain compositionality, then we can be sure that the only true semantic content abides in them. Since compositionality is the non-negotiable trademark of propositional content, this provides a firm basis for thinking that thoughts must be logically independent from, and prior to, language in the order of things.

The substantive lemma is that 'language is pretty clearly not compositional' and its unpacking warrants close scrutiny. The heart of the argument depends on the truth of two further premises (the first of which is advanced as straightforward empirical observation): (i) language is strikingly elliptical and inexplicit about the thoughts it expresses; and (ii) language couldn't be strikingly elliptical and inexplicit about the thoughts it expresses if language were compositional in anything like strict detail (Fodor, 2001: 11).

Consequently because of its indeterminacy, natural language is in no position to supply the basic constituents needed to underwrite a recombinant and constructive semantics. The sentences of natural language are ambiguous and inexplicit in ways that their underlying thought-contents putatively are not, hence only the latter could possibly specify what is meant by a speakers on given occasions. Or to put this in a more revealing way, because natural language utterances are not precise on all points, the truth conditions of a speaker's expressions must be fixed at the level of underlying thought contents. It is what a speaker 'has in mind' that fleshes out the true content of their intended meaning with absolute precision. This is consistent with the received view that public language is nothing more than an imperfect medium for conveying thoughts. Given this, it is easy to see the full force of Fodor's argument. Since compositionality is, as he puts it, a 'non-negotiable' feature of propositional thinking it must be accounted for. Since natural language is in no position to do this, we have *no choice* but to suppose that fully determinate underlying thoughts do the requisite work. To account for semantic determinacy Mentalese sentences must exist and they must have certain properties which natural language expressions borrow from them. *Ex hypothesi*, thought and language do not exist on an equal footing (e.g., semantically speaking, natural language sentences could not even be translations of the LOT; their meaning is transduced from it).

We might wonder: Is the crucial supporting premise, presented here as a matter of empirical fact – that ordinary language is intrinsically indeterminate – true? Assessed against its capacity to support a truth-conditional semantics, it certainly seems so. Natural language is both syntactically and semantically inexplicit in important respects and thus notoriously unable, at least without supplement, to sponsor such. In isolation, the surface syntactic forms of many of its sentences are inherently ambiguous. To take a stock example, the word 'flying' in 'They are flying planes' can be construed either as part of a verb phrase or the first component of compound noun: reading it the one way as opposed to the other completely alters the meaning of the sentence. Semantic inexplicitness has several forms too, including incompleteness, and lexical and logical ambiguity. In daily life, confusions are often bound up with the use of referent-shifting demonstratives ('Does your dog bite?', said of a dog you are holding but which does not belong to you) or the use of quantifiers in an unspecified domain of discourse ('Everyone out of the pool!' meant of some pertinent group and not of all people, which would clearly make the imperative ridiculous). Often, meeting demands of conversational implicature makes ordinary discourse telegraphic, curtailed and incomplete in these sorts of ways. Hence, the all too frequent use of the phrase: 'You know what I mean' (Dunbar, 2000: 241).

Even so, Fodor's argument rests on a highly questionable philosophical assumption that *all* acts of communication *must* be understood in truth-conditional terms.[14] The success of his proof of the 'priority of thought thesis' (and by implication the truth of the LOTH) rests on making another substantive philosophical assumption. And again, the assumption in question looks to be closely connected to, if not directly sponsored by, the very 'model' of thought that is being defended. For what independent grounds do we have for thinking (other than to satisfy certain explanatory needs) that the thoughts we express *in* language are *initially* any more determinate than the natural language sentences used to convey them (at least that they are so *prior* to being *made* such by expressing them and reflecting on them)? Since the language of thought sentences are not accessible to consciousness, one might wonder why anyone would be persuaded that a truth-conditional semantics is the correct way to understand *all* acts of communication. What evidence or argument is there to support this claim?

Certainly, we have been given no reason to suppose that *all* communication necessarily rests on its participants locking on to one another's determinate thoughts. They are more likely to be using public norms in order to clarify what is said, meant and thought (Gauker, 2003: 91). Effective day-to-day, pragmatic communication, which often is nothing more than a kind of contextualized coordination, is not predicated on interpreting others absolutely correctly or by recovering exactly what they think at a subterranean level. This does not require representing the thoughts of others in terms of completely unambiguous propositions.[15]

It may be objected that even if not *all* linguistic interactions require the formation and interpretation of determinate thoughts, some certainly do: specifically, those of the compositional, truth-conditional variety. Careful thinking and communication may be less widespread than some suppose but it does exist. Undeniably, specifying relatively unambiguous propositions is necessary for certain purposes, such as explicit logical reasoning, analysis and claim making. Certain practices – legally binding promise making, engaging in theoretical debates and developing argu-mentative proofs – require us to be precise in our thinking and utterances. But, and this is the important question, to exactly what degree? This will vary from case to case.

Since to *completely* clarify what one thinks would involve charting *all* possible inferential relations, it is not clear that anyone has ever had or expressed an *absolutely* determinate thought. To encode *all* the possibilities relevant to making even a single proposition entirely unambiguous – so that there could be no confusion about its scope, reference or background presuppositions, and the like would require the representation of a poten-tially infinite series of rules. This was one major take-home lesson of Wittgenstein's *Tractatus* (Hutto, 2003/2006: ch. 2). Worse still, reifying the 'contexts of utterances' as required to fully specify the truth-conditions for any given proposition and imagining these to be represented in LOT constructions begins to look like the most rampant form of Platonism we've seen to date (Sperber and Wilson, 1998: 186). We can avoid all of this by resisting certain deep-seated philosophical intuitions and accepting that even our best thinking (and speaking) is only ever approximate. Even if we take great care to shape our thoughts and to choose our words, we fall quite a long way short of the high standards demanded of an ideal lan-guage (or an ideal language of *thought*). Nevertheless, *some* linguistic utterances – at least *some* of the time – exhibit enough determinacy to enable compositional operations, such as those involved in ringing the changes of a coherent argument, developing a plan, or generating new expressions out of existing constituents of the public lexicon.

All this shows is that different types of expression are used for different purposes. Most utterances (indeed, most thoughts) are not put to traditional logical work; they are merely expressive or used for mere coordinating purposes. If one demands that *all* linguistic expressions have the same degree of exactitude required of expressions used for certain fact-stating purposes, then it goes without saying that 'natural language as a whole' will be downright vague in all sorts of ways. But since this is an unreason-able, and question-begging, demand it is no good trying to run an argu-ment in defence of the 'primacy of thought over language' on the grounds of a general linguistic indeterminacy. Such a move is defeated by the fact that *some* of our utterances are determinate enough to serve as the basis for generative, systematic thinking. All compositionality requires is that the words of the public lexicon are stable *enough* to be recombined in appropriate norm-governed ways, time and time again. The fact is that they are. There is no *need* to postulate a 'language of thought' in order to account for this.

Fodor's 'argument' is revealed to be nothing more than a rather complex philosophical demand. Indeed, it is just the sort of demand that the young Wittgenstein was initially inclined to make – one which he only later recognized to be an imposition of his own thinking. The forging of models by 'analogy' in the attempt to give philosophical 'explanations' and the practice of defending these by self-sustaining logical arguments are all symptoms of deep-seated philosophical confusion.

Baker is right that this kind of confusion involves being blinded by one 'form of representation'. But this is only *part* of the problem. Those in the grip of a picture are normally inclined to more complex 'self-protecting' errors and they are driven by more complicated motives. Making an example of Fodor was meant to bring out this *complexity*. His case shows why undoing the 'knots' of philosophical confusion requires great patience. Thus:

> In order to fully eliminate disquiet, we must still uncover the motives which give rise to the error. We will see how this error is based on a whole series of mix-ups.

> (VOW: 109)

Baker's diagnosis is weak in that the claim that one is blinded by a single dominant aspect fails to capture the true depth of the trouble. It also suffers from another problem, for it is not as if all forms of representation are *equally* legitimate (albeit one-sided). Returning to the case of Augustine, it is not as if his 'picture' is an adequate but merely limited representation of language, as Baker suggests. A great deal of language does, as a matter of fact, 'defy being cast in its net'. At best, it might describe a truncated form of our language or a part of it, but it is not an adequate way of representing the whole of it. This seems to be Wittgenstein's verdict as well:

> Augustine, we might say, does describe a system of communication; only not everything that we call language is this system. And one has to say this in many cases where the question arises 'Is this an appropriate description or not?' The answer is: 'Yes, it is appropriate, but only for this narrowly circumscribed region, not for the whole of what you are claiming to describe.'

> (PI: 3)

In a similar way, the author of the *Tractatus* made the mistake of thinking that certain features of fact-stating discourse were inherent in all sense-making language. His truth tables, like Beck's tube map, perspicuously represent the possibilities of first-order logic. His mistake was to think that in showing this he had also revealed the ultimate bounds of sense and nonsense, the true limits of thought. Strictly speaking, what he says about the general form of the *proposition* is quite correct – the only trouble is that not all uses of language involve trading in propositions. His mistake was to *impose* a structure derived from one small part of language and to imagine that it applied to the whole of it. While this was a serious mistake, a key difference between the young Wittgenstein and philosophers such as Fodor is that Wittgenstein was never under the illusion that he was advancing a philosophical *theory*. This only goes to show that there are many ways that one might be misled; there are many different types of philosophical confusion, many ways to go wrong (as Aristotle would say). One might fail to realize *that* one is making a philosophical mistake but this can be compounded, as it is in Fodor's case, by a failure even to see *how* one is making such mistakes systematically.

4   Positive philosophy

The above hopefully provides some insight into how certain 'forms of representation' can mislead; how they can be misused in various ways. But it also suggests a sister strategy for using such 'representations' correctly in clarifying certain topics for certain purposes. Freed of misleading explanatory and crude descriptive ambitions, such tools can be used restrictively, case by case, to provide genuine insights. Baker is just wrong to suppose that in rejecting 'theoretical' philosophy Wittgenstein promotes a purely negative, therapeutic method that leads to relativism. Removing misconceptions and recontextualizing our practices in a way that leaves them open to be illuminated by other non-philosophical investigations is one way to pursue a more positive end. By using perspicuous representations with care, and understanding what this comes to, a positive philosophy is on the cards after all.

Notes

1. Some New Wittgensteinian promoters of the therapeutic programme have – in ways similar to Baker – taken to denying the very possibility of a 'non-theoretical' elucidatory philosophy. They claim that we face a hard choice

of either endorsing theoretical accounts or recognizing that philosophy is therapeutic through-and-through. I respond to this in the postscript to the second edition of *Wittgenstein and the End of Philosophy* (Hutto, 2006).

2. Of course, acknowledging this does not commit one to the other extreme of supposing that everything is in constant flux. It is worth remembering that there are typically strong forces keeping most things of interest to philosophers stable across time (see Hutto, 2003/2006: ch. 6).

3. These writings were particularly important in framing Baker's later thinking about Wittgenstein. As Katherine Morris reports: 'in Baker's view', 'Waismann's complex personal and working relationship with Wittgenstein makes his work ... an important resource for understanding Wittgenstein, if used with caution' (Morris, 2004a: 25).

4. Baker takes Wittgenstein's query – 'Is this a "Weltanschauung"?' – at the end of PI: 122 to be advanced with the utmost seriousness (see Baker, 2004: fn. 29).

5. Wittgenstein famously claims that philosophers incline to free and easy talk about mental processes while leaving their nature undecided (PI: 308). It seems that, for Fodor, this is an appropriate prelude to theorizing.

6. Given their starting point, it is hardly surprising that contemporary analytic philosophers neither understand nor appreciate what is unique in Wittgenstein's proposed methodology. Although Wittgenstein has a prominent place in the canon, his insights on method and their implications for the possibilities of philosophy are typically misrepresented, downplayed or ignored.

7. On this score, Fodor is not so much blinded by science as by its (presumed) method – i.e., as characterized by philosophers!

8. Alarm bells should sound when an *explanandum* and its *explanans* look so alike.

9. This last remark may have been autobiographical, given what we know about Tractarian views of the relation of thought and public language expressions. The similarities between the Tractarian view and Fodor's are very strong. Fodor replicates nearly all the errors of the early Wittgenstein – precisely the ones that the 'later' Wittgenstein fought so hard to purge. These include commitment to: semantic atomism and determinism; the idea that truth-conditional content is the only kind of linguistic content; the idea that linguistic meaning derives from, and is the expression of, the underlying thought contents; that thought content is compositional through and through (indeed, Fodor goes further by resurrecting Russell's views that the principles of logic are representations with which we are in some way intellectually acquainted). It seems that the same old mistakes are still being propounded with new voice talents. Philosophers are still failing to heed the lessons of history.

10. It is possible to tell a story about the latter in terms of uniquely human mimetic abilities (see Hutto, 2006b).

11. For example, some have claimed that the failure to find any sentences in the brain discredits the 'language of thought hypothesis' (Churchland, 1991: 65). Yet, from the very start, Fodor has maintained that his 'hypothesis' must not be confused with a crude thesis about how such a mental architecture is implemented at the neural level. All that is required is that the higher-order symbolic operations are somehow implemented at the neural level. Mentalese symbols

are natural 'computational' kinds that have a higher level of existence, but this is consistent with their being spatio-temporal particulars, with genuine causal powers in the same way as the entities of interest to other special sciences. Thus one can be fully committed to their reality without assuming that they make any appearance or leave a trail at the neural level. In line with token materialism, although every symbol kind is also a physical kind, there need be no robust or systematic correlations between the symbolic and the neural. This is certainly an internally consistent position, but as far as empirical hypotheses go, it makes the claim that symbols of *the lingua mentis* are natural kinds very awkward to falsify. At least, no evidence for or against it can be amassed by carrying out physiological or neuroscientific investigations into the actual working of brains.

12. Accordingly, it is a prerequisite for having a natural language that we should have a prior language of equally expressive power (Fodor, 1975: 32–3). For 'you cannot learn a language whose terms express semantic properties not expressed by the terms of some language you are already able to use' (ibid.: 61).

13. Many are suspicious of this argument because it leads to a regress. But the language of thought is meant to 'solve' the problem by being a language that one does not need to learn. If one could account for its semantics by some other route, the problem would indeed be solved. But the fact is that there is no adequate story about how Mentalese content is acquired.

14. This idea is still alive and well as the following example from Elugardo and Stainton reveals: 'Imagine Andrew walks into a room, holds up a cigarette, and says "From France" to Sylvia. We think it is obvious that, in this case, Andrew could easily convey a proposition. Let us agree that Andrew communicates, about the cigarette, that it is from France. A singular proposition. He can do this because, as will be obvious to both Andrew and Sylvia, what Andrew means clearly is not the property λx.from-France(x). How could he mean that?' (Elugardo and Stainton, 2003: 257). The authors go on to argue that because what Andrew means to convey is greater that what he actually says, Sylvia must somehow decode his utterance in order to make sense of it. What Andrew meant to convey was a complete proposition; what he uttered was only a fragment of one – a mere prepositional phrase.

15. As Ruth Millikan observes, 'Classification for purposes of communication ... does not correspond to a single general domain. The domains that are involved in ordinary informal communication typically are severely restricted by context, varying radically from one speaker-hearer pair and from one occasion to another. For this reason, words whose natural extensions have very vague boundaries can still be used in specific communicative contexts to classify objects precisely. I refer to what I want simply as 'red' but given the books on my table it is clear enough what object I want, even though the entire domain of red things shade off gradually into pink things, purple things, orange things and so forth' (Millikan, 2000: 35–6). It is by these means that we 'effect accurate hearer classifications in context' (ibid.: 37).

References

Abse, D. (1977) *Collected Poems, 1948–1976* (London: Hutchinson).

Alanen, L. (2003) *Descartes' Concept of Mind* (Cambridge, MA, and London: Harvard University Press).

Albritton, R. (1959) 'On Wittgenstein's Use of the Term "Criterion"', *Journal of Philosophy* 56; rpt in Canfield (1986): 1–14.

Albritton, R. (1966) 'Postscript 1966', in G. Pitcher (ed.), *Wittgenstein: The Philosophical Investigations* (New York: Doubleday 1966), 15–16.

Asch, S. E. (1987) *Social Psychology* (Oxford: Oxford University Press).

Baker, G. P. (1974) 'Criteria: A New Foundation for Semantics', in Canfield (1986), 234–68.

Baker, G. P. (2004) 'Philosophical Investigations §122: Neglected Aspects', in Morris (2004a), 22–51.

Baker, G. P. and Hacker, P. M. S. (1984) *Scepticism, Rules and Language*. Oxford: Blackwell.

Baker, G. P. and Hacker, P. M. S. (1985) *Wittgenstein: Rules, Grammar and Necessity. Volume 2 of An Analytical Commentary on the Philosophical Investigations* (Oxford: Basil Blackwell).

Bearn, G. C. F. (1997) *Waking to Wonder: Wittgenstein's Existential Investigations* (New York: SUNY)

Bennett, M. and Hacker, P. M. S. (2003) *Philosophical Foundations of Neuroscience* (Oxford: Blackwell).

Bennett, P. (1978) 'Wittgenstein and Defining Criteria', in Canfield (1986), 49–63.

Blatchford, R. (n.d.) *My Favourite Books* (London: The Clarion Press).

Bourdieu, E. (1998a) 'Une conjecture pour trouver le mot de l'énigme: La conception peircienne des catégories', *Philosophie* 58: 14–37.

Bourdieu, E. (1998b) *Savoir faire. Contribution à une théorie dispositionnelle de l'action* (Paris: Éditions du Seuil).

Bourdieu, P. (1990) *The Logic of Practice* (Cambridge: Polity), trans. from *Le sens pratique* (Paris: Minuit, 1980).

Bouveresse, J. (1970) 'La notion de grammaire chez le second Wittgenstein', in *Wittgenstein et le problème d'une philosophie de la science* (Paris: Éditions du CNRS), 173–89.

Bouveresse, J. (1982) 'L'animal cérémoniel: Wittgenstein et l'anthropologie', annexe aux *Remarques sur le Rameau d'Or de Frazer* (Lausanne: L'Age d' Homme, 1982).

Bouveresse, J. (1987) *Le Mythe de l'intériorité: Expérience, signification et langage privé chez Wittgenstein* (Paris: Éditions de Minuit).

Bouveresse, J. (1988) *Le Pays des possibles. Wittgenstein, les mathématiques et le monde réel* (Paris: Minuit).

Bouveresse, J. (1995a) 'Règles, dispositions et habitus', *Critique* 579/580: 573–94.

Bouveresse, J. (1995b) 'Le réel et son ombre. La théorie wittgensteinienne de la possibilité', in P. Egidi (ed.), *Wittgenstein: Mind and Language* (Dordrecht: Kluwer Academics Publishers), 59–81.

Bouveresse, J. (1995c) *Wittgenstein reads Freud* (New Jersey: Princeton University Press).

Bouveresse, J., Laugier, S. and Rosat, J.-J. (eds) (2002) *Wittgenstein, dernières pensées* (Marseille: Agone).

Brown, H. I. (1986) 'Sellars, Concepts and Conceptual Change', *Synthese* 68: 275–307.

Bruner, J. S. (1983) *In Search of Mind* (New York: Harper and Row).

Bühler, Karl (1930) *Die geistige Entwicklung des Kindes*, 3rd edn (Jena: Verlag von Gustav Fischer).

Campos, J. and Sternberg, C. (1981) 'Perception, Appraisal, and Emotion: The Onset of Social Referencing', in M. Lamb and L. Sherrod (eds), *Infant Social Cognition: Empirical and Theoretical Considerations* (Hillsdale, NJ: Lawrence Erlbaum), 273–314.

Canfield, J. V. (1975) '"I know that I am in pain" is senseless', in J. Canfield (ed.), *The Philosophy of Wittgenstein, Volume 8: Knowing, Naming, Certainty and Idealism.* (New York: Garland Publishing, 1986), 113–29.

Canfield, J. V. (1981) *Wittgenstein: Language and World* (Amherst: The University of Massachusetts Press).

Canfield, J. V. (1986) (ed.) *The Philosophy of Wittgenstein, Volume 7: Criteria* (New York: Garland Publishing).

Canfield, J. V. (1993) 'The Living Language: Wittgenstein and the Empirical Study of Communication', *Language Sciences* 15:3: 165–93.

Canfield, J. V. (1995) 'The Rudiments of Language', *Language & Communication* 15:3: 195–211.

Canfield, J. V. (2003) *Philosophy of Meaning, Knowledge and Value in the 20th Century* (London: Routledge).

Cavell, S. (1969) *Must We Mean What We Say?* (Cambridge: Cambridge University Press).

Cavell, S. (1979) *The Claim of Reason: Wittgenstein, Skepticism, Morality and Tragedy* (New York: Oxford University Press).

Chomsky, N. (1968) *Language and Mind* (New York: Harcourt, Brace & Word).

Churchland, P. M. (1991) 'Folk Psychology and the Explanation of Human Behaviour', in *The Future of Folk Psychology*, ed. J. D. Greenwood (Cambridge: Cambridge University Press), 51–69.

Cioffi, F. (1998) *Wittgenstein and the Question of Pseudo-Science* (Chicago: Open Court).

Cockburn, D. (1994) 'Human Beings and Giant Squids', *Philosophy* 69: 135–50.

Cohen, S. (2000) 'Contextualism and Skepticism', *Philosophical Issues* 10: 94–107.

Collett, P. (1977) 'The rules of conduct', in P. Collett (ed.), *Social Rules and Social Behaviour* (Oxford: Blackwell).

Coulter, J. (1985) 'On Comprehension and "Mental Representation"', in Gilbert and Heath (1985), 8–23.

Coulter, J. (1999) 'Discourse and Mind', rpt in Shanker and Kilfoyle (2002), III, 143–61.

Cowley, S. J. (1997) 'Conversation, Co-ordination and Vertebrate Communication', *Semiotica* 115:1: 27–52.

Cowley, S. J. (2004) 'Simulating Others: The Basis of Human Cognition?', *Language Sciences* 26:3: 273–99.

Cowley, S. J. and Love, N. (forthcoming) 'Language and Cognition or How to Avoid the Conduit Metaphor', forthcoming in U. Oskulska and A. Duszek (eds), *Bridges and Walls in Metalinguistic Discourse* (Berlin: Peter Lang).

Cowley, S. J., Moodley, S. and Fiori-Cowley, A. (2004) 'Grounding Signs of Culture: Primary Intersubjectivity in Social Semiosis', *Mind, Culture and Activity* 11:2: 109–32.

Crary, A. and Read, R. (eds) *The New Wittgenstein* (London: Routledge, 2000).

Davies, M. and Coltheart, M. (2000) 'Pathologies of Belief', *Mind & Language: Pathologies of Belief* 15:1: 1–46.

Denis, M. (1890) in 'Définition du Néo-Traditionnalisme', cited in D. Riout, *Qu'est-ce que l'art moderne?* (Paris: Gallimard, 2000).

Dennett, D. C. (1987a) *The Intentional Stance* (Cambridge, MA.: MIT Press, Bradford Books).

Dennett, D. C. (1987b) 'Styles of Mental Representation', in Dennett (1987a), 213–25.

Dennett, D. C. (1987c) 'Instrumentalism Reconsidered', in Dennett (1987a), 69–81.

Dennett, D. C. (1991) *Consciousness Explained* (Boston, MA: Little, Brown).

Descombes, V. (2001) 'Relation intersubjective et relation sociale', in J. Benoist et B. Karsenti (eds), *Phénoménologie et sociologie* (Paris: Presses Universitaires de France), 127–55.

Diamond, C. (1989) 'Rules: Looking in the Right Place', in D. Z. Phillips and P. Winch (eds), *Wittgenstein: Attention to Particulars* (Basingstoke: Macmillan), 12–34.

Diamond, C. (1991) *The Realistic Spirit, Wittgenstein, Philosophy, and the Mind* (Cambridge, MA: MIT Press).

Diamond, C. (1966–67) 'Secondary Sense', in Diamond (1991), 225–43.

Diamond, C. (2000) 'Does Bismarck Have a Beetle in His Box? The Private Language Argument in the Tractatus', in Crary and Read (2000), 262–92.

Dostoevsky, F. (1972) *The Devils* (London: Penguin).

Dreyfus, H. L. (1992/1999) *What Computers Still Can't Do: A Critique of Artificial Reason* (Cambridge, MA: The MIT Press).

Drury, M. O'C. (1967) 'A Symposium', in K. T. Fann (ed.), *Ludwig Wittgenstein: The Man and His Philosophy* (New York: Dell), 68–9.

Dunbar, R. I. M. (2000). 'On the Origin of the Human Mind', in P Carruthers and A Chamberlain (eds), *Evolution and the Modern Mind: Modularity, Language and Meta-Cognition* (Cambridge: Cambridge University Press), 238–53.

Elder, C. R. (1994) *The Grammar of the Unconscious: The Conceptual Foundations of Psychoanalysis* (Pennsylvania: The Pennsylvania State University Press).

Elman, J. L., Bates, E. A., Johnson, M. H., Karmiloff-Smith, A., Parisi, D. and Plunkett, K. (1996) *Rethinking Innateness: A Connectionist Perspective on Development* (Cambridge, MA: MIT Press).

Elugardo, R. and Stainton, R. J. (2003) 'Grasping Objects and Contents', in *Epistemology of Language*, ed. A. Barber (Oxford: Oxford University Press), 257–302.

Empson, W. (1949) *Seven Types of Ambiguity*, 2nd edn (London: Chatto and Windus).

Fodor, J. A. (1975) *The Language of Thought* (Cambridge, MA: Harvard University Press).

Fodor, J. A. (1994) The Elm and the Expert: Mentalese and Its Semantics (Cambridge, MA: MIT Press).

Fodor, J. A. (2001) 'Language, Thought and Compositionality', *Mind & Language* 16:1: 1–5.

Fodor, J. A. (2003) *Hume Variations* (Oxford: Oxford University Press).

Fodor, J. A. (2004a) 'Having Concepts: A Brief Refutation of the Twentieth Century', *Mind & Language* 19:1: 29–47.

Fodor, J. A. (2004b) 'Reply to Commentators', *Mind & Language* 19:1: 99–112.
Fogelin, R. J. (1976) *Wittgenstein* (London: Routledge & Kegan Paul).
Franklin, J. (1979) *Joe Franklin's Encyclopaedia of Comedians* (Secacus, NJ: The Citadel Press).
Frege, G. (1962) 'Über Sinn und Bedeutung', in G. Patzig (ed.), *Funktion, Begriff, Bedeutung* (Göttingen: Vandenhoeck & Ruprecht), 40–66.
Freud, S. (1900/1953) *The Interpretation of Dreams, The Complete Psychological Works of Sigmund Freud*, vol. 5 (London: Hogarth Press).
Freud, S. (1922/1955) 'Medusa's Head', *The Complete Psychological Works of Sigmund Freud*, vol. 18 (London: Hogarth Press).
Frith, U. and Happé, F. (1999) 'Theory of Mind and Self-Consciousness: What Is It Like to Be Autistic?', *Mind & Language* 14:1: 1–22.
Garfinkel, H. (1967) *Studies in Ethnomethodology* (Englewood, N. J.: Prentice Hall).
Gasking, D. and Jackson, C. (1951) 'Ludwig Wittgenstein', *Australian Journal of Philosophy* 29: 234–48.
Gauker, C. (2003) *Words Without Meaning* (Cambridge, MA: MIT Press).
Gilbert, G. N. and Heath, C. (eds), (1985) *Social Action and Artificial Intelligence* (Vermont: Gower Publishing).
Glock, H.-J. (1996) *A Wittgenstein Dictionary* (Oxford: Blackwell).
Good, D. (1985) 'Sociology and AI: The Lesson from Social Psychology', in Gilbert and Heath (1985), 82–103.
Hacker, P. M. S. (1993) *Wittgenstein, Meaning & Mind: Volume 3 of An Analytical Commentary on the Philosophical Investigations, Part I: Essays* (Oxford: Blackwell).
Hamlyn, D. W. (1976) 'Thinking', in H. D. Lewis (ed.), *Contemporary British Philosophy: Personal Statements* (London: Allen & Unwin, 1976), 100–12.
Hanfling, O. (1991) 'I Heard a Plaintive Melody', in A. Phillips Griffiths (ed.), *Wittgenstein Centenary Essays* (Cambridge: Cambridge University Press, 1991), 117–35.
Hanfling, O. (2002) *Wittgenstein and the Human Form of Life* (London: Routledge).
Hanly, C. (1972) 'Wittgenstein on Psychoanalysis', in A. Ambrose and M. Lazerowitz (eds), *Philosophy and Language* (London: Allen Lane), 73–94.
Hark, M. R. M. ter (1990) *Beyond the Inner and the Outer: Wittgenstein's Philosophy of Psychology* (Kluwer: Dordrecht).
Hark, M. R. M. ter (2000) 'Uncertainty, Vagueness & Psychological Indeterminacy', *Synthese* 124: 192–220.
Hark, M. R. M. ter (2004) 'Patterns of Life: A Third Wittgenstein Concept', in Moyal-Sharrock (2004b), 125–43.
Harman, G. (1973) *Thought* (New Jersey: Princeton University Press).
Harré, R. and Secord, P. F. (1972) *The Explanation of Social Behaviour* (Oxford: Blackwell).
Harré, R. and Tissaw, M. A. (2005) *Wittgenstein and Psychology* (Aldershot: Ashgate).
Hebb, D. O. (1958) *A Textbook of Psychology* (London: W. B. Saunders).
Hertzberg, L. (2001) 'The Sense Is Where You Find It', in T. McCarthy and S. Stidd (eds), *Wittgenstein in America* (Oxford: Oxford University Press), 90–103.
Hertzberg, L. (2005) 'The Limits of Understanding', *SATS* 6: 5–14.
Hirsh-Pasek, K. and Golinkoff, R. (2000) *The Origins of Grammar: Evidence from Early Language Comprehension* (Cambridge, MA: MIT Press).
Hilton, T. (1985) *John Ruskin: The Early Years* (New Haven: Yale University Press).
Hobson, P. (2000) *The Cradle of Thought* (Oxford: Oxford University Press).

Husserl, E. (1913/2001) *Logical Investigations*, vol. I, 2nd edn, trans. J. N. Findlay (London: Routledge).

Hutto, D. D. (1999) *The Presence of Mind* (Amsterdam: John Benjamins).

Hutto, D. D. (2003/2006) *Wittgenstein and the End of Philosophy: Neither Theory nor Therapy* (Basingstoke: Palgrave).

Hutto, D. D. (2005) 'Voices to be Heard', *The British Journal for the History of Philosophy* 13:1: 149–61.

Hutto, D. D. (2006a, forthcoming) 'Against Passive Intellectualism: Reply to Crane', in R. Menary (ed.), *Consciousness and Emotion: Special Issue on Radical Enactivism*.

Hutto, D. D. (2006b, forthcoming) 'Four Herculean Labours: Reply to Hobson', in R. Menary (ed.), *Consciousness and Emotion: Special Issue on Radical Enactivism*.

Hutto, D. D. (2007) *Folk Psychological Narratives: The Socio-Cultural Basis of Understanding Reasons* (Cambridge, MA: MIT Press).

Huxley, A. (1976) *After Many a Summer* (London: Triad/Panther).

Hyman, J. (1999) 'How Knowledge Works', *Philosophical Quarterly* 49: 433–451.

James, W. (1890) *The Principles of Psychology*, vol. 1 (New York: Holt).

James, W. (1896/1948) *The Figure in the Carpet in The Lesson of the Master and Other Stories* (London: John Lehmann), 149–84.

Kenny, Anthony (1967) 'Criterion', in P. Edwards (ed.), *Encyclopedia of Philosophy* (New York: MacMillan).

Kihlstrom, J. F. (1987) 'The Cognitive Unconscious', *Science*, n.s. 237: 1445–52.

Klein, P. (1981) *Certainty: A Refutation of Skepticism* (Minneapolis: University of Minnesota Press).

Kolers, P. and von Grunau, M. (1976) 'Shape and Color in Apparent Motion', *Vision Research*, 16: 329–35.

Kosslyn, S. M. and Koenig, O. (1995) *Wet Mind: The New Cognitive Neuroscience* (New York: Free Press).

Lagerspetz, O. (1998) *Trust: The Tacit Demand* (Dordrecht: Kluwer Academic Publishers).

Leslie, A. (1987) 'Pretence and Representation: The Origins of "Theory of Mind"', *Psychological Review* 94: 412–26.

Lycan, G. (1971) 'Non-Inductive Evidence: Recent Work on Wittgenstein's "Criteria"', in Canfield (1986), 109–25.

MacIntyre, A. C. (1958) *The Unconscious: A Conceptual Analysis* (London: Routledge & Kegan Paul).

Malcolm, N. (1959) *Dreaming* (London: Routledge & Kegan Paul).

Malcolm, N. (1963) *Knowledge and Certainty* (Englewood Cliffs, NJ: Prentice-Hall).

Malcolm, N. (1972–73/1977) 'Thoughtless Brutes', in *Thought and Knowledge* (Ithaca, NY: Cornell University Press), 40–57.

McDowell, J. (1982) 'Criteria, Defeasibility, and Knowledge', *Proceedings of the British Academy*, 68:1: 456–79.

McGinn, Marie (1998) 'Criterion', in *Routledge Encyclopedia of Philosophy*, ed. E. Craig (New York: Routledge).

McMullin, E. (1984) 'A Case for Scientific Realism', in J. Leplin (ed.), *Scientific Realism* (Berkeley: California University Press), 8–40.

Meinong, A. (1983) *On Assumptions* (Berkeley: University of California Press).

Mill, J. S. (1958) *Autobiography* (London: Oxford University Press).

Millikan, R. G. (2000) *On Clear and Confused Ideas* (Cambridge: Cambridge University Press).

Moore, G. E. (1966) *Philosophical Papers* (New York: Collier Books).

Morris, K. (ed.) (2004a) *Wittgenstein's Method: Neglected Aspects* (Oxford: Blackwell).

Morris, K. (2004b) 'Introduction', in Morris (2004a), 1–18.

Moyal-Sharrock, D. (2004a) *Understanding Wittgenstein's On Certainty* (Basingstoke: Palgrave Macmillan).

Moyal-Sharrock, D. (ed.) (2004b) *The Third Wittgenstein: The Post-Investigations Works* (Aldershot: Ashgate).

Moyal-Sharrock, D. and Brenner, W. H. (eds) (2005) *Readings of Wittgenstein's On Certainty* (Basingstoke: Palgrave Macmillan).

Nowicki, S. and Duke, M. P. (1992) *Helping the Child Who Doesn't Fit In* (Atlanta, GA: Peachtree Publishers).

Nowicki, S. and Duke, M. P. (2002) *Will I Ever Fit In The Breakthrough Program for Conquering Adult Dyssemia* (New York: The Free Press)

Parfit, D. (1987) *Reasons and Persons* (Oxford: Oxford University Press).

Pascal, B. (1671/2006) *Pensées*, trans. W. F. Trotter (Eulogos), section 252.

Pascal, R. (1960) *Design and Truth in Autobiography* (London: Routledge & Kegan Paul).

Pears, D. (1971) *Wittgenstein* (London: Fontana).

Peirce, C. S. (1873/1958/1966) 'The Logic of 1873', in *Collected Papers of Charles Sanders Peirce*, vol. VII, ed. A.W. Burks (Cambridge, MA: The Belknap Press of Harvard University Press), 194–219.

Perry, R. B. (1996) *The Thought and Character of William James* (Nashville, TN, and London: Vanderbilt University Press).

Pinker, S. (1994) *The Language Instinct: The New Science of Language and Mind* (London: Penguin).

Polanyi, M. (1966) *The Tacit Dimension* (New York: Doubleday).

Pollock, J. and Cruz, J. (1999) *Contemporary Theories of Knowledge*, 2nd edn (Lanham, ML: Rowman & Littlefield).

Proust, M. (1968) *The Captive* (London: Chatto & Windus).

Putnam, H. (1988) *Representation and Reality* (Cambridge, MA: MIT Press).

Putnam, H. (1990) *Realism with a Human Face* (Cambridge, MA: Harvard University Press).

Read, R. (2004) 'Throwing Away the Bedrock', *Proceedings of the Aristotelian Society* 105: 1, 81–98.

Rhees, R. (1971) 'The Tree of Nebuchadnezzar', *The Human World*, 4: 23–6.

Rhees, R. (1974) 'Correspondence and Comment', *The Human World*, 15/16: 153–63.

Ryle, G. (1949) *The Concept of Mind* (Harmondsworth: Penguin Books).

Ryle, G. (1979) 'Adverbial Verbs and Verbs of Thinking', in *On Thinking* (Oxford: Basil Blackwell), 17–32.

Ryle, G. (1990) *Collected Papers*, vol. 2 (Bristol: Thoemmes).

Sacks, O. (1985) *The Man who Mistook his Wife for a Hat* (London: Duckworth).

Sacks, O. (1995) *An Anthropologist on Mars* (London: Picador).

Sampson, G. (1997) *Educating Eve* (London: Cassell).

Sellars, W. (1956/1997) *Empiricism and the Philosophy of Mind* (Cambridge, MA: Harvard University Press).

Shanker, S. (1998) *Wittgenstein's Remarks on the Foundations of AI* (London: Routledge).

Shoemaker, S. (1963) *Self-Knowledge and Self-Identity* (Cornell, NY: Cornell University Press).

Shotter, J. (1980) 'Action, Joint Action and Intentionality', in M. Brenner (ed.), *The Structure of Action* (London: Blackwell), 28–65.

Shotter, J. (2003) 'Cartesian Change, Chiasmic Change – the Power of Living Expression', *Janus Head: Journal of Interdisciplinary Studies in Literature, Continental Philosophy, Phenomenological Psychology and the Arts* 6:1: 6–29.

Singer, P. (1979) *Practical Ethics* (Cambridge: Cambridge University Press).

Sorce, J., Emde, R. N., Campos, J. J. and Klinnert, M. D. (1985) 'Maternal Emotional Signalling: Its Effect on the Visual Cliff Behavior of One-Year-Olds', *Developmental Psychology* 21: 185–200.

Soussignan, R. (2002) 'Duchenne Smile, Emotional Experience, and Autonomic Reactivity: A Test of the Facial Feedback Hypothesis', *Emotion* 2:1: 52–74.

Sperber, D. and Wilson, D. (1998) 'The Mapping Between the Mental and the Public Lexicon', in *Language and Thought: Interdisciplinary Themes*, ed. P. Carruthers and J. Boucher (Cambridge: Cambridge University Press), 184–200.

Striano, T. and Rochat, P. (2000) 'Emergence of Selective Social Referencing in Infancy', *Infancy* 1/2: 253–64.

Stroll, A. (1994) *Wittgenstein and Moore on Certainty* (Oxford: Oxford University Press).

Tilghman, B.R. (1984) *But Is It Art?* (Oxford: Basil Blackwell).

Tomasello, M. (1999) *The Cultural Origins of Human Cognition* (Cambridge, MA: Harvard University Press).

Tomasello, M. (2003) 'On the Different Origins of Symbols and Grammar', in M. Christiansen and S. Kirby (eds), *Language Evolution* (Oxford: Oxford University Press), 94–110.

Tomassi, P. (2001) 'Logic After Wittgenstein', *Nordic Journal of Philosophical Logic* 6:1: 43–70.

Von Eckardt, B. (2003) 'The Explanatory Need for Mental Representations in Cognitive Science', *Mind & Language* 18:4: 427–39.

Wegner, D. (2003) 'The Mind's Best Trick: How We Experience Conscious Will', *Trends in Cognitive Science* 7: 65–9.

Winch, P. (1967) *The Idea of a Social Science and Its Relation to Philosophy* (London: Routledge & Kegan Paul).

Winch, P. (1980-81) 'Eine Einstellung zur Seele', in *Trying to Make Sense* (Oxford: Basil Blackwell), 140–53.

Wisdom, J. (1953) *Philosophy and Psychoanalysis* (Oxford: Blackwell).

Woolf, V. (1982) *The Diaries of Virginia Woolf*, vol. 3, 1925–30, ed. Ann Olivier Bell (London: Penguin).

Wright, C. (1982) 'Anti-Realist Semantics: The Role of Criteria', in G. Vesey (ed.), *Idealism Past and Present* (Cambridge: Cambridge University Press), 225–48.

Ziff, P. (1981) 'Quote: Judgements from our Brain', in I. Block (ed.), *Perspectives on the Philosophy of Wittgenstein* (Oxford: Blackwell), 201–11.

Zoshchenko, M. (1974) *Before Sunrise*, trans. G. Kern (Ardis: Ann Arbor).

Index